D1029339

FOUNDATIONS OF HEGEL'S SOCIAL THEORY

FOUNDATIONS OF HEGEL'S SOCIAL THEORY

Actualizing Freedom

FREDERICK NEUHOUSER

HARVARD UNIVERSITY PRESS

Cambridge, Massachusetts

London, England

2000

Library of Congress Cataloging-in Publication Data

Neuhouser, Frederick.
    Foundations of Hegel's social theory : actualizing freedom /
    Frederick Neuhouser.
        p. cm.
    Includes bibliographical references and index.
    ISBN 0-674-00152-4 (alk. paper)
    1. Hegel, Georg Wilhelm Friedrich, 1770–1831—Contributions in sociology.
2. Social sciences—Germany—Philosophy—History—19th century.
3. Sociology—Germany—History—19th century.   I. Title.
HM477.G3 N48   2000
301'.01—dc21   00-020264

For my mother and father

ACKNOWLEDGMENTS

I would like to express my gratitude to the many individuals and institutions who have contributed to the writing of this book. I am especially indebted to the three philosophers whose teaching, writings, and criticism of my work have most shaped my understanding of Hegel: Raymond Geuss, Allen Wood, and Michael Theunissen. In addition to reading and criticizing large portions of this manuscript, each has been a living example to me of how Hegel and the philosophical tradition that follows from him can be fruitfully appropriated through a combination of sympathy and analytic rigor.

I am also indebted to Bill Bristow, who painstakingly checked all of the book's notes and polished its German translations. More important, my conversations with Bill during the past ten years are among the most philosophically rewarding I have known; they have played an immeasurable role in shaping my interpretation of Hegel. Michael Hardimon has been a constant source of good ideas and imaginative suggestions since I began this project. I am grateful to him for his detailed criticism of my work, as well as for our many joint reading projects, which greatly sharpened my understanding of Hegel (and others). I am also much indebted to David Brink, Dudley Knowles, Tony Laden, and Robert Pippin, who read and helpfully commented on large portions of the manuscript.

I owe a different kind of intellectual debt to Ann Robertson, whose classes on Marx and Kant at Wabash College first aroused my interest in Continental social philosophy and taught me to strive for clarity and precision. Her ideas and style inform this study in ways that may be difficult to see but are real nonetheless.

Most of my ideas in this book were born and attained whatever maturity they have during the period 1988–1995, when I regularly taught courses on Hegel and Rousseau at Harvard University. I owe my greatest intellectual debt to the scores of students in those classes who patiently endured my attempts to articulate what I did not understand and persistently plagued me with questions I could not answer.

In addition, I would like to thank the Alexander von Humboldt-Stiftung for its generous financial support of two separate research leaves in Berlin, during which I wrote a large part of the book's first draft. I am also grateful to the editors of *The Philosophical Review* and the *Bulletin of the Hegel Society of Great Britain,* who published early versions of two of the chapters of this book and graciously gave their permission to reprint them in modified form here. Chapter 3 was first published as "Freedom, Dependence, and the General Will" in *The Philosophical Review* 102 (July 1993), and part of chapter 7 appeared as "Ethical Life and the Demands of Conscience," in the *Bulletin of the Hegel Society of Great Britain* 37 (May 1998).

I owe a personal debt to Eleanor Schuker, of New York, and Steven Cooper, of Cambridge, Massachusetts, whose weekly (and often more frequent) conversations with me taught me the value of knowing my own particularity. My contact with them not only transformed me personally but also altered my philosophical outlook in ways they cannot possibly know. I am also grateful to Uday Dhar, who was an unfailing source of encouragement, companionship, and intellectual stimulation during the early years of this project; without him this book would never have been started.

Finally, to Jason Hill, my companion and secret sharer, I express my deepest gratitude for upsetting my life when I needed it most, for showing me new ways of doing philosophy, and, most important, for bringing me to myself.

CONTENTS

ABBREVIATIONS OF WORKS CITED

Hegel

All translations from Hegel's works are my own, although I have benefited immeasurably from consulting both Knox's and Nisbet's translations of *The Philosophy of Right*.

Numbers preceded by "§" without further bibliographic information refer to paragraphs of *Grundlinien der Philosophie des Rechts*, vol. 7 of Hegel's *Werke* (Frankfurt am Main: Suhrkamp, 1986), available in English as *Elements of the Philosophy of Right*, ed. Allen W. Wood, trans. H. B. Nisbet (Cambridge: Cambridge University Press, 1991), and as *Philosophy of Right*, trans. T. M. Knox (London: Oxford University Press, 1967). Hegel's remarks (*Anmerkungen*) are indicated here by "A," his additions (*Zusätze*) by "Z," and his handwritten marginal notes by "N." "§151+Z" refers to both paragraph 151 and its addition.

Other works of Hegel are cited as follows:

E   Part III of the *Enzyklopädie der philosophischen Wissenschaften, Werke*, vol. 10; in English: *Hegel's Philosophy of Mind*, trans. William Wallace (Oxford: Oxford University Press, 1971); cited by section (§) number.

EL   Part I of the *Enzyklopädie der philosophischen Wissenschaften: Die Wissenschaft der Logik, Werke*, vol. 8; in English: *Hegel's Logic*, trans. William Wallace (Oxford: Oxford University Press, 1975); cited by section (§) number.

LHP   *Vorlesungen über die Geschichte der Philosophie, Werke*, vol. 18–20; in English: *Lectures on the History of Philosophy*, trans. Elizabeth Haldane and Frances H. Simson (New York: Humanities Press, 1968); cited by English and German page numbers.

NL   *Über die wissenschaftlichen Behandlungsarten des Naturrechts, Werke*, vol. 2; in English: *Natural Law: The Scientific Ways of Treating Natural Law, Its Place in Moral Philosophy, and Its Relation to the Positive Sciences of Law*, trans. T. M. Knox (Philadelphia: University of Pennsylvania Press, 1975); cited by English and German page numbers.

PH   *Vorlesungen über die Philosophie der Geschichte, Werke,* vol. 12; in English:
        The Philosophy of History, trans. J. Sibree (New York: Dover, 1956); cited
        by English and German page numbers.

PhG   *Phänomenologie des Geistes, Werke,* vol. 3; in English: *Phenomenology of
        Spirit,* trans. A. V. Miller (Oxford: Oxford University Press, 1977); English
        cited by paragraph (¶) numbers, German by page numbers.

VPR1   *Die Philosophie des Rechts: Die Mitschriften Wannenmann (Heidelberg 1817/
        18) und Homeyer (Berlin 1818/19),* ed. Karl-Heinz Ilting (Stuttgart: Klett-
        Cotta, 1983), cited by page number.

VPR2   *Philosophie des Rechts: Die Vorlesung von 1819/20 in einer Nachschrift,* ed.
        Dieter Henrich (Frankfurt am Main: Suhrkamp, 1983).

VPR4   *Vorlesungen über Rechtsphilosophie,* vol. 4, ed. Karl-Heinz Ilting (Stuttgart:
        Frommann-Holzboog, 1973). Includes student transcriptions of Hegel's
        lecture notes by K. G. von Griesheim (1824–1825) and D. F. Strauss
        (1831).

Rousseau

For Rousseau I have taken the English translations and made minor amendments
where necessary.

"SC, I.4.vi" refers to book 1, chapter 4, paragraph 6 of *On the Social Contract* (SC),
ed. Roger D. Masters, trans. Judith R. Masters (New York: St. Martin's Press, 1978).

Other works of Rousseau's are cited as follows:

DI   *Discourse on Inequality,* in *The First and Second Discourses,* trans. Roger D.
        Masters and Judith R. Masters (New York: St. Martin's Press, 1964).

DSA   *Discourse on the Sciences and Arts,* in *The First and Second Discourses,*
        trans. Roger D. Masters and Judith R. Masters (New York: St. Martin's
        Press, 1964).

Emile   *Emile,* trans. Allan Bloom (New York: Basic Books, 1979).

GM   *Geneva Manuscript,* in *On the Social Contract,* ed. Roger D. Masters, trans.
        Judith R. Masters (New York: St. Martin's Press, 1978).

GP   *The Government of Poland,* trans. Willmoore Kendall (Indianapolis:
        Hackett, 1985).

OC III *Oeuvres Complètes,* ed. Bernard Gagnebin and Marcel Raymond (Paris:
        Gallimard, Bibliothèque de la Pléiade, 1959–1969), vol. 3.

PE   *Political Economy,* in *On the Social Contract,* ed. Roger D. Masters, trans.
        Judith R. Masters (New York: St. Martin's Press, 1978).

RSW   *The Reveries of the Solitary Walker,* trans. Charles E. Butterworth (New
        York: Harper and Row, 1979).

Kant

I have used the following abbreviations for works by Kant:

KRV   *Critique of Pure Reason,* trans. Norman Kemp Smith (New York: St. Martin's Press, 1963). Cited by first edition (A) and second edition (B) page numbers.

KU   *Critique of Judgment,* trans. Werner S. Pluhar (Indianapolis: Hackett, 1987). Cited by § number.

MS   *The Metaphysics of Morals,* trans. Mary Gregor (Cambridge: Cambridge University Press, 1996); cited by Prussian Academy page numbers.

Introduction

This book is about the philosophical foundations of Hegel's social theory. Its aim is to understand the basic structure of that theory by articulating the normative standards Hegel takes himself to be employing when he asserts that a particular set of social institutions is rational, or good. The book's central concern can be formulated as the question: What, on Hegel's view, makes a rational social order rational? In focusing on this question, the book sets itself a task that is both interpretive and philosophical. That is, it aspires not only to be faithful to the letter of Hegel's texts but also to present his theory in a way that shows it to be a philosophically compelling account of rational social institutions. For a historian of philosophy who is motivated by both of these ambitions, Hegel's social theory proves the perfect object of study. This is because, on the one hand, Hegel's abstruse but intricately constructed texts offer a nearly limitless supply of hermeneutic challenges and pleasures and, on the other, because persistence in decoding his tortured idiom is rewarded by the discovery of a social theory that is unsurpassed in its richness, its philosophical rigor, and its insights into the nature of good social institutions. In short, reconstructing Hegel's social theory is not only highly engaging as an interpretive exercise; it is also a philosophical venture that promises to enrich our understanding of what constitutes a rational social order.

In order to avert a possible misunderstanding of the project I mean to undertake here, it is necessary to say a further word about the kind of foundations the book seeks to investigate. In the present context it would be quite natural to take 'philosophical foundations' to refer to the

1

metaphysical doctrines that form the subject matter of Hegel's *Logic*. These doctrines are foundational for Hegel's philosophy in the very robust sense that they aspire to articulate the basic structure of rational thought in general and to grasp the underlying character of all that is real. If the term is understood in this sense, articulating the foundations of Hegel's social theory would involve showing how the norms that define the rational social order have their source in a more general metaphysical account of how any entity whatever must be constituted if it is to qualify as rational and hence (as Hegel would have it) as truly "real" (*wirklich*).

Alternatively, talk of foundations in Hegel's philosophy might be construed as alluding to the historical account the *Phenomenology of Spirit* provides of how the modern world came to regard the norms it upholds, including those relevant to social theory, as authoritative. This genetic account of the norms that define modernity could be thought of as foundational with respect to social theory because the narrative Hegel tells there aims not merely to recount how a particular set of norms came into the world but also to establish their rational validity. Because the *Phenomenology* seeks to reveal the forms of consciousness it considers as the results of necessary developments—as *rationally necessary* in a sense that is too complex to articulate fully here—its account of how the norms of modernity arise functions at the same time as a demonstration of their rational validity. If understood in this sense, the project of uncovering the "foundations" of Hegel's social theory would consist in justifying the normative standards employed by that theory by showing them to be the necessary end point of a historical process driven by the aim of finding a stable, logically consistent set of norms that fully satisfies the aspirations of reason as Hegel conceives them.

Neither of these alternatives captures the sense in which I shall be concerned with the foundations of Hegel's social theory here. Although both are projects worthy of attempting—for neither, in my view, has yet been satisfactorily carried out—the ambitions of this book are, philosophically speaking, more modest. That is, the book's aim is neither to examine the deepest metaphysical foundations of Hegel's social theory nor to reconstruct the *Phenomenology*'s meta-justification of the social and political norms Hegel thinks are authoritative for the modern era. Its task, rather, is simply to articulate as clearly as possible what those norms are and to do so in a way that makes it possible to appreciate the considerable richness and power that Hegel's vision of the rational social order possesses. This project is philosophically less ambitious than the other two I have mentioned because it does not aspire to uncover what Hegel himself would consider to be the deepest philosophical foundations of his social theory. Although not concerned with foundations in either of the two senses distinguished earlier, the present study is nevertheless foundational in that it focuses not on the (already widely familiar) institutional details of Hegel's theory—issues such as the scope of the monarch's powers or the patriarchal structure of the family—but rather on the more fundamental question concerning the nature of the normative criteria Hegel uses in judging that a particular set of institutions constitutes a rational social world. Its principal task is not to recount which institutions Hegel endorses but to understand the types of reasons he appeals to in making those judgments. In other words, it seeks to articulate the philosophical underpinnings of Hegel's social theory by clarifying and, where necessary, reconstructing the basic normative standards at work in its vision of the rational social order.

The choice to adopt this more modest approach to Hegel's social theory is not based on a studied conviction that the two alternative projects would be philosophically unrewarding (for such a conclusion would be warranted only on the basis of exhaustive attempts to reconstruct and defend the positions of the *Logic* and *Phenomenology*). Rather, it reflects the belief that our grasp of Hegel's social theory has not yet penetrated even to the level at which it will be treated here—that, in other words, our understanding of Hegel's theory remains plagued by the simple lack of a precise and coherent statement of the normative standards that underlie its vision of the rational social order. It is already widely known that Hegel's aim in his social theory is to defend what he takes to be the three central social institutions of the modern era: the nuclear, bourgeois family; civil society (the market-governed realm of production and exchange); and the (more or less) liberal, constitutional state. Yet despite the fact that there exist numerous treatments of Hegel's social theory by philosophers, it is surprisingly difficult to find one that goes beyond a description of the institutions Hegel favors to provide a systematic, philosophically sensitive account of the arguments that underlie his claims.[1] By reconstructing Hegel's account of the basic normative standards that define the rational social order, the present project aims to remedy precisely this deficiency.

The choice to restrict the focus of this book to foundations of the sort just described rests on a further, more controversial conviction regarding the relatively self-standing character of the parts of Hegel's elaborate philosophical system: even though Hegel's social theory is undeniably embedded within a more comprehensive philosophical vision—one that includes views about the nature of ultimate reality and the meaning of human history—it is possible, to a surprisingly large extent, to understand his account of what makes the rational social order rational and to appreciate its force even while abstracting from those more fundamental doctrines. It would not be productive to attempt to argue directly for this assertion here; instead, the book itself—its sustained attempt to make good sense of Hegel's theory in relative detachment from its deepest foundations—ought to be taken as a protracted, indirect argument for the fruitfulness of its approach. Its ultimate success or failure in constructing a view that is coherent and compelling will be the most reliable test of the thesis that Hegel's social theory is, to a considerable extent, a self-standing position. One reason this thesis is more plausible than it might initially seem comes to light once we begin to say more about the content of the normative standards at issue.

In one respect Hegel's answer to the question, What makes the rational social order rational? is surprisingly simple. It can be captured in a single word: *freedom*. Thus, formulated in the most general terms possible, Hegel recognizes the family, civil society, and the constitutional state as rational institutions because they play essential roles in realizing the central value of freedom. Since freedom is the fundamental concept here, the principal task of a project that aims to examine the normative standards at work in Hegel's social theory will be to articulate the conception of freedom the theory invokes and to show how that conception grounds Hegel's claims as to which institutions satisfy the demands of reason. This feature of Hegel's theory explains in part why it is not unreasonable to suppose that it can be usefully explored in relative detachment from the rest of his philosophy. For if such a project succeeds both in making sense of the ideal of freedom Hegel employs and in showing how the central institutions of modernity work to realize that ideal, considerable progress will have been made in establishing the forcefulness of Hegel's view. That is, most contemporary readers will be able to recognize Hegel's view as compelling if they can see how it is grounded in a plausible conception of freedom, even though they may lack access to his account of how freedom came to be the authoritative value of modernity or to his metaphysical arguments establishing that self-legislating reason (a type of freedom) constitutes all reality—nature, history, and the social world as well.

This naturally leads one to ask whether it is possible to make sense of the conception of freedom that grounds Hegel's social theory in abstraction from the rest of his philosophy. The intuition that guides this study is that, contrary to appearances, Hegel's conception of freedom is far less idiosyncratic—far less tied to distinctively Hegelian categories of thought—than is generally assumed. Again, the ultimate test of this thesis will be how successful the attempt to give such an account proves to be. But it may help to diminish the inevitable suspicion that this undertaking is doomed from the start to consider that, despite Hegel's unique and forbidding mode of expression, he himself regards his conception of freedom as the product of a long and comprehensive dialogue with the philosophical tradition that precedes him. For this reason, an important part of the project I shall undertake here will consist in uncovering the important but often obscured connections between Hegel's conception of freedom and those of his better understood predecessors—Kant, Spinoza, and, most significant of all, Rousseau.

Although the normative standards employed by Hegel's theory can be summed up in a single word, articulating the content of his conception of freedom proves to be, not surprisingly, a difficult and complex task, one that takes up most of the seven chapters that follow. The complexity of this task is compounded by the fact that not just one but three conceptions of freedom play major roles in Hegel's social theory: personal freedom, the freedom of moral subjectivity, and what I shall call here *social freedom*. Although all three are essential to Hegel's account of the rational social order, social freedom is both the most prominent and the least understood. Moreover, the idea of social freedom represents the most distinctive innovation of Hegel's theory and its single most important contribution to social and political philosophy. For these reasons it will be the main focus of this study. 'Social freedom' is not, however, a term that Hegel himself uses. It is employed here to designate the peculiar freedom that is central to Hegel's account of *Sittlichkeit* (or "ethical life") in Part III of the *Philosophy of Right*, a freedom that Hegel sometimes refers to as "substantial freedom" (*substantielle Freiheit*) (§§149, 257). Social freedom is not the freedom to do as one pleases (which is, roughly speaking, personal freedom), nor is it the freedom that consists in being the source of the normative principles that govern one's actions (which is the freedom, or autonomy, of moral subjectivity). Rather, it is a distinctive species of freedom that can be realized only by and within certain social institutions, most notably, those Hegel takes to be the three central institutions of modernity.[2] As we shall see in more detail later, this conception of freedom is particularly difficult to grasp, in part because it is both a freedom that individuals achieve through certain ways of participating in their social institutions and a freedom that can be predicated of those institutions themselves, insofar as they are rational. Although a great deal has been written about the special role social membership plays in Hegel's social theory, previous interpreters have failed to articulate precisely what *social* (or "substantial") freedom is, why it makes sense to regard it as a kind of freedom, and what relationship social institutions must have to this freedom in order to qualify as rational.[3] Given the obscurity with which Hegel presents his positions, this failure may not be surprising, but without answers to these questions it is impossible to find his account of social institutions philosophically compelling.

The book's basic strategy for articulating the normative structure of Hegel's theory is to argue that its fundamental concept, social freedom, has deep affinities with the conception of freedom implicit in Rousseau's political theory, especially in his claim that citizens of the rational state win their freedom "through the general will."[4] The basic thought here is that Hegel's puzzling assertion that social freedom has both a subjective and an objective component can be illuminated by showing how Rousseau's conception of political freedom has a similar two-part structure. The central claim of Rousseau that Hegel appropriates is that social freedom incorporates two main elements: first (the *objective* component), rational laws and institutions must furnish the basic social conditions necessary for realizing the freedom (in a variety of senses) of all individuals; and, second (the *subjective* component), it must be possible for all social members to affirm those freedom-realizing laws and institutions as good and thus to regard the principles that govern their social participation as coming from their own wills. As will become clearer in what follows, one of the main advantages of understanding Hegel's conception of freedom as a descendant of Rousseau's is that doing so shows Hegel's social theory to be more attentive to the freedom (and other interests) of *individuals* than is implied by the common view of Hegel as the proponent of a totalitarian social order that sacrifices the essential interests of individuals to some mysterious "freedom of the whole."

In both content and approach this book has much in common with two recent books on Hegel's practical philosophy that have made valuable contributions to making Hegel's views more accessible to contemporary English-speaking philosophers: Allen Wood's pathbreaking work, *Hegel's Ethical Thought*, and Michael Hardimon's excellent study, *Hegel's Social Philosophy: The Project of Reconciliation*.[5] As I have already indicated, the most important respect in which the present book differs from its predecessors is that it takes as its focus a sustained and systematic analysis of the conceptions of freedom that undergird Hegel's vision of the rational social order. But beyond this general point, two further, specific differences are worthy of mention.

First, this book will have very little to say about the topic that serves as the organizing theme for Hardimon's study, reconciliation. At first glance this might appear to signal a deep and substantive disagreement over what is normatively fundamental in Hegel's theory. A moment's reflection on how the concepts of freedom and reconciliation are related in Hegel's theory, however, reveals that this need not be the case. It is certainly true that the idea of reconciliation plays a major role in Hegel's thought. Indeed, he regards it as the principal aim of philosophy in general. In comprehending the whole of reality (*Wirklichkeit*) as informed through and through by the categories of rational thought, philosophy is supposed to reveal to human subjects that their world is not fundamentally alien to their basic aspirations—including the need to find the world good and intelligible to human reason—but rather an arena within which those aspirations can be satisfied. Thus, by demonstrating the rationality of the world, philosophy reconciles us to it. But Hardimon's indisputable claim that reconciliation is the driving aim of Hegel's account of the rational social order is not in conflict with the view taken here, namely, that social freedom is the core normative concept of his theory. On the contrary, the two theses are complementary. Whereas the doctrine of reconciliation gives an account of the particular good that results from comprehending the social order we inhabit as rational, the doctrine of social freedom specifies (the greatest part of)[6] what Hegel must show to be true of our social order if we are to see it as rational and thus to be reconciled to it. In other words, social freedom is the central element of Hegel's answer to the normative question, What about the modern social order makes it *worthy of* reconciliation?

Although this difference in focus need not point to a substantive dispute over the content of Hegel's theory, it might very well mark a disagreement about where the principal philosophical importance of the theory lies. In my view, emphasizing the concept of reconciliation (while downplaying the role of freedom) runs the risk of diverting attention from the substantial critical potential Hegel's theory possesses and hence of reinforcing its ill-deserved reputation as an antiquated, inherently reactionary theory designed solely for the purpose of justifying the existing social order of its time. Critics of Hegel have long complained that his emphasis on reconciliation makes his social theory into little more than an ex post facto justification of the status quo. This simple objection to the project of reconciliation is clearly based on a misunderstanding of it. As Hardimon correctly explains, Hegel's belief that philosophy's aim is to reconcile modern individuals to their social order depends on a logically prior judgment that the modern social order is good and therefore worthy of being reconciled to.[7]

Still, even if the doctrine of reconciliation does not fall prey to the simplistic criticisms that have often been made of it, there are good reasons for not putting it at the center of a contemporary reconstruction of Hegel's theory. One of these reasons is simply that the normative standards that inform the theory, though conceptually prior to the doctrine of reconciliation, are still widely misunderstood or, worse, thought not to exist at all.[8] The second reason is that focusing on the normative structure of Hegel's theory serves to highlight the logical space that lies between his account of the criteria in terms of which the rationality of a social order is to be judged and his further claim that the institutions of modernity in fact meet those criteria. Distinguishing these two parts of Hegel's theory makes it easier to see that it is conceptually possible to reject his claim that modern social institutions in fact satisfy the demands of reason while endorsing the normative standards that underlie that claim. In other words, the approach taken here draws special attention to the possibility that we might come to find the normative standards Hegel employs compelling but deny that reconciliation to our social order is the implication of accepting them. In doing so, it intentionally leaves space for the kind of appropriation of Hegel's theory that critical theorists of our own century have attempted.[9] This is an important fea-

ture of my project because my first objective in resuscitating Hegel's social theory is not to promote satisfaction with the present state of affairs
but to articulate and reveal the force of the very demanding standards
Hegel thinks social institutions ought to measure up to. Whether the appropriate response to Hegel's theory is reconciliation or radical critique
can be settled only once we have achieved a more thorough understanding of its normative foundations.[10]

The most important respect in which this study differs specifically
from Wood's is announced in the books' respective titles: his is a work in
ethical philosophy, mine in social theory. Yet despite this difference in
how the projects are characterized, the subject matters of the two books
overlap considerably. This is due to the fact that Hegel views his account
of what constitutes a rational social order—his treatment of *Sittlichkeit*,
or "ethical life"—as providing answers to the basic questions of both
ethical (or moral) philosophy[11] and, as I call it here, social theory. This
feature of Hegel's view is potentially the source of much confusion, since
these two sets of questions are normally taken to constitute distinct
fields of philosophical inquiry. Yet even within the framework of Hegel's
thought, it is possible to demarcate ethical philosophy from social theory by distinguishing between the basic aims each strives to achieve:
whereas ethical philosophy is concerned primarily with understanding
the nature and foundation of moral obligation, social theory aims to lay
out the basic principles that define the rational social order and to specify which institutions best realize those principles. What makes it possible for these two projects to converge in Hegel's system is that he attempts to ground both of them in the same first principle: the concept of
practical freedom, or the self-determined will. This means that Hegel intends to employ a single philosophical strategy to answer the basic questions of both ethical philosophy and social theory, a strategy that consists, most fundamentally, in asking after the conditions, both internal
and external to the will, that must obtain if the ideal of practical self-
determination is to be realized. Thus, on Hegel's view both the content
of ethical duties and our obligation to fulfill them have their ultimate
source in the imperative enjoined on us to realize our nature as self-
determining beings. Moreover, his ethical philosophy culminates in a
theory of social institutions, because it is through their participation in
rational social institutions that individuals are thought to achieve the
highest degree of practical self-determination available to them.

My project differs significantly from Wood's, as well as from most previous discussions of Hegel's theory of *Sittlichkeit*, in that it abstracts from the main concerns of ethical philosophy and focuses instead on topics traditionally assigned to social theory. My reasons for adopting this approach are twofold. First, I believe that Hegel's positions on the standard issues of ethical philosophy have thus far been the object of much more genuinely philosophical attention than his answers to the questions of social theory. Second, I am more skeptical about the prospects for success of Hegel's view considered as an ethical philosophy, especially its claim to be able to give a complete account of our duties, and of moral obligation in general, without appeal to anything like the (allegedly) formal, abstract, and individualistic principles of Kantian moral theory.[12] But whatever the reasons for delimiting the scope of my inquiry in this way, it is important to recognize that in doing so I give myself not so much a *different* subject matter from Wood's as a *less inclusive* one. This is because the account of the rational social order I intend to focus on here is developed within the broader framework of Hegel's ethical philosophy and constitutes just one part of that more comprehensive project.

Since certain ways of detaching Hegel's social theory from the rest of his thought are bound to result in distortions of his views, it is necessary to be clear about the sense in which the present study abstracts from the main concerns of ethical philosophy. Most important, it does not attempt to reconstruct Hegel's social theory by abstracting from his views concerning the kinds of lives it is ethically best for human beings to lead and what about those lives makes them good. An attempt to understand the normative foundations of Hegel's social theory cannot ignore his answers to these indisputably ethical questions. There are two reasons for this: first, part of what makes rational institutions good (according to the social theory) is that they enable their members to lead the ethically best lives available to human individuals; second, what accounts for the goodness of those lives from the perspective of Hegel's ethical philosophy is part and parcel of the end he ascribes, as social theorist, to rational institutions—namely, freedom. By contrast, the ethical question I intend to bracket here is whether a conception of the rational social order such as Hegel provides is suited to play the central role he thinks it must in ethical philosophy's quest to give a comprehensive account of our moral duties and to understand the source of our obligation to fulfill them. In other words, I shall attempt to articulate the vision of the rational social order Hegel endorses, together with his (inherently ethical) reasons for doing so, without evaluating his controversial claim that such a vision can serve as the foundation for ethical theory in its entirety.

Two further points about my use of the term 'social theory' will help to demarcate the object of this inquiry more precisely. First, by calling Hegel's account of the rational social order a *theory* rather than a *philosophy*, I do not mean to suggest that it stands either outside the bounds or on the margins of what is properly considered philosophy. Hegel's social theory is a patently philosophical account of what rational social institutions are and of what about them makes them good. Nothing of substance would be affected by referring here instead to Hegel's "social philosophy." At most, the term 'social theory' is meant to signal that in his account of *Sittlichkeit,* or at least in those aspects of it that interest me here, Hegel shares deep affinities with a long line of thinkers—a line initiated by Smith and continued by Marx, Durkheim, Weber, and the Frankfurt School—whose theories (profitably, in my view) straddle the boundary between empirical social science and normative philosophy. What these theories have in common is that they offer, or presuppose, a vision of the good social order that is grounded in both a detailed, empirical understanding of how existing institutions function and an acknowledged commitment to normative criteria that are (in the broadest sense) ethical. Although Hegel's theory is undoubtedly more thoroughly permeated by philosophical concerns than the others, its detailed accounts of the specific features of rational institutions—modern civil society is the best example here—rely heavily on empirical knowledge of the contemporary social world. This characteristic of Hegel's view is deeply connected to the view expressed in his well-known remark in the preface to the *Philosophy of Right* that philosophy's task is not to invent social institutions of its own and to prescribe them to the world. Although speculative philosophy, for Hegel, is able to furnish us with a general notion of the ideals social institutions ought to live up to—it provides us with an initial, abstract understanding of the nature of freedom—it lacks by itself the imaginative force that would be required to elaborate a concrete vision of the specific form in which those ideals can be realized in the world and of how institutions would have to be constituted in order to do so. In order to provide such a vision of the rational social order, speculative philosophy must be complemented by a thorough acquaintance with the facts of history and contemporary social reality.

Second, 'social' ought not to be thought of as defined in contrast to 'political', thereby implying that the domain of social theory is restricted to a society's nonpolitical institutions. As Hegel conceives it, the realm of *Sittlichkeit* is made up of three central institutions—the family, civil society, and the state—and each of these constitutes the subject matter of one of the three main divisions of his "social" theory. This means that Hegel's social theory includes an account of rational political institutions and so must regard itself as offering answers to the traditional questions of political philosophy. Again, nothing of real substance would be affected by amending the title of this book to refer to the foundations of Hegel's "social and political theory." One reason for not describing Hegel's position in this way, however, is that doing so tends to obscure the important fact that his treatments of political and nonpolitical institutions constitute a single, unified theory. This is true in (at least) two quite different senses.

First, Hegel's view of the rational state is logically inextricable from his account of civil society and the family in the following respect: for Hegel it is impossible to achieve a complete grasp of the state's proper functions and ends without understanding the functions and ends (and deficiencies) of its two subordinate, nonpolitical institutions. For example, one of the primary duties of the Hegelian state is to ensure the survival and proper functioning of both the family and civil society. This implies that determining the tasks of the rational state—determining the kinds of legislation it ought to enact, for instance—presupposes an understanding of the proper ends of a society's nonpolitical institutions and of the ways in which they are vulnerable either to decay from within or to encroachment from without. A further example of how the central issues of Hegel's political theory are defined within the context of his broader social theory is found in his treatment of the problem, inherited from Rousseau, of how members of the state are to acquire a general (or universal) will. For Hegel, as for Rousseau, achieving society-wide consensus on the laws that govern the polity and claim to express its collective will is a crucial function of political institutions because the freedom of citizens depends on their ability to assent to the laws that constrain and direct their own actions. Yet Hegel sees that because citizens are also members of a highly differentiated civil society—because they enter the political realm with diverging particular interests—this central problem of politics can be solved only by taking into account certain basic extrapolitical features of a society such as the nature of its economic classes (or estates) and how membership in each is likely to affect the stance citizens will be able to take to issues concerning the collective good. Here, too, political philosophy proceeds only on the basis of a broader social theory.

The second sense in which Hegel's account of *Sittlichkeit* constitutes a unified theory is that it employs a single model to understand the essential character of both political and nonpolitical institutions. Although Hegel acknowledges many important, mutually complementary differences among the family, civil society, and the state, he takes these institutions to share one basic feature: each functions by fostering among its members a distinctive kind of particular identity—as family member, as member of a profession, and as citizen of a nation-state—that enables it to solve, in its own fashion, a version of the general problem Hegel views as central to his project of understanding the role social institutions play in the realization of freedom, namely, how can particular and universal wills be harmoniously united within the individuals who belong to and sustain the social order's three main institutions? The core idea behind Hegel's answer to this question is that individuals can be brought to will and work freely for the collective good of the social groups to which they belong, insofar as doing so is at the same time a way of giving expression to a particular identity that they take to be central to who they are. Because each of the identities associated with the institutions of *Sittlichkeit* involves thinking of oneself as having substantive, noninstrumental attachments to other individuals, adopting those identities goes hand in hand with a concern for the good of one's fellow social members and of the group as a whole.[13] This means that participation in the family, civil society, and the state is both universally beneficial and particularly satisfying, since to act on the basis of one's identity as a family member, as a member of a profession, or as a citizen is at the same time to work for the good of the whole.

Since one of my aims in this book is to make the foundational ideas of Hegel's social theory accessible to contemporary philosophers outside the Hegelian tradition, it may be helpful to close this introduction by briefly indicating some of the central claims of Hegel's view that continue to be of relevance today. Three of the most important of these claims have already been alluded to:

1. A social or political philosophy that conceives of freedom only in its negative guise—as the absence of external hindrances to doing what one pleases—is founded on an impoverished conception of freedom.[14] Although safeguarding a sphere of negative (or personal) freedom for each social member is an essential task of the rationally ordered society, it alone represents only a partial realization of the freedom available to modern individuals. Most important, personal freedom must be supplemented by *social freedom*, which includes the ability of individuals both to endorse (or will) laws and practices that promote the collective good and to find their own particular identities through their social participation.

2. One task of the rational social order is to sustain the kinds of social structures that enable individuals to escape the anomie, alienation, and sense of rootlessness that have come to characterize Western societies of the twentieth century. The powerful social forces unleashed by the free market—including the tendency to rationalize all forms of social life in accord with the imperative of economic efficiency—must be balanced by a concerted effort to foster and protect social structures that address the need of all its members (not merely the educated elite) to experience their social world as a meaningful place within which they can pursue projects worthy of human subjects and, through social recognition, gain a stable sense of their own dignity.

3. Political philosophy ought not to be carried out as though it were an autonomous, self-standing discipline. An account of the proper ends of the state must be grounded in a broader social theory that incorporates both a knowledge of the functioning and potential of existing institutions and a general understanding of the ways in which institutions can furnish the social conditions that enable their members to lead lives of human excellence.

In addition to these points, two claims that have not yet been mentioned are also central to Hegel's theory and of contemporary importance:

4. Social institutions ought not to be understood as external structures into which already constituted individuals choose to enter in order to pursue ends or satisfy needs that they acquire prior to, or outside of, social life. Rather, social theory must acknowledge that

a society's basic institutions inevitably construct the subjectivity of their members in fundamental ways. Because these institutions have the power to form individuals into subjects of particular sorts, one of the concerns of social theory must be to ask what kinds of individuals the institutions it evaluates are likely to create. More precisely, social theory must reflect on the kinds of subjective capacities individuals require in order to realize themselves as free (in the various relevant senses) and on the roles institutions can play in equipping their members with those capacities.

5. The values of individuality and social membership are not to be thought of as competing or mutually exclusive ideals. In fact, each of these ideals, properly understood, can be realized only in conjunction with the other.[15] More specifically, Hegel's account of *Sittlichkeit* enables us to understand how social roles that are not necessarily chosen by the individuals who occupy them can nevertheless be the source of an important species of freedom for them (social freedom); it explains how social members can be free even while bound by the demands of (rational) social practices and laws.

Finally, there is a further reason that contemporary philosophers ought to be interested in the reconstruction of Hegel's social theory offered here: understanding his conception of social freedom and how it can ground a social theory enables us to begin to reconcile many of the differences often thought to divide communitarians and liberals. Contrary to common perceptions—perceptions reinforced by the attempts of some communitarians to style themselves as his intellectual descendants—Hegel does not stand squarely on one side of this contemporary debate. Rather, one of Hegel's most important and explicit aims in his social theory is to integrate liberalism's concern for the fundamental rights and interests of individuals with certain aspects of romantic political thought, including its tendency to view the social order as an organism (rather than as a collection of equal and essentially identical individuals) and to emphasize the importance of substantive, identity-constituting attachments to social groups.[16] In addition to his unequivocal endorsement of universal individual rights (the rights of personhood outlined in "Abstract Right"), Hegel parts ways with most communitarians in maintaining that there exist universally valid ("absolute") criteria by which the goodness of a particular society's institutions and practices can be judged.

Yet despite these fundamental differences, the widely perceived affinities between Hegel and communitarians are not merely illusory. What makes Hegel's theory more than just another version of liberalism is that it accords central importance to the need of human individuals—call it a spiritual need—to experience themselves as belonging integrally to a greater social reality, a reality whose significance and being transcend their own particular projects and finite life span. Although, in my view, the best examples of liberal thought do not, strictly speaking, rule out the possibility of satisfying this need within a liberal society, part of what makes them liberal is that they do not count it among the fundamental concerns of political (or social) theory. Indeed, the precise opposite is more nearly the case, since a good deal of the liberal tradition can be understood as motivated by a desire to avert the familiar dangers bound up with the powerful human longing to have a part in the life of a being larger than oneself. But, despite these indisputable dangers, a social theory that fails to take notice of this human need—or, even worse, denies it—runs a risk of at least equal gravity. For, as the thinkers immediately following Hegel were to recognize, when human needs of this magnitude and durability are disavowed, rather than acknowledged and addressed, they do not simply dissipate but reassert themselves instead in estranged and more malevolent guises. Hegel's social theory continues to deserve our attention today, not least because it represents modern philosophy's most comprehensive attempt to do justice to this human need while accommodating the concern for the moral dignity of individuals that motivates liberal political thought. In the end, of course, we may be forced to conclude, in agreement with postmodernists and many liberals, that a synthesis of this sort is destined to fail, whether because the longing to find one's social order a home cannot in principle be satisfied, or because such a social order is no longer a possibility for us. Even in this case, though, Hegel's social theory would retain a certain value as a testimony to the powerful, perhaps inextirpable urge of human beings to find their social world hospitable, coherent, and good. Rather than being a philosophy of reconciliation, Hegel's theory would then represent, at best, the keeping alive of a now unsatisfied but hope-inspiring utopian impulse or, at worst, a defiant cry of protest at the forlornness of an alien, godforsaken world.

1

Hegel's Conception of Social Freedom: Preliminaries

In this chapter my aim is to begin to articulate the conception of freedom that grounds Hegel's account of the three basic institutions—the family, civil society, and the state—that together make up the social realm he calls *Sittlichkeit,* or ethical life. The first order of business is to situate this conception of freedom—"social freedom," as I refer to it here—with respect to other conceptions of freedom that figure prominently in Hegel's philosophy. Second, I shall attempt to elucidate the general project of Hegel's social theory by briefly sketching the philosophical problems that the idea of social freedom is meant to solve. As we shall see, this project has both a historical and a logical (or conceptual) formulation. That is, social freedom is Hegel's response to a question about whether and how a variety of historically significant conceptions of freedom can be reconciled with one another, as well as to the more abstract question of what constitutes a coherent and fully adequate conception of (practical) freedom. The third and fourth sections of this chapter deal with two questions that have ultimately to do with the relation between Hegel's conception of social freedom and his notoriously obscure doctrine of absolute spirit, or *Geist.* The first of these has to do with who, or what, is properly regarded as the bearer of social freedom: Is it individuals, or only some supra-individual social entity, that embodies freedom in this sense? The second concerns the extent to which the intelligibility of Hegel's conception of social freedom depends on his view of the historical mission of absolute spirit: Can this conception of freedom be recognized as such outside the context of Hegel's theodicy, or does it amount to nothing more than the idea of individuals realizing

17

their "true" nature by serving the ends of absolute spirit? Finally, the chapter closes with a brief and preliminary account of what I call the "dual nature" of social freedom.

Other Conceptions of Freedom in Hegel's Philosophy

Like abstract right and morality, the topics of the first two divisions of Hegel's *Philosophy of Right*, *Sittlichkeit* is characterized as a "realm of actualized freedom" (§4). Hegel's claim is not simply that the rational social order brings about the social conditions that make freedom possible; rather, *Sittlichkeit* is itself said to be an actualization,[1] a making real, of freedom (§142): "In *Sittlichkeit* freedom *is*" (VPR1, 248). But what conception of freedom is at work in Hegel's claim that freedom is realized in the family, in civil society, and in the state? What sense does it make to say that freedom *is* in these social institutions? What will emerge in the course of addressing these questions is that Hegel's theory of *Sittlichkeit* is founded on a distinctive conception of freedom—the "social freedom" referred to earlier[2]—which, according to that theory, is realized only in a rationally structured society. Social freedom is to be understood as distinguishable from, though not conceptually or existentially independent of, the other two main conceptions of practical freedom that appear in the *Philosophy of Right* and serve as the grounding concepts of abstract right and morality, namely: *personal freedom* and *moral freedom* (or, equivalently, the freedoms of personhood and moral subjectivity). But before sorting out the three kinds of *practical* freedom that figure most prominently in the *Philosophy of Right* as a whole (personal, moral, and social freedom), it is necessary to say a few words about the concept of freedom in the most general sense in which it appears in Hegel's thought. In this widest sense, the concept of freedom extends beyond the boundaries of practical philosophy (the sphere treated of in the *Philosophy of Right*) to include nonpractical—that is, theoretical or, more precisely, "speculative"—forms of freedom.

The idea most fundamental to Hegel's general concept, or "formal definition,"[3] of freedom is *self-determination* (*Selbstbestimmung*). In general, an entity is free, on Hegel's view, when it is determined by itself—when it is the source of its own determinations, or properties (*Bestimmtheiten*)—rather than determined by an "other" (that is, by something alien or external to itself).[4] A being whose determinations come from itself can also be said to be independent of, or unlimited by, anything other than itself. It is independent, or free—one could also say "self-sufficient"—in the sense that it relies on nothing outside of itself in order to be what it is. A being of this sort, then, would stand in no essential relation to anything other than itself but rather would be wholly self-related or, in Hegel's language, "with itself" *(bei sich)*. In fact, Hegel sometimes defines freedom as the absence of all genuine externality, or foreignness,[5] and he commonly employs variations of the term 'being-with-oneself' *(Beisichselbstsein)* to designate this essential characteristic of freedom in its most general sense (§§7, 23; E §384Z; VPR1, 215). Yet this formula by itself is misleading, insofar as it suggests that a free being must be—and therefore also that it is *possible* for something to be—purely and immediately self-related. Such a view, however, stands in conflict with one of Hegel's fundamental metaphysical doctrines, namely, that there are and can be no "immediate" entities or, in other words, that every being acquires its determinacies—every being is what it is—only through its relations to some other.[6] But if this is indeed the case, it would appear that no determinate being could possibly qualify as free according to Hegel's definition, since determinacy requires otherness, and freedom requires independence from the same.

That Hegel recognizes this dilemma and means to resolve it is made clear in his expanded version of the formula cited earlier, which defines freedom not simply as "being-with-oneself" but as "being-with-oneself-in-an-other" *(Beisichselbstsein in einem Anderen)*.[7] This expanded definition of freedom (freedom still in its most general sense) is supposed to give expression to the possibility of reconciling an entity's necessary relatedness to an other with its being "with itself" and therefore self-determined. As Hegel conceives it, essential independence from the other can be achieved not through the abolition of that other—not by simply making the other cease to be—but only by doing away with ("negating") the otherness, or alien character, of the other: "Spirit's freedom is an independence from the other that is achieved not *outside* the other but *in* the other" (E §382Z; emphasis added). Freedom, then, is a state of being-with-oneself that is attainable only through a process best characterized as the overcoming of otherness. It is an important consequence of this view that, ultimately, only a being endowed with *consciousness*—and not, say, Spinoza's immediately self-identical substance—can achieve true self-determination. This is because only a conscious being is capable of the complex feat required of something free. For only a conscious being can allow its other to continue to exist while simultaneously negating its otherness *by taking a certain view of it*—that is, by comprehending it in such a way that it ceases to appear as alien. Throughout Hegel's philosophy, then, freedom is always thought of as the end point of some process in which a being becomes constituted as what it is through its relations to an other and then abolishes the alien character of its other by apprehending it as identical to itself (in a sense in need of further specification), thereby becoming related only to itself. (It is perhaps helpful to note in this context that the young Hegel took love to be the paradigm for freedom conceived of as being-with-oneself-in-another. There is an obvious sense in which a loved one continues to be an other for the person in love, while at the same time, through an act of conscious identification with the loved one's needs and well-being, the demands those needs place upon the lover cease to appear as something foreign or limiting.)

This characterization of freedom can be made less abstract by considering one of the forms in which being-with-oneself-in-an-other appears in Hegel's philosophy. For Hegel, as for Aristotle, the highest activity human beings can engage in is philosophical contemplation. But unlike Aristotle, Hegel thinks of this contemplation as a form of *freedom,* indeed the highest, most complete form of self-determination possible: speculative freedom. Philosophical contemplation can be regarded as a species of freedom because, as Hegel conceives it, it is a process through which individuals come to be reconciled to a world that initially appears to them as radically "other"—that is, as hostile or indifferent to their basic aspirations as rational subjects. In other words, the task of Hegelian philosophy is to show that a world that originally appears to be both dominated by evil and impervious to rational comprehension is in fact, in its basic features, both good and thoroughly intelligible to human reason.[8] To apprehend the fundamental rationality and goodness of reality as a whole is to learn that, contrary to appearances, the world we inhabit is not alien to our deepest aspirations but is instead a realm within which rational subjects can be "at home," or "with themselves."[9] For a subject to achieve freedom in the speculative sense, then, is for it to overcome its original alienation from the world by finding itself (its aspirations as a rational subject) to be fully realized in an other (the world), which, when comprehended philosophically, ceases to confront the subject as an external, inhospitable other.

It is very important to distinguish the speculative freedom just described from the practical freedom that is supposed to be realized within the rational social order. Whereas the former could be considered a type of theoretical freedom (since reconciliation is achieved by *comprehending* the world philosophically), the freedom at issue in the *Philosophy of Right*—the sphere of "objective spirit"—is explicitly practical in character. This is to say that it is a freedom that pertains to the *will* and is realized through real activity within the external world. (This explains why the *Philosophy of Right* must be founded on an introductory account of the .re of the will and its freedom [§§5–28].) The distinction between speculative and practical freedom must not be taken to imply that the latter is somehow blindly voluntaristic, in contrast to the intellectual character of the former. Practical freedom, too, will involve certain cognitive relations to oneself, to others, and to the world. (Free social participation, for example, will require a certain understanding of oneself and one's relation to others if being bound by a general will is not to turn out to be subjection to an external other.) The point here is not that practical freedom is voluntaristic but that, unlike the speculative freedom achieved through philosophical contemplation, it is primarily a phenomenon of the will and realized through action.[10]

Articulating what practical freedom is turns out to be an extremely complicated enterprise, since, as indicated previously, it appears in a number of distinct forms (personal, moral, and social freedom). The task of understanding practical freedom in its various forms (but especially as social freedom, the basis of the theory of *Sittlichkeit*) will occupy us for the remainder of this book. For now, however, it is sufficient to bear in mind that, in all its guises, practical freedom differs from speculative freedom in that it always involves—is always realized through—practical engagement with the existent world. Subjects who are practically free enjoy a species of being-with-themselves-in-an-other, but unlike speculative freedom, it is a being-with-self that comes about through some practical relation to the world. Such subjects relate to a world that has been, and continues to be, determined by them—that is, transformed by their own activity and in accord with their own wills. Thus, formulated very generally, the aim of Hegel's treatment of the various forms of practical freedom in the *Philosophy of Right* is to provide an account of the different ways a subject's activity within the world can be its *own*, proceeding from its *own* will rather than from an external source.[11]

Although my principal aim here is to understand Hegel's conception of social freedom and the foundational role it plays in his social theory, it is impossible to do this without briefly considering the two species of practical freedom that precede "Ethical Life" in the *Philosophy of Right*: personal and moral freedom. This is necessary for two reasons. First, what is distinctive about social freedom is best brought to light by contrasting it with the two other configurations of practical freedom. Second, reconstructing Hegel's conception of social freedom requires articulating its relation to these other forms, since, as we shall see in more detail in chapter 5, one of the constitutive features of a social order in which this freedom is realized is its capacity to secure the social conditions of practical freedom in its other guises. In other words, part of our account of social freedom will consist in showing how it plays an essential role in realizing the types of freedom appropriate to persons and moral subjects.

Before examining what distinguishes personal from moral freedom, though, it will be helpful to say a bit more about practical freedom in general. I mentioned earlier that practically free subjects are "with themselves in an other" because their activity makes the world into something determined by them: through that activity their willed ends become determinations of the world. But there is a further, more substantive sense in which the forms of practical freedom represent a kind of being-with-oneself-in-an-other. In all three of these forms the practical activity at issue not only determines the world but also plays an essential part in the *self-actualization* of its agents—that is, it is activity through which individuals actualize, or give reality to, certain conceptions they have of themselves.[12] This means that each type of practical freedom is based on a distinctive self-conception that, when successfully expressed in action, acquires a real existence in the world. I shall say more in chapter 3 about what it is for individuals to actualize their self-conceptions in the institutions of *Sittlichkeit,* but even prior to that account it is not difficult to appreciate how self-actualization might be regarded as a form of being-with-oneself-in-an-other: when I give reality to my self-conception by acting upon the world, the reshaped world no longer confronts me as something alien but instead reflects back to me a confirmatory image of who I take myself to me. Practical freedom, on this conception, could be said to consist in the fact that "I can intuit and recognize myself in my activity or in the products of this activity in the world."[13]

It is important to add, however, that Hegel's account of practical freedom cannot be fully explicated by this notion of self-actualization alone. For it is not the case that actualizing any self-conception whatever constitutes practical freedom. Rather, in all three forms of practical freedom that Hegel considers the self-conceptions acted upon also have freedom as their *content*. In other words, even apart from the question of whether they are realized in the world, the self-conceptions at issue here can be recognized as conceptions of the subject as free, where 'free' means, very generally: possessing a self-determining will, a will that is the source of its own determinations (the ends it resolves to act upon). The crucial implication of this—a point that is completely obscured in Hegel's own exposition—is that 'freedom' enters into an account of each of the forms of practical freedom at two places and in two distinguishable senses. In the first sense, being free is a matter of successfully translating one's self-conception into the world (and thereby achieving a kind of being-with-oneself-in-an-other). In its second usage, freedom is defined simply, and in terms less distinctively Hegelian, as having a self-determined will—as the will's being the source of its own determinations, or ends (in a variety of senses to be further specified later). Thus, in all three of its forms practical freedom will involve (1) successfully acting upon a conception of oneself as (2) a being who possesses a self-determining will in one of the three senses recognized by Hegel's social theory, namely: as person, moral subject, or social member (of ethical life).

Since appealing to the idea of a self-determining will is an intuitively plausible way of giving content to the concept of freedom, Hegel's inclusion of that element in his understanding of practical freedom means that it will be easier than is commonly thought to recognize the alleged freedoms of personhood, moral subjectivity, and ethical life as genuine configurations of freedom without invoking his unique metaphysical views, including his definition of self-determination as being-with-oneself-in-an-other. The point of this observation is not to deny the importance or legitimacy of the claims Hegel means to be making in connection with the idea of being-with-oneself-in-an-other. On the contrary, the aspiration this idea points to—the aspiration to experience the world as a home—is both fundamental to Hegel's thought and a topic that philosophy in general cannot afford to ignore or ridicule. The point, rather, is that the idea of being at home in the world—which, one could argue, is more aptly captured by the phrase 'absence of alienation' than by 'freedom'—does not exhaust Hegel's understanding of practical freedom, which, because it also incorporates the more familiar notion of a self-determining will, turns out to be much closer to ordinary conceptions of freedom than it initially appears to be.

In summary, then, each configuration of practical freedom will have two components, which (in a discussion of personhood) Hegel characterizes as: "[1] something subjective that knows itself as free and . . . [2] an external realization (*Realität*) of this freedom" (E §385Z). In other words, each configuration will consist of both a distinctive conception of what it is for the will to be self-determining and an account of what it means for that conception to be actualized in the world we inhabit, taking into account the basic features of that world, including natural laws, the basic facts of human psychology, the plurality of individual subjects, and so on.[14] Perhaps it is best to illustrate the dual structure common to all forms of practical freedom by considering the example of personal freedom, the first and simplest configuration of freedom treated in the *Philosophy of Right*.

Personal freedom is the concept that grounds Hegel's theory of individual rights, which is the main concern of the first main section of the *Philosophy of Right*, "Abstract Right."[15] The type of self-determination at issue in personhood is the will's choosing of its own ends. Persons are characterized by a set of given drives and desires that have the capacity to motivate them to act, but they are persons by virtue of the fact that their wills are not simply determined by the drives and desires they happen to have. Rather, persons have the ability to reject some of their desires and to embrace others; they possess, in other words, a "resolving" (or deciding) will *(ein beschließender Wille),*[16] a will whose mode of self-determination consists in deciding which among one's given inclinations to satisfy and in which concrete ways to do so (§12). Hegel also calls this conception of the self-determining will the "arbitrary will" *(Willkür)*[17] (E §492) in order to emphasize that such a will qualifies as self-determined (on this conception) simply by virtue of its having chosen which ends to act upon, regardless of the reasons for having chosen as it did. The basic thought underlying the idea of personal freedom, then, is that an act is my own—it proceeds from my will rather than from an external source—if it is the result of a desire I resolve to act on, a desire that *affects* my will (provides me with a possible motive for action) but does not by itself *determine* it.

The doctrines of abstract right are arrived at by asking how individuals who conceive of themselves as self-determining in this sense could actualize their self-conceptions in the world and, most important, how the social order must be constituted if its inhabitants are to be able to do so. Hegel's answer is that an individual realizes the freedom of the arbitrary will by having at his disposal a portion of the external world, made up of will-less entities, or "things" *(Sachen)* (§42), within which his own arbitrary will has unlimited sovereignty[18] and from which other wills, as potential sources of obstacles to his own freely chosen ends, are excluded. The thought of an exclusive, external domain of activity that is subject to an individual's arbitrary will is the central idea behind Hegel's theory of abstract right, and it is the boundaries of such a domain that the principles of that theory are supposed to define. The principles of abstract right accomplish this end by ascribing to individual persons a set of rights guaranteeing them the liberty to do as they please with those things that are properly regarded as subject only to their own wills—their lives, their bodies, and the material things they own—all of which together constitute their *property (Eigentum)*.[19] Individuals realize their personal freedom, then, when they inhabit a social world that secures for them a private sphere of action within which they are unhindered by external agents, both other individuals and the state, from pursuing the ends that, as possessors of arbitrary wills, they choose as their own.[20] In having exclusive say over the things that make up their private external spheres, persons enjoy a certain kind of being-with-oneself-in-an-other and, thus, are (practically) free.[21]

Moral freedom, the concept that grounds "Morality,"[22] the second division of the *Philosophy of Right,* is a more complex configuration of freedom and is based on a correspondingly more complex conception of a self-determining will, which Hegel calls the moral subject.[23] Moral subjects are self-determining not only in the sense that they are able to choose which among their given desires they want to take as ends for action; they also have the capacity to determine their wills, not merely arbitrarily, but in accord with their own principles or, more precisely, in accord with their own understanding of what is (morally) good. The self-determination associated with moral subjectivity is more complex than that of personhood, not only because it involves determining one's will in accord with normative principles (principles that define one's understanding of the good), but also because those principles themselves count as "one's own" in the sense that, as a moral subject, one has the capacity to reflect rationally on such principles and to affirm, reject, or revise them. Individuals actualize moral freedom, then, when they subscribe to a rationally held vision of the good, determine their ends in accord with it, and successfully realize that vision in the world by bringing about the good through their own actions.[24] According to this conception of practical freedom, such actions count as the subject's own—as proceeding from its own will rather than from an external source—because they follow from normative principles that the subject itself rationally endorses.

It is more difficult in the case of moral subjectivity than in that of personhood to see how social institutions are implicated in the actualization of freedom. One connection between social theory and moral freedom becomes clearer if we bear in mind that the latter requires that individuals' wills be subject only to principles they themselves recognize (and affirm) as good. In Hegel's words, one implication of his view of moral subjectivity is that "ethical . . . determinations ought not to make claims on the behavior of the human being merely as external laws or as the dictates of an authority. Instead, they ought to find assent, recognition, or even justification in his heart, disposition [*Gesinnung*], conscience, insight, etc." (E §503A). Thus, the rational social order will need to satisfy what Hegel describes as the most important right of moral subjects (§132), namely, that all practical dictates governing their lives, including the prevailing laws and imperatives of social life, be accepted as good and affirmed as such by the subjects whose actions they determine. (One way the rational social order accommodates this right of moral subjects is addressed by Hegel's doctrine of the subjective component of social freedom—the "subjective disposition" of social members—which is the topic of chapter 3.) But there is a further respect in which this account of the self-determining will is relevant to social theory: from the perspective of moral subjectivity, it is not enough that social members in fact regard their social order as good and therefore worthy of their support; that perspective also requires that this attitude be rationally defensible, that the factually affirmed social order also be worthy of that affirmation. A set of institutions that actualizes moral freedom, then, must be capable of withstanding the rational scrutiny of its members. A social order that prohibits rational criticism, or whose appearance of worthiness could not survive such questioning, might be capable of gaining the actual assent of the majority of its members, but it is not one that satisfies the demands placed on it by the moral subject. (This aspect of moral subjectivity and its implications for social theory will be the topic of chapter 7.)

Social Freedom and the Project of Hegel's Social Theory

Thus far I have spoken of the three configurations of practical freedom as though they were separate and unrelated phenomena. In fact, however, Hegel thinks of them as constituting a hierarchically ordered ensemble, with social freedom at the top, followed (in order of decreasing rank) by the freedoms of moral subjectivity and personhood. Understanding what Hegel means to convey by this picture will help to bring into focus the project he takes himself to be carrying out in his theory of *Sittlichkeit*. The fact that Hegel locates a form of freedom above another in the hierarchy says two things about its relation to the lower form: first, that it represents a "richer" (§32Z)—a more complex and substantive—configuration of self-determination; and, second, that the lower form is *dependent* on the higher in the sense that, without the higher form, the lower cannot be actualized in the world in a manner fully consistent with the essential character of a self-determined will.[25] This second point implies that it is possible to arrive at a full account of the configurations of practical freedom through a single series of ("dialectical") arguments that, beginning with the lowest form of practical freedom and proceeding to the highest, investigates the conditions required for each to be adequately realized (realized in a manner fully consistent with the essential character of a self-determined will). In each instance[26] a consideration of those conditions will reveal how a lower form falls short of being completely adequate to the concept of self-determination and thus point out the necessity of the configuration immediately above it in the hierarchy.

Let me now spell out these points in the case of the two forms of practical freedom just defined. First, Hegel regards the freedom of moral subjectivity as higher than that of personhood because it embodies a more complex and substantive form of self-determination. The species of will associated with personhood—the arbitrary, resolving will—is self-determining in the sense that it, and nothing outside it, determines (chooses) the particular ends it will act upon. But the sense in which these chosen ends "come from the will itself" can be very weak indeed. Since all that

is required for such a will to qualify as self-determined on this conception is that its ends not be determined by something other (not be immediately determined by its given desires), this form of self-determination
is compatible with caprice or whim—in other words, with a choosing of
ends that is nothing more than unregulated spontaneity. (It is important
to remember here that, despite his claim that personal freedom is the
least substantive form of practical freedom, Hegel regards the self-determination of the arbitrary will as a genuine instance of freedom and
therefore as having a value to which the rational social order must give
its due, a task it accomplishes by enforcing the principles of abstract
right.) The will of a moral subject, in contrast, determines its ends in a
more substantive way: it chooses in accord with an understanding of the
good that is its own in the sense that it regards its principles of the good
as open to rational criticism and subject to revision. The intuition behind Hegel's claim that moral subjectivity involves a higher form of freedom than personhood is that an action determined in accord with a subject's rationally grounded understanding of the good represents a more
substantive expression of who that subject is—more of itself is invested
and embodied in such a deed—than an action undertaken arbitrarily or
for reasons peripheral to the subject's self-understanding.

The second point implicit in the assertion that the freedom of moral
subjectivity is higher than that of personhood is that the latter requires
the former in order to be actualized in a manner consistent with the essential character of a self-determined will. This claim is not spelled out
in a straightforward manner in Hegel's text but is inscribed in one of its
structural features, namely, the fact that "Abstract Right" precedes "Morality" in the text's progression toward a fully adequate conception of
practical freedom, the later stage allegedly emerging out of the earlier
with the necessity characteristic of Hegel's notorious dialectical transitions. Although the workings of such transitions in Hegel's texts are
highly obscure and controversial, his general intent in the present case
is relatively clear. It is to show that, on its own, the form of the self-
determining will associated with personhood falls short of the ideal of
complete self-determination in some way and therefore must be supplemented by another, more complex configuration of freedom, that of the
moral subject. Hegel's argument for this claim can be reconstructed as
follows.

As I said earlier, personal freedom, when actualized, consists essentially in a relation between an arbitrary will and the will-less entities (things) that such a will can appropriate and make use of in pursuing its freely chosen ends. Thus, the freedom of a person is actualized when it has exclusive, arbitrary control over a determinate portion of the external world that constitutes its property. If it were possible to imagine a world inhabited by a single arbitrary will, its freedom actualized in its dominion over things, there would be no basis for regarding the freedom of the arbitrary will as incomplete and in need of some further configuration of the will in order for self-determination to be fully realized. But when we consider the conditions under which the freedom of the arbitrary will can be realized in a world shared by more than one person— when we take into account the plurality of individual wills—we see that personal freedom cannot be the only kind of self-determination the inhabitants of such a world enjoy. More precisely, it cannot be the only freedom they enjoy, if they are to achieve the ideal of having wills that are fully self-determined.[27] A person living in a world in which the personal freedom of a plurality of individuals was guaranteed could not be fully self-determined if he possessed only an arbitrary will, for there would be a respect in which his actions would be subject to laws that were not internal to his own (merely arbitrary) will. The reason for this is that realizing the personal freedom of a plurality of individuals requires that the actions of all be subject to constraints. That is, their actions must be bound at least by those principles (the principles of abstract right) that specify which of an individual's actions are inconsistent with the personhood of others. Thus, one of the conditions for the actualization of personal freedom in a world shared by more than one person is that the actions of individuals conform to what Hegel presents as the fundamental command of abstract right: "Respect others as persons" (§36). The rational social order will codify the principles of abstract right into a system of laws and make use of external legal sanctions to enforce them, but if the persons whose actions are governed by those principles are to be fully self-determined (and therefore not bound by external constraints), they must be able to grasp the rational purpose behind the principles of abstract right, affirm them as their own, and determine their actions in accord with them. They must, in other words, possess the more complex structure of will that Hegel associates with moral subjectivity.[28]

Until we have given a more complete characterization of social freedom, it will be impossible to articulate satisfactorily how it represents a more complex and substantive conception of self-determination than its predecessors and how it is required for their actualization. On the basis of the preceding, however, we can say something of a general and pre-liminary nature about how a consideration of the conditions under which the first two forms of freedom can be actualized helps to define the basic tasks faced by Hegel's account of *Sittlichkeit*. The transition within the *Philosophy of Right* to social theory proper—to an account of the institutions that constitute the rational social order—is motivated by the insight that the lower forms of freedom can be realized only if a number of social conditions obtain. (These conditions will be discussed in more detail in the chapters that follow, but for now it is sufficient to have in mind, as examples, how legal institutions are required for the enforcement of abstract right and how institutions, such as the family, form their members into individuals who possess the subjective capaci-ties necessary for the exercise of their freedom.) One of the principal tasks of rational social institutions, then, will be to secure those condi-tions that make it possible for their members to realize personal and moral freedom. (This set of issues will be treated in chapter 5, as part of the objective component of social freedom.) Further tasks of Hegel's so-cial theory come to light when we recall that the conditions of the lower forms of freedom must also be brought about in a manner consistent with the essential character of self-determination. In other words, the means by which social institutions secure those conditions may not themselves violate the ideal of a self-determined will. This requirement, as Hegel interprets it, translates into two further criteria the rational so-cial order must meet. The first concerns the wills of the individuals who make up that order: individual social members, as the bearers of the in-stitutions of *Sittlichkeit*, must be able to relate subjectively to those insti-tutions in a way that is consistent with their being determined only by their own wills at the same time that they participate in, and reproduce, their social order. (This requirement is the subjective component of so-cial freedom, the concern of chapter 3.) The second of these criteria, by far the least intuitively evident aspect of Hegel's social theory, is based on the following thought: if the ideal of self-determination is to be fully re-alized in the process of securing the conditions of the lower forms of practical freedom, it is not enough that the human individuals who make up the social order have self-determined wills; it must also be the case that the social order as a whole, regarded as a living, self-reproducing system, itself embodies the characteristics essential to a self-determined will. (This feature of Hegel's view, a part of the doctrine of objective freedom, will be examined in chapter 4.)

Let me now reformulate these points in a way that makes clearer how Hegel's doctrine of social freedom can be understood as the necessary final step of a quasi-logical[29] project that seeks to arrive at—or dialectically "deduce"—a fully adequate conception of practical freedom, starting only with the bare idea of a will that is undetermined by anything external to it. The deduction begins with the simplest possible conception of a self-determined will—the arbitrary will characteristic of personhood—and demonstrates the necessity of supplementing that conception with a more complex form of freedom (moral freedom) by showing how personal freedom by itself is inadequate to the task of eliminating all subjection to a foreign will. (Since personal freedom cannot be universally realized unless the actions of all accord with the principles of abstract right, persons can avoid determination by a foreign will only if they are also able to will those principles that constrain their actions— that is, only if they are capable of the kind of self-determination that constitutes moral subjectivity.) This more complex form of freedom remedies the shortcoming of its predecessor, but it also gives rise, in typical dialectical fashion, to a new set of problems that require their own solution via an even richer conception of self-determination.

What, then, are the deficiencies of personal and moral freedom that necessitate the introduction of social freedom? As was the case in the previous transition from personal to moral freedom, the inadequacies of an earlier conception of freedom come to light by envisaging the conditions under which they can be realized in the world. The relevant problems associated with the realization of personal and moral freedom are of two main types: first, the wills that characterize persons and moral subjects fall short of complete self-sufficiency—they depend on something outside of themselves in order to be real—in the sense that actually being constituted as a person or a moral subject presupposes that one has undergone various social processes of character formation, or "education" (*Bildung*). Among other things, social members must learn to think of themselves as discrete individuals with their own particular interests and sovereign wills (in order to be a person), and they must acquire the capacity to internalize the principles that govern their interaction with others (in order to be moral subjects). Second, moral subjectivity falls short of true self-sufficiency in a further respect: considered on their own—in abstraction from their places within the basic institutions of society—moral subjects lack the resources they need in order to give concrete, nonarbitrary content to the concept of the good. While socially detached moral subjects may sincerely desire to realize the good, in the absence of a more concrete vision of the projects and forms of life that best promote the freedom and well-being of all (the good), they cannot know what specific actions their allegiance to the good requires of them. As Hegel formulates the critique, moral subjectivity is "abstract," "empty," and "formal" (§§134–137, 141); it fails to satisfy the criteria for a fully self-determining will because it cannot by itself give sufficient determinacy to its own reigning concept.[30]

The thought that leads to Hegel's doctrine of social freedom is that the solution to both of these problems lies in an account of good (or rational) social institutions. Thus, for Hegel, rational social institutions are charged with the dual task of socializing their members into beings who possess the subjective capacities required to realize the freedoms of personhood and moral subjectivity, and of providing a social framework that gives definition to the particular projects that imbue their individual lives with purpose and provide determinate content for their understanding of the good. Each of these tasks points to an important respect in which the systematic realization of personal and moral freedom depends on the existence of rational social institutions. That such institutions secure the conditions necessary for realizing personal and moral freedom should not, however, lead us to think that Hegel's theory values social membership for purely instrumental reasons (merely as a means to the realization of the two lower forms of practical freedom). This is emphatically not the case. On the contrary, if the problems posed by the lower forms of freedom are to be solved in a way that remains true to the ideal of complete self-determination, this solution must itself give rise to a new and more substantive configuration of the self-determining will, one that finds expression, in this case, in the idea of social freedom. In other words, the means by which the rational social order secures the necessary conditions of personal and moral freedom must themselves embody a kind of self-determination of the will; more than being *merely* means to the realization of freedom, they are at the same time an instance of it. (Here it may help to recall Hegel's claim: "In *Sittlichkeit* freedom *is*.")

Bringing together the various requirements this new form of self-determination is supposed to meet will provide us with a concise statement of its essential features, as well as an outline of the structure of much of the discussion to follow: In addition to (1) securing the necessary conditions of the lower forms of freedom (part of the objective component of social freedom and the subject matter of chapter 5), social freedom will incorporate self-determination in two further, distinctively Hegelian senses. These are (2) individual social members will be self-determining in the sense that, because their self-conceptions are linked to the social roles they occupy, their participation in the institutions of *Sittlichkeit* is not only voluntary but also an activity through which they constitute—give real determinacy to—their very identities. (This is the subjective component of social freedom, the concern of chapter 3.) And, (3) the social order itself—the ensemble of institutions together with their members—constitutes a self-determining whole, one that is more thoroughly self-sufficient than any individual on its own can in principle be. (This is a further part of the objective component of social freedom and the topic of chapter 4.) Thus, the actions of socially free individuals will count as their own—as proceeding from their own will rather than from an external source—in a dual sense: first, their social participation will be expressive of their own consciously held self-conceptions (for example, as mother, teacher, and citizen of a particular state); and, second, in acting in accord with their self-conceptions they actually produce the totality of social conditions that make their own (personal and moral) freedom possible, along with the holistically defined "self-determination" (or self-sufficiency) of the social whole. (As we shall see in more detail later, these two senses in which the actions of socially free individuals can be considered "their own" form the basis of what I call the subjective and objective aspects of social freedom.)

We have just seen how Hegel's doctrine of social freedom can be understood as the culmination of a kind of logical inquiry, one that seeks to develop a concrete conception of practical freedom that is fully adequate to its core notion of complete self-determination. There is, however, a second way of viewing Hegel's philosophical project here—not as a conceptual investigation into the nature of freedom but as the response to a sociocultural problem that arises at a particular point in history and defines the basic predicament of a new world-historical age (Hegel's, as well as, presumably, our own). On this reading, the central task of Hegelian social theory is to find a way of bringing together three distinct

and potentially conflicting visions of freedom (personal, moral, and social freedom) that the post-Enlightenment age has inherited from its
past and continues, even now, to find compelling. Implicit in this understanding of Hegel's project is the thought that, for us today, a social order
that excluded one or more of these forms of freedom could not be regarded as a fully rational, satisfying world. Indeed, from this perspective,
the rational social order could be defined as one that fulfills the aspiration of its members to achieve self-determination in all three of its
guises.

Hegel himself endorses this reading of his project. That he does so is
evidenced both by his general claim that "world history is nothing but
the development of the concept of freedom" (PH, 456/XII, 539–540)
and by his practice of identifying each of the forms of practical freedom
with a particular historical era. (Moreover, as these points make clear,
this understanding of his project does not at all conflict with the first,
since for Hegel the movement of world history simply reflects the logical
structure of reason itself; in other words, each of the moments of "the
Concept" (*der Begriff*) has its day, as it were, in the march of world history.) Hegel's claim is that the idea of personal freedom, with its emphasis on "the abstract freedom of the individual," comes to us from ancient
Rome (PH, 279/XII, 340). It first finds expression in the Roman legal
practice that recognized all citizens of the empire (with the exception of
slaves)[31] as personae possessing a determinate set of personal and property rights. The idea of moral freedom, in contrast, is a product of the
modern world. It first appears in the theology of the Reformation (in the
view that the word of God is present in the heart of all believers), but it
is most clearly articulated in Kant's conception of the autonomous moral
subject that is bound only by principles immanent to its own reason.

The third conception of freedom that Hegel's social theory attempts to
incorporate is more difficult to characterize. It comes from classical
Greece—or, more accurately perhaps, from the picture Hegel and his
contemporaries had of that world. This kind of freedom—the classical
forerunner of Hegel's *social* freedom[32]—is bound up with the circumstance that the inhabitants of ancient Greece (at least its free male citizens) had such a deep subjective attachment to their polis that their social membership could be said to constitute a central part of their own
identities. For the ancient Greeks, participation in the life of the polis
was valuable for its own sake (and not simply as a means to achieving external, egoistic ends), as well as the source of the goals, projects,

and social roles that were central to their understanding of themselves. Hegel regards the subjective relation Greek citizens had to their polis as a kind of freedom for two reasons. First, the fact that citizens did not regard the good of their polis as distinct from, or antagonistic to, their own good enabled them to obey the political laws that governed them—laws directed at the good of the polis as a whole rather than at the particular good of its members—without experiencing those laws as external constraints on their wills. Second, the classical polis was the source of a distinctive and important kind of satisfaction for its members. It provided a social framework that gave meaning to their individual lives and served as the primary arena within which, by fulfilling their roles as citizens, they won what Hegel calls their "sense of self" through the recognition of their fellow beings. In short, the social world of ancient Greece was experienced as a "home" by those who inhabited it.

For Hegel one of the central questions facing post-Enlightenment culture is whether it is possible for a social order to realize all three of these conceptions of freedom. His social theory is an attempt to show that, contrary to appearances, the three basic institutions of modernity— modern forms of the family, civil society, and the state—are able, working in concert, to accommodate each of these ideals. The idea of social freedom plays a central role in this argument, for, in its modern form, it integrates the freedom of ancient Greece with the two forms of freedom that succeed it historically. Modern social freedom achieves this integration in two different respects: First, socially free individuals have a subjective relation to their social order that is similar to the one Greek citizens had to theirs but also crucially different from it in that, in the case of modern social members, having identity-constituting attachments to one's institutions is compatible with conceiving of oneself as an *individual*—that is, as a person with rights and interests separate from those of the community and as a moral subject that is able and entitled to pass judgment on the goodness of existing social norms and practices. Second, the institutions within which modern individuals achieve their particular identities objectively promote personal and moral freedom in the sense that, when functioning properly, one of their effects is to bring about the various social conditions that make the realization of those freedoms possible.

In the next sections of this chapter, before beginning the extended discussion of social freedom that is to follow, I want to turn to two questions, both of which have to do with the relation between Hegel's conception of social freedom and his doctrine of absolute spirit, namely, who, or what, is the bearer of social freedom? (Is it individuals, or some supra-individual social entity, that is properly said to be socially free?) And, can social freedom be recognized as a plausible conception of freedom independently of Hegel's understanding of absolute spirit and its historical mission, or does the idea of social freedom simply reduce to the view that human individuals are most free when they realize their "true" nature by serving the ends of absolute spirit?

In order to gain entry to these issues, it will be helpful to consider what the answers to these two questions would be if posed with respect to personal and moral freedom. First, it is quite easy to regard both as genuine instances of freedom without appealing to distinctively Hegelian views about the nature of reason, history, or absolute spirit. This is because, in contrast to other conceptions of freedom that figure in Hegel's thought, personal and moral freedom are grounded in easily recognizable conceptions of the *self-determining will*. As indicated previously, persons possess self-determining wills in the sense that they choose which of their desires are to determine their actions, and moral subjects are self-determining in the sense that their wills are determined by principles they recognize as their own. Second, both are clearly species of *individual* freedom. The freedoms characteristic of persons and moral subjects are individualistic in (at least) the sense that 'personally free' and 'morally free' are predicates that can be, and typically are, meaningfully applied to individual agents. It is (for the most part) individuals rather than groups who qualify as persons and moral subjects, and hence individuals are also the principal bearers of the freedoms associated with each.

It is more difficult to find answers to these questions in the case of social freedom. That is, it is far from clear whether social freedom can be understood as a kind of *self-determination of the will* (and hence as a genuine species of practical freedom) and whether it, like personal and moral freedom, is a property of *individuals*. Until now most interpreters either have explicitly answered these questions in the negative—denying both that social freedom is a species of self-determination of the will and that individuals are its bearers—or have failed to spell out in sufficient detail how the freedom realized in *Sittlichkeit* can be otherwise understood. This circumstance has had a significant impact on the philosophical reception of Hegel's social theory, both present and past, for without being able to show how social freedom is a form of practical freedom enjoyed by individuals, its account of the rational social order ends up looking highly unattractive. If, for example, the freedom actualized in rational social institutions turns out to be something other than a freedom of the will (for example, something akin to realizing one's true "spiritual" nature as a vehicle of absolute spirit), then Hegel's theory appears to be thoroughly dependent on a metaphysics—indeed, a theodicy—that few of us today are willing to accept. Alternatively, if social freedom, said to be the *highest* form of practical freedom, is only the property of a social order considered as a whole and not also of individuals, it becomes difficult to resist the familiar charge that Hegel's theory ends up sacrificing the essential interests of individuals to the collective ends of the social organism.

That such positions have unattractive consequences does not, of course, prove that Hegel did not hold them. In my reconstruction, however, I shall try to show that traditional readings of Hegel's account of *Sittlichkeit* have gone astray with respect to both of these issues. I shall argue, in other words, that social freedom can be understood as a species of self-determination of the will (in a sense that is independent of Hegel's theodicy of absolute spirit) and that it can be meaningfully predicated of individual social members (or, equivalently, that individuals in a rational social order can meaningfully be said to enjoy a distinctive form of practical freedom beyond the freedoms of personhood and moral subjectivity). By way of clarifying the two main pitfalls my account of social freedom means to avoid, I shall examine two recent interpretations—those of Karl-Heinz Ilting and Charles Taylor—that attribute to Hegel the very positions I am claiming he (rightly) rejects. I shall begin with the second of these issues, whether social freedom can be ascribed to the individual members of a rational social order.

Is Social Freedom a Freedom of Individuals?

Hegel begins Part III of the *Philosophy of Right* with the pronouncement: "Ethical life is the *Idea of freedom*" (§142). This statement is reformulated in the same paragraph as the claim that ethical life is the "concept of freedom" that has acquired a real existence in the world and in the consciousness of its members. The question I mean to address here is, *whose* freedom is it that gets actualized in the institutions of *Sittlichkeit*? Is this freedom a property that belongs only to the social whole in question, or does it also pertain to the individuals who compose the whole? In other words, is it the ensemble of ethical institutions itself—the family, civil society, and the state—that is free (in some peculiarly Hegelian sense of freedom yet to be determined), or is it the individual members of those institutions who enjoy the freedom distinctive of *Sittlichkeit*? The question whether social freedom is a property of a social order as a whole or of its constituent parts (human individuals) is ultimately a question about the extent to which Hegel's social theory embraces a *holistic* account of the basic values that rational social institutions are supposed to achieve. So before addressing this question directly, it will be helpful to make the concept of holism more precise by distinguishing three ways in which the properties of composite entities (such as a social whole) might relate to the units of which those entities are made up (in our case, the individual members of society).

Consider a group of differentiated cells, each of which on its own lacks the basic capacities essential to the sustainment of life but which, when united in the appropriate way, constitute a living organism capable of carrying out the biological functions necessary for its continued survival. It is possible to ascribe a number of kinds of properties to such an organism; we could say of it, for example, that it has mass, that it is alive, and that it is self-sustaining. If we now ask whether and under what conditions these properties of the organism can also be ascribed to its individual cells, we see that a different response is called for in each of the three cases. The first of the organism's properties, that of having mass, also holds of each of its constituent cells and does so regardless of whether those cells are organically united into a living being. Having mass, then, is a property individual cells have on their own, independently of their relations to other cells. The second property, that of being alive, can also be ascribed to the organism's individual cells—it is possible to characterize a single cell as "living" and to distinguish it from a neighboring cell that is now dead—but being alive is an attribute each possesses only when joined together with other cells so as to constitute a whole that is capable of the basic functions of life. Being alive, then, could be considered a holistic property in the sense that it pertains to the parts of a composite entity only by virtue of their having a certain relation to the whole of which they are the parts. The third of the organism's properties, its being self-sustaining, is holistic in a stronger sense: it can be ascribed only to the organism as a whole, not to the individual cells that compose it. We can say of an individual cell that it participates in, or is a member of, a self-sustaining entity but not that it itself is self-sustaining. Since Hegel's conception of social freedom is clearly not a property of the first type, the question before us is whether it is best understood as holistic in the stronger or weaker of the two senses distinguished here: Is social freedom something that individual social members achieve by virtue of being situated within a rationally structured society, or is it a property of their social order considered as a whole?

There is ample textual evidence to support the view that Hegel conceives of social freedom as a strongly holistic property in the sense just distinguished. In one typical passage Hegel refers to *Sittlichkeit* as "the free whole" *(das freie Ganze)* (VPR1, 271), and in another he identifies "the ethical whole" *(das sittliche Ganze)* with "the actualization of freedom" (258Z). The same idea is expressed even more explicitly in the following quotation: "The rationality of ethical life [*das Sittliche*] resides in the fact that it is the system of the determinations of the Idea. In this way ethical life is freedom, or the will that has being in and for itself as something objective . . . The determinations of ethical life constitute the concept of freedom" (§145 + Z; emphases omitted).[33] Since there is clearly some force to the claim that the freedom distinctive of *Sittlichkeit* is first and foremost a property of the rational social order considered as a whole rather than of its constituent parts, I shall first spell out this idea in enough detail to be able to see how it might be developed into a plausible interpretation of Hegel's position. (I shall expand upon these thoughts in chapter 4 with the aim of making them more compelling than they will appear to be here, but a preliminary discussion of them is necessary now in order to give some minimal content to the suggestion that social freedom is a strongly holistic property.) In spelling out this interpretive possibility I shall refer to the work of one interpreter who emphasizes this aspect of Hegel's view, Karl-Heinz Ilting.[34]

The claim that social freedom is a strongly holistic property immediately raises questions about the intelligibility of such a notion: Under what conception of freedom could social wholes be said to be free and to be so independently of whether or not the individuals who compose them are also free in that sense? What could it mean to say that the family, civil society, and the state are themselves, in Ilting's words, "configu-

rations . . . of the free will," or that "freedom *exists as a concrete [ethical]*
community" and resides in "*the structure*" of that community?[35] The key
to making sense of this position lies in understanding Ilting's interpretive claim that only the ethical community as a whole "is fully adequate
to the 'concept' of freedom."[36] Making use of the terms employed earlier
in the discussion of the concept of freedom in general, this claim can be
reformulated as follows: among all entities that can plausibly be counted
as wills, the rational social order as a whole most fully embodies the
qualities that define the ideal of (practical) self-determination;[37] that is,
the rational social order as a whole comes closer than other configurations of the will to being the source of its own determinations and independent of anything external to itself. Implicit in this claim is the thesis
that the more individualistic forms of will that precede *Sittlichkeit* in the
Philosophy of Right—the person and the moral subject—approximate
but do not fully correspond to the concept of self-determination. Not
surprisingly, giving some content to this claim will help illuminate the
view, alluded to earlier, that social freedom is a richer and more substantive type of freedom than the two preceding forms.

A fully satisfying reconstruction of the arguments underlying the position that social freedom is a property of the social order as a whole
would require a more tortuous excursion into Hegel's metaphysics than
can be undertaken here. Nevertheless, it is possible for us to get a sense
of the general idea behind that view by returning to the concept of self-
determination and taking a closer look at what Hegel believes to be contained within it.[38] As Hegel understands it, the concept of self-determination entails two properties that are especially significant for his account of a fully self-determined will: such a will must (1) have a self-
sufficient existence and (2) exhibit the distinctive logical structure possessed by what Hegel calls "the Concept" *(der Begriff)*.[39] Explaining the
requirement of existential self-sufficiency is relatively straightforward. It
derives from the thought that if a being were dependent on anything external to itself for its continued existence, then it would not be fully self-
determined. In the context of Hegel's social theory, self-sufficiency refers
primarily to the capacity for self-reproduction.[40] A self-sustaining society, one that is capable of reproducing itself with all of the qualities essential to it, is self-sufficient, then, in the relevant sense.

The requirement that a self-determined will exhibit the structure of
the Concept is considerably more difficult to explain because it is more

intimately bound up with a distinctively Hegelian metaphysical thesis. 'The Concept' is Hegel's name for the basic structure that informs all of actuality (*Wirklichkeit*)—that is, all of existence that is susceptible of rational comprehension. Since the free will is taken to be a part of that existence, it too must exhibit the structure of the Concept. Hegel characterizes this structure in a variety of ways,[41] but for our purposes here its most important feature is what he calls "the interpenetrating unity of universality and individuality" (*die sich durchdringende Einheit der Allgemeinheit und der Einzelheit*) (§258A), a feature that he also, in the same passage, identifies as the essence of rationality in general (*die Vernünftigkeit, . . . abstrakt betrachtet*). Hence in order to qualify as self-determined in the sense at issue here (and therefore also as rational), a will must be composed of universal and particular[42] elements that are arranged so as to constitute a specific kind of (rational) unity, the nature of which must still be explicated.

The thought that is supposed to make sense of this second requirement of a self-determined will derives from a metaphysical claim, fundamental to all of Hegel's thought, about the form any self-determined being must assume if it is to have a real existence in the world. Hegel's idea is that, in contrast to an abstract, universal concept (such as the bare concept of self-determination with which Hegel's philosophy begins), any really existing entity is necessarily a particular being with particular properties, or determinacies (*Bestimmtheiten*). But if a really existing being is fully to realize the ideal of self-determination, its particular properties must be more than external or contingent; they must be "self-determined" particular properties, which in this case means that they are determined by—or, better, fully adequate to—the being's abstract concept, or essence. It is primarily this match between a being's essential nature and its particular qualities that Hegel refers to when he invokes the notion of an interpenetrating unity of universality and particularity. As will be described in more detail in chapter 4, self-determination in this sense amounts to what we would be more likely to call organic structure. A being that is self-determined in this sense is an articulated, teleologically organized whole (§260A)—that is, a being made up of distinguishable, relatively autonomous components, each of which contributes in its unique way to the well-being or proper functioning of the whole. (In Hegelian language, a part that can be understood as having the specific properties it has because of their suitability for furthering the ends of the whole is a particular that is (qualitatively) "determined" by the universal, and the being so organized is, regarded as a whole, "self-determined.") Although it no doubt strikes us as odd to think of organic structure as a kind of self-determination (and as even odder perhaps to regard it as a species of *freedom*), it is easier to appreciate Hegel's reasons for associating this structure with rationality. On this view, a social whole is (in at least one significant respect) rational, or intelligible to reason, when its various parts fit together so as to constitute a coherently organized whole. Since the idea of self-determination understood as teleological organization does play a major role in Hegel's social theory, it will be useful to point out briefly two principal ways in which it does so.

First, "the interpenetrating unity of universality and particularity," as applied to the rational social order, designates a unity of universal and particular *wills,* understood in the following sense: the particular ends pursued by the individuals of a rational social whole are in harmony with, and contribute positively to, the achievement of universal ends, the content of which is defined by what the social whole requires in order to exist and to reproduce itself as the kind of being it essentially is. (To take one of Hegel's simplest examples: in civil society[43] the individual's pursuit of his particular ends through his own productive labor is harmonious with, and contributes positively to, the achievement of a universal end of civil society, the production of the societal wealth required for the community to reproduce itself.) But the "interpenetrating unity" said to exist among universal and particular wills refers not only to a harmony of the two; it also points to their mutual dependence. The social whole's universal will is dependent on the particular wills of individuals, since it is only through them that its universal ends can be realized. Conversely, the particular wills of individuals are dependent on the universal, because their particular ends can be achieved only by participating in the life of the social whole.

Understood in this sense, the unity of universality and particularity designates a relation among wills that exists (in slightly different forms) within each of the three main spheres of *Sittlichkeit.* Yet the idea of an interpenetrating unity of universality and particularity plays more than this intra-institutional role in Hegel's social theory; it also specifies the relations that hold among the three social institutions themselves. This second aspect of Hegel's view comes to light in those passages (for example, §260+Z) where he associates the family and civil society with particularity, identifies the state with universality, and then locates the rationality of the ethical social whole in the fact that the spheres of particularity stand in a relation of harmony and mutual dependence to the sphere of universality. Identifying the family and civil society with particularity expresses the idea that these two spheres, in their own distinct ways, serve the purpose of fostering and accommodating the particularity of individual social members. Through their participation in civil society and the family, individuals develop and express identities as distinct human beings and acquire and pursue specific interests that distinguish them from other members of society. As citizens of the state, on the other hand, individuals attain a universal existence in the sense that they gain an identity that is shared with all other citizens and learn to discern and to be moved by the best interest of the whole, even though this may conflict with some interests they have by virtue of their particular positions within civil society or the situations of their own particular families. In this context the demand that the social world exhibit a "self-determined" unity of universality and particularity translates into the requirements that the three principal spheres of *Sittlichkeit* coexist in basic harmony and that they depend on one another for their continued existence as stable, well-functioning social spheres.[44]

Thus, Hegel's conception of a self-determining will, when fully articulated, translates (roughly) into the thought of a plurality of particularities that are qualitatively determined by the universal and unified into an organism that is capable of reproducing itself as a whole, along with the diverse particularities required for its continued existence as the kind of being it essentially is. My primary purpose here is not to defend this conception of self-determination or the metaphysical views upon which it rests but merely to show how it enables us to give some meaning to the claim that social freedom is a property of the rational social order considered as a totality. If the essential features of a self-determined will are its being self-sustaining and its possessing the (Conceptual) structure of a teleologically organized whole, then it is not difficult to see how the institutions of *Sittlichkeit,* taken together, meet the standards for practical self-determination more adequately than any merely individual will. Moreover, it becomes clear (on the assumption that this is all there is to social freedom) why one might claim that the type of freedom distinctive of *Sittlichkeit* belongs *only* to the social world as a whole and not to the individuals who compose it. On this view individuals could be said to *partake of* social freedom, insofar as they belong to a social order that, considered as a whole, embodies the essential features of a self-determined will. But since individual social members do not themselves exhibit the qualities required of a fully self-determined will—individuals, for example, are not existentially self-sufficient—they cannot properly be said to be bearers of social freedom.

The question that confronts us now is whether the conception of the self-determined social whole just outlined exhausts Hegel's conception of social freedom, or whether there is also a sense in which individual social members could be said, through their membership in the institutions of *Sittlichkeit,* to achieve a species of self-determined will beyond the freedoms they enjoy as persons and moral subjects. If the latter is the case, then social freedom will not merely be a holistic property of the third type distinguished earlier; it will also be a holistic property of the second, weaker type (a property that can be ascribed to the individuals that make up the social whole but only insofar as they are united within that whole in the appropriate manner). A common response to this question, perhaps even the most natural one, is to opt for the first of these alternatives and ascribe social freedom exclusively to the social whole and not to the individual members who compose it. This view, which I shall call the strongly holistic interpretation of social freedom, is unambiguously endorsed by Ilting in passages such as the following:

> What is designated as "free" [in *Sittlichkeit*] is no longer the "free individual" but the ethical [*sittliche*] "substance" as the "universality" (community) in which individuals live as "organic moments" in such a way that their individuality is recognized and has acquired a "being." . . . [T]he abstract "concept" of the free will of an individual has now developed into the "idea" of freedom as an ethical community, i.e., freedom exists now *as Sittlichkeit.* In the ethical community, therefore, freedom has reality through and in the disposition [*Gesinnung*] of a subjective will, and the latter has its foundation and substance in the freedom of an ethical community.[45]

According to Ilting, then, the freedom of *Sittlichkeit* is a quality possessed exclusively by the ethical community as a whole; individuals are said to find in the community their "foundation and substance," as well as a recognition of their individuality, but not social freedom itself.

What is immediately striking about the strongly holistic interpretation is that it appears to attribute to Hegel a conception of freedom that is blatantly unattractive as a foundation for social theory. The view Hegel is alleged to hold appears to be unattractive in two respects. First, the conception of freedom said to be realized in *Sittlichkeit* derives from such an abstract notion of self-determination that it is difficult to see what connection the described phenomenon has to anything human beings normally recognize and value as practical freedom. Even if we grant that the ethical community Hegel describes instantiates the formal qualities he attributes to the fully self-determining will, what reason does that give us for regarding the "freedom" of such a community as something good? Second, ascribing to Hegel a strongly holistic conception of social freedom appears to commit him to a highly objectionable view concerning the relation between the good of a rational society and the good of its individual members. For if the highest good realized in *Sittlichkeit,* social freedom, consists in properties that can be ascribed only to the community as a whole, not severally to the individuals who compose it, then the primary good of the rational social order appears to be realizable independently of the good of individuals. This point concerns more than just the theoretical issue of how Hegel conceives of collective goods. It has a more practical relevance as well, for it is closely connected to the much discussed question whether Hegel's social philosophy is inherently totalitarian: if the primary good of society is thought to exist independently of the good of individuals (and if the collective good has priority over individual goods), then the philosophical groundwork seems to be in place to justify the view, often attributed to Hegel, that the good of the community may (and perhaps even must) be achieved at the expense of the good of individuals.[46]

To a sympathetic reader these considerations alone might seem to be a good reason for calling Ilting's strongly holistic interpretation of social freedom into question. In fact, however, the situation is more complex than it appears, for both of these objections can be met (at least in part) by the defender of the strongly holistic view. Although I shall ultimately reject this interpretation of social freedom, I shall do so not because it necessarily saddles Hegel with a hopelessly reactionary social theory— on the contrary, it does not—but rather because it misrepresents the position Hegel actually held and in doing so overlooks one of the most important (and appealing) features of Hegel's social philosophy, namely, his account of the distinctive kind of freedom that *individuals* enjoy as members of the rational community. In order to get clear on precisely what is at issue in rejecting the strongly holistic account of social freedom, we must first see why this account need not be as indifferent to the good of individuals as it initially seems to be.

Although the strongly holistic interpretation locates the primary good of the social order in properties that can belong only to the community considered as a whole (self-sufficiency and organic structure), it need not regard this collective good as achievable independently of the good of individuals. On the contrary, it is open to the strongly holistic interpretation—and this is the route taken by all plausible versions of that interpretation, including Ilting's—to make the realization of the good of individual social members *indispensable* to the attainment of the primary social good. A justification for positing an essential connection between the good of individuals and the good of the whole can be derived from the basic requirement that the fully self-determining social whole unify universal and particular wills in accord with the structure of the Concept. For, as mentioned earlier, the interpenetrating unity of universality and particularity implies an interdependence of the universal and particular such that the ends of the universal will can be achieved only insofar as individuals pursue and attain their own particular ends. What the strongly holistic interpretation does imply is that the good of individuals that is necessarily realized within the rational social order is not to be conceived of as a distinctive type of *freedom* (social freedom) but rather as what Ilting describes as the development and recognition of social members' *individuality*.[47] On this interpretation, then, the institutions of *Sittlichkeit* are good for individuals not because they are the source of some distinctive species of freedom (beyond the freedoms of personhood and moral subjectivity) but because they allow them to realize their individuality—that is, the rational social order secures the conditions necessary for individuals' freedom as persons and moral subjects and constitutes a social world within which they can pursue and satisfy their own particular ends, including their need to be recognized by fellow social members as individuals of value and standing within the community.

This account of how the good of individuals is realized in the rational social order is not, strictly speaking, incorrect, for Hegel does regard individuality in the sense articulated earlier as an important good that individuals achieve as members of *Sittlichkeit*. But individuality in this sense is neither the only nor the primary good individuals enjoy in the ethical community. In contrast to the strongly holistic interpretation, I shall argue that Hegel's theory of *Sittlichkeit* includes a distinctive conception of freedom that can be meaningfully ascribed to the wills of individual social members and that this aspect of social freedom is viewed by Hegel as the most important practical good individuals realize in the ethical community. This conception of freedom will be holistic in the weaker of the two senses distinguished previously: like individual cells that can severally be called alive but that have this property only by being joined together with other cells so as to form a biological organism, socially free individuals themselves acquire a species of self-determined will that depends on (and consists in) their being united with other individuals into the three kinds of social groups that make up the institutions of *Sittlichkeit*. Asserting this view does not make it necessary to reject the basic interpretive claim underlying the strongly holistic conception of social freedom, namely, that Hegel thinks of the institutions of *Sittlichkeit* themselves as embodiments of freedom. On the contrary, it is indisputable that Hegel regards the family, civil society, and the state as "free" entities and that he does so because, taken together, they approximate the self-sufficiency and organic structure characteristic of a fully self-determining will. What is incorrect about the strongly holistic account is its assertion that the conception of freedom that grounds the theory of *Sittlichkeit* is exhausted by this claim. Essential to Hegel's position as well, I shall argue, is the view that individual members of *Sittlichkeit* achieve a distinctive form of freedom that is realized in their social participation and extends beyond their freedom as persons and moral subjects.[48] In other words, the interpretation I develop here attempts to take more seriously than previous commentators have done those passages in which Hegel says explicitly of individual social members that they have their "actual" (E §514) or "substantial freedom" (§§149, 257) in ethical institutions.[49]

But apart from the fact that my rejection of the strongly holistic interpretation seems to be required by the texts themselves, why is it important to emphasize that individuals realize a distinctive sort of freedom, and not merely their individuality, as members of *Sittlichkeit?* What in the end does this interpretive difference amount to? It is difficult to give a perspicuous answer to these questions in advance of the full account of social freedom to be provided in chapters 3 through 5, but perhaps the following remarks will help to indicate the significance of this difference in a preliminary way: As long as individuality (including the freedoms of personhood and moral subjectivity) is taken to be the sole good individuals achieve through their membership in *Sittlichkeit,* it is possible to think of social members as little more than the cogs of a social mechanism who perform their distinctive functions by pursuing their own specialized, particular ends but lack any cognitive or voluntative relation to the mechanism as a whole. The most important implication of including social freedom among the goods realized by individuals in *Sittlichkeit* is that doing so imposes an additional requirement on the rational social order: in order for the ideal of practical self-determination to be fully realized, the rational ends of the social organism must be achieved in such a way that not only the whole as such but also its parts themselves (human individuals) possess wills that are undetermined by anything external to themselves. Formulated in these terms, it is possible to see this requirement as closely related to Rousseau's principle that a legitimate social contract must be one in which each individual, while united with the rest, "nevertheless obeys only himself and remains as free as before" (SC I.6.iv). And, again like Rousseau, Hegel's strategy for satisfying this requirement will depend on individual social members consciously identifying with the universal will—the set of laws or principles—that governs the operation of the whole to which they belong.[50] In Rousseauean terms, then, what my interpretation of Hegel's social theory brings to light is its claim, not always fully explicit in Hegel's texts, that in order for the freedom distinctive of *Sittlichkeit* to be realized, individual social members must possess general wills. Or, as Hegel himself puts it: "The individual has and enjoys his freedom [in the state] by knowing . . . and willing the universal" (PH, 38/XII, 55).[51] The strongly holistic interpretation, in contrast, obscures this important feature of Hegel's position. This, however, constitutes a significant misrepresentation of that theory, for there is a world of difference between a view that holds that the most important mission of social members is to satisfy their individuality in and through their social participation and one that also requires that, in doing so, individuals know and affirm the laws that govern their activity as their own, thereby avoiding determination by an external other.

It can easily appear that the interpretation I propose here has the disadvantage of making social freedom consist in two quite unrelated states of affairs (the self-sufficiency and "self-determined" organic structure of the social whole, on the one hand, and the free wills of individual social members who embrace the general will, on the other). But in fact this is not the case. While it is true that on my account social freedom incorporates two different forms of self-determination (one strongly, the other weakly holistic), it remains a unitary phenomenon because the realization of each is bound up with the realization of the other. The requirement that the general will be willed by all individuals can be thought of as simply part of what it means for a social order to exhibit an interpenetrating unity of universality and particularity and hence as implicit in the idea of a fully self-determined social whole. Conversely, the features of the social order that allow us to call it self-determined in the strongly holistic sense are (at least part of) what makes it possible for individuals to regard it as good and to embrace the interests of the social order as their own, thereby avoiding subjection to a foreign will when laboring for the collective good.

This suggestion raises a number of questions, including to what extent Hegel's basic approach to social theory can ultimately be distinguished from the methodological atomism that informs Rousseau's theory (and social contract theory in general). Central to this question is the issue of whether, and in what sense, Hegel takes the good of the social order to be reducible to the good of the individuals that compose it. Is it the case, as has recently been asserted, that Hegel, along with social contract theorists, subscribes to the view that "collective goods have value because they have value *for individuals*"?[52] And if that (or some closely related) assertion is true, what sense are we to make of Hegel's repeated and emphatic rejections of the social contract tradition? I return to these important foundational issues in chapter 6, after having laid out Hegel's conception of social freedom in full detail in chapters 3 through 5.

Is Hegel's Conception of Social Freedom Parasitic on His Theodicy?

Charles Taylor's account of the freedom that is realized in *Sittlichkeit* appears to be in agreement with Ilting's interpretation, insofar as it emphasizes that "Hegel is not talking of the idea of merely human freedom, but rather of the cosmic Idea" and that "the will whose autonomy men must realize is not that of man alone but of *Geist* [spirit]."[53] Yet Taylor's insistence that *Sittlichkeit* realizes spirit's freedom rather than "merely human freedom" is meant not to exclude but to be compatible with the claim that human individuals, too, achieve their freedom in *Sittlichkeit*. While this idea—that *Sittlichkeit* is founded on a supraindividual conception of self-determination that includes the freedom of individuals— does capture an important feature of Hegel's position, Taylor fails to give a satisfying account of the specific sense in which individuals possess self-determined wills as members of the rational social order. On Taylor's view, sense can be made of the claim that individuals achieve a distinctive freedom in the institutions of *Sittlichkeit* only by appealing to the notion that the essential nature of human individuals consists in their roles as "vehicles" of cosmic spirit. Individuals realize their freedom by participating in rational social institutions only because such institutions play a necessary role in the historical process through which spirit comes to consciousness of, and thereby realizes, its true nature. In other words, the institutions of *Sittlichkeit* form part of a cosmic order, the rational structure of which is dictated by the nature of spirit. But, Taylor claims, since spirit constitutes their own essential nature, individuals who belong to *Sittlichkeit* live within an order that "flows from [their] own nature properly understood," and such individuals are free, "since to be governed by a law [that] emanates from oneself is to be free."[54] The wills of individual social members are free, then, only in the sense that their social participation is dictated by the norms of a social world whose structure ("immediate unity, separation, and mediated unity") reflects the structure of cosmic spirit and therefore their own true nature as well.[55] This account does in fact ground Hegel's social theory in a kind of self-determination (although one could ask whether it really counts as a self-determination of the *will*), but it is the self-determination of a cosmic subject that produces a world in accord with the Concept, understood here as a universal that "produces a particular content out of itself." The social freedom enjoyed by individuals in the institutions of *Sittlichkeit* turns out, then, to be a form of self-actualization: individuals lead a social life appropriate to the kind of beings they essentially are.

There are a number of reasons to be dissatisfied with an interpretation of *Sittlichkeit* that construes the social freedom of individuals solely in terms of their participation in the larger historical project of spirit's self-realization. Not the least of these is that a reading that relies so heavily on Hegel's philosophy of history makes it difficult for us to regard his account of *Sittlichkeit* as a plausible view. As Taylor himself concedes, it is "not easy to grant" Hegel's basic claim that "man is the vehicle of cosmic spirit" and that the social world "expresses the underlying formula of necessity by which this spirit posits the world."[56] But once these theodicean claims are rejected, there is, on Taylor's interpretation, very little left to the claim that individuals realize a distinctive type of freedom as members of *Sittlichkeit*.

A second reason for resisting Taylor's interpretation is that it raises doubts, similar to those raised by the strongly holistic account of social freedom, about whether Hegel's understanding of the good of social institutions accords sufficient importance to the good of the individuals who belong to those institutions.[57] Strictly speaking, Taylor's interpretation cannot be accused of sacrificing the good of individuals to collective social ends, because it simply *identifies* the primary good of individuals with their participation in spirit's historical project of self-realization and regards rational social life as an essential moment of that project. So, given this understanding of the essential nature (and highest good) of individuals, any social order that serves the ends of spirit will automatically serve the ends of individuals. Yet it is precisely this step—identifying the primary good of individuals with the ends of a supraindividual organic whole to which they allegedly belong—that is problematic. An account of Hegel's social theory that simply starts from this assertion can be faulted, at the very least, for failing to show how (or whether) rational social institutions secure a recognizable human good for their members. Left unexplicated, Hegel's claim about the essentially spiritual nature of human individuals is too obscure to serve as the basis of a persuasive account of how rational social institutions realize the good of their members. If this claim is to carry some weight, it must be possible to say more than Taylor's reconstruction does about why it is valuable for individuals to participate in spirit's projects. In the chapters that follow I shall try to show that Hegel has a more complicated account of the relation between the good of individuals and the ends of the social whole and that his social theory depends upon showing how, by participating in rational social institutions, individuals realize a good (practical freedom) that is recognizable as an essential human good independently of a theory about their nature as vehicles of cosmic spirit.

These first two objections could be said to come from a perspective external to Hegel's own thought, insofar as they rely on a conception of what Hegel's position must be like if "we" are to be able to recognize it as plausible and appealing. One could agree with these objections to Taylor's account and still regard it as a faithful interpretation of Hegel's view. Both of these philosophically dissatisfying features of Taylor's reading, however, can be traced back to an interpretive mistake and hence to an error that can be recognized as such even internal to Hegel's thought: Taylor's interpretation fails to grasp the freedom realized in *Sittlichkeit* as a species of *practical* freedom and thus contradicts Hegel's own understanding of the *Philosophy of Right* as grounded, in its entirety, on the idea of a self-determined will. Taylor is able to give a meaning to the claim that individuals achieve social freedom in *Sittlichkeit* only by stretching the concept of practical freedom to include what would more accurately be described as inhabiting a social world whose structure reflects both the essential order of the cosmos and the true nature of human beings. (Construed this broadly, even Plato's social philosophy could be said to be grounded in a conception of the will's "freedom.") In contrast to the freedoms of personhood and moral subjectivity, the concept of social freedom for Taylor seems not to involve any meaningful sense in which individuals are voluntatively self-determined (as opposed to being "self-determined" in the vaguer sense of inhabiting a social world whose features are determined by the same structure that defines one's own essential nature). But since Hegel explicitly grounds his *Philosophy of Right* on the concept of practical freedom, a convincing interpretation of his social theory must be able to make a plausible connection between the institutions of *Sittlichkeit* and a kind of self-determination that can be recognized as a freedom of the will. Moreover, if such a connection can be drawn, Hegel's position will become less vulnerable to the first two objections raised here against Taylor's interpretation. For then it will be possible to see the institutions of *Sittlichkeit* as securing for its members an important and recognizable human good (self-determination of the will) without appeal to Hegel's theodicy of cosmic spirit.[58]

The Dual Nature of Social Freedom: A Preliminary Sketch

Now, in the final paragraphs of this initial chapter, it is time to turn more directly to the questions that will be central to my investigation into the philosophical foundations of Hegel's social theory, namely, What is social freedom? How can Hegel's vision of the self-determined social whole be seen as a plausible account of the rational social order? In what sense does participating in the institutions of *Sittlichkeit* actualize the freedom of individual social members? The first step in addressing these questions is to explain Hegel's claim that social freedom involves two main elements. This feature of social freedom is asserted in Hegel's statement that *Sittlichkeit* consists in "the unity of objective freedom . . . and subjective freedom" (§258A), as well as in his claim that "*Sittlichkeit* is [1] objective, real freedom that [2] has an existence in self-consciousness befitting of freedom" (VPR1, 248). In the second characterization of *Sittlichkeit* freedom appears in two guises, once as "objective, real freedom" and once as a subjective phenomenon (a "self-consciousness befitting of freedom"). By connecting *Sittlichkeit* to freedom in these two ways, Hegel both avows the dual nature of social freedom and provides us with a clue as to what its two parts are: First, social freedom has both an objective and a subjective component, elements that correspond to what Hegel elsewhere calls the objective and subjective moments of *Sittlichkeit* (§§144, 146). The former he equates with "the laws and institutions" of the rational social order (§144, E §538); the latter is said to consist in the frame of mind, or "disposition" (*Gesinnung*), of individual social members.[59] Second, Hegel's use of the terms 'objective freedom' and 'subjective freedom' implies that each of the two components of social freedom, viewed in abstraction from its relation to the other, can be understood as a kind of freedom in its own right: Freedom is said both to "have its actuality in the subjective disposition" of individuals (as subjective freedom) and to be "objective and real" (as objective freedom) in the institutions of the rational social order (VPR1, 248). One could say, then, that social freedom consists in an objective and a subjective freedom, both of which are realized in the institutions of *Sittlichkeit*.

This preliminary gloss on the dual nature of social freedom already raises two important sets of questions that will guide my inquiry throughout the next four chapters: First, why is it necessary to conceive of social freedom as a unity of two elements? What is the rationale for dividing an account of the social order that best realizes practical freedom into two parts, one concerned with the nature of rational laws and institutions (the objective aspect), the other with the disposition or frame of mind of social members (the subjective aspect)? Second, what sense is to be made of the claim that each of these components of social freedom can be regarded as a kind of freedom in its own right (objective and subjective freedom)? And, singling out objective freedom as the more mysterious of the two, what can be meant by saying that freedom becomes "objective and real" in the institutions of *Sittlichkeit*? My strategy for answering these questions will be to examine first how the very same issues arise within Rousseau's political philosophy, since, as I shall argue in detail in the following chapter, his account of the legitimate political order is based on a similarly structured conception of freedom that (implicitly) invokes the same categories of objective and subjective freedom.[60] The main reason for taking this apparently circuitous route is that the conception of freedom we shall find in Rousseau is closely related in content to Hegel's conception of social freedom yet relatively free of the obscure terminology and metaphysical apparatus that makes Hegel's conception so difficult to understand. Thus, even in those places where the two theories diverge, Rousseau's understanding of political freedom will make an excellent point of reference in contrast to which the distinctive features of Hegel's position can be brought clearly into view.

2

Rousseau: Freedom, Dependence, and the General Will

In his *Lectures on the History of Philosophy* Hegel credits Rousseau with an epoch-making innovation in the realm of practical philosophy, an innovation said to consist in the fact that Rousseau is the first thinker to recognize "the free will" as the fundamental principle of political philosophy.[1] Since the whole of Hegel's own practical philosophy is explicitly grounded in an account of the will and its freedom, Hegel's assertion is clearly intended as an acknowledgment of his deep indebtedness to Rousseau's social and political thought.[2] What is not so clear, however, is how this indebtedness is to be understood: In what sense do the political theories of Hegel and Rousseau share the same first principle? In this chapter I intend to follow up on this interpretive suggestion of Hegel's by elaborating, much more explicitly than he himself does, the sense in which Rousseau's political thought is founded on the principle of the free will. While accomplishing this task will put us in a better position to clarify the obscure philosophical strategy behind Hegel's own social theory, my primary interest in this chapter is to illuminate the foundations of Rousseau's political thought, especially its account of the connection between freedom and the general will. I argue that it is necessary to distinguish two ways in which Rousseau takes the general will to secure, or realize, the freedom of individual citizens, namely, by functioning as an embodiment as well as a precondition of such freedom. Understanding both of these points will lead us to see that Rousseau's thought rests on two distinct, though not incompatible, accounts of how citizens whose actions are constrained by the general will are in fact subject only to their own wills and therefore free in their obedience to the general will.

55

As we shall see, these two accounts are implicitly based on distinct conceptions of political freedom, which, for reasons I discuss later, can be characterized as "subjective" and "objective" conceptions of freedom. My claim is that to ignore either of these conceptions is to leave out an essential element of Rousseau's understanding of how citizens achieve their freedom within the rational state.

Hegel sets out his understanding of Rousseau's contribution to political philosophy in a brief summary of his predecessor's basic position: "The human being is free; this is certainly his substantial nature. This freedom is not something that is surrendered in the state; rather, it is first constituted therein. Natural freedom, the predisposition [*Anlage*] to freedom, is not actual freedom, for it is in the state that freedom is first actualized" (LHP, vol. III, 401–402/XX, 307).[3] Two points emerge from this characterization of Rousseau's view that are relevant to understanding what it means to found political philosophy on the principle of the free will. The first involves a claim about the essential nature of human beings, which is said to consist in *freedom:* human beings live up to their true essence when they possess free wills; or, as Rousseau himself puts it, "to renounce one's freedom is to renounce one's status as a man" (SC, I.4.vi). The second point formulates the most basic principle of political philosophy by asserting an essential connection between human freedom and the state: "The state is the actualization of freedom." The key to understanding Rousseau's social philosophy (and ultimately Hegel's as well) lies in grasping the nature of the relation that is said to hold between freedom and the state. Above all, what is meant by the claim that the state "actualizes" freedom? To say that the state actualizes freedom is to imply that without the state freedom is not actual or real—or, in the words of Hegel cited here, that human freedom is first constituted in the state. On this view, the role of the state with respect to freedom is not, as Locke would have it, one of simply preserving and extending a freedom that individuals can possess independently of their membership in a political community. For Rousseau the freedom that defines our nature as human beings is first constituted in the state and therefore depends on the state for its very existence. Thus, the most basic thought of Rousseau's political philosophy can be formulated as follows: The justification of the rational state resides in the fact that such a state plays an indispensable role in constituting human beings as bearers of free wills and is therefore essential to the fulfillment of their true nature as free beings.

Elaborating this basic thought of Rousseau's will involve, above all, specifying how the rational state actualizes the freedom of its members. There are at least two ways one might conceive of the relationship between the state and freedom. First, the state might be thought of as bringing about a set of social conditions that *make possible* but do not themselves constitute the freedom of its members. On this view, the state would actualize freedom by fulfilling (at least some of) the conditions that enable individuals to possess a free will. Membership in a rational state would then be a precondition of the actualization of one's essential freedom. A second possibility would be to understand political membership not as something that conditions but remains external to the freedom of citizens but rather as a mode of relating to the social world that is itself an instance of freedom. That is, being part of a rational state might be regarded as constitutive of, or as *embodying,* the freedom of the individuals who compose it. This is especially plausible if, as in the case of Rousseau, the rational state is held to be a democratic one in which (at least a part of) the freedom of citizens consists in their self-legislating activity. This set of conceptual possibilities can be summed up by saying that the rational state might relate to the freedom of its members either as a *precondition* or as an *embodiment* of that freedom.

An intriguing, and complicating, feature of Rousseau's political philosophy—one that also characterizes Hegel's theory of *Sittlichkeit*—is that it views the state as standing in *both* of these relations to the freedom of its members: membership in the rational state makes freedom actual by being both its precondition and its embodiment. This interpretive claim immediately raises a question concerning the coherence of Rousseau's position: How can the state stand in both of these relations to one and the same thing? The key to answering this question in the case of Rousseau is to associate each of these relations with one of the two kinds of political freedom distinguished in the *Social Contract,* both of which are actualized only in the state. In short, Rousseau's view will be that membership in the state *embodies* moral freedom, which is defined as a species of autonomy, or as "obedience to the law one has prescribed for oneself" (SC, I.8.iii).[4] At the same time, political membership is a *precondition* of civil freedom, which Rousseau takes to be the ability of individuals to act unconstrained by the particular wills of others within a sphere of activity deemed by society to be external to the vital interests of the community as a whole. For now I shall consider moral and civil freedom simply to be two distinct kinds of freedom and only later ask about the relationship between them.

Freedom through the General Will

Having indicated the general direction in which my interpretation is headed, I turn now to a more detailed examination of Rousseau's views as he himself presents them. I shall be concerned to articulate not only Rousseau's understanding of how a rational state actualizes the freedom of its members but also his reasons for maintaining that a free will can exist *only* as part of a rational political order. The place to begin such an investigation is the central concept of Rousseau's political theory, the general will. For the general will is both a *political* concept—it embodies the principles of political association—and the principle that accounts for the *freedom* of the state's individual members. This dual function of the general will is expressed in the statement that "it is through the general will that [individuals] are citizens and free" (SC, IV.2.viii; translation amended). In what follows I begin to elucidate Rousseau's thought that it is through their political attachments, or "through the general will," that individuals exist as free.

Rousseau invokes the concept of the general will in order to solve what he takes to be the fundamental problem of political philosophy—namely, to devise a form of political association that reconciles the associates' need for social cooperation with their essential natures as free beings (SC, I.6.iv). The difficulty of this task lies in the fact that effective social cooperation must be regulated by a collective will in accord with the common good, whereas the freedom of individuals requires that their wills be subject to no will other than their own. Since the need to cooperate with others requires individuals to adjust or curtail their actions in accord with interests beyond their own particular (or private) good, they seem to have no option but to submit their wills to a will other than their own and thus cease to be free. As is well known, the key to Rousseau's solution to this problem lies in his doctrine of the general will. If this solution is to succeed, the general will must regulate social cooperation in accord with the common good and at the same time be the will of the individuals whose behavior it governs. If the latter condition is met, then individuals who subject their actions to the general will can be said to be free, for in doing so they obey only their own will. Thus, individuals can achieve freedom through the general will only if the general will is also their own will. But what is involved in the latter condition? In what sense and under what circumstances can the general will be understood as the will of each individual? It is this question, more than any other, that must be answered if we are to grasp the strategy behind Rousseau's solution to the fundamental problem of political philosophy.

The most straightforward way of understanding how the general will can be the will of individual citizens is offered by the "social autonomy" model of freedom.[5] This conception of the freedom that is actualized in the rational state involves the thought of individuals who consciously identify with the general will in the sense that they regularly recognize and embrace the common good as their own deepest interest. Conceiving of freedom in this way depends upon seeing the general will (and the legislation that derives from it) as expressing a consciously shared conception of the common good: if the general will is grounded in an understanding of the common good that is both shared and affirmed by the individuals who make up the state, then in submitting to laws that derive from the general will, they remain subject only to their own wills and therefore free. This model requires not only that individuals be able to come to a theoretical agreement about what constitutes the common good but also that they be capable of *willing* the common good. This requirement is based on the thought that if one had theoretical insight into the common good without any conscious, voluntative relation to it—if one were able to discern the common good but unable to affirm or endorse it—then actions regulated by a conception of the common good could not be said to derive from one's own will. Thus, if individuals are to remain free while subject to the general will, they must will the common good. But what is involved in such willing? In the first place, individuals must *have* a general will, which simply means that they can be moved by considerations of the common good, that something's being in the common interest can count for them as a reason for acting to attain it. But having a general will in this minimal sense is not sufficient to ensure that one will be free (subject only to one's own will) in a society where the general will prevails. The reason for this is that one may have a general will without it being one's *dominant* will. For individuals who have general wills do not therefore cease to have particular wills,[6] and these particular wills can—indeed, very often do—come into conflict with what the common good dictates. Thus, individuals who inhabit a state in which the general will prevails (a society in which the general will, through law, effectively regulates the actions of individuals) can be considered free only if, as individuals, they possess *properly ordered* wills—that is, wills that are disposed to subordinate purely particular interests to the common good in cases where the two conflict. Such wills belong to individuals whose identification with the shared ends of the association is sufficiently strong to outweigh, at least most of the time, their commitment to purely particular interests. Thus, according to the social autonomy model of freedom, individuals remain free in a society governed by the general will only if they are internally constituted as *citizens,* which requires both that they can be motivated by the common good and that, as a rule, their general will speaks to them in a louder voice than their particular will.

It is not difficult to see that the freedom depicted by the social autonomy model is an inherently political species of freedom that can be actualized only within the rational state. Moreover, this model views the state as essentially involved in the actualization of freedom not because political membership satisfies preconditions of being free but because such membership is itself an embodiment of freedom—more precisely, an embodiment of a form of *moral freedom,* or autonomy, which consists in individuals governing their lives by laws they all help to frame in accord with a shared conception of the common good. Although this conception of freedom does play a prominent role in Rousseau's political thought, the relationship between the freedom of individuals and the general will is more complex than this model, taken by itself, can allow for. This point is brought out most forcefully by two troublesome passages of the *Social Contract.* The first of these is the site of Rousseau's well-known but poorly understood remark that "whoever refuses to obey the general will shall be constrained to do so by the entire body, which means only that he will be forced to be free" (SC, I.7.viii). The second passage occurs in Rousseau's discussion of voting procedures in the assembly. There he asserts that the citizens of a well-constituted state are free, even when required to submit to particular laws that do not conform to their own understanding of what the common good prescribes: "when the opinion contrary to mine prevails, that proves nothing except that I was mistaken, and what I thought to be the general will was not. If my particular opinion had prevailed, I would have done something other than what I wanted. It is then that I would not have been free" (SC, IV.2.viii).[7] Although these passages occur in different contexts, they both express the idea that one achieves freedom by being subject to the general will, even if one does not consciously recognize the general will as one's own. There must be, then, for Rousseau a sense in which the general will's being the will of each individual does not depend on the individual's recognition of it as such—that is, there must be a sense in which the general will can be said to be my will (one might say: my deepest or truest will), even though I may lack the kind of subjective relation to it that is ordinarily taken to constitute willing. I may fail to discern the common good or to make it the object of my striving, and yet the general will is understood to be *my* will and my subjection to its dictates freedom. That Rousseau intends to make such a claim seems to me incontrovertible; what is less certain is whether it is possible to make sense of this position, including its apparently perverse implication that an individual can be free even when required to act contrary to her own assessment of what she wants to do. The social autonomy model of freedom, however, is unable to make sense of such a position, and so, if we are to understand this aspect of Rousseau's view, we must look beyond this model for an alternative—or, better, a supplement—to the conception of freedom as social autonomy. The best way to do this is to examine more closely Rousseau's notorious claim that in the rational state it is possible for individuals to be forced to be free.

I shall begin by reviewing the passage in question in its entirety:

> In order for the social compact not to be an ineffectual formula, it tacitly includes the following engagement, which alone can give force to the others: that whoever refuses to obey the general will shall be constrained to do so by the entire body; which means only that he will be forced to be free. For this is the condition that, by giving each citizen to the homeland, guarantees him against all personal dependence; a condition that creates the ingenuity and functioning of the political machine, and alone gives legitimacy to civil engagements which without it would be absurd, tyrannical, and subject to the most enormous abuses. (SC, I.7.viii)

The most common way of explicating this difficult passage is to take Rousseau simply to be arguing that citizens have a rightful obligation to obey the general will and that therefore the state's coercive power can be legitimately directed against them when they fail to do so.[8] This obligation to obey the general will is usually understood to derive from citizens' previous (actual) consent to the terms of the social contract, which include a promise to abide by those laws arrived at through agreed-upon procedural principles of majority rule. If Rousseau's passage is understood in this way, the issue it addresses appears to be not a distinctively Rousseauean problem but the problem faced by any social contract theory of providing an account of the citizen's obligation to comply with legitimately constituted legislation and of the state's corresponding right to use coercive force to ensure such compliance. Moreover, insofar as this interpretation views the *Social Contract* as grounding the citizen's obligation to obey the law in the obligation incurred through his original promise to do so, Rousseau's position comes out to be essentially indistinguishable from that of other social contract theorists, including Locke. But this reading, regardless of its merit as an account of the obligation citizens have to obey, fails to address the passage's central, and most puzzling, assertion—namely, that being forced to comply with the general will is nothing more than being "forced to be free." In other words, the most fundamental question raised by this assertion is not how citizens come to have an *obligation* to obey the general will but how their being forced to fulfill that obligation can be consistent with—indeed, constitutive of—their being *free*.[9] What sense can it possibly make to say that the would-be offender, forced to obey, is doing nothing other than following his own will?

It is sometimes said that the citizen who is forced to obey the general will can be thought of as simply being forced to follow his own will, insofar as the general will embodies those principles that he himself, in moments of undisturbed reflection, recognizes as the object of his own deepest commitment. In such a case the principles that define the general will would constitute the citizen's own constant (and therefore true) will, and the occasional impulse to follow his particular will in opposition to the general will would be a temptation to act contrary to what he, by his own acknowledgment, most wants to do.[10] Thus, disobedience to the law would represent a species of weakness of will, and one's original consent to the social contract—more specifically, one's agreement to subject oneself to the law-enforcing powers of the state—could be seen as the will's strategy for binding itself to a principle it explicitly endorses but finds difficult to follow in every situation. Being forced to subordinate one's divergent particular will to the general will would then simply be to have one's actions brought into line with one's own constant will; but this would amount to nothing more than being forced to do what one most wants, which could also be described as being forced to be free.

This interpretation has the advantage of being able to give some meaning to the idea that one can be forced to be free; its disadvantage is that the explication it offers is not the one Rousseau himself suggests in the lines immediately following his famous utterance. Considering the amount of confusion the phrase 'forced to be free' has generated among interpreters, it is surprising to discover that Rousseau explicitly points out to us the thought that is supposed to make sense of his otherwise paradoxical formulation: "For this [the stipulation that individuals be constrained to follow the general will] is the condition that, by giving each citizen to the homeland, *guarantees him against all personal dependence*" (SC, I.7.viii; emphasis added). It is quite clear, I believe, that Rousseau intends for this sentence, which is linked to its predecessor by the explanatory 'for', to be recognized as holding the key to the riddle posed by the expression 'forced to be free'. That is, he means for us to take seriously the thought expressed by this sentence—namely, that universal compliance with the general will effectively safeguards citizens from personal dependence and that this protection from dependence is so bound up with their freedom that obedience to the general will can be said to make them free, even when their obedience is not voluntary in the ordinary sense of the term. My aim in what follows will be to make sense of this difficult thought and thereby to elucidate one of the ideas that lies at the heart of Rousseau's conception of freedom and its relation to the political order. Doing so will require a discussion of two sets of questions raised by Rousseau's claim: First, how are we to understand the notion of dependence, and in what relation does it stand to the concept of freedom? If freedom is not simply identical with independence, why does Rousseau believe the two concepts to be so closely connected? The second set of questions concerns the relation that allegedly holds between the general will and the independence of citizens—most important: What is behind the assertion that the general will, if adhered to, safeguards citizens from personal dependence?

Dependence and Freedom

Rousseau's claim that compliance with the general will makes citizens free because it safeguards them from personal dependence could be taken to imply that freedom simply consists in the absence of dependence and that therefore *independence* is synonymous with *freedom*. This view, which some interpreters have taken, appears to be reinforced by the fact that Rousseau more than once treats these two terms as though they were interchangeable.[11] But adopting this view will have serious consequences for any attempt to make sense of Rousseau's philosophical project. For the fundamental problem to which his project as a whole is directed can be coherently formulated only by distinguishing freedom from independence. That such a distinction is required becomes clear once we recognize that Rousseau starts from the supposition that dependence is a fundamental, ineliminable feature of human existence. Although, as we shall see, he regards this dependence as having negative implications for our ability to be free, dependence does not strictly preclude freedom's being actualized. In fact, Rousseau's thought can be understood as aiming, above all, to show how the basic dependence of human beings can coexist with their freedom. If this task is to be anything other than a logical impossibility, it must presuppose a conceptual distinction between freedom and independence. That Rousseau's thought operates with such a distinction cannot be gathered from his actual usage of the terms *liberté* and *indépendance*. Yet a careful reading of his central works, especially his *Discourse on Inequality,* compels one to conclude that this distinction, if only implicit in Rousseau's texts, is indispensable to his philosophy of freedom.[12]

How, then, is the distinction between freedom and independence to be drawn? Rousseau's concept of independence is best understood as closely related to the notion of self-sufficiency. As such, it can be defined only with reference to the more basic concept of *need*: to be independent is to be self-sufficient with respect to the satisfaction of one's needs, and dependence is simply the lack of such self-sufficiency. Thus, human beings are dependent in the broadest sense of the term when they must rely on resources outside of themselves in order to have their needs satisfied. Although Rousseau recognizes two species of dependence in general—dependence on things and dependence on other human beings—it is the latter category that is of primary importance to him. The reason for this can be traced back to his belief that dependence on things alone—that is, on things other than human individuals or groups—has little impact on one's ability to be free (*Emile,* 85). Thus, Rousseau portrays the independent individual as one who "has no need to put another's arms at the end of his own" (*Emile,* 84); in other words, he is able to satisfy his needs without the cooperation of other human beings. The primitive gatherer of fruit, reliant on the beneficence of nature but not on the assistance of others, is therefore not dependent in the sense that most interests Rousseau.

Thus, a consideration of Rousseau's concept of independence leads directly into his account of human needs. Although this aspect of Rousseau's thought is sufficiently rich to merit a lengthy treatment of its own, I shall restrict myself here to those points that are most relevant to elucidating the connection between dependence and freedom. It is important to note first that in this context the concept of need refers always, and only, to *perceived* needs. Characterizing a need as "perceived" does not imply that it is *merely* a perceived need (but not, say, a real or true need). Although Rousseau's texts do provide resources for distinguishing true (or real) needs from false (or illusory) needs,[13] this distinction is irrelevant here. What is important for understanding dependence is not some objective quality of needs (for example, whether they are in fact essential to one's well-being, properly understood) but their subjective character—that is, the way they present themselves to and influence the behavior of the subject to whom they belong. All needs, whether real or illusory, have the potential to give rise to dependence, as long as they are perceived as needs by the subject.

There are two subjective qualities of needs that make them crucial to the phenomenon of dependence—namely, the *force* and the *constancy* with which they present themselves to subjects as inducements to action. First, needs are powerful determinants of behavior and psychological well-being. The feeling of lack that accompanies an unfulfilled need possesses an urgency that is not easily ignored or endured. An unquenched thirst or an unrequited love has the power to torment individuals and to drive them to desperate action. It is this forceful quality of needs that accounts for the nearly irresistible hold that relations of dependence come to have over individuals who become entangled in them. Second, needs possess a constancy that many inclinations do not; in contrast to whims or fleeting desires, needs constitute an enduring part of the subject's appetitive makeup: when needs go unsatisfied, the urges to which they give rise do not simply disappear but continue to make their demands felt by the subject. Moreover, satisfying a need once does not amount to extinguishing it, for needs typically give rise to recurrent feelings of lack, which demand that the process of satisfaction be repeated. Whether fulfilled or unfulfilled, needs are not easily gotten rid of. This feature of needs is important, because it is what makes dependence an enduring state rather than merely a momentary phenomenon.

The needs that figure most prominently in Rousseau's thought fall into two main classes. The first comprises those goods (for example, food, clothing, shelter) that are involved essentially in the reproduction of life and whose significance for the human being derives primarily from the requirements of his physical constitution. The second class is made up of needs that have their origin not in our biological nature but in a form of self-love that Rousseau calls *amour-propre,* a passion that gives rise to the distinctively human yearning "to have a position, to be a part, to count for something" (*Emile,* 160).[14] *Amour-propre,* which is fundamental to our nature as spiritual (or moral) beings, is capable of manifesting itself in numerous ways and therefore of giving rise to an extremely diverse set of concrete needs. The need to be thought handsome or clever, the need to be loved, the need to have one's will and preferences respected—all are grounded in the promptings of *amour-propre* and can be understood as particular forms of the basic need generated by that passion: the need to have a recognized standing among beings of one's own kind or, in other words, the need to be acknowledged by one's fellow beings as possessing a value that makes one worthy of their esteem. This twofold classification of needs is summed up by Rousseau in a footnote to the Second Discourse: "all our labors are directed to only two objects: namely, the commodities of life for oneself, and consideration among others" (DI, 223).[15]

These two kinds of needs give rise to the two main types of dependence with which Rousseau is concerned: *economic* and *psychological* (or psychomoral) dependence.[16] The former consists in dependence on others in the production or acquisition of necessary commodities. It is a necessary consequence of the two most important economic facts of modern (and most of premodern) society: the material division of labor (for example, into tillers of the soil and workers of metal) and the division of society into economic classes of rich and poor (or, in more precise terminology, into owners and nonowners of the means of production). Psychological dependence is dependence on others for the recognition one needs in order for one's sense of one's value or standing among others to be reflected and thus confirmed in the external world. Rousseau's writings abound with sharply observed examples of dependence that he takes to be of this second type: the artist whose self-esteem requires his audience's applause, the lover who cannot endure being denied his beloved's affection, the citizen who values the honor of his countrymen more than his own life.[17]

It would be a mistake to conclude, as some interpreters have done, that Rousseau regards one species of dependence as of greater consequence than the other; on the contrary, he sees correctly that economic and psychological dependence pose equally serious threats to individuals' freedom. Yet one interesting feature of his view is that it ascribes far more importance to *amour-propre* than to biology in its explanation of human dependence. The explanatory primacy of *amour-propre* manifests itself in two ways. First, *amour-propre* has a more immediate connection to dependence than does purely physical need. In addition to his vivid depictions of human dependence, Rousseau offers accounts, usually in narrative form, of the conditions under which the fact of human need gives rise to a state of dependence. In the Second Discourse Rousseau argues that dependence, understood as an enduring condition, is not a necessary consequence of our biological nature alone.[18] Savage individuals, isolated and independent, are able to satisfy their purely physical needs without the regular cooperation of their fellow beings. Physical needs result in dependence only when the production of necessary commodities acquires certain *social* characteristics (which itself presupposes that these needs have become more complicated and less easy to satisfy). That is, it is only with the division of labor, occasioned by the advent of metallurgy and agriculture, and with the subsequent division of society into rich and poor that individuals become economically dependent on other humans for the satisfaction of their physical needs. In contrast, the relation between psychological dependence and the needs of *amour-propre* is more straightforward. For the object of *amour-propre*'s striving is such that its attainment requires by its very nature the involvement of others. The individual's yearning for a recognized standing among others cannot be satisfied by the individual himself, nor by subhuman beings.[19] Thus, in the case of *amour-propre,* neediness is inseparable from dependence; the existence of psychological dependence presupposes no conditions beyond those of *amour-propre* itself: a simple awareness of oneself as an individual, a certain constancy of social intercourse, and the mental capacity to make comparisons between oneself and one's fellow beings.

Amour-propre has primacy over purely physical needs in Rousseau's account of dependence in a second sense: the needs of *amour-propre* not only give rise on their own to psychological dependence but also play an important, perhaps dominant, role in the constitution of economic dependence. This is most easily seen in the fact that many of the needs that make us dependent on the labor of others (for example, the need for a sufficiently stylish wardrobe) stem directly from the promptings of *amour-propre*. Although the possession and consumption of things cannot by itself satisfy *amour-propre*, commodities frequently play a central role in individuals' strategies for gaining the respect of others. A less obvious but equally important point is that with the development of society, biologically based needs quickly cease to be purely biological in nature. What counts as a "commodity of life" is not determined by a fixed, strictly biological quantity (for example, the minimum required for survival and reproduction). Rather, our conception of the necessities of life changes with historical development and presupposes a conception of the minimal standard of living that is consistent with a humane existence. Thus, these biologically based needs come to be determined in part by considerations as to the kind of physical existence that it is *fitting* for human beings to have and hence by considerations that ultimately have their source in *amour-propre*. To fail to achieve this minimal standard is to lead a less than human existence, a circumstance that is incompatible with the recognized standing that *amour-propre* strives to attain. This blurring of the distinction between physical and psychological needs is due to the fact that for beings in whom *amour-propre* has begun to operate—and that includes all *human* beings—no aspect of one's existence remains untouched by the concern for one's standing among others. Even those needs that derive most immediately from our biological nature take on a psychological significance and become essential to achieving self-esteem, as well as the esteem of our fellow beings.

Freedom, in contrast to independence, is defined without reference to the concept of need. It refers, rather, to a condition of the *will* and, more precisely, to a particular relation between the will and the world. The meaning of freedom is captured in a rough way by Rousseau's characterization of the free being as "one who does his own will" (*Emile,* 84). Freedom, it would seem, consists in an agreement of will and action; individuals are free when they "do what accords with their will" (RSW, 84). At times, however, Rousseau insists upon a slight but significant revision of this formulation: "Freedom does not consist so much in doing one's will as in not being subjected to the will of others" (OC III, 841).[20] What is the import of defining freedom negatively (as the absence of subjection to a foreign will) rather than in the more straightforward manner suggested earlier? Rousseau's endorsement of the negative formulation implies that "doing one's will" is too exclusive a definition of freedom and, hence, that there are instances in which one does not do what one wants without therefore being unfree. What Rousseau must have in mind are instances in which the force that prevents me from doing my own will comes from the "necessity of things" rather than from a foreign will.[21] That is, I may fail to do what I want because I lack the requisite strength, or because of limits imposed by the laws of nature. In such cases Rousseau will agree that my will has been frustrated but deny that my freedom has been compromised.[22] Rousseau's concept of freedom, then, cannot be defined simply as a correspondence between an individual's will and his deeds. Such a definition equates freedom with the successful translation of will into action, and in doing so it overlooks a central characteristic of freedom, a characteristic that makes freedom, for Rousseau, an inherently moral phenomenon, namely, that freedom (as well as its opposite) always refers to a relation between one will and another: to be unfree is to obey a foreign will, and freedom is always being free of the will of another. We can do justice to this aspect of Rousseau's conception of freedom by replacing our initial characterization of the free individual as "one who does his own will" with the following: the free individual is one who *obeys* only his own will or, more explicitly, one who *obeys no will* other than his own.[23]

This rather meager formula is not, of course, Rousseau's final word on the topic of freedom. It would be more accurate to describe it as his starting point. For although the thought of "obeying only one's own will" captures what is essential to the idea of freedom, it is still a long way from a full account of what a free human existence would look like and how such an existence could be actualized. It is no exaggeration to say that Rousseau's thought as a whole is devoted, above all else, to the task of providing just such an account. Central to this project is the question that could be said to inform each of Rousseau's major works: Under what conditions is human freedom possible? How must the world be constituted—both the external, social world and the inner, psychological world—in order for individuals to be able to obey only their own wills? It is in this context that the topic of dependence makes its entry into Rousseau's philosophy, for dependence on others represents the most important obstacle to the actualization of freedom.

With this thought I return to the question posed at the beginning of this section: What relation exists between freedom and dependence? Although, as we have seen, the concepts of freedom and independence can be distinguished in thought, the phenomena to which they refer are closely connected in reality. The general nature of this connection is expressed in Rousseau's remark that dependence on others is "detrimental to freedom" (*Emile*, 85). One could also say that dependence is the *source* of subjection and, more precisely, that it is the source of subjection in two distinct senses: First, dependence is a condition that *makes possible* the subjection of one will to another. It allows us to make sense of the otherwise puzzling phenomenon of obeying a foreign will instead of one's own.[24] For in certain, easily imaginable circumstances, requiring the cooperation of others for the satisfaction of one's needs makes it necessary, or gives one powerful incentives, to abandon one's will in favor of another's. But Rousseau makes the even stronger claim that dependence is *necessary* for subjection to arise: "since the bonds of servitude are formed only from the mutual dependence of men and the reciprocal needs that unite them, it is impossible to enslave a man without first putting him in the position of being unable to do without another" (DI, 140).[25] Rousseau's talk of "bonds of servitude" indicates that it is the enduring subjection of one will to another that requires dependence as its condition. For isolated instances of yielding to a foreign will can occur even in the absence of dependence; a simple threat of violence, for example, can result in obedience to another, and such encounters are conceivable even for the thoroughly independent beings of the original state of nature. Enduring subjection, however, is possible only for dependent beings—that is, for beings whose lack of self-sufficiency requires them to have ongoing interactions with others.

Second, dependence for Rousseau is more than just a necessary condition of subjection. Insofar as it is relatively extensive and exists in its natural form (that is, prior to being restructured in the ways advocated by Rousseau's philosophy),[26] dependence *virtually guarantees* that individuals will be unfree. This is to be attributed in part to the nearly irresistible force with which unsatisfied needs impel individuals to seek satisfaction. Beings who constantly have to choose between getting what they need and following their own wills cannot be expected to opt consistently for freedom over satisfaction. But dependent individuals will regularly find themselves in this unhappy position only if their relations of dependence are so constituted that they give rise to systematic conflicts among wills. Hence, Rousseau's view that the loss of freedom is a virtually unavoidable consequence of unrestructured dependence is also based on a supposition about the inevitability of conflict among the desires and particular interests—and hence among the wills—of interdependent individuals in the absence of an imposed order that harmonizes those interests. The division of society into economic classes that have directly antithetical material interests is but one of Rousseau's examples of a common form of dependence that guarantees a systematic conflict among wills.[27]

We are now in a position to consider how Rousseau's understanding of the relation between freedom and dependence dictates the basic terms of his solution to the fundamental problem of political theory, that of devising a structure for the ongoing social cooperation of human beings that allows for each individual to exist as free. First, however, it is important to note that Rousseau's formulation of his task—his specification of freedom as the end to be realized—bears witness to the important fact that freedom, not independence, is the supreme value of his political thought (and, indeed, of his philosophy in general). Rousseau's view is not merely that freedom stands above independence in the hierarchy of values, but that independence has no intrinsic value. Indeed, whatever value Rousseau ascribes to independence is completely parasitic on the value of freedom. Thus, to the extent that Rousseau considers independence to be good, he does so not because it is intrinsically valuable, nor because self-sufficiency is the surest means to the satisfaction of one's needs, but solely because of the positive contribution independence can make to the ability of individuals to avoid subjection to foreign wills. By the same token, dependence is regarded not as bad in itself but as bad only insofar as it is detrimental to the freedom of the dependent individual.

Rousseau's view of dependence as the source of subjection suggests one obvious response to his central question concerning the conditions under which freedom can be actualized, namely, the perfect independence of all individuals. Further, it suggests that a political solution to the problem of subjection could be found in eradicating dependence on others in all of its forms, since to eradicate dependence would be to eliminate the condition that both makes subjection possible and virtually ensures that it will come about. Indeed, the link between dependence and subjection is a theme that occurs so frequently and with such urgency in Rousseau's texts that it is easy to get the impression that the eradication of dependence is the only possible remedy for the subjection of individuals. In the Second Discourse, however, Rousseau in effect considers, and emphatically rejects, just this solution. His portrayal of the original state of nature can be seen as an attempt to imagine what life would be like for individuals who enjoyed a freedom predicated on complete self-sufficiency. The beings Rousseau depicts are perfectly "free and independent" (DI, 156) (and free *because* they are independent); they obey no wills other than their own and are able to do so only because they are self-sufficient. Yet Rousseau makes it clear that such freedom, even if it were practically possible, would come at too high a cost. His refusal to look to the original state of nature for the solution to dependence is based less on his belief about the impracticality of returning to the state of nature than on his view that such a solution would not be desirable. For the radical independence that makes such freedom possible can be maintained only in the absence of all enduring attachments to others. But, as Rousseau makes clear, the unencumbered beings of the original state of nature are not, and cannot be, *human* beings, for the absence of enduring social bonds precludes the existence of a wide variety of goods and capacities that are essential to being human and are of sufficient intrinsic value that freedom may not be obtained at their expense: perfect independence makes impossible not only conjugal love (one of "the sweetest sentiments known to men") but also language, reason, virtue, and subjectivity itself.[28]

In accord with this view, Rousseau's strategy for reconciling the ineliminable dependence of human beings with the freedom that constitutes their essential nature will focus less on the eradication of dependence than on its restructuring. This strategy implies that human dependence admits of being reorganized in such a way that it ceases to be incompatible with freedom. The principles that are to guide the restructuring of dependence—at least the political component of this restructuring[29]—can be found in Rousseau's conception of the general will. For, as we have seen, Rousseau claims that it is the individual's (forced or voluntary) compliance with the general will that "guarantees him against all personal dependence." Thus, Rousseau intends for the general will to be understood as willing a set of social and political institutions that alter the nature of individuals' dependence on others so as to eliminate, or at least significantly reduce, those aspects of dependence that make it inimical to freedom. My task now is to understand how his conception of the general will accomplishes this.

Dependence and the General Will

A clue to the basic idea behind Rousseau's proposed restructuring of dependence can be found in the statement, cited previously, in which the general will is said to guarantee individuals against "personal" dependence. This suggests that Rousseau's political solution to the problem of freedom involves transforming the dependence on individual persons into a dependence on the community as a whole. This suggestion is confirmed by Rousseau's remark later in the *Social Contract* that in the rational polity "each citizen is in a position of perfect independence from all the others and of excessive dependence upon the city" (SC, II.12.iii). But what does it mean to depend upon the city, as opposed to the individual persons who compose it, and how does depersonalizing dependence in this way make it possible for individuals to be free? In another context Rousseau says that the only social remedy for "dependence on men" is "to substitute law for man" (*Emile*, 85). Hence the "dependence upon the city" Rousseau envisages can be described more accurately as a dependence on the well-constituted republic, that is, on a community effectively governed by law that faithfully reflects the general will. As we shall see later, however, it is best to characterize the social arrangement endorsed by Rousseau not as one in which one species of dependence (dependence on other individuals) is *replaced* by another (dependence on the law-governed republic) but rather as a social order in which the ineliminable relations of dependence among individuals are preserved but *regulated* by a system of well-founded law and thereby made less injurious to freedom.

The question to be answered, then, is how the rule of law orders the dependence of individuals such that dependence on others can coexist with freedom. A great deal could be said about Rousseau's view of the rule of law and its virtues; in what follows I merely outline three ways in which Rousseau believes law to be capable of restructuring dependence such that the freedom of individuals can be actualized. Although these three points can and should be distinguished from one another, they all share one fundamental attribute: in each case law mitigates the harmful consequences of dependence by establishing *equality* (in various senses) among citizens. This close connection between law and equality is explicitly recognized by Rousseau: "[Law] reestablishes, as a right, the natural equality among men" (PE, 214).[30] He also acknowledges the deeper philosophical point that my interpretation of his position emphasizes, namely, that law aims at the equality of citizens not because equality is valuable in itself but because it furthers the end of freedom.[31] Each of the following three points, then, can serve as a particular illustration of the general idea that bringing equality to mutually dependent individuals helps to safeguard them from the subjection into which their dependence is otherwise likely to deliver them.

The first way that law is to restructure dependence is by ensuring that citizens enjoy a significant (but not fully specified) level of *material equality.* The legislation of a well-constituted republic does not seek to establish an absolute equality of wealth among its citizens but only to impede the development of great material inequalities that are the inevitable consequence of unregulated economic activity.[32] Rousseau's concrete proposals range from laws that restrict inheritance or levy taxes on luxury goods to the suggestion that the existence of a class of property-less individuals—more precisely, a class of individuals who own no means of production other than their own labor power—is incompatible with the freedom of citizens.[33] More important than the details of Rousseau's proposals is the idea behind them: narrowing the distance between the extremes of wealth alleviates the economic dependence of the less advantaged and thereby reduces the likelihood that they will have to submit to the will of another in order to satisfy their material needs. Yet lessening, or even eliminating, the differences between classes does not do away with all economic dependence, for as long as there is a material division of labor within society, individuals will rely upon the cooperation of others in order to obtain the necessities of life. What distinguishes the material division of labor from the division of society into economic classes is that the former is compatible with a high level of equality among individuals, whereas the latter is not. Moreover, it is this difference that makes the material division of labor a less harmful form of dependence than the existence of classes, for interactions among mutually dependent individuals who meet on an equal footing are less likely to result in the sacrifice of freedom than those among highly unequal beings. Thus, legislation directed at bringing about the material equality of individuals should be understood as aiming not so much at a lessening or eradication of economic dependence as at its equalization.

In this first instance the capacity of law to restructure dependence is due not to a formal feature of law in general but to a particular end Rousseau ascribes to law, the promotion of material equality. That law can be said to have such a content for Rousseau is a reflection of the fact that the general will (of which law is simply a determinate expression) is more than a set of purely formal criteria for the legitimacy of legislation; the general will, as Rousseau conceives it, also has a content in the sense that it wills certain broadly defined but nonvacuous ends. In some places, however, Rousseau implies that the rule of law per se, regardless of the law's content, shields citizens from some of the pernicious consequences of dependence on others.[34] This suggests that Rousseau sees law as capable of restructuring dependence in a second way that relies solely on the formal character of law as such. The feature of law that Rousseau draws on in this context is its universality. Although more will need to be said about the kind of universality that is relevant here, it will involve some form of the idea of "bearing equally on all." Thus, the universality of law implies that those who are under it enjoy a species of equality, distinct from the material equality discussed earlier, which can be characterized as the *formal equality of citizens before the law.* The nature of this equality is roughly captured in the idea that the law is no respecter of persons; it regards individual citizens as abstract units that (in a sense to be specified) count as equals. This raises two questions in need of further attention: In what precise sense do citizens count as equals before the law, and how does this formal equality function as an antidote to dependence?

Although Rousseau's claim here is difficult to pin down precisely, the general thrust of his idea is that the rule of law helps to protect individuals from the capricious wills of those on whom they depend.[35] Capricious wills are (for the most part) unconstrained by principles and are therefore inconstant, unpredictable, and arbitrary. Being dependent on capricious individuals poses a serious threat to one's freedom, because it is virtually inevitable that wills exhibiting only random motion will come into frequent collisions with other (random or nonrandom) wills. Rousseau's idea, then, must be that the laws of a rational state effectively order capricious wills by placing external constraints on what those wills may demand of others. Thus, without decreasing the level of their interdependence, the rule of law helps preserve the freedom of individuals by shielding them from one of the most freedom-endangering consequences of dependence. While the basic thought here is plain enough, it is not at all evident why Rousseau believes that this capacity of law follows simply from its formal character as *universal* law. This claim is tersely formulated in Rousseau's remark that "any condition imposed on each by all can be onerous to no one" (OC III, 842). Here law is said to be universal in two distinct senses: it is imposed *on each* and *by all.* Not surprisingly, these two kinds of universality reappear in Rousseau's statement of what makes a general will general, namely, that it "applies to all" and "comes from all" (SC, II.4.v). But how can the universality of law in either of these senses account for its ability to protect individuals from the capricious wills of those on whom they depend?

In a number of passages Rousseau appeals only to the first kind of universality—the universal *applicability* of law—when making the point that law protects individuals from capricious wills. An example of this is his statement that "the worst of laws is worth even more than the best master, because every master has preferences and the law never does" (OC III, 842–843). Law, in both its formulation and its enforcement, applies to all and tolerates no exceptions; "magistrates themselves are obliged to obey them" (OC III, 491). By making no distinctions among particular individuals, the law effectively creates a kind of equality among citizens—a guarantee of equal treatment under the law—that, at least within the domain of activity governed by law, deters one of the modes of behavior characteristic of capricious wills: the differential treatment of individuals on the basis of arbitrary preferences. But the universality of law in this sense alone still leaves plenty of room for what we would consider arbitrary treatment, not perhaps of particular individuals but of classes of individuals.[36] For the law 'Only property owners may have access to the means of public communication' can be scrupulously applied to all citizens and still be arbitrary in an important sense. For this reason it is important to take into account the second sense in which law is said to be universal, namely, that it is imposed by, or comes from, all. The universality referred to here is best understood not as the actual participation of all citizens in the process of framing laws but as a condition that places a constraint on the content of admissible legislation by requiring that laws be possible objects of the rational consent of all citizens.[37] Since laws (like the one suggested earlier) that violate a fundamental interest of a class of citizens cannot be regarded as capable of gaining the rational consent of those citizens, they lack universality in this sense. The requirement that laws come from all implies a kind of equality of citizens before the law that consists in the fact that each citizen is regarded as having fundamental interests that no law may violate and that count as equal to the fundamental interests of every other citizen in the framing of legislation. Laws that are universal in this sense can be seen as a response to the problem posed by dependence on others, because by safeguarding (at least some of) the fundamental interests of individuals, such laws block one important kind of arbitrary treatment by capricious wills to which dependent individuals are otherwise susceptible.

The third way in which the rule of law transforms personal dependence into dependence on the republic is by making the community itself into a source of the esteem sought by individuals as a consequence of their *amour-propre*. Law accomplishes this by ensuring that individuals enjoy an *equality of respect* as citizens. This function of law is a direct consequence of its universality in the sense just discussed. For safeguarding the fundamental interests of individuals has the effect of securing for them a kind of recognized standing within the community that is itself a form of respect. Moreover, the availability of this respect is not contingent on the mutable opinions of particular individuals but is assured by a guarantee as reliable as the rule of law itself. Securing equality of respect for all citizens is essential to Rousseau's project, since *amour-propre* is (arguably) the single most important source of dependence on others. Rousseau, of course, does not believe that the recognized standing individuals achieve as citizens of a law-governed community is sufficient to satiate *amour-propre* in all its manifestations. His view, rather, is that one's standing as a citizen represents a partial but not insignificant confirmation of one's value for others, which, because it relies only on the institution of law, makes individuals less dependent on particular persons for the satisfaction of their need to possess a standing among their fellow beings.

Concluding Remarks: On the Possibility (and Impossibility) of Being Forced to Be Free

Having examined the connections between freedom and dependence, on the one hand, and between dependence and the general will, on the other, I am now in a position to reconstruct Rousseau's response to the central question that arises from his claim that being constrained to follow the general will is nothing more than being forced to be free: In what sense do the dictates of the general will constitute one's own will as an individual, even when one fails to recognize them as such? Rousseau's answer consists in the following thought: by restructuring human dependence such that subjection to the will of others ceases to be a virtually inevitable consequence of dependence, the general will brings about the objective social conditions that must be present if individuals are to be able to avoid subjection to a foreign will. The general will, then, can be said to be an individual's own *true* will, even when he does not consciously recognize it as such, because the general will wills the conditions necessary in order for his freedom (along with the freedom of all others) to be actualized. Identifying the general will with the true will of each individual is based on the idea that the individual will, apart from whatever particular ends it may embrace, necessarily, and most fundamentally, wills its own freedom. But in willing a certain end (its freedom), it must also will the conditions that make that end attainable. A will that chooses to act in ways that are inconsistent with what is required for the actualization of its own freedom cannot be regarded as "doing its own will" and therefore cannot be considered truly free. Such a will—one that in effect wills its own subjection—is a self-negating, therefore contradictory, will.

This set of claims rests upon an understanding of how freedom is actualized through the general will—call it the freedom-through-personal-independence model—that, in contrast to the social autonomy interpretation, views the rule of laws informed by the general will not as itself an embodiment of citizens' freedom but as the latter's precondition. Moreover, the kind of freedom that is claimed to be actualized on this view is

not moral freedom (because it does not necessarily involve determining one's actions in accord with self-given laws) but rather the negatively defined freedom that Rousseau calls civil freedom. That is, the general will's restructuring of dependence creates for individuals not merely the abstract right but the real possibility to act unconstrained by the will of others within a sphere of activity external to the community's vital interests. Rousseau's political thought, then, contains two distinct accounts of how individuals actualize their freedom through the general will, accounts that differ with respect to both (1) the nature of the relation claimed to hold between freedom and the general will and (2) the type of freedom said to be actualized: According to the first, membership in the state is (1) a *precondition* of (2) a negatively defined *civil freedom,* insofar as the rule of law effectively mitigates the freedom-endangering consequences of dependence; according to the second, membership in the state is (1) an *embodiment* of (2) *moral freedom* (or social autonomy), insofar as citizens are ruled by laws they construct for themselves in accord with a shared conception of the common good.

Can Rousseau consistently maintain both of these accounts of how freedom is actualized through the general will, or are the two views incompatible? In order to answer this question we must first locate more precisely the point at which the two views threaten to collide. The fact that Rousseau ascribes two kinds of freedom to the members of a rational state is not itself problematic, for civil and moral freedom are to be understood not as two rival conceptions of freedom but simply as two different forms that the freedom of citizens assumes. Being free of constraints imposed by the wills of other individuals and being subject only to self-given laws are merely two different ways of satisfying the basic condition of freedom, which stipulates that one obey no will other than one's own. Neither is there a problem in Rousseau's assertion that the two kinds of freedom exist side by side within a single state. Since the sphere of moral freedom can extend only as far as the domain of law itself, and since the latter is not so extensive as to determine everything individuals do, the limits of the domain of law demarcate a sphere within which citizens enjoy a freedom that can be characterized only negatively, as a condition of not being constrained to obey the particular wills of other individuals.

If there is a tension between these two accounts, it resides not in the distinction between civil and moral freedom itself but in the way each account conceives of the relation that must hold between individual wills and the general will, if the general will is to be considered the will of each individual. In other words, the point of difference concerns the kind of relation that individuals who are in fact subject to the general will must have to that will if their subjection to it is to count as obedience to their own will and therefore as freedom. According to the social autonomy model, the general will counts as the will of individuals only by virtue of a certain *subjective* relation individuals can have to the general will, a relation that consists in a conscious affirmation of the principles that inform the general will. For this reason the freedom depicted by the social autonomy model could be characterized as a species of "subjective freedom." For the freedom-through-personal-independence model, however, the general will's being the will of each individual depends not on a subjective quality of individual wills but on an *objective* feature of the general will itself, namely, that what it wills is a set of conditions that, if realized, has the effect of freeing individuals from their otherwise necessary subjection to the arbitrary wills of others. Because the freedom one enjoys in this scenario is independent of one's subjective relation to the principles that structure the social world, it could be termed a kind of "objective freedom." Thus, the tension between these two accounts comes to the fore when the requirements of objective and subjective freedom come into conflict—that is, in those instances where individual citizens of a well-constituted state do not consciously affirm the principles by which they are governed, principles that, objectively speaking, are necessary for their own freedom. In other words, the conflict becomes manifest in precisely those situations where Rousseau speaks of individuals being forced to be free.

The question to be answered, then, is whether it is possible to bring together Rousseau's distinct accounts of freedom into a single coherent theory. The key to resolving the tension between these two models of political freedom lies not in embracing one at the expense of the other but in recognizing that, while each on its own represents a genuine species of freedom, each is also, in the absence of the other, a limited or merely partial freedom. This is obvious enough in the case of being forced to be free: to fail to affirm the principles that in fact constrain one's actions is to fall short, in an important way, of the ideal of being subject only to one's own will. While the notion of objective freedom provides the conceptual resources that make it possible to speak coherently of being forced to be free, such one-sided freedom remains a kind of unfreedom from the point of view of the subjective requirements of free willing. But the claim that each of the two conceptions is only partial freedom is no less true for the purely subjective freedom envisaged by the social autonomy model. The full freedom of citizens must consist in more than their simply having the appropriate subjective attitude to the principles by which they are governed, since to affirm principles that are ultimately destructive of one's freedom is itself a kind of unfreedom—that is, a failure to will in accord with one's own true will and its fundamental aspiration to be able to pursue its ends in the world free of external determination. Thus, the basic point underlying Rousseau's dual account of how citizens actualize their freedom through the general will can be formulated as the claim that each of the two conceptions of freedom isolated here constitutes a necessary but not sufficient condition of achieving what Rousseau regards as full political freedom. According to this reconstruction, then, two independent conditions, one subjective and one objective, must be met in order for individuals to actualize full political freedom: (1) the laws that govern citizens must be objectively liberating—they must effectively mitigate the freedom-endangering consequences of dependence on other individuals; and (2) citizens must also stand in the appropriate subjective relation to the laws that govern them—that is, the principles that inform the laws must be consciously embraced by citizens as their own.

In the chapters that follow I shall argue that Hegel's social theory, grounded in a version of "the free will that wills the free will" (§27), invokes a conception of social freedom that has precisely the structure I have attributed here to Rousseau's understanding of political freedom. That is, Hegel retains Rousseau's central idea that rational social institutions stand in a twofold relation to the freedom of their members—they are both preconditions and embodiments of that freedom—while making explicit that the subjective affirmation of the principles that govern social life is a necessary component of a fully actualized freedom, thereby insisting, in contrast to the view Rousseau is normally thought to have, that individuals cannot be forced to be free.

3

The Subjective Component of Social Freedom

Having seen how Rousseau's understanding of political freedom incorporates two main elements—a subjective and an objective component— we are now in a position to begin to articulate Hegel's own conception of social freedom, which, as I have already suggested, possesses a two-part structure similar to Rousseau's. Our return to Hegel's social theory will be facilitated by recalling his claim, introduced at the end of chapter 1, that *Sittlichkeit* is "the unity of objective freedom . . . and subjective freedom" (§258A), where the former refers to the laws and institutions of the rational social order (§144, E §538) and the latter denotes a certain frame of mind, or disposition *(Gesinnung),* of social members that is "befitting of freedom" (VPR1, 248).

The basic idea underlying Hegel's bipartite account of social freedom can be given a preliminary formulation by bringing together two thoughts, versions of which we have already encountered in my discussion of Rousseau's conception of political freedom: First, in calling the laws and institutions of *Sittlichkeit* "objective freedom," Hegel means to claim that there is a sense in which rational laws and institutions *objectively* embody freedom—that is, they realize a kind of freedom independently of whatever subjective relation (such as affirmation, rejection, or indifference) social members might have to their laws and institutions. On the basis of such a conception, freedom can be said to be realized (in at least a limited sense) simply by virtue of the fact that rational (that is, freedom-procuring) laws and institutions are in place and are sustained over time by their members' participation. As I have suggested previously, one part of Hegel's doctrine of objective freedom derives from a premise he inherits from Rousseau concerning the socially conditioned nature of individuals' freedom. According to this premise, individuals can realize themselves as free only if a variety of social conditions first obtain that make that freedom possible. Thus, one of the important ideas behind Hegel's identification of the laws and institutions of *Sittlichkeit* with objective freedom is the claim that such laws and institutions bring about and maintain the social conditions necessary for individuals to realize themselves—to acquire a real existence within the world—as bearers of self-determined wills. Matters are complicated, however, by the fact that this account of objective freedom omits a crucial feature of Hegel's doctrine that distinguishes it from his predecessor's: for Hegel rational laws and institutions embody objective freedom not only in the Rousseauean sense that they secure the necessary preconditions of the freedom of individual social members, but also in the sense that together they constitute a social order that, as a whole, approximates the essential properties of a fully self-determining being. (Further discussion of this distinctively Hegelian feature of objective freedom will be postponed until chapter 4.)

The second thought behind Hegel's conception of social freedom is expressed in the demand that objective freedom acquire "an existence in self-consciousness befitting of freedom." The idea here is that members of *Sittlichkeit* whose behavior conformed to the requirements of rational laws and institutions, but who lacked the appropriate subjective relation to those laws and institutions, would fall short of the ideal of freedom in an important respect. This claim follows from a point about the subjective conditions of self-determined action: individuals who inhabit a rational social world are required (by the sanctioning power of laws and social norms) to determine their actions in accord with the dictates of freedom-procuring laws and institutions, and, insofar as they do so, they enjoy objective freedom in the sense explicated earlier. But the mere fact that individuals conform to the requirements of rational laws and institutions is not sufficient to ensure that their activity is *subjectively* free— that is, free in the sense in which someone's actions can be said to come from his own will, or to be freely willed (as opposed to involuntary, coerced, or, as Hegel would say, determined by an external other). As just described, the lack of subjective freedom is a situation in which the activity of individuals is subject to principles (embodied in laws and institutions) that remain external to their own wills. Since the social participation of such individuals is determined not by their own wills but by something external to them, their actions in the social world are not, subjectively speaking, their own. If social members are fully to realize the ideal of self-determination, then, it is not enough that they merely live in accord with principles that make them free from an objective point of view; they must also have a conscious voluntative relation to those principles that makes their social activity subjectively self-determined—that is, they must in some fashion know and will those principles as their own.

If social freedom is the unity of these objective and subjective elements, then *individuals* can be said to enjoy social freedom when three conditions are met: first, their laws and institutions effectively secure the real social conditions of their own freedom;[1] second, their institutions constitute a "self-determining" social whole; and, third, they have a conscious, voluntative relation to rational laws and institutions that makes their social participation into (subjectively) free activity. If we add to these considerations Hegel's claim (discussed later in the second part of 3) that a will's self-determination is not complete until it successfully translates its ends into reality, we arrive at the following abstract account of what it is for individuals to enjoy social freedom: the socially free individual *freely* and *effectively* wills the laws and social institutions that are *the real conditions of his or her own freedom* and that, taken together, *constitute a self-determining social whole*. In more Hegelian language, a socially free individual can be said to possess a will that "has itself [its freedom] as its content, object, and end" (§21) and therefore to be an embodiment of "the free will that wills the free will" (§27), or of what Hegel calls the "absolutely free will" (*der an und für sich freie Wille*) (§22A). In the next three chapters I shall attempt to make sense of Hegel's idea that the distinctive freedom realized in the rational social order is to be understood as a unity of objective and subjective freedom. This will require a detailed examination of both components of social freedom with a view to articulating what each of them is and in what sense each can be thought of as a species of freedom. In this chapter I consider the kind of self-consciousness that belongs to socially free individuals, and in the following two I investigate what it means for laws and social institutions to embody objective freedom.

Social Members' Subjective Disposition

According to Hegel, individuals who enjoy social freedom stand in a subjective relation to their social institutions that is "befitting of freedom." This subjective relation—what I shall refer to throughout as the "subjective disposition" *(subjektive Gesinnung)* (VPR1, 248) of social members—can be thought of as a "frame of mind," or a conscious attitude individuals have toward the social institutions to which they belong.[2] Their subjective disposition is befitting of freedom in the sense that it is only by virtue of this disposition that they experience their social participation, which necessarily involves conforming to the norms embodied in laws and social institutions, as their own freely willed activity. This section will address the three principal questions that arise from Hegel's claims concerning the subjective component of social freedom: In what does the subjective disposition of socially free individuals consist? How does it make their social participation into subjectively free (that is, freely willed) activity? And, finally, what conception of freedom, or self-determination, is at work in Hegel's claim that freedom is realized through this disposition?

The terminology Hegel most commonly uses to describe the subjective disposition of socially free individuals does not at first seem to provide a promising set of conceptual tools with which to construct either a theory of rational social institutions or an account of how individuals achieve their freedom in such institutions. The subjective disposition appropriate to *Sittlichkeit* is repeatedly characterized as an attitude of trust *(Vertrauen* or *Zutrauen)* on the part of individuals toward the social institutions to which they belong (§268; E §515; VPR2, 129). Moreover, this trust is said to be predicated on what Hegel describes as a relation of "identity" *(Identität,* §147A), or "unity" *(Einheit,* §158+A), between individuals and their social institutions. (From here on I shall refer to this relation between individuals and institutions as an "identical unity" in order to distinguish it from the very different concept of identity I introduce later.)[3] This identical unity is said to consist in individuals' perception of their social institutions as undifferentiated from themselves (§147) or, equivalently, in a form of consciousness in which those institutions cease to be "an other" for social members (§268). Hegel expands on this description of the identical unity of social members and their institutions in his introductory account of *Sittlichkeit:* where social freedom is realized, the laws and powers of institutions "are not something *alien* to the subject; rather the subject bears *spiritual witness* to them as to *its own essence,* in which it possesses its *sense of self (Selbstgefühl)* and lives as within an element that is undifferentiated from itself—a relation that at first is more identical than even *faith* and *trust*" (§147).[4]

Hegel's emphasis on the concept of trust and his insistence that such trust is possible only if individuals see themselves as undifferentiated from their social world appear either to be flatly at odds with the claim that individuals achieve their freedom in *Sittlichkeit* or else to imply that Hegel holds to that thesis only by doing violence to our common notions of what it means to be free. For if the rational social order requires an identical unity of social members and their institutions, it seems that individuals can achieve social freedom only at the expense of their ability to distance themselves reflectively from social norms and hence only by surrendering their capacity for individual self-determination. In what follows I shall try to dispel the force of these initial impressions by undertaking a detailed analysis of what Hegel takes the subjective disposition of socially free individuals to consist in and how he understands that disposition to be essential to their existence as free, or self-determined, individuals. The first and most important part of this task will be to investigate what it means, on Hegel's view, for individuals to regard themselves as being identically unified with their social institutions.

In the third section of "*Sittlichkeit*" Hegel spells out the content of the subjective disposition appropriate to free social membership in terms of three distinct elements: socially free individuals are said to be conscious of their identical unity with their social institutions insofar as they regard those institutions as (1) their purpose, or end (*Zweck*), (2) their essence (*Wesen*), and (3) the product of their own activity (§257).[5] The first of these elements can be thought of as a kind of *voluntative* unity, a oneness of wills, that obtains between individuals and their institutions. As we shall see, socially free individuals have wills that are identically unified with their institutions in two senses: they regularly and willingly take the collective ends of social institutions as their own, and they do so not in the sense that they regard their participation in such institutions as merely instrumental to achieving some external good but in the more substantive sense that they take that participation to be valuable for its own sake. The second element, identical unity with respect to "essence," refers to a relation of unity between social members and their institutions at the level of individuals' self-conceptions or, as I shall refer to them later, their *practical identities*.[6] That is, the practical identities of social members—their understanding of who they are as particular individuals—are (in a sense to be explicated) constituted by and expressed through their social membership. According to the third, socially free individuals regard themselves as identically unified with their social institutions in the sense that they are aware of themselves as the *producers* (more accurately, the *re*-producers) of their institutions: they see those institutions as sustained by and therefore dependent on their own collective activity.

Before examining each element of the subjective disposition of free social members, it is important to say a word about the role this account plays in Hegel's theory. The point of the doctrine of subjective freedom is not to claim that individuals ought to adopt a certain attitude toward their institutions regardless of what those institutions are like. The point, rather, is to articulate the kind of conscious relation individuals would have to have to their social order if the full panoply of freedoms available to the modern world were to be fully realized. In other words, the doctrine of subjective freedom is an account of the disposition social members have when the social order is functioning as it should (and *can*, in the modern world). Rather than functioning as a set of demands made primarily on individuals, Hegel's account of the subjective disposition of *Sittlichkeit* yields a set of standards that rational social institutions must measure up to. For, as we shall see in succeeding chapters, one of the questions the doctrine of objective freedom has to answer is, How must institutions be constituted so their members are able to adopt the attitude to them that Hegel regards as constitutive of subjective freedom? In other words, What must be true of the social order if individuals are to regard themselves as identically unified with it?

1. UNITY OF WILL.   The voluntative unity of individuals with their social institutions consists in two distinct, though closely related, phenomena. The first of these Hegel refers to as "the identical unity of the particular will and the universal [or general] will" (VPR2, 124). The identical unity at issue here is, most fundamentally, a harmony in *content* between the particular wills of individual social members and what Hegel, following Rousseau, calls the "general [or universal] will" of the social institution in question. This kind of voluntative unity obtains when individuals need only pursue their own particular ends in order for the good of the social whole (the ends of the universal will) to be achieved. Hegel's point here has its origins in Adam Smith's understanding of the harmony that exists between individual and collective inter-

ests in a free market economy. Hegel explicitly incorporates Smith's insight into his own account of how particular and universal wills relate to each other within the market-governed relations of civil society: "In furthering my end I further the universal, and this in turn furthers my end" (§184Z). It is not difficult to see why Hegel was impressed by the kind of relation between individual and collective interests that underlies Smith's account of the market. Such an arrangement (one in which there is a unity of particular and universal wills) makes it possible for the collective good of a social whole to be achieved through the free (uncoerced) activity of its individual members. Since individuals realize the universal will by pursuing their own particular ends, they achieve the ends of the whole by following only their own wills and, hence, freely. Moreover, since the achievement of individuals' particular ends also depends on the flourishing of the whole, the relations between individuals and the collective good within the market economy approximate Hegel's ideal, discussed in chapter 1, of an "interpenetrating unity" of universality and particularity.

Although the harmony of interests that characterizes the market-governed relations of civil society counts as an "identical unity of particular and universal wills" in the broadest sense in which Hegel uses that phrase, there is an important respect in which it falls short of the more thoroughgoing unity of particular and universal wills that figures most prominently in his theory of Sittlichkeit. This point is expressed in Hegel's characterization of civil society as merely a "relative totality" (§184) in which universal and particular wills, although identically unified (in content), remain external to one another. What Hegel has in mind is the fact that in civil society particular wills typically realize the good of the whole only, so to speak, behind the backs of individual members. The particular wills of individuals are in harmony with the universal will independently of any conscious relation, cognitive or voluntative, that individuals might have to the good of the social whole. The situation is different, however, in the two institutions Hegel takes as the paradigmatic instances of ethical social wholes, the family and the state (§142N). The family member differs from the member of civil society in that the former possesses a will that is universal not only objectively but subjectively as well. This means that the family member (when subjectively constituted as such) stands in a conscious relation to the family in its entirety, a relation that involves both a conception of what is good for the family as a whole and an ability to be moved practically by considerations relating to that good, even when doing so conflicts with the particular interests one has as a separate individual.

This way of characterizing the will of a family member raises an important question concerning Hegel's use of the term 'particularity': If the family member wills in accord with its understanding of what is good for the whole, then in what sense is that will also, at the same time, a particular will? In order to get clear on Hegel's concept of particularity, it will be helpful to recall first how Rousseau uses the term 'particular' (or 'private') when characterizing the wills and interests of social members. A particular will, as Rousseau defines it, "tends only toward [one's] particular [or private] advantage" (SC, III.2.v). Particular interests for Rousseau, then, are the interests one has when regarded as a wholly separate individual, unattached to others through sentiment or obligation.[7] On this definition, a particular will is the same thing as a purely self-interested, or egoistic, will. It is important to note that nothing in Rousseau's concept of a particular will implies that the particular will of one individual must differ in content from the particular wills of others. It is perfectly conceivable, for example, that two particular wills might desire the very same piece of food or, more important, that they might seek identical types of self-interested ends, such as freedom and security. In fact, the intelligibility of Rousseau's political project—the very possibility of a social contract, as he conceives it—rests on the assumption that there exist certain particular interests that are both shared by all individuals and most effectively pursued through social cooperation. If there were no such "universal" particular interests—particular interests common to all human beings—there would be no basis for the agreement of unassociated individuals to join forces within society and submit to the dictates of a general will.[8]

Since Hegel considers the will of a family member to be a particular will (or, more precisely, a will that is at once particular and universal), and since such a will is clearly not purely egoistic, 'particular' must signify something different for Hegel than it does for Rousseau. But if particular interests, for Hegel, are not the interests one has as a separate, unattached individual, what kinds of interests are they? Two points are essential to understanding Hegel's concept of a particular will. First, particularity for Hegel is always associated with the twin ideas of qualitative determinacy and difference from others. To be a particular being in this sense is to have at least one determinate quality (or "determination") that is not common to all other beings of the same species and that therefore distinguishes its bearer from (at least some) other members of that species. To call a human will particular, then, is to say that it possesses a determinate content (an end or set of ends) that is not shared by all human wills and that therefore marks it as qualitatively distinct from (at least some) other human wills. This is also to say that the ends of a particular will derive not from some universal feature of human beings as such but from the determinate, and therefore distinctive (though not necessarily unique),[9] position that the bearer of that will occupies in the world. The particular ends I embrace as a family member—to care for the particular members of my family in ways appropriate to my particular place within it—distinguish my will not only from the wills of the members of other families (my end is to care for *this* family) but also from the wills of the other members of my own family (since I care for this family in accord with *my* place within it). Given this conception of particularity, it is no longer puzzling how a will could be both particular (having a determinate content that distinguishes it from other wills) and nonegoistic. Moreover, as the example of the family member makes clear, there is nothing in this concept of particularity that precludes a particular will from also being "universal" in one prominent sense of the term (consciously directed at the good of a certain social whole).

The second defining feature of a particular will, the one more important to our purposes here, is that particular wills are attached to their ends through inclination[10] rather than abstract reason (reason that tells us what we ought to do independently of, and possibly in opposition to, what we are inclined to do). This means that individuals have a motivation for acting on their particular ends independently of any reflection on those ends from the standpoint of a purely rational being who abstracts from its particular characteristics, including its particular relations to others. To say that the wills of family members are both particular and universal, then, is to say that family members are subjectively constituted such that they are typically inclined to act in ways that further their family's good as they understand it and that such action for the sake of the whole (or for other members of the group) is experienced by them not as indifferent or contrary to their own good but as intrinsic to it.[11] This kind of unity of particular and universal wills—a feature that distinguishes family members and citizens from members of civil society—could also be described by saying that individual social members consciously embrace the ends of their social institutions as their own.

Thus, as Hegel applies the term to wills and interests, 'particular' does not imply 'egoistic'. At the same time, nothing in the definition of 'particular' excludes the possibility of a particular interest being purely egoistic. A desire to spend the afternoon lying in the sun, for example, satisfies both of Hegel's criteria for particularity: it distinguishes my will from (at least some of) my fellow humans, and I am motivated to seek it by inclination rather than universal reason. In other words, within the class of particular interests as Hegel defines them, it is necessary to distinguish those that are also particular in Rousseau's sense (purely egoistic) from those that are also "infused with universality" (directed at a nonegoistic end, such as the family's good). When discussing Hegel's theory, I shall reserve the term 'private' to describe interests of the first kind in order to avoid confusing them with those of the second.[12] It is, of course, the latter sort of particular interests that figures crucially in Hegel's account of the subjective disposition of *Sittlichkeit,* and of how social members can work for the collective good without sacrificing their (subjective) freedom.

The voluntative unity of individuals and their social institutions includes a second component that is closely related to, yet conceptually distinct from, the point just discussed: social members who are voluntatively identical with their social institutions regard "the universal interest" of those institutions as "their final end" (*Endzweck*) (§260). That is, individuals view their membership and participation in the institutions of *Sittlichkeit* as having an intrinsic value beyond the merely instrumental value they have as means for the attainment of their private ends. Moreover, the collective, or universal, interests served by their social participation are said to be not only final ends but also their "highest," "absolute" ends (§258, E §514). Thus, their activity for those interests not only has for them an intrinsic value; it is also their most highly valued activity. These features of the subjective disposition of social members are most visible in Hegel's description of the family and state, where family members and citizens are said to view both their own activity and their ties to others within those institutions as final ends (VPR1, 252; §260). It is not surprising that the institutions in which individual members consciously embrace the good of the whole as their own (namely, the family and the state) are also institutions in which members see their participation as having an intrinsic and overriding value. But, according to Hegel, even in civil society, where a conscious concern for the good of the whole is not required, individuals regard their social activity as an important and intrinsic good. Individuals' participation in the economic sphere—which consists, most fundamentally, in their socially productive labor—is clearly of instrumental value to them, insofar as it is a means to the satisfaction of their naturally based needs. Yet it is crucial to Hegel's understanding of civil society as a realm in which social freedom is realized that membership therein has more than a purely instrumental significance for its members. As we shall see in more detail later, socially free individuals are able to experience their activity in civil society (and in the other two spheres as well) as intrinsically valuable and of supreme importance because it is through their socially recognized, productive labor that they constitute themselves as beings of standing, both "in their own eyes and in the eyes of others" (§207).

Finally, Hegel's thesis that rational social institutions are characterized by an identical unity of universal and particular wills should not be understood as asserting the implausibly strong claim that members of such institutions maximize their private good—their good as wholly separate individuals—if and only if they carry out their social roles.[13] On the contrary, in performing their roles within the institutions of *Sittlichkeit* social members are regularly called upon to forgo the pursuit of (some of) their private ends. Hegel's point, rather, is that members of a rational social world—one in which social freedom is realized—are subjectively constituted so as to be willing to subordinate their private interests to universal ends and to be able to do so not out of selflessness but because they regard their activity on behalf of those universal ends as intrinsic to their own (particular) good.[14] But embracing the good of the whole as their own is a possibility for social members only insofar as they conceive of themselves as something more than discrete, unattached beings whose interests are wholly private. In other words, the voluntative unity at issue here is predicated on individuals having conceptions of themselves as beings for whom membership in the family, civil society, and the state is intrinsic to who they are. This thought leads us directly to the second element of the subjective disposition appropriate to social freedom, the unity between social members and their institutions with respect to their "essence." It is this feature of Hegel's view that enables us to understand how forsaking egoistic ends in favor of the good of the whole can be regarded not as a sacrifice of self but as its very opposite, namely, activity through which social members achieve their selfhood by establishing for themselves identities as determinate (and therefore particular) individuals.

2. UNITY OF ESSENCE.   Although the preceding account of the voluntative unity of social members and their institutions articulates the content of Hegel's claim that socially free individuals regard their institutions as their own end, it leaves unanswered the important question of how such a voluntative unity is possible. What is it that allows individuals to embrace the interests of their families and their state as their own? Why do they regard their participation in these institutions, and in civil society, as valuable for its own sake? The answers to these questions are to be found in the second, more fundamental, part of Hegel's account of the subjective disposition of socially free individuals: the voluntative unity of individuals and their social institutions follows from and is made possible by their consciousness of those institutions as identical (or "one") with "their own essence" (E §514).

Four preliminary points about this unity of essence will help bring into focus the phenomenon Hegel has in mind. First, the kind of unity at issue here differs from the voluntative unity discussed earlier in that it concerns not individuals' wills but their "essences," or what I shall call (at the risk of compounding the confusion already caused by Hegel's equivocal talk of identity) their *practical identities*. So, with respect to their practical identities (a concept that will be explicated straightaway), free social members are said to be one with their institutions. It is important to note that this way of formulating Hegel's position points to what is surely the most difficult interpretive problem associated with the doctrine of the subjective disposition of *Sittlichkeit*: given the wide variety of meanings 'identity' can have, precisely what sense of the term is at issue here? Clarifying this aspect of Hegel's view will take up a major part of the present chapter, but doing so is necessary if we are to avoid some of the common mistaken (and unattractive) readings of his claim that socially free individuals are, with respect to their essence, "identical with" their social institutions.

The second point helps to clarify the concept of a practical identity by specifying the aspect of social institutions from which individuals' practical identities derive. What social members regard as their own essence is not, *in the first instance,* social institutions themselves but the particular roles they occupy within them:[15] members of *Sittlichkeit* have identities as mothers or fathers, as farmers or teachers, as citizens of this or that land.[16] The third point follows directly from the second: the kind of practical identity at issue here is not a generic or "abstract" universal essence—some essential property we all share as, say, rational beings, or as members of the human race—but rather a *particular* identity that makes social members the particular individuals they are and distinguishes them qualitatively from one another.[17] My positions within the institutions of *Sittlichkeit* make up my "essence" (or core) as an individual in the sense that my particular roles as mother (of these children), teacher (of this subject), and citizen (of this nation) are fundamental constituents of my identity—constituents that are central to my being the particular individual I take myself to be. It is important to bear in mind, especially in light of widespread misunderstanding of Hegel on this point, that Hegel's emphasis here on the particular identities of social members does not imply that he denies the need for individuals to have identities as abstract, universal beings as well. Both persons and moral subjects, as Hegel defines them, are universal in precisely this sense.[18] The point, rather, is that what is at the core of the kind of self-determination specific to *Sittlichkeit* are the ways in which individuals, through their social participation, win identities as particular beings. Later I shall expand upon and qualify the claim that the practical identities involved in the subjective dispositions of social members are particular rather than universal. For now, however, it is sufficient to construe Hegel's assertion that socially free individuals regard their families, civil society and the state as their own essence, and hence as undifferentiated from themselves, as expressing the claim that the roles they occupy within those institutions are (in a sense still to be explicated) constitutive of their practical (particular) identities.

The fourth point comes into view by considering Hegel's various formulations of his claim about the practical identities of social members: individuals are said to "win their substantial self-consciousness" in the institutions of *Sittlichkeit* (§162), to "arrive at an intuition [*Anschauung*] of themselves" within their "common social life" (VPR2, 125), and to find their "consciousness and sense of self [*Selbstgefühl*]" as members of social wholes (§261A). These statements clearly indicate that the practical identities attained within *Sittlichkeit* are *self-conscious* identities,

identities that necessarily include a self-conception, a conscious under-standing of who, fundamentally, one is (as a particular individual). This is not to say, however, that these identities are merely self-conceptions. For through their social membership individuals not only come to con-ceive of themselves as husbands and plumbers and citizens; they also objectively realize their identities as such, which is to say that their con-ceptions of who they are are confirmed by their social world and thereby take on an objective—a socially recognized—existence. As is appropri-ate for an account of the subjective disposition of *Sittlichkeit,* Hegel's own statements here emphasize the self-conscious element of the identi-ties of social members, but, as we shall see later, his view involves claims about the socially constituted nature of both who they take themselves to be and who in reality they are. Hegel's view that the members of *Sittlichkeit* regard their social institutions as "their own essence" could be restated, then, as the claim that for socially free individuals member-ship in the basic social institutions—more precisely, the ensemble of particular roles they occupy within those institutions—is constitutive of their practical, self-conscious identities. This formulation raises an im-portant question that must be considered in some detail if we are to un-derstand Hegel's view: What exactly does it mean to speak of the practi-cal *identities* of individuals, and in what sense are their social roles *constitutive of* these identities?

The claim that the roles social members occupy within *Sittlichkeit* are constitutive of their identities must not be interpreted, as it sometimes has been, to mean that individuals simply are (are nothing more than) the bearers of the particular roles they occupy. It is not Hegel's view that social members are, or ought to be, so closely identified with their roles that they are unable to distance themselves reflectively from their social attachments and question the value of those attachments and the in-stitutions of which they are a part.[19] Although Hegel believes that this was true of the inhabitants of classical antiquity—their relation to their social roles was one of *unmediated* unity—he denies that the identities of individuals in the modern world (beginning, roughly, with the Prot-estant Reformation) can be reduced without remainder to the social roles they occupy. Indeed, if individuals' social attachments were consti-tutive of their identities in this strong sense, they could not be said, on Hegel's own terms, to be fully free in those attachments. Or perhaps it is more accurate to say that such individuals would not be free in their social attachments in the manner appropriate to modern subjects; that is, they would lack the capacity for the kind of self-determination characteristic of moral subjectivity.[20] For, according to Hegel, the will of a modern individual necessarily includes as one of its elements "the I's pure reflection into itself" (§5), which is one of the essential features of moral subjectivity. In the case of moral subjects, free willing involves more than simply having (and acting upon) a set of ends; it also presupposes the ability to abstract from any of one's given properties or ends—to consider any particular property or end as external to who one is—in order then to reject it or to embrace it as one's own. This is why Hegel thinks of, and explicitly describes, the relation modern individuals typically have to their social institutions as a unity that is mediated by reflection (§147A).[21] While it is not the case that social freedom *consists in* this ability to distance oneself from one's social roles, the unity between individuals and institutions it involves must nevertheless be *compatible with* the self-determination appropriate to moral subjectivity. If Hegel's basic project of harmonizing the demands of modern moral subjectivity with the requirements of free social membership is to get off the ground, it must at least be conceptually possible for individuals to enjoy the social freedom characteristic of *Sittlichkeit* while maintaining their status as moral subjects. But if the social attachments of modern individuals are not constitutive of their identities in the sense considered here, we must find another way of understanding Hegel's assertion that, with respect to their essence, social members are one with their institutions. If it is not the case that individuals are simply identical with (nothing more than the bearer of) their social roles, in what sense are these roles constitutive of their identities?

A second, more natural way of understanding Hegel's view is to take it as a thesis about the social origin of individuals' identities. On this interpretation, the identities of social members are constituted by their social world in the sense that they are the products of that world: their characters and values, their understanding of who they are as individuals, are shaped, if not completely determined, by the ways they are socialized by the institutions in which they are raised.[22] While Hegel believes this to be true of individuals who grow up within the institutions of *Sittlichkeit*, it is not what is at issue in his claim about the socially constituted nature of their practical identities. The most important part of Hegel's view is a thesis concerning not the origin of social members' practical identities but their content. The roles that socially free individuals occupy within the institutions of *Sittlichkeit* are constitutive of their identities in the sense that those roles provide the basic framework in terms of which individuals define themselves. The point is not simply that individuals acquire whatever identities they come to have from the institutions within which they are brought up but that they regard their ongoing participation in their families, in civil society, and in the state as fundamental to who they are.

In what sense, then, are social roles constitutive of the practical identities of free social members? Hegel's claim involves two main points, each of which articulates a distinct sense in which social roles are constitutive of an individual's identity. First, to say that individuals define themselves in terms of their social roles is to say that these roles, and the attachments to others that these entail, furnish social members with the projects[23] and final ends that figure most prominently in their practical engagement with the world. The social roles of socially free individuals are constitutive of their practical identities in the sense that they regard the ends and projects they have by virtue of occupying those roles as their most important, life-defining aims. Those ends and projects are what gives meaning to individuals' lives and makes them worth living, and for this reason they can be said to constitute (make up) the essential core, or substance, of who those individuals are.[24] Their membership in the family, their citizenship, and their roles as productive members of civil society are the sources of what socially free individuals take to be their most important practical commitments and are thus the features of themselves that play the largest part in shaping their activity in the world. This is no doubt what Hegel means when he says that the ends socially free individuals pursue in their social participation are their "highest" final ends, but what about his further claim that those ends are "absolute" (E §514)? In this part of his practical philosophy Hegel frequently associates 'absolute' and 'unconditioned' with the idea of moral duty (§§135, 137, 258). It is plausible, then, to ascribe to him the view that finding one's identity in one's social roles involves regarding the norms associated with those roles as morally binding. Thus, to take the ends I have as a parent or citizen as absolute is to see myself as having an obligation to realize them.[25] The absolute, or obligatory, character of such ends is linked to the fact that I regard my social roles as making up the essential core, or substance, of who I am. Acting in ways that are contrary to my roles as parent or citizen would represent a repudiation of something I take to be essential to who I am and hence a threat to my very being as a self.[26]

The second respect in which an individual's social roles are constitutive of his practical identity is expressed in the claim that a free social member's "sense of self"—his "self-feeling" (*Selbstgefühl*, §261A)—depends in some way on fulfilling his roles. Since 'sense of self', as it is used here, is roughly synonymous with 'self-esteem',[27] this assertion makes a claim about the centrality of individuals' social participation, their occupying and performing of their particular roles, in establishing for themselves identities as individuals of value or standing. Socially free individuals are said to regard their social membership as fundamental to their own "worth and dignity" (VPR1, 252; §152) and to be motivated to fulfill their roles not out of considerations of "advantage" (*Vorteil*) but because "they have their dignity" in doing so (§155N). By performing their social roles, and performing them well, they secure the esteem of others and ultimately their self-esteem as well. They achieve, in other words, the *recognition* of their fellow social members and thereby satisfy an aspiration that Hegel (again, following Rousseau) regards as fundamental to being a self, namely, the aspiration to "be someone," to count as a being of value both for oneself and for others. To have an identity as a member of a social whole, then, is not only to have a practical commitment to fulfilling one's roles but also to know one's social commitments as a substantial source of one's sense of self, to find in them one's identity as a self that matters.

The recognition individuals win as members of the institutions of *Sittlichkeit* is not the only kind of recognition that plays an important role in Hegel's social and political philosophy. The securing of individuals' formal rights as persons—the concern of "Abstract Right"—represents another way in which individuals are recognized by their social order as beings of intrinsic worth. But the recognition specific to the theory of *Sittlichkeit* differs from that accorded to persons in a significant respect: whereas a system of abstract rights recognizes individuals as persons (and hence as abstractly universal beings, formally indistinguishable from all others), membership in *Sittlichkeit* involves a recognition of individuals' *particularity*—of their worth as the particular beings they are. This is most apparent in the family, where the bonds among individuals are rooted in an attachment to others that is highly object-specific, namely, the love family members feel for one another. As the member of a family, one is loved because of the particular individual one is; to experience this love is to have the value of one's particular qualities affirmed by others or, in Hegelian terms, to achieve recognition as a particular being.[28] In civil society, too, social members achieve recognition on the basis of who they are as particular beings rather than as abstract individuals. The identities acquired by members of civil society are particular identities because they derive from, and are defined in terms of, individuals' exclusive membership in a determinate estate *(Stand)*, or profession (§207). In order to achieve "recognition and honor" (E §527) as a self-sufficient, productive member of civil society, one must establish oneself as a competent and conscientious practitioner of a socially useful occupation. This, however, is no frivolous undertaking but a life-long project that involves directing one's efforts and developing one's skills in accord with a conception of oneself as exercising a particular vocation—as farmer or teacher or harness maker. An individual comes to have a standing within civil society, then, only by "stepping into determinate particularity" (§207), that is, only by taking on a determinate and exclusive professional identity that both makes him into a particular someone and distinguishes him from (the majority of) his fellow members of civil society.

Thus far I have emphasized that the practical identities individuals win within *Sittlichkeit* are particular rather than (abstractly) universal identities. While this point brings out a crucial feature of Hegel's view, it is also misleading if taken to imply that these identities are *merely* particular. For, like the case of particular wills discussed earlier, the particular identities of social members can also be said to be infused with a kind of universality; more precisely, they are infused with universality in three different senses of that term. The first and most obvious sense is that, although the identities acquired within *Sittlichkeit* are particular in the sense that they distinguish individuals qualitatively from one another, they are at the same time "thickly social" in content. This point is brought out nicely by Hegel's characterization of the subjective disposition appropriate to the family as one in which the family member gains "the self-consciousness of his individuality *within this unity* . . . , so that he or she exists within it not as a person in his or her own right [*für sich*] but as a *member*" (§158).

The thickly social nature of social members' practical identities shows itself most plainly in the practical consequences of those identities, that is, in the kinds of actions individuals who have such identities are typically motivated to undertake. As we saw earlier, members of ethical life are characterized by a capacity to subordinate their private interests to collective ends and to do so willingly, without experiencing the social need for such behavior as an external constraint on their wills. They possess, in other words, general, or universal, wills (where 'universal' simply means collective or social, in contrast to private or egoistic). But, as I suggested earlier, the ability of socially free individuals to have universal wills in this sense is itself grounded in the more fundamental fact that they have practical identities of a certain kind, namely, identities that are universal, or thickly social, in the sense articulated in the preceeding quote: they have conceptions of themselves as essentially *members* of social wholes rather than as separate, self-sufficient individuals.

To say that the particular identities of members of *Sittlichkeit* are thickly social is to say, most fundamentally, that they are identities in which the particular relations they have to other concrete individuals play an essential, constitutive role in defining who they are rather than being accidental determinations, external to their self-conceptions. In jointly pursuing the shared projects that follow only from such relations, and in finding recognition of my worth as a particular being within them, "I win myself"—my "substantial self-consciousness"—through my relations to others, and to be deprived of these relations is to experience oneself as "defective and incomplete" (§§158Z, 162). Thickly social identities, then, involve substantial bonds to other individuals—both in the sense that they are deep-felt, enduring attachments to others and in the sense that they make up an essential part of the content, or substance, of who I take myself to be. Moreover, these social bonds are not attachments to others in the abstract—for example, to all rational beings as such—but are grounded essentially in certain determinate, particular qualities of those to whom one is attached (most obviously, their membership in one's own family, trade, or nation).

Thus, the identities acquired within *Sittlichkeit* are of a different kind from those (abstractly universal) identities individuals have as persons or moral subjects. Insofar as I conceive of myself as a person, I think of myself as a sovereign, self-standing unit of free agency, indistinguishable in essence from all other such units. As a person, other individuals enter into my self-conception and my practical undertakings only negatively and even then only as abstract beings stripped of their determinate qualities; that is, others have significance for me only as an external limit on my otherwise arbitrarily willed activity and as agents from whom I have the right to demand that they, too, refrain from trespassing the boundaries of my own private sphere. My identity as a person implies no positive obligations to others, and the ends I set myself in acting upon that identity need take no account of their needs or well-being. As a moral subject, one's relations to others enter into one's self-conception in a more substantive fashion, since the very standpoint and ends the moral subject adopts cannot be formulated without reference to other subjects. For example, relations to others are constitutive of the moral subject's will in the sense that the good, which the moral will by definition takes as its end (§131), includes as one of its constitutive elements "*universal well-being*" (§130). This means that the moral will, in setting ends for itself in accord with its conception of the good, takes into account the needs and well-being of others. While other individuals have more than a merely negative significance for the moral subject, its self-conception and the relations to others it implies are abstractly universal rather than particular in the sense that they are the same in principle for all rational beings, as opposed to being grounded in particular qualities of the individuals involved.

There is a second sense in which the particular identities individuals win through their membership in the three basic social institutions are infused with universality: although it is possible to characterize social roles in terms so specific that they distinguish their bearers as unique individuals, qualitatively distinct from all others, the fundamental content of those roles does not differ radically from individual to individual, as if they were simply the expressions of caprice or idiosyncrasy. Despite an infinite variety among the concrete circumstances that enter into the particular identities acquired within *Sittlichkeit*, they are also, at a fundamental level, *shared* identities that secure a significant degree of commonality among the basic self-conceptions, and hence the substantive interests, of social members. While these identities can be understood as deeply particular in the sense that they can be defined in terms of the distinctive place one occupies (as mother rather than father) within a group of specific, concrete individuals (the Garcías rather than the Chatterjees), they are nevertheless grounded in basic social roles— mother and father, doctor and worker—that also inform the identities of other social members. Having an identity as the husband of a certain wife or the farmer of a particular tract of land includes not only an awareness of one's uniqueness as an individual but also a view of oneself as exemplifying a general type, as subsumable under the concepts 'husband' and 'farmer'. While such concepts are not universal in the sense of applying to all social members as such (and are therefore not "abstractly universal"), they possess a degree of universality that gives a more than merely particular content to the identities individuals attain in ethical life.

Finally, Hegel is committed to maintaining that the particular identities of social members are infused with universality in a further, weightier sense of that term. Although this version of that claim has been less apparent to many of Hegel's interpreters than those discussed previously,[29] it is nevertheless essential to his general philosophical project. That is, the task of providing a philosophical justification of modern social institutions, as Hegel understands it, involves demonstrating that those institutions, including the set of role-centered, particular identities that accompany them, are universal in the sense that they can be shown to be rational from a perspective that has validity not merely for individuals who are already subjectively "at home" in their positions within modern ethical life but for all thinkers.[30] Thus, to say that these particular identities are universal in this weightier sense is to say that they are objectively rational or, in other words, that they form an integral part of a social system that, as a whole, satisfies the fundamental demand of universal reason, namely, that freedom (here: freedom of the will) be realized in the world. It is an important feature of Hegel's view that the particular identities acquired within *Sittlichkeit* need not be *subjectively* universal in the sense at issue here—they need not be seen as satisfying universal reason by all who have them, nor embraced by them for that reason—in order to *be* rational in this sense.

3. INSTITUTIONS AS THE PRODUCT OF INDIVIDUALS' ACTIVITY. I shall have less to say about this aspect of social members' unity with their institutions than the previous two, not because it is less important to Hegel's theory, but because it is considerably easier to grasp. By distinguishing this third component of the subjective disposition appropriate to ethical life—social members' consciousness of their institutions as the product of their own activity—Hegel means to draw our attention to two

closely related features of the subjective aspect of social freedom. The first of these consists in individuals' awareness that the social world to which they belong depends for its very existence upon their own wills. One of the fundamental facts to be taken account of by a social theory based on freedom is that individuals enter the institutions to which they belong by birth rather than through a free act of will. They neither fashion their basic social institutions from scratch nor even (for the most part) choose which ones they will belong to. On the contrary, social members appear to be more the products than the producers of their institutions, since both *who* they are and *that* they are depend upon their belonging to a social world, or to what Hegel (in view of this fact) calls a social "substance." The point being made here, however, is that socially free individuals are not *merely* accidents of their social substance (E §514) for the reason that the latter, too, depends upon the former for its being *(Sein)*—that is, the social substance attains a sustained existence only through the collective activity of the individuals who compose it. While the social world is undeniably prior to and independent of the will of any of its individual members, the institutions that make it up cannot be maintained and reproduced without the widespread, voluntary participation of those individuals.[31] It is for this reason that Hegel goes so far as to say of socially free individuals that they are conscious of themselves as "*bringing about*" their institutions "through their own activity" (E §514) and thereby know those institutions as extensions of themselves, the results of their own (re)productive activity.[32]

The assertion that members of *Sittlichkeit* are conscious of their institutions as products of their own activity is meant to point to a further "satisfaction of the will" enjoyed by social members that Hegel likewise counts as part of their social freedom. This consciousness is said to comprise not only the knowledge that the continued existence of their institutions depends on them but also the perception of those institutions as "something achieved in the here and now" *(ein erreichtes Diesseits)* (E §514), as opposed to an ideal realizable only in some world beyond *(jenseits)* their own. Insofar as social members take their institutions as their own ends and participate in the successful reproduction of their social world, their consciousness of the actual existence and flourishing of those institutions serves as a confirmation that the social world they desire to live in is not a utopian dream but an achievable goal and provides them with a satisfaction that comes from seeing their ends realized in the world. This consciousness, then, involves their perceiving in the world that their wills have real effects; it is the knowledge that they have not merely striving, but also *effective,* wills. Hegel's inclusion of this point in his account of the subjective disposition appropriate to ethical life is based on the thought that a will's self-determination is not complete—it has not achieved its satisfaction—unless it has succeeded in translating its ends into reality (§§8–9). That Hegel considers this satisfaction to be a component of social freedom shows that the freedom on which his theory of *Sittlichkeit* is based is more than simply a capacity or possibility for action; it also requires that the will's ends be realized, resulting in a kind of harmony between the will and the world.[33]

As we shall see in more detail in the following chapter, Hegel's inclusion of this feature among the essential components of the subjective disposition necessary for social freedom has the effect of requiring as one of the conditions of "objectively free" social institutions that they be "substantial" in the sense of self-reproducing—or, as Rawls would say, that they enjoy a stability over generations. The justification for including this consideration in an account of social freedom becomes clearer when one imagines the situation of social members who willed a set of institutions that were in fact incapable of having a sustained existence in the world. (One might think here of inhabitants of the former eastern bloc who identified with the ends of socialism but had the misfortune to live in a socialist society whose Stalinist structure, perhaps because it allowed too small a space for the expression of its members' particularity, made it incapable of being sustained over time by the uncoerced activity of those members.) Such individuals, unable to find the social world they will as "something achieved in the here and now," would be denied one of the fundamental satisfactions to which the will inherently aspires, that of seeing its ends translated into reality. Having one's will frustrated in this way represents for Hegel a kind of unfreedom—or, better perhaps, it represents a failure of the free will to complete itself by giving real existence (*Dasein*) to its willed determinations.

The Subjective Disposition of *Sittlichkeit* as Self-Determination

Having examined the three main components of the subjective disposition appropriate to ethical life, it is time to consider how this account figures into Hegel's basic strategy for providing a justification of the institutions of *Sittlichkeit* on the grounds that they play an essential role in the realization of freedom. What is it that makes this subjective disposition "befitting of freedom"? In what sense are individuals who have this subjective relation to their social institutions free, or self-determined? The most important part of this task will be to articulate the conception of freedom that underlies Hegel's view by attempting to lend coherence to his obscure and divergent remarks on the connection between freedom and *Sittlichkeit*.

In some passages Hegel appears to equate the subjective component of social freedom with the disposition of social members itself, implying that the subjective freedom they enjoy as members of *Sittlichkeit* consists simply in a state of consciousness—specifically, in their awareness of their identical unity (in the senses explicated earlier) with their social institutions. The clearest instance of this is found in Hegel's treatment of patriotism, the subjective disposition appropriate to membership in the state (§268). In this passage Hegel first characterizes patriotism as a species of trust, which he defines as "the consciousness that my substantial and particular interest is contained and preserved in the interest and end of an 'other' (here the state)." He then goes on to equate this trust itself with freedom via the claim that through this trust the state "ceases to be an 'other' for me, and *in this consciousness* I am free" (emphasis added). This way of characterizing the freedom social members win through their subjective disposition is easily recognized as a version of Hegel's well-known formula, cited in a variety of contexts, that serves as his most general definition of freedom: freedom, in all of its many Hegelian guises, is said to be a state of being-with-oneself-in-an-other (*Beisichselbstsein in einem Anderen*) or, more perspicuously perhaps, a being-at-home-in-an-other.[34] Yet this one-sentence explication of the subjective component of social freedom is clearly unsatisfactory on its own. Apart from obvious questions it raises about the plausibility of equating trust with freedom (an issue to which I return later), it is seriously misleading if taken for the whole of what there is to say about the freedom social members win through their subjective dispositions. For if this being-with-oneself-in-an-other is thought to consist merely in a *consciousness* of one's identity with the other—simply in a kind of *attitude* one has to the social world—it seems to be more a theoretical stance to the world than a practical one and, as such, closer in character to the speculative freedom achieved in philosophical contemplation—in apprehending the world as a manifestation of one's own (spiritual) nature—than to something recognizable as practical freedom.[35] Yet social freedom, belonging to the realm of what Hegel calls "objective spirit," is clearly meant to be a species of practical freedom—a freedom of the *will*—and hence a freedom that is essentially bound up with the real, practical activity through which the will realizes its subjective (inner) ends in the objective (external) world (§§8–9).[36] As we shall see later, the attitude of trust social members have to their institutions can indeed be characterized as one form of being-at-home-in-an-other, and therefore as a kind of freedom, but this attitude itself is derivative of their "being-with-themselves" in their social institutions in a way that is more clearly practical in nature, a being-with-self that individuals achieve only in and through their actual participation in the institutions of *Sittlichkeit*. Social members who have the subjective disposition described above are subjectively free, not simply because they are aware of themselves as one with their social institutions but because they "*live* within them as within an element undifferentiated from themselves" (§147; emphasis added).

How, then, is the subjective disposition of socially free individuals bound up with their practical freedom? Or, equivalently, in what sense is the social participation of such individuals subjectively free (freely willed) activity? A partial answer to these questions can be formulated in terms that do not appeal to any distinctively Hegelian views about the nature of practical freedom. This formulation is suggested by bringing together two of Hegel's statements concerning the relation between the wills of individuals and their social institutions: while the institutions of *Sittlichkeit* are "*ethical powers* that govern the life of individuals" (§145), social participants can be said to be subjectively free because, given the appropriate subjective disposition, they "do not perceive [this] universal as a foreign power" (VPR2, 123). This way of conceiving of the subjective aspect of social freedom can be understood as a direct consequence of the voluntative unity (in the sense indicated earlier) that holds between individuals and their social institutions: insofar as there is a unity in content between the particular wills of social members and the general will of the institution as a whole, those members do not perceive the imperatives of social participation as antagonistic to their own wills. Using the same terms Rousseau would employ to characterize the freedom enjoyed by citizens who identify with the general will of their political association, the social participation of members of *Sittlichkeit* can be said to be free because, in acting in accord with the general will, they are subject to no will other than their own; they are, in effect, determined only by their own wills.

It is clear, however, that Hegel also regards the members of *Sittlichkeit* as subjectively free in a peculiar sense that goes beyond the conception of freedom implicit in the preceding paragraph and distinguishes his social theory from all others, including Rousseau's. This is evidenced by numerous passages, such as the following, in which the freedom of individuals is equated with their achieving "substantial self-consciousness" (§162) or a "sense of self" (§147) through their social participation: "By acting as ethical beings [*als Sittliche*] humans free themselves. Their living together in *Sittlichkeit* is their liberation; for in that living together they arrive at an intuition [or perception] of themselves" (VPR2, 125). The connection Hegel asserts here between freedom and "intuiting" oneself can only be understood in the context of his thesis, examined earlier, concerning the inherently social nature of individuals' particular identities. By participating in the institutions of *Sittlichkeit,* social members arrive at an intuition of themselves; they are able to perceive who they are by looking at their real existence in the world. In other words, social members find in the external, social world a confirmatory reflection of who they take themselves to be, and they are able to do so because it is by participating in that world that they establish objectively realized identities as particular individuals. To describe the identities acquired by social members as objective and real is to say, above all, that they consist in more than merely subjectively held conceptions of who they are; these identities are real because they have taken on an existence in the external world, and they are objective because they hold not only privately for themselves but also for the other subjects who share their world.

The claim that individuals achieve objectively real identities through their social participation includes two theses concerning the connection between identity and social participation that are worth distinguishing: First, social members give objective, real existence to their conceptions of themselves, insofar as they actually pursue and realize the practical projects implied by their self-conceptions. As members of *Sittlichkeit,* they do not merely imagine themselves to be mothers, plumbers, and citizens; they in fact become such beings by carrying out the activities that the roles of mother, plumber, and citizen require. In translating their conceptions of themselves into the external world, they give objective reality to their otherwise merely subjective identities. Thus, the social participation of the members of *Sittlichkeit* can be said to have a self-expressive character, insofar as it is an activity through which they externalize, or give expression to, their conceptions of who they are. Included in this notion of self-expression is the idea that in giving real existence to their self-conceptions social members inevitably interpret the social roles they embrace and therefore express them in a way that reflects, to a limited extent, their own understanding of what those roles require of them. Although Hegel himself does not explicitly recognize this aspect of social members' self-expressive activity, the need to do so becomes clear when one considers that social roles are seldom defined in such detail that they fully determine the particular actions that are supposed to follow from them. Thus, every mother knows that it is her duty as a parent to discipline her children in order to make them capable of self-restraint as adults, but social expectations alone do not suffice to specify which forms of punishment are appropriate or the precise circumstances in which disciplinary measures are called for. While social members define their identities in terms of social roles they do not themselves create, executing those roles within the world is less like a mechanical translation of norms into action than an interpretive performance in which individuals determine their actions in accord with their own ideas about how best to exemplify the roles they take as their own.[37]

The sense in which individuals objectively realize their identities through their social participation is not fully captured by the thought of translating some subjective, or inner, content (a conception of who one is) into the external world. This point, the second of the two referred to above, follows from the fact that having an identity as a husband or citizen involves more than successfully carrying out the projects that husbands and citizens are supposed to undertake. Saying that individuals have their identities in their social roles also implies that their occupying those roles is a substantial source of their sense of self, or their consciousness of themselves as individuals of value or standing. Since achieving this sense of self is dependent on the recognition of one's fellow social members, which itself is won by fulfilling one's roles well, individuals' social activity provides them with a form of self-consciousness, and hence a form of selfhood, they could not have independently of that social participation. This implies that their practical activity within the institutions of *Sittlichkeit* is not only *self-expressive* in character (the externalization of a subjectively held self-conception) but also *self-constituting* in the sense that, more than simply expressing a previously existing self-conception, it serves actually to constitute social members as *selves*—that is, as individuals who count as beings of value not only for others but also for themselves. This is why their labor for universal ends, rather than being a "selfless" activity, is the very opposite, namely, a form of self-assertion; for it is through such activity that social members posit, or establish, their identities as particular selves. Moreover, it is precisely this connection between selfhood and social membership that allows them to regard their social participation as valuable in itself, even as their highest, absolute end.

Thus, Hegel regards individuals' social participation as subjectively free not only because their subjective dispositions enable them to embrace the general will of the groups to which they belong as their own (and hence to comply willingly with the dictates of their social institutions) but also, and more important, because their social activity "comes from themselves" in the stronger sense that it is through such activity that they express and constitute their own identities as particular individuals. How, though, is this to be interpreted as *self-determination?* There are, I think, two senses in which the social members Hegel describes can be characterized as self-determining. First, their practical activity is mediated, or determined, by their conceptions of who they are, of what is essential to their identity. These self-conceptions are articulated in terms of a set of basic projects that structure their lives and provide guidelines for determining the content of their wills—that is, for determining which desires it is appropriate for them to have and to act upon, and which desires they should reject as inconsistent with the kind of individuals they take themselves to be. In carrying out their social roles, then, socially free individuals engage in activity that is self-determined in the sense that it is determined in accord with their understanding of their own practical identities. The second sense in which Hegel sees the social participation of individuals as a form of self-determination is directly connected to the thought that through such participation they realize their particular self-conceptions and constitute themselves as beings of value. The type of self-determination carried out here could be characterized as an act of *giving real determinacy to the self*[38]— and hence as a kind of *self-realization*—for it is precisely this activity that makes one into a determinate self—a particular individual with a real, socially recognized standing in the world. Bringing together the various points made thus far about the freedom social members attain through their subjective dispositions, we could say that the social participation of such individuals is free because it is successfully executed activity, undertaken for its own sake and informed by a conscious, voluntary adoption of universal ends, which, at the same time, is expressive of individuals' particular identities and a substantial source of their status as selves of recognized value, or standing.

This account of the type of self-determination realized in the subjective disposition of free social members will no doubt give rise to the objection "But that's not what we normally mean by 'freedom,' nor is it the kind of freedom a social theory ought to be most concerned with." The proper response to this objection is that the doctrine of subjective freedom constitutes only a part of Hegel's social theory and makes no claim, by itself, fully to answer the question "what freedom is" (or what "real" freedom consists in). Its aim, rather, is to provide an account of a specific type of "self-determination" that individuals are able to achieve as members of a rational social order. If Hegel succeeds, as I believe he does, in bringing to light an important good—a kind of determining of oneself—that can be won through certain forms of social participation, then the appropriate response to his view is not to object, "But that's not what freedom is," but to ask—as Hegel himself goes on to do—whether this form of self-determination is compatible with the realization of freedom in other, more familiar guises. Demonstrating that social freedom is compatible with both personal and moral freedom is one of Hegel's most urgent theoretical aims, and examining how he does so will be a central task of this book's final four chapters.

"The True, Ethical Disposition": Trust

Hegel no doubt intends for us to think of the self-expressive and self-constituting activity of social members as a kind of being-with-oneself-in-an-other. For in their social participation individuals are with-themselves-in-an-other in the sense that they enter into practical relations with other social members that are constitutive of their own identities; they are who they are (as particular individuals) only in those relations to others. Having grasped this point, we are in a position to consider the phenomenon, alluded to earlier, that Hegel more explicitly associates with being-with-oneself-in-an-other, namely, the attitude of *trust* that socially free individuals are said to have to their social institutions. In the passage cited earlier Hegel offers a definition of this frame of mind, which he elsewhere calls "the true, ethical disposition" (E §515): "*trust* (which can pass over into more or less educated insight), [is] the consciousness that my substantial and particular interest is contained and preserved in the interest and end of an 'other' (here the state) in its relation to me as an individual" (§268). Two aspects of this definition are in need of closer consideration here, the first of which makes reference to the cognitive content of trust, the second to what we might call its subjective form.

In this passage, as in many others (E §515; VPR1, 99), Hegel locates the central feature of trust in its cognitive content, which he specifies as the belief held by social members that their own fundamental interests are inseparably intertwined and in essential harmony with both the ends of their basic social institutions and the fundamental interests of the other individuals to whom they are bonded in those institutions. Thus, trust is essentially nothing other than the enduring confidence individuals have that their institutions are for them a "home"—that is, a social world that is hospitable not only to the attainment of their private ends (such as the needs acquired and satisfied through participation in the market economy) but also to the satisfaction of their "substantial" (fundamental) interest in realizing their freedom and, inseparable from that, their identities as particular beings. It is easy to see, then, that Hegel's view of trust rests on his account of how social members win their particular identities, since it is the thickly social content of those identities that makes it possible for them to regard the family, civil society, and the state as the arenas within which they realize their deepest aspirations, including the aspiration to be a particular self. Hegel asserts that the attitude of trust itself, and not merely the self-determining *activity* of individuals, represents a species of freedom because he thinks of the cognizance of being at home within the social world as a kind of satisfaction of the will: it is the enduring assurance that one inhabits a world whose basic framework makes it capable in principle of accommodating one's most fundamental practical ends. To lack this assurance, or to be convinced of the opposite, is to doubt, or to despair of, the possibility of achieving one's deepest aspirations in the present world; it is to see that world as an abiding source of frustration of one's will and hence to be subjectively estranged, or alienated, from it.[39]

The second noteworthy feature of the definition of trust given here is its allusion to what I am calling the subjective form of that attitude. Hegel's parenthetical remark that trust "can pass over into more or less educated insight" implies that the essential content of that attitude—the belief that one's own basic interests are "contained and preserved" in the ends of one's social institutions—is capable of assuming a variety of subjective forms, ranging from an immediate, unreflective faith in one's social institutions to a fully grounded, philosophical comprehension of their rationality. Although this point is often ignored by interpreters, it is unambiguously asserted in numerous passages (§147A; VPR2, 123–124), and, more important, it is indispensable to Hegel's basic aim of showing that the freedom specific to membership in *Sittlichkeit* is compatible with the demands of modern (moral) subjectivity, including the requirement that the subject be bound only to principles whose rationality he or she is able to recognize (§132). This common misunderstanding of Hegel's view is surely due in part to the natural tendency to think that trust must be blind or unconditional, and hence an attitude that by its very nature excludes rational reflection. Hegel himself sometimes encourages such misreadings (though less frequently than their prevalence would suggest), especially in those places where he fails to distinguish as clearly as he should between the subjective disposition characteristic of ancient *Sittlichkeit,* which could be described correctly as simple, unwavering, and immediate, and the disposition most appropriate to modern social membership, which could not.[40] Another likely source of confusion is that Hegel often associates trust, even in the case of modern *Sittlichkeit,* with habit, or with what he refers to as social members' "second nature" (§§151+Z, 268+Z). But the force of Hegel's emphasis on habit is to make a point about how socially free individuals are motivationally constituted—that their desires, dispositions, and values are formed (*gebildet*) by their upbringing such that their social participation is largely spontaneous, or "comes naturally" to them—not to attest to an incompatibility between rational reflection and free, unalienated social membership. The fact that one is in the habit of walking the streets at night without taking special precautions (to take an example of Hegel's that has lost its resonance for us) does not imply that one would be unable to give a rational justification of that practice if asked, or that one could not be brought to call it into question by experiences or arguments that cast doubt upon its advisability. While it is true that particular acts done out of habit are done unreflectively, it is not the case that habit itself (or trust) is inherently antithetical to reason, since agents of habit are able to reflect on, and even change, the habits they have.

What is most important from the point of view of Hegel's theory of *Sittlichkeit* (and hence for the phenomenon of social freedom) is the cognitive content of trust and the absence of alienation it represents, not the subjective form in which it is present. If what procures the freedom associated with trust is the belief that one's social world is basically hospitable to one's deepest practical aspirations, then the subjective side of social freedom is in no way diminished when that belief is founded on reason rather than on unquestioning faith. This also implies that the belief central to trust can be held in a relatively unreflective form—it can be immediate trust—and still be social freedom (assuming it is at the same time a *true* belief). A theory of modern ethical life does require, however, that the trust ascribed to social members *be capable* of being grounded in rational insight and hence that it be able to survive good-faith reflection on the merits of existing social institutions. Moreover, in order to accommodate the requirement that moral subjectivity be realizable for all, the rationality of the social world cannot be visible only from the perspective of an esoteric philosophical doctrine accessible only to the few but must in principle allow of being made transparent to the average social member. Thus, it must be possible for individuals who conscientiously reflect on their social world to come to recognize its rationality, which is to say that they must be able to arrive at an understanding of the essential roles their institutions play in the realization of freedom. In other words, in order to realize the full range of freedoms available to them as modern subjects, social members not only must have the subjective disposition described in this chapter but also must be in a position to understand *what makes it rational* for them to have such an attitude to their social order; they must, in other words, be able to grasp the basic elements of Hegel's doctrine of objective freedom, the topic of chapters 4 and 5.

4

Objective Freedom, Part I:
The Self-Determining Social Whole

In the preceding chapter we saw that Hegel locates the subjective component of social freedom in the ability of individuals to identify with their particular social roles and, by extension, with the social institutions within which those roles are defined. The members of *Sittlichkeit* are able to comply willingly with the basic demands of social institutions—their social participation is their own, freely willed activity—because it is through such participation that they constitute and give expression to their particular identities. But, as the following passage indicates, Hegel's conception of social freedom is not exhausted by his account of the subjective disposition of social members: "The right of individuals to their . . . freedom is fulfilled by their belonging to ethical actuality, for their [subjective] *certainty* of their freedom has its *truth* in such objectivity; in the ethical sphere they actually possess their own essence, their inner universality" (§153). The claim expressed here is that in order to ascribe social freedom to individuals, it is not sufficient simply to establish that they subjectively identify with a given set of existing institutions. Beyond this subjective "certainty" on the part of social members that their social world constitutes a home, that world must in "truth" *be* a home, which means, according to this passage, that it must enable its members to realize their true essence—"their inner universality" or, as we shall see later, their practical freedom.[1] This point could also be formulated as the claim that for social freedom to be fully realized, the institutions with which social members subjectively identify must also be objectively *worthy* of that identification, which is to say that they must meet the criteria Hegel sets out for *rational* social institutions; they must embody, in Hegel's words, "that which is inherently (or 'in itself') rational" (*das an sich Vernünftige*) (§258A).[2]

Thus, my present task—one that will occupy me for the next two chapters—is to examine both the content and the philosophical justification of the criteria Hegel employs in evaluating the "inherent" rationality of social institutions. In carrying out this task I shall need to address two sets of questions: First, what general features must characterize a social institution if it is to be considered rational "in itself" (and therefore objectively worthy of being the object of individuals' subjective identification)? Second, how is the inherent rationality of such institutions related to the freedom of their members? Or, more precisely, why does membership in those institutions constitute an essential part—the "objective component"—of individuals' social freedom?

The fundamental concept in Hegel's account of the inherent rationality of social institutions is what he calls "objective freedom" (§258A; E §538; VPR1, 248; PH, 43/XII, 61). Social institutions are inherently rational, and therefore worthy of being the object of individuals' subjective identification, when they conform (in the ways to be articulated later) to the requirements of objective freedom. The concept of objective freedom is an indispensable part of Hegel's theory of *Sittlichkeit*, for it is what enables that theory to provide a more robust justification of social institutions than one grounded simply in the subjective attitudes of its members. If one fails to give the concept of objective freedom its due, Hegel's argument in defense of a given set of institutions can do no more than point to the fact that the members of those institutions are subjectively constituted so as to be able to identify with them; it remains powerless to explain why, beyond the mere fact of their identification, it is rational for them to do so. In other words, objective freedom is Hegel's answer to the question: What features of the family, civil society, and the modern state make it rational, or good, that individuals subjectively identify with those institutions (rather than others) and lead their lives within them?

Another way of bringing out the significance of the doctrine of objective freedom is to focus on the kinds of reasons it gives individuals to endorse their social institutions. As we saw in chapter 3, Hegel's account of the subjective component of social freedom located the primary motive for social participation in the interest social members have in giving expression to their particular self-conceptions and in constituting themselves as beings with a socially recognized worth. In contrast, the doctrine of objective freedom addresses the issue of whether social members also have reasons for endorsing their institutions independently of the fact that they view their membership in their families, civil society, and the state as essential to their own particular identities. Thus, the doctrine of objective freedom figures into Hegel's claim about the inherent rationality of the institutions of *Sittlichkeit* because it furnishes individuals with reasons for endorsing their institutions that are valid not merely from the perspective of social members who are already subjectively at home in their particular social roles but from the perspective of *all* thinkers (or, more precisely, from the perspective of all thinkers who take an interest in the realization of freedom, which for Hegel just is the perspective of universal reason).[3] In other words, this part of the theory of *Sittlichkeit* is meant to ensure that social members' endorsement of their institutions is capable of surviving reflection on those institutions undertaken from the universal perspective—in Hegel's terms, the "abstractly universal" perspective—that is definitive of moral subjectivity. This means that Hegel's social theory claims for itself the power to convince even individuals who lack an immediate subjective attachment to their institutions that those institutions are in fact worthy of their endorsement. Such subjectively alienated social members can be reconciled to their social world by being shown that its institutions are inherently rational (or embody objective freedom), which is to say that they play a necessary role (to be further specified later) in the realization of practical freedom.[4]

Although it is clear that Hegel intends to employ a notion of objective freedom that will enable him to claim that rational institutions play a necessary role in the realization of freedom independently of the subjective dispositions of social members, it is not easy to determine what content he gives to that notion. For despite the crucial role this idea plays in his account of *Sittlichkeit,* Hegel only rarely makes explicit use of the term 'objective freedom', and where he does, he fails to clarify both what it means and how it functions in his theory. Not surprisingly, Hegel's obscurity with respect to this fundamental issue has had grave consequences for the philosophical reception of his social theory. Most important, it has engendered a nearly universal confusion among interpreters—a confusion that also manifests itself in contemporary attempts to revive the Hegelian doctrine of *Sittlichkeit*—concerning the basic philosophical strategy Hegel means to employ to justify the social institutions he endorses. It is primarily in order to clarify this basic strategy that I turn now to an examination of objective freedom.

The task that faces us is to explicate what it means to say, as Hegel does, that *Sittlichkeit* is "objective freedom" (VPR1, 248). We can begin by noting that the modifier 'objective' refers here to three qualities of the freedom under discussion, qualities that correspond to the three senses of objectivity Hegel distinguishes in his introduction to the *Philosophy of Right*. First, objective freedom is real, or true, freedom (§26, α), as op-posed to what is merely taken to be freedom. This is not to say that ob-jective freedom is the whole of practical freedom—on the contrary, it constitutes only one component of social freedom—but rather that it "truly accords with the concept of the [free] will" (§26), or, in less He-gelian language, that it conforms in fact, and not merely in appearance, to what is required in order for practical freedom to be realized. In its second sense, 'objective' refers to anything that has an existence in the external world (§26, γ). To use Hegel's example, a will that achieves its ends by acting in the world makes itself objective in this sense. Objec-tive freedom, then, will be a freedom that exists externally (in existing laws and institutions) rather than merely inwardly (subjectively) in the (unrealized) wills of agents.

In its third usage, applying the predicate 'objective' to a thing signifies that the thing is what it is independently of any consciousness of it as such on the part of subjects (§26, β). In this sense of the term one could say (to borrow an example from Kant) that the laws of nature have an objective causal force, whereas the moral law does not, since its causal force depends on agents' consciousness of it as a binding law. This third sense of objectivity is both the most important for our purposes and the most difficult to grasp in connection with freedom. To speak of objective freedom in this sense is to imply that there is a kind of freedom that can be ascribed to practical beings independently of any subjective (that is, conscious) relation they might have to whatever is said to constitute their objective freedom. In the context of Hegel's social theory, the doc-trine of objective freedom implies that there is a meaningful, albeit lim-ited, sense in which individuals are free simply in virtue of inhabiting an inherently rational (objectively free) social world, regardless of their subjective relation to the laws and institutions of that world. In other words, a social world that is objectively free secures a kind of freedom for its members "whether it is recognized and willed by individuals or not" (§258A).

How, then, are we to understand the contention, fundamental to Hegel's social theory, that rational laws and institutions embody a kind of freedom whose existence is independent of the conscious knowledge and will of social members? It is important to note here that the opening chapters of this book already provide us with the conceptual resources for developing two quite different accounts of objective freedom, one derived from Rousseau's political theory and the other from Hegel's distinctive conception of a self-determined will as one that has a self-sufficient existence and exhibits the organic structure of the Concept. As I argued in chapter 2, Rousseau's doctrine of the general will rests on a conception of freedom that qualifies as objective in the three senses indicated here. This aspect of Rousseau's position is most visible in his claim, implicit in his talk of citizens' being forced to be free, that the effective enforcement of the general will makes individuals politically free (in at least a limited sense) independently of their conscious relation to that will. For Rousseau, political institutions informed by the general will can be taken to embody a sort of objective freedom, insofar as they secure the real conditions necessary for individuals to possess a free will (one that is undetermined by any foreign will). What this means more specifically is that freedom-procuring institutions restructure the natural, prepolitical dependence of individuals in such a way that subordination to the wills of others ceases to be an inescapable consequence of human neediness. Two general features of objective freedom in its Rousseauean guise are worth highlighting here: first, the objectively free character of rational laws and institutions resides in their status as necessary *conditions* of freedom; second, the freedom conditioned by such laws and institutions is quite straightforwardly ascribable to the wills of *individual* social members.

The other way of conceiving of objective freedom is to understand it in terms of the claim, discussed in chapter 1 in conjunction with the strongly holistic interpretation of social freedom, that the institutions of *Sittlichkeit,* taken as a whole, come closest to embodying the structure of a fully self-determined will. Thus, the family, civil society, and the modern state could be equated with objective freedom because they constitute a system of fully self-sufficient institutions that exhibits the structure of the Concept and is capable of reproducing itself, along with all of the diverse particular qualities essential to its being what it is. On this interpretation, objective freedom would be understood not as a set of conditions that make it possible for freedom to be realized but as an embodiment of a sort of freedom that is thought to reside in the rational, "self-determined" structure of the social world. Contrary to initial appearances, such a reading would still allow for social freedom to be attributed to the individual members of *Sittlichkeit,* because insofar as they subjectively identified with their social institutions, their social participation would be free in the sense articulated in chapter 3. Moreover, this freedom could be said to be true freedom—more than simply a matter of their subjective "certainty"—because such individuals would identify not with an arbitrary set of institutions but with inherently rational ones, with institutions "made necessary by the idea of freedom" (§148A). The distinctive feature of this interpretation, rather, is that it takes *one* of social freedom's two components—the objective freedom in terms of which the inherent rationality of social institutions is defined—to consist in a strongly holistic quality, one that is attributable to a system of institutions but not to individuals themselves. In other words, the property of the social world that makes it rational for social members to identify with the institutions of *Sittlichkeit* (rather than with others) is located in the fact that only those institutions, considered as a whole, approximate Hegel's criteria for a completely self-determined will and are for that reason necessary in order to satisfy the demand that practical freedom be fully realized in the world.[5]

In which of these two directions are we to proceed, then, in reconstructing Hegel's doctrine of objective freedom? There is no doubt that the relevant texts appear to favor the second of these interpretations. One clear example of this tendency is found in the passage in which Hegel first lays out the distinction between objective freedom and the subjective component of *Sittlichkeit:* "The *rationality* of ethical life [*das Sittliche*] resides in the fact that it is the *system* of the determinations of the Idea. In this way ethical life is freedom, or the will that has being in and for itself as something objective . . . It is because the determinations of ethical life constitute the concept of freedom that they are the substantiality or universal essence of individuals" (§145+Z).[6] Although it is beyond dispute that Hegel intends to appeal to his distinctive conception of self-determination in order to give content to the assertion that the institutions of *Sittlichkeit* embody objective freedom, a compelling reconstruction of his position along these lines faces a formidable challenge: How is it possible to lend plausibility to the claim that the social world's self-sufficiency and its being structured in accord with the Concept (or "the determinations of the Idea") make it inherently rational and therefore objectively worthy of its members' endorsement? In response to this question it is not sufficient simply to note that Hegel's claim has its source in his peculiar metaphysical views concerning the nature of reason and the structure of reality *(Wirklichkeit)*. The difficulty posed by this conception of objective freedom is not one of locating its source in another part of Hegel's philosophical system but of showing concretely how a claim with obscure metaphysical origins can be fruitfully applied to the problems specific to social theory.

While the Rousseauean conception of objective freedom has the advantage of being the intuitively more plausible alternative, explicit textual evidence that Hegel held such a view is very difficult to find.[7] I shall argue here, however, that with respect to the issue of objective freedom, Hegel's account of *Sittlichkeit* exhibits a much deeper affinity with Rousseau's political theory than is apparent from the surface of his texts. More specifically, I shall argue that Hegel's assertion that the institutions of *Sittlichkeit* embody objective freedom includes as one of its central components the Rousseauean claim that such institutions, independently of the conscious will or knowledge of their members, secure the conditions necessary for their individual members to acquire self-determined wills. Moreover, the conception of self-determination at issue in this claim is not parasitic on the strongly holistic conception of self-determination discussed previously. That is, the contention that rational social institutions are conditions of individuals' freedom does not simply reduce to the assertion that social members are objectively free because they are part of a "self-determined" social whole. In other words, I shall show that for Hegel the inherent rationality of social institutions resides (at least in part) in the fact that such institutions make it possible for social members to realize the more individualistic forms of freedom, most prominently those associated with personhood and moral subjectivity. This position is implicit in Hegel's statement that personhood and moral subjectivity "cannot exist on their own" but "must have ethical life as their bearer *(Träger)* and foundation [*Grundlage*]" (§141Z). Yet my interpretive claim will be fully convincing only after I have shown in detail that Hegel's accounts of the inherent rationality of the particular institutions that make up ethical life, especially his treatments of the family and civil society, are in fact devoted in large part to the task of demonstrating how those institutions effectively secure the conditions necessary for the freedom of individuals to be realized.

The suggestion that the theory of *Sittlichkeit* tacitly relies on both conceptions of objective freedom does find some support in my earlier claim (in chapter 1) that one of the aims of the *Philosophy of Right* is to fulfill the "logical" (or conceptual) task of articulating the content of a coherent and fully adequate conception of practical freedom. Bearing this project in mind, it is possible to see how both of the conceptions of objective freedom I have distinguished here are essential to Hegel's project. First, if practical freedom is to be realized in the world, the social order must be constituted so as to bring about the social conditions required in order for the "lower," more straightforwardly individualistic forms of self-determination (personal and moral freedom) to be realized. (The realization of these conditions constitutes objective freedom in its Rousseauean guise.) But, second, if the conditions of the lower forms of freedom are to come about in a manner that is fully consistent with the ideal of a self-determined will—if practical freedom is to be *completely* realized—the social order that secures them must itself be a self-determining entity, that is, a living, self-reproducing system that, because structured according to the Concept, exhibits the basic features that any rational (self-determined) entity must possess. (This is the distinctively Hegelian conception of objective freedom.)

The following two chapters will be devoted to filling in the details of my claim that Hegel's defense of the three basic modern social institutions makes use of both conceptions of objective freedom. As we shall see in the remainder of this chapter, Hegel regards those institutions as inherently rational because together they make up a social whole that fully realizes the ideal of self-determination. In chapter 5 I shall explore the claim that a further requirement of inherently rational institutions is that they make it possible (in ways to be specified later) for their individual members to have self-determined wills.

I shall begin my discussion of the first part of the doctrine of objective freedom by considering one of Hegel's more perspicuous formulations of the basic thought behind his appeal to a strongly holistic conception of self-determination within the realm of social theory: "The state exists as living spirit only as an organized whole, differentiated into the particular functions [*Wirksamkeiten*] that derive from the single concept of the rational will (even if not known as such) and continually produce it as their result" (E §539; emphasis omitted).[8] This quote provides a concise statement of the four properties contained in Hegel's holistic conception of self-determination that will be of importance for my analysis of objective freedom: the self-determined social order is a (1) *teleologically organized*, (2) *self-reproducing* whole that is (3) *articulated into specialized, semiautonomously functioning components* ("differentiated into particular functions") whose specific qualities and relations to one another are (4) *determined by the Concept* ("derive from the single concept of the rational will").[9] In chapter 1 I gave a brief account of Hegel's reasons for thinking of an entity that exhibits these properties as self-determined, or free. My concern in this chapter is not to defend this use of the term 'freedom' but to articulate the thought that underlies it by showing what these properties amount to in the context of Hegel's social theory and how they translate into a plausible (though incomplete) account of the features of a rational social world.

As a first step it is necessary to say a few words about the meaning of 'rational' as it is applied here to the social world. In what respects and from what perspective are the institutions of *Sittlichkeit* judged to be rational? Because this part of Hegel's doctrine depends on a strongly holistic conception of self-determination, the features of the rational social world it picks out will be properties the society exhibits as a whole rather than properties that belong to its individual parts as such. These properties will reside primarily in certain relations that obtain among the various components of a society, and so the rationality at issue here will inhere in the organization of those components, or in the internal structure of the social world.[10] Thus, Hegel's holistic conception of self-determination can be thought of as specifying the relations in which the parts of a social order must stand to one another in order for it to qualify as a *rationally organized* whole.

It is important to note that a social order of this kind will appear rational only from a standpoint that affords a view of the social order as a whole and hence only to someone who is able to transcend the limited perspectives bound up with some particular position within it. While this suggests the perspective of an outside observer who, perhaps for purely aesthetic reasons, takes pleasure in contemplating a well-organized whole, it would be erroneous to conclude that only an outside observer—someone who does not belong to the social order in question—could be interested in whether it is rational in this sense. The social order differs crucially from other kinds of organisms in that its parts—individual social members—not only have the capacity to step out of their particular circumstances and regard the entity they compose as a whole but also take an interest in doing so. This ability of the parts to take a stance with respect to the whole is precisely what makes the social order a higher, more spiritual being than a mere biological organism. In other words, Hegel views human individuals as more than particular beings with parochial perspectives; he takes them also to be universal beings—moral subjects, as it will turn out—who care about the character of the whole to which they belong. Within the present context this implies that social members not only aspire to affirm their particular lot within society but also take an interest in whether the world they inhabit constitutes a coherent, intelligible whole (in a sense to be defined later).

My present task, then, is to determine what view of rational organization is implied by Hegel's holistic conception of self-determination. One way of giving content to the concept of rational organization would be to define it in terms of the coordination of social members' private ends. For such a view, the ends of individuals would be characterized independently of their membership in the group in question, and the social order would count as rationally organized if it met some standard for the effective coordination of those ends (for example, that overall more of such ends are realized in society than could be realized outside it or, alternatively, that each member realizes more of his ends through social cooperation than when acting separately). Regardless of the specific standard used, such a view locates the proper end of social organization in the effective coordination of individuals' private ends, and it regards a social whole as rational to the extent that it realizes that end. Even though this conception takes private ends to be the only basic elements that enter into the construction of a social will, it makes sense to think of the social order as having an end of its own (and therefore as subject to being judged rational or not), because an end is ascribed to the organization of society that may not be found among the ends of any of its individual members.

It is clear, however, that this is not the conception of rational organization on which the theory of *Sittlichkeit* is based, for it is precisely this way of defining the rationality of the state that Hegel criticizes in his frequent and spirited attacks on the social contract tradition. (This raises the question, to be considered in chapter 6, whether Hegel's famous critique rests on the dubious presupposition that social contract theory is committed to such a conception of what makes a state rational.) It is not the case, of course, that Hegel simply rejects this conception of rational organization as irrelevant to social theory but only that he assigns it a very limited role. Insofar as one of the functions of social institutions is to help social members achieve certain kinds of private ends (for example, those derived from their need for the means of survival), rational institutions, on Hegel's account, too, must be effective coordinators of those ends. This sort of consideration figures most prominently in Hegel's defense of civil society, one component of which consists in the familiar claim, espoused by a wide variety of non-Hegelian social theorists as well, that a market-based system of production and exchange is a rational form of organization because of its ability to coordinate effectively the private economic ends of its individual participants (§§182–184).

If the conception of rational organization just described is not central to Hegel's social theory, what does he propose in its place? As the passage cited at the beginning of this section suggests, the theory of *Sittlichkeit* appeals to the idea of teleological organization in order to give content to the notion of a rational social whole. Thus, the kind of rational organization Hegel's theory demands of the social order will be akin to the rationality sought by a biologist who is examining an unfamiliar form of life or by a critic who seeks to interpret a work of art. Both attempt to understand their respective objects by posing the question: How do the various parts of this entity work together to form a coherent, harmonious whole? What each of these investigators seeks to find in his object is a purposive order that bestows a kind of intelligibility on the object as a whole. Comprehending an object as teleologically organized includes, minimally, two elements: first, a conception of the essential end, or telos, of the entity as a whole—an idea of what its proper function consists in; and, second, an understanding of how the makeup of its parts is determined by that end or, in other words, how their determinate features can be explained in terms of what the entity as a whole requires in order for its end to be realized.[11] Apprehending this order provides insight into what can be called the object's inner rationality, for it enables one to grasp the reason for its being constituted just as it is by referring to an end internal to the object itself.

The version of teleological organization that informs the theory of *Sittlichkeit* includes a third feature (referred to earlier as the articulation of the whole into specialized, semiautonomous components), which, although clearly borrowed from the example of a complex biological organism, is fruitfully exploited in Hegel's account of the social organism. When a body is constituted such that it must carry out a variety of complex functions in order to realize its end, it normally relies on the cooperation of differentiated, highly specialized components. In biological organisms this specialization typically takes the form of a network of functional subsystems, each of which operates with a significant degree of autonomy, even though all are ultimately subordinated to the end of the whole and dependent on its proper functioning. Despite these limits to their self-sufficiency, the relative autonomy of specialized subsystems makes it possible to speak as if they had their own distinctive ends, or their own proper function. This means, then, that the relation between the organism and its parts can be meaningfully characterized as one of mutual dependence. That is, it is not just that the proper functioning of the whole is dependent on each component carrying out its particular task, but the parts, too, depend on the whole (more accurately, on their being united with the other parts so as to constitute a properly functioning whole) in order to realize their own distinctive ends. This relation of mutual dependence between parts and whole is one feature of the "interpenetrating unity" of universality and particularity that, as we saw in chapter 1, Hegel equates with rationality (§258A).

What this third feature adds to the concept of teleological organization is the idea that the fully rational organism, whether social or biological, attains its dominant end only through a multiplicity of highly differentiated, relatively autonomous components: "The different parts within the state must exist as members with their own distinctive organization, which are self-standing in themselves and bring forth [or] reproduce the whole" (VPR1, 151). What makes such an organized whole rational for Hegel is not merely that it is highly *efficient* in achieving its ends but, more important, that it allows for, indeed requires, the flourishing of independent particularity. Thus, it attains its dominant end not by squelching diversity but by bringing its diverse elements into a harmonious, purposeful arrangement, thereby preserving the qualitative richness that difference implies.[12] The contemplation of such a teleologically organized whole affords the observer the rational satisfaction that comes from seeing how diversity is both given its due and at the same time ordered so as to serve the ends of the whole to which it belongs— or, in Hegelian language, from seeing how particularity and universality are brought into a relation of "interpenetrating" unity. That Hegel conceives of a rationally organized whole in this way—as one in which there exists a relation of harmony and mutual dependence between the proper functioning of the whole and that of its semiautonomous, particular components—is explicitly confirmed by his definition of rational existence ("actuality," or *Wirklichkeit*) in the following Addition to the *Philosophy of Right*: "The state is actual [*wirklich*], and its actuality consists in the fact that the interest of the whole is realized in particular ends. Actuality is always the unity of universality and particularity; it is universality's being broken apart into particularity, which appears as self-standing, even though it is supported and maintained only in the whole" (§270Z).

It is obvious, however, that simply articulating the conception of rational organization that underlies Hegel's theory of *Sittlichkeit* is not sufficient to establish its suitability as a criterion for a rational social order. It is natural (for us moderns) to want to dismiss this aspect of Hegel's view on the grounds that the ideal of rationality implicit in the notion of teleological organization, whatever its value for the biologist or critic, is out of place in the realm of normative social theory. Why, after all, ought the social world to exhibit the same kind of harmony and unity of purpose that characterize a work of art or a living organism? Our resistance to Hegel's position is not easily set aside, for it has its source (or at least one of its sources) in our deep-seated aversion to a central feature of teleological organization, indeed to the very feature that distinguishes it most clearly from the alternative conception of rational organization discussed earlier, namely, the effective coordination of private ends. The main difference between these two conceptions is not that a teleological view thinks of the social whole as having its own ends distinct from those of its individual members as such, for, as we have seen, this is true of the first conception as well. The difference resides, rather, in whether primacy is given to the whole or to the individual members as such in determining the ends ascribed to the social whole. More precisely, the teleological view thinks of the social whole as having ends that are conceptually prior to the ends of its parts as such, whereas for its rival the proper ends of the social whole can be exhaustively constructed out of its members' private ends.

This point brings us back to the heart of the controversy discussed in chapter 1 concerning whether the holism that informs the theory of *Sittlichkeit* is sufficiently respectful of the essential interests of individuals or whether it sacrifices those interests to the collective ends of the social organism. Rather than attempt to defend Hegel against this charge by considering in the abstract what a commitment to the ideal of teleological organization in general entails, I suggest that we proceed by first examining in concrete detail how his social theory actually makes use of this ideal. Moreover, I propose that for now we regard Hegel's position concerning the primacy of the whole as a heuristic point that is relevant to the order of exposition of his doctrine but reserve judgment as to whether it also has substantive implications for his understanding of the ends he attributes to the social world as a whole. In other words, let us bracket for now the very intricate question that will be central to our assessment of Hegel's relation to the social contract tradition in chapter 6, namely, to what extent his account of the properties of the rational social whole admits of reconstruction from a standpoint that begins only with a conception of the essential interests of individuals.

Hegel's most explicit employment of his conception of rational organization in the *Philosophy of Right* occurs in his discussion of the structure of the state (construed here narrowly, as the political realm per se rather than as the entire complex of political and nonpolitical institutions). It is most clearly visible in his account of the three basic powers—the crown, together with the executive and legislative powers—that make up the state's "internal constitution" (§§272–329). Here, however, I shall consider only what I take to be the most fundamental way in which the ideal of teleological organization informs Hegel's social theory, namely, as the basis for an account of the rational structure of the social world as a whole. More specifically, I shall attempt to reconstruct and render plausible Hegel's assertion that the modern social world qualifies as rationally structured because its three basic institutions—the family, civil society, and the state—are constituted so as to form a whole that exhibits the properties of teleological organization outlined previously. In other words, I shall investigate the content and force of Hegel's claim that the three institutions of *Sittlichkeit* represent interdependent, semiautonomous social spheres whose specialized and complementary functions work together to make the modern social world into a self-reproducing, rationally intelligible whole. In doing so I shall proceed in roughly the order suggested in my statement at the beginning of this section of the four properties contained in Hegel's holistic conception of self-determination. Recall that the self-determined social world was defined there as a (1) teleologically organized, (2) self-reproducing whole that is (3) articulated into specialized, semiautonomously functioning components whose specific qualities and relations to one another are (4) determined by the Concept.

I have already described the general features of the conception of teleological organization that is at work in the theory of *Sittlichkeit*. The first step in acquiring a more concrete understanding of how this conception functions as an ideal for social organization is to specify the ends Hegel attributes to the social world as a whole. What precisely is it that constitutes "the interest of the whole" (§270Z), or the "general business" *(allgemeines Geschäft)* (VPR1, 150) of the social organism? The most easily recognized of these ends comes into view by thinking, once again, of the example of a biological organism: a rationally organized society must have at its disposal the materials and capacities required for its own reproduction. This thought alone brings to light an important piece of Hegel's account of what makes the structure of modern *Sittlichkeit* rational, namely, that each of its spheres exercises a distinct function necessary for the material reproduction of society: the family furnishes society with human individuals; civil society supplies the material goods needed for the sustainment of life; and the state carries out the function of coordinating the two spheres (in that its legislation is aimed, in part, at shoring up the two subordinate institutions and ensuring that neither flourishes at the other's expense).

Yet what the social organism needs in order to realize its end of self-reproduction cannot be fully specified in terms of its material requirements alone, for the simple reason that the social organism is something more than a merely material being. The institutions of *Sittlichkeit* make up what Hegel calls "objective spirit," and thus, like any "spiritual" being, a social whole exists (to use Hegel's language) not only as *substance* but also as *subject* (PhG, ¶17; 23). In other words, human society is not simply a material entity but one that exists also as (human) consciousness. More precisely, the social world functions only in and through the conscious wills, attitudes, and beliefs of its constituent parts (human beings), all of which exist within that world as individuated bearers of consciousness. The fact that the social world is made up of parts that are themselves discrete units of subjectivity (in a sense to be further determined) marks, as Hegel recognizes, an extremely important difference between social and biological organisms. Taking note of this difference is crucial to our project here not only because it affects the content of Hegel's view on a number of significant issues but also because the ways in which he understands and accommodates the fact that the social world is made up of individual subjects will bear importantly on our assessment of the acceptability of his holistic starting point.

In our attempt to determine what the social organism requires to reproduce itself, and to do so with reasonable efficiency, the social world's ontological status as a spiritual rather than merely material entity is of considerable importance, for it imposes conditions on the rationally organized society that concern not just its objective structure but also the subjective makeup of the agents of social reproduction. Most important, it implies that in order for a society to reproduce itself as the kind of being it is, its individual members must be subjectively constituted so as to be capable of carrying out socially required functions of their own accord—that is, through activity that is motivated from within rather than induced by an external, coercive apparatus. If we recall the account given in chapter 3 of the subjective disposition appropriate to ethical life, the strategy behind Hegel's response to this requirement of the social organism comes clearly into view: the need for reliable reproducers of social institutions—for social members who are capable of regularly and willingly overriding their private interests for the sake of universal ends—can be met only if individuals' activity in the service of universal ends affords them a more substantial satisfaction than can be had from the pursuit of private ends alone. Thus, the demand that the rational social world be constructed so as to allow its members to find and realize their practical identities as particular individuals within their social activity can be understood as grounded both in society's need for an internally driven mechanism of reproduction and in the requirement that individuals, in accomplishing this social task, not be subject to a foreign will. This point suggests that it might be appropriate to regard Hegel's account of the subjective disposition of *Sittlichkeit* as an important piece of his solution to a basic problem of social theory that admits of a distinctly Rousseauean formulation: How is society to accomplish its "general business" in a way that is compatible with the freedom of each participating individual?[13]

While this formulation highlights a genuine and deep affinity between Hegel's and Rousseau's approaches to social theory, it would also be misleading if it were taken to imply that the telos of the social whole for Hegel is conceptually independent of the freedom of individual social members and that the basic problem the theory of *Sittlichkeit* faces is one of reconciling the claims of these two distinct and competing ends (the end of the whole and the freedom of its members). A more accurate representation of Hegel's position, I believe, is one that sees the concern for individuals' freedom as deriving from, and therefore as internal to, the end of the social whole properly understood. On such a view, the end of the social order as a whole would be conceived of such that the realization of individuals' freedom would appear not as an extraneous desideratum but as an essential part of the work of a properly functioning society. It is in fact possible to interpret Hegel's position in precisely this way once we realize that the telos he attributes to society as a self-sustaining entity is not mere self-reproduction but self-reproduction in accord with its own essence; the social organism's end, in other words, is to reproduce itself *as the kind of being it essentially is.*

The essential nature of the rational social order is, of course, to realize itself as free, or self-determining, but in which of the many senses of self-determination encountered thus far? Although Hegel never addresses this question in precisely this form, it is of utmost importance to recognize that his conception of the telos of the social whole includes not only self-determination in its strongly holistic sense but also the practical freedom of its individual members. Thus, it belongs to the essence of the rational social whole to reproduce itself in a way that also accommodates the greatest possible freedom of its individual parts. This crucial feature of Hegel's theory, though nowhere made explicit, shows itself in the importance the *Philosophy of Right* accords to the more individualistic forms of freedom—personal and moral freedom, the accounts of which occupy two of the work's three main parts—and it is expressed more directly in the very important statement, made in the midst of one of Hegel's most extensive discussions of rational social organization, that "the individuals of the mass are themselves spiritual natures" (§264).[14] As its context makes clear, this statement is not intended to express the point (though it, too, would be true for Hegel) that the essential nature of human individuals is to belong to a community that, taken as a whole, exhibits the properties of a spiritual being. Rather, the claim that individuals themselves are spiritual beings is meant to convey precisely what it appears to, namely, that it is the essence of human individuals to replicate within themselves, albeit approximately and on a miniature scale, the qualities that define a spiritual being. Further, it implies that a social world that failed to give this fact its due would fall short of the ideal implicit in the requirement that it reproduce itself as the kind of being it essentially is (because it would neglect the kind of beings its individual parts essentially are). Whatever else follows from Hegel's statement ascribing a spiritual status to individuals themselves—its full import will become clear only in succeeding chapters—it means above all that providing for the *freedom* of its individual members is part and parcel of the social organism's proper functioning. In Hegel's account of *Sittlichkeit* the social world fulfills this aspect of its essential nature not only by constituting an arena within which its members acquire particular identities that enable them to embrace the universal will of their institutions as their own (and hence to be self-determined when acting in accord with that will) but also by securing the conditions necessary for them to realize their freedom as individual persons and moral subjects.

One important consequence of this way of construing the telos of the social whole is that the two possibilities sketched here for giving content to the notion of objective freedom—one derived from Rousseau's account of the general will, the other from Hegel's holistic conception of self-determination—no longer appear as competing alternatives. For the crucial assumption that the parts of the social world must themselves achieve the forms of self-determination appropriate to them as individuals in order for the whole to realize its essential end means that the Rousseauean conception of objective freedom—defined broadly as that which secures the conditions of the freedom of individual wills—turns out, on Hegel's view, to constitute one essential element of society's telos as a whole.

Once we have determined the proper end of the social organism, the next step in apprehending the modern social world as a rationally organized whole is to discover how its composition is determined by that end or, in other words, how the specific functions of its parts—in our case the three basic institutions of *Sittlichkeit*—are necessary if the social world is to be able to reproduce itself in accord with its essential nature. Hegel gives expression to this aspect of his conception of rational organization in the following passage: "The living self-production [*Sich-selbst-Hervorbringen*] of the spiritual substance consists in its organic activity: . . . the articulation and division of its general business and power into . . . different powers and businesses. The fact that the final end is brought about out of the determinate workings of the different spheres of business . . . constitutes the inner necessity of freedom" (VPR1, 150; emphases omitted). I have already noted how each of the spheres of modern *Sittlichkeit* makes a unique contribution to producing what is materially required for the social order's self-maintenance. Assigning these distinct reproductive functions to the different social institutions makes it possible to see the latter as articulated spheres within a social whole that carry out their specialized tasks by functioning as relatively autonomous subsystems. It becomes meaningful, for example, to make the family, the economy, and the state into objects of study in their own right and to ask about each: How does this sphere carry on its distinctive business? Through what particular mechanisms does it accomplish its own part of the general task of society's material reproduction? Moreover, because the essential end of the social order also includes the freedom of its individual members, a further task of Hegel's theory is to demonstrate how its basic institutions function so as jointly to secure the conditions necessary for personal and moral freedom to be realized. The details of this important part of Hegel's account of how the general business of society is realized through the cooperation of distinct, independently functioning social spheres will be the main topic of chapter 5.

The claims of the previous paragraph can be formulated more succinctly as follows: Hegel's appeal to the notion of a teleologically organized whole in order to give content to the concept of a rationally structured society implies that one of the central tasks of his social theory is to delineate how the institutions of modern *Sittlichkeit*, when working in concert, are especially well-suited to achieve the two primary ends of the social organism as a whole, namely, its material reproduction and the formation of conscious agents of social reproduction who are free as persons and moral subjects. It is in this way that the Hegelian social theorist demonstrates the necessity of such institutions or shows that, in Hegel's words, "they constitute the inner necessity of freedom." Necessity, of course, is to be understood here as teleological necessity: the family, civil society, and the modern state are claimed to be necessary *in order for the social organism to realize its proper end.*

Although central to Hegel's account of a rational social world, the points just made do not yet exhaust the content of his claim that the modern social world is rationally organized. For Hegel's conception of rational organization includes a further, much more obscure element that is bound up with his metaphysical doctrine of the Concept, as developed in the part of his philosophical system known as the Logic. This aspect of Hegel's social theory is alluded to in the passage cited at the beginning of this section in which the particular spheres that make up the rational society are said to "derive from the single concept of the rational will." It is also what is at issue in Hegel's numerous statements to the effect that the composition of *Sittlichkeit* as a whole reflects the logical structure of the Concept.[15] As I indicated in chapter 1, 'the Concept' (*der Begriff*) is Hegel's term for the basic structure that is said to inform not only reason—the cognitive faculty of the "subject"—but also the "object" of that faculty, actuality itself (*Wirklichkeit*). This is to say that for Hegel 'the Concept' names both the structure reason requires of its objects if they are to satisfy its demand that the world be intelligible through and through, as well as the structure that can be demonstrated (by philosophy) to underlie the whole of that world. In Hegel's more grandiose language, the doctrine of the Concept can be said to ground his philosophy's famous claim to establish the thoroughgoing identity of subject and object. The relevance of this metaphysical thesis to social theory lies in its claim to be able to give a distinctive content to the notion of a rationally organized social world (because it purports to specify the structure of *any* entity that is fully intelligible to reason). More specifically, Hegel appeals to his account of the three essential constituents of any rationally ordered whole—the "moments" of immediate unity, difference, and mediated unity[16]—in order to determine the number and nature of the parts required by the social world in order to qualify as rational. Thus, in the context of the theory of *Sittlichkeit*, the doctrine of the Concept translates into the requirement that the social world be composed of three distinguishable social spheres, each corresponding to one of the three moments of the Concept. The rationally organized social world, then, is one whose basic institutions allow the moments of immediate unity, difference, and mediated unity to attain full and com-

patible expression.[17] From the perspective of Hegel's metaphysical position, such institutions are judged to be rational not because they are
well-suited to achieving a particular set of ends specific to the social organism (and hence "rational" in a sense that can be grasped independently of any distinctively Hegelian theses about the nature of reason)
but rather because the whole they constitute is inherently rational in the
sense that it embodies the very structure of reason itself.

The specific doctrines of Hegel's Logic have proved exceptionally re-
sistant to the efforts of generations of sympathetic commentators to reconstruct them into a philosophically compelling metaphysical system.
Rather than defend this aspect of Hegel's social theory by attempting to
make plausible the metaphysics from which it derives (a challenge I
forgo less for lack of space than for lack of ability), I shall restrict myself
to the more modest, but not necessarily less rewarding, task of showing
how Hegel exploits the resources of his doctrine of the Concept to make
a powerful point about the nature of the modern social world, the force
of which is appreciable without a mastery of Hegelian logic. This procedure, of course, stands in opposition to that of interpreters who insist on
the seamless integrity of Hegel's thought and therefore reject out of hand
any attempt to explicate a part of his philosophy in detachment from its
metaphysical foundations. In contrast to this interpretive approach, I regard it as a testimony to the depth of Hegel's philosophical achievement
that his theory of *Sittlichkeit* can be shown to provide a compelling account of the rational social world independently of a prior commitment
to his metaphysics. For this means, in agreement with Hegel's own self-
understanding, that the particular pieces of his all-embracing system are
more than simply the result of mechanically applying an abstract conceptual formula to the different problem areas of philosophy. Rather, as I
shall try to show in the case of his social theory, Hegel at his best reveals
an astounding ability to employ his distinctive metaphysical doctrines to
provide insight into the complex phenomena peculiar to the various do-
mains of philosophical inquiry.[18]

The point I have in mind comes into view if we think of the Concept
not as specifying the structure of intelligible reality *überhaupt* but as a
highly abstract account of the kind of inner articulation required of a
self-conscious being, whether individual or collective, in order for it to
be a whole, fully integrated subject (or, in Hegel's terminology, in order
for it to realize its essential nature as "spirit"). When we add to this the

consideration that the family, civil society, and the state are (for reasons to be considered later) associated with the Conceptual moments of immediate unity, difference, and mediated unity, respectively, it becomes clear that Hegel means to claim that the modern social world, composed of these institutions, qualifies as a spiritual, therefore thoroughly rational, whole.

The aspect of this doctrine I want to emphasize here—what I consider its rational kernel—comes more clearly into focus when we consider Hegel's reasons for associating the three institutions of *Sittlichkeit* with the moments of the Concept.[19] In this context immediate unity, difference, and mediated unity refer primarily to the structure of the institutions with which they are linked. More specifically, they designate the type of unity that characterizes the institution in question, as well as the kind of relations among its individual members that such unity involves. The point here is that while the family, civil society, and the state all embody a kind of social unity—in each case the group in question can be said to have a collective end, or general will—each embodies a unity of a different sort. The family, for example, counts as an instance of immediate unity because love is the principal bond that unites family members and makes it possible for them to have a collective will, each regarding the good of other members and of the family as a whole as his own good. Familial love represents an immediate attachment to others because it has its origin not in thought, which is mediated or reflective, but in "natural feeling" (in both sexual love and the love between parent and child). As Hegel puts it, "within family life . . . one experiences *Sittlichkeit* in the form of *undeliberated* love and trust" (VPR2, 144; slightly amended). It is important to note here that the unity of the family is not only immediate but also "substantial," in contrast to "formal" or "external" unity (§§157–158; VPR1, 250). This means that familial love, and the trust that issues from it, are the basis of substantial attachments among family members, where 'substantial' refers to the fact that one's having such attachments (to other particular individuals) makes up the substance of who one is—or, to use the terminology developed in chapter 3—that those attachments are (partially) constitutive of one's identity as a particular individual. It follows from this that members of substantial social unities do not regard their participation in them as merely or primarily a means for satisfying their own private ends. Rather, their membership in such groups is the source of new, socially shared final ends such that, for example, participation in the life of one's family becomes an end in itself. For the members of substantial unities "social union as such is itself the true content and end, and the proper destination [*Bestimmung*] of [such] individuals is to lead a universal [that is, shared or collective] life" (§258A).

Civil society, in contrast, represents the moment of difference—or "atomism" (E §523)—because those who participate in the economic sphere do so as separate, independent individuals who work and trade in order to satisfy their own particular needs, especially those that derive from their status as natural beings. In civil society individuals are joined together in what Hegel calls "formal universality" (as opposed to the substantial unity of the family) and are said to have merely "external" relations (§§157, 181), both to one another and to the economic order as a whole. These basic features of the economic sphere are due to the crucial fact that in modern civil society production and exchange are market-regulated. This means that while there are rules—laws of the market—that in fact govern the apparently independent activities of economic agents and unite them into a coherent system of production and exchange, the operation of those rules remains external to both the wills and consciousness of the individuals involved. Within such a system, individual producers and traders contribute to the realization of a social end—the efficient increase of overall social wealth—but they do so without either knowing or willing that end as their own. The relations members of civil society have to other individuals and to the economic order in general are external in the sense that, as economic agents, they need be, and typically are, motivated only by their own private ends rather than by the ends of other participants in civil society or by the collective end that they in fact (but unwittingly) bring about. In this sphere individuals' relations to others and to society itself appear to them as primarily of instrumental value, since they serve as the means to achieving a set of ends (including the protection of their person and property) they have independently of their association with others in civil society: "universality as such is not an end in and for itself but rather a means for the existence and maintenance of individuals" (VPR1, 208). (It is important to bear in mind that this is a simplification of Hegel's account, since civil society in its fully rational form also includes certain groups, the corporations, in which members partially shed the perspective of independent individuals and acquire bonds of solidarity with the fellow members of their trade or estate. Yet even these bonds are said to develop directly out of one's egoistically motivated productive activity and are therefore still grounded in one's role as an independent individual who pursues private ends.)

Finally, the modern state as Hegel understands it embodies the moment of mediated unity. As such, it incorporates two prominent structural elements of the previous spheres: the substantial unity of the family and the element of difference, or atomism, characteristic of civil society. Hegel, following Rousseau, conceives of the state, or political sphere, as the public realm where legislation is framed and executed in accord with a shared conception of the good of society as a whole—as the arena, in other words, where the general will is given both a determinate content and a real existence. The state incorporates the atomism of civil society because citizens enter the political sphere with diverse, independently established identities as particular individuals whose family ties and positions within civil society provide them with divergent particular interests. Because the moment of difference is not to be suppressed by the state but rather incorporated into it, the principal concern of Hegelian politics is to find a way of integrating the particular wills of individual citizens with the general will not only through the framing of laws that further the good of the whole but also by subjectively transforming citizens so as to enable them to embrace the general will as their own. The latter requirement poses a by now familiar problem: What enables citizens to assent to social policies that sometimes subordinate their private interests to the good of the whole? Hegel's response here is to appeal to the same idea that underlies his account of the substantial unity of the family: individuals are capable of embracing the ends of the state as their own only if they are able to experience their roles as citizens as a source of their own selfhood (§261A). Thus, in order for individuals to will the general will (in order for them to be citizens in the full sense of the term) the state must be a substantial unity in which individuals' relations to their fellow citizens—their being joined together as a single nation, or people (*Volk*)—provides them with a shared, "universal" project, the carrying out of which is for them both an end in itself and a substantial source of the value they ascribe to their own lives.

This, however, raises a further question: What is the source of the more than merely instrumental ties that citizens are said to have to one another? What kind of attachment in the political sphere substitutes for the bond of love that unites individuals in the family? It is tempting to assume that Hegel's appeal to the idea of national identity implies that the ties among citizens are akin to bonds of brotherhood, having their roots in a prereflective attachment citizens feel to one another by virtue of their all belonging, through birth, to a single people. The ability of citizens to embrace the general will, then, would be parasitic on a lovelike concern they feel for the welfare of their compatriots prior to (independently of) the dealings they have with one another within the specifically political institutions of their society. Yet Hegel repeatedly emphasizes that there is a fundamental qualitative difference—one that makes the state an instance of mediated rather than immediate unity— between the attachments of the family and those within the state. The unity that characterizes the latter, Hegel insists, is not grounded in immediate feeling or any other "bond of nature" (VPR1, 250) but is instead a "union through laws" and therefore a "unity that is known, conscious, expressly pronounced, and thought" (§157N).[20] The state, then, embodies the Conceptual moment of mediated unity because the tie that binds citizens together—the bond that endows them with a single will— comes into being only through a collective act of legislating *reason:* in giving itself laws, the state establishes for itself principles that are universally binding, explicitly known, and consciously endorsed through a process of public reflection on the common good.[21] The state, Hegel says, differs from the family in that it "*knows* what it wills and knows it in its *universality,* as something *thought;* it therefore functions and acts in accord with conscious ends, recognized principles and according to laws that . . . are present to consciousness" (§270).

Hegel's claim that the substantial attachments among citizens first get fully constituted through the enacting of laws implies that the specific workings of the legislative process play a crucial role in his account of how the modern state solves its central problem of bringing citizens to embrace the general will as their own. For Hegel the key to achieving this integration of wills lies in a certain (ideal) feature of the act of legislation itself, namely, its "publicity" (§§314–315), or, as I shall refer it to here, the *public transparency* of the process through which the general will acquires a determinate content. The legislative process in the rational state is transparent not only in the sense that it is open to public view but also in the more substantive sense that the rational basis of the laws that issue from it is clearly articulated and accessible to all citizens.

There are two main ideas behind Hegel's claim that the public transparency of the legislative process helps to enable citizens to will the general will. The first idea is that citizens come to apprehend their laws as rational—as reflecting the interests of the whole—when they see how those laws emerge from public deliberation that is aimed at discerning the collective good and that gives due consideration to the input of all major interest groups of society.[22] For Hegel, in contrast to Rousseau, the demand that resulting laws "come from all" requires not that each individual participate in the legislative process—a requirement Hegel thought impracticable in large, modern societies—but only that all basic interest groups be fairly represented in the legislative process (§309Z). Second, in addition to seeing their laws as universally rational (rational from the perspective of the whole), citizens must also be able to regard the general will as in some way continuous with their own particular wills. The public transparency of the legislative process works to this end by allowing citizens to become spectators of the real process— which Hegel calls a "spectacle," or *Schauspiel* (§315Z)—through which their particular interests are taken into account—*recognized* as having a weight—in arriving at the necessary social compromise among competing particular interests. This distinctively political way in which individuals find particular satisfaction in the universal is predicated on their identification with (at least one of) the principal actors that occupy the legislative stage, namely, "the associations, communities, and corporations" (§308) to which, as members of civil society, they belong prior to their political involvement. Insofar as individuals see their corporate deputies as representations of themselves—and hence as representing their own particular interests—they are able to experience the recognition accorded to corporate interests in the legislative process as a kind of recognition of themselves as particular beings.

Given his metaphysical doctrine of the Concept, together with the claim that the family, civil society, and the state embody its three characteristic moments, it is possible to appreciate the general idea behind Hegel's assertion that the modern social world is a spiritual, thoroughly rational whole. But this assertion, properly understood, is more than simply a claim about the abstract structure required of the social world in order for it, as a whole, to count as a spiritual entity. It is also a claim about the different kinds of social membership *individuals* need to experience in order to exist as whole, fully developed subjects. This point becomes clearer when we realize that the idea of a Conceptually organized social world not only specifies the necessary internal structure of the three basic institutions and the relations that must obtain among their members but also gives an account of the different kinds of *identities* required of individuals if they are to participate freely in such institutions. Focusing on the latter point suggests that Hegel's demonstration of the Conceptual structure of *Sittlichkeit* includes the claim that the modern social world is rational (in part) because it allows its members to develop and express different, complementary types of identities, each of which is indispensable to realizing the complete range of relations to others (and to self) that are available to human subjects and worthy of achieving. On this view, then, to lack membership in any of the three basic institutions would be to miss out on an important part of what it is to be a fully realized (individual) self.

Before filling in some of the details of this interpretation, it is necessary to consider a fundamental (and partially justified) objection to the suggestion that Hegel intends for his doctrine of the Concept to serve as an ideal not only for the structure of the social world as a whole but also for the internal composition of individual social members. This dispute, it will easily be recognized, is just one specific aspect of the larger debate over the extent to which the theory of *Sittlichkeit* is holistic in its foundations—or, in other words, over the extent to which the basic properties of the rational social world can also be ascribed severally to the parts of that world, namely, to individual social members. Implicit in this objection is the interpretive claim, opposite to my own, that for Hegel only *Sittlichkeit* taken as a whole realizes (or approximates) the rational structure attributed to a spiritual entity and that an individual comes as close as he or she can to achieving this ideal simply by occupying a specialized position within such a rationally structured whole.[23]

There are indeed textual grounds for attributing such a strongly holistic position to Hegel on this issue. First, there is one important class of individuals, namely, women, who, though not denied the formal rights of personhood,[24] are unambiguously excluded from membership in two of the three institutions of *Sittlichkeit,* the state and civil society (§§164Z, 166, 301A; VPR1, 98, 253–254). In other words, it is clearly the case that Hegel believes (and finds it untroubling) that women realize the ideal of spirituality not by embodying the three moments of the Concept within themselves but only by participating in the life of a larger whole that does so. Second, there are suggestions that Hegel also means to consign large groups of men to a spiritual fate not unlike that of all women. This impression is created by Hegel's apparent exclusion of many (male) members of the first two estates of civil society[25]—the agricultural and commercial estates—from participation in the political sphere, with the consequence that life in the state appears to be the nearly exclusive province of the civil servants who make up the "universal" estate.[26] This suggests that the strongly holistic position—the idea that the spiritual status available to individuals consists only in their being part of a Conceptually organized whole—is more deeply rooted in Hegel's social theory than if it were restricted to the single case of women (and hence easier to dismiss as merely the consequence of chauvinistic assumptions about the natural superiority of men).

While Hegel's exclusion of women from the state and civil society is indisputable, the textual issues involved in the second case are considerably more complex. I shall argue here that although support for both positions can be found in the relevant texts, a comparison of early with later sources reveals that Hegel's thought underwent an unmistakable development from the more strongly holistic position described earlier to the view that a defining aim of the rational social order is to allow for all (male) individuals to incorporate, as fully as possible, each of the types of identities associated with membership in the three basic social spheres. This development is brought out most vividly by considering two parallel passages from different versions of the *Rechtsphilosophie*, the first of which is taken from student transcripts of Hegel's lectures in 1818–1819: "It can appear hard that the whole of *Sittlichkeit* gives over a part of its individuals to the limitedness of family life or to the necessity of bourgeois life [in the sphere of civil society]. On the one hand, that is a necessity; on the other hand, there is reconciliation in this necessity" (VPR1, 270). Less than two years later, in the first published version of the *Philosophy of Right*, this passage is replaced by §§262–264, which contain the following statement (already partially cited earlier) regarding the spiritual nature of individual social members: "Individuals . . . are themselves spiritual natures. As such, they contain within themselves a dual moment, namely, the extreme of *individuality*, which knows and wills *for itself*, and the extreme of *universality*, which knows and wills the substantial. For this reason individuals achieve their right to both of these sides only insofar as they have actuality as both private and substantial persons" (§264). From a position that allows itself to be reconciled to the necessity that large numbers of individuals be given over to the narrowness of a purely domestic existence, or to a life restricted to the pursuit of one's profession, Hegel moves to a view that recognizes the right of all (male) individuals to participate in social life as a family member, as the practitioner of a socially productive occupation, and as a citizen all at once.[27] As he puts the point more plainly in his lectures of 1819–1820: "the human being [*der Mensch*] fails to achieve his destiny [*Bestimmung*] if he is only a father, only a member of civil society, etc." (VPR2, 127–128).[28]

The passage cited earlier (§264) introduces a further complication into the present discussion because it refers to individuals as embodying only two extremes (individuality and universality) rather than the three moments one would expect, given the tripartite structure of the Concept. This becomes less puzzling, however, when we realize that Hegel not infrequently (for example, at §260+Z) lumps the family and civil society together, calling them the spheres of particularity[29] and contrasting them both with the state, which he identifies as the universal sphere. Associating the family and civil society with particularity expresses the idea that, viewed from a perspective that looks at the social world as a whole, these two spheres serve the purpose (in their own distinct ways) of fostering and giving expression to the particularity of social members. That is, through their participation in civil society and the family individuals develop and express identities that distinguish them qualitatively from other members of the state and provide them with divergent, potentially conflicting ends and interests. Yet Hegel's practice of subsuming the family and civil society under the single rubric of particularity is not inconsistent with the expected threefold classification, because membership in each sphere is associated with a distinct kind of particular identity, depending on whether the social unity in question embodies the Conceptual moment of difference or immediate unity.

We have already seen how Hegel distinguishes the family from civil society on the basis of the kinds of relations—whether (immediately) "substantial" or "external"—that hold among the members of the group in question: as a family member, one's relations to others make up part of the content of one's identity (with the consequence that the good of those others, and of the family as a whole, become one's own, consciously embraced final ends), whereas the ends that are consciously pursued by members of civil society are private, and their relations to others have for them primarily an instrumental value. But, as I suggested previously, the difference in the ways individuals relate to one another within these two institutions implies a corresponding difference in the kinds of particular identities that are acquired and expressed in those spheres. The most fundamental difference between these identities can be expressed as follows: in the family one conceives of oneself as essentially a *member* of a particular social unity (§158), as someone who depends on one's attachments to these concrete others for being who one is, while the participant in civil society conceives of himself as an independent individual, a pursuer of private ends and projects who achieves a self-sufficient existence by supporting himself through his own productive activity. The identity of a family member, then, is characterized by the fact that other individuals figure positively into his self-conception rather than functioning negatively, as a limit or boundary of the self over and against which he defines who he is. Thus, the family distinguishes itself from civil society in that participation in the former provides individuals with particular identities that are won, paradoxically, only through a kind of surrendering of self, namely, through abandoning the standpoint of an independent, separate self motivated only or primarily by its own private ends.

Implicit in Hegel's account of *Sittlichkeit* is the idea that each of these kinds of identities possesses a distinct, independent value for the individual who has them and that experiencing particularity in both of these forms is essential to realizing (or approximating) the full range of possible modes of selfhood. To miss out on any of these forms of social membership, then, is to be deprived of one of the basic ways of being a self and hence to suffer an impoverishment of one's life (in this one respect). One way of bringing out this point more forcefully is to recall how membership in each sphere brings with it different kinds of practical projects, each possessing its own distinctive pleasures and rewards: while family members engage in consciously shared projects that are defined and limited by the good of others to whom they are attached through love, civil society is the sphere in which individuals (in the words of one commentator) "pursue their own welfare in their own way, choose their own way of life, and enter into voluntary relations with others who are likewise free choosers of their own ends and activities."[30] Another way of bringing out the importance of participating in both spheres is to consider how each form of social membership provides individuals with a different way of having their particularity affirmed by others. In civil society the recognition individuals achieve is conditional on their competence as productive social members and is therefore earned "through their own activity, diligence, and skill" (§207). In contrast to this, recognition in the family, because it is based on love, represents an affirmation of the particular being one is that is independent of one's usefulness to others and of what one has made oneself into. Whereas in civil society "I must give myself the form of universality, make myself into something for others [in order to achieve recognition], . . . in the family I am valued [*ich gelte*] on the basis of what I immediately am" (VPR2, 148)—that is, my particular qualities are affirmed by others for no reason at all other than that they happen to be mine.

In contrast to the spheres of particularity, membership in the state offers individuals the possibility of achieving a universal existence by taking part in "a public life dedicated to the substantial universal" (§157). The state is the realm of universality because within it citizens acquire an identity that is universally shared (that is, shared with all other citizens of one's land), and because they learn to discern and to be moved by the good of the whole, even though this sometimes conflicts with interests they have by virtue of their specific positions in civil society or the distinctive situations of their own families. Hegel's claim is that individuals whose practical engagements are restricted to family life and to the pursuit of their own private good within the economic sphere lead unnecessarily narrow lives that fall short of realizing the full range of possibilities for selfhood offered by the modern world. Participation in the realm of politics is important not merely because it is requisite for individuals to meet the Rousseauean requirement that they have wills undetermined by an external other (since by affirming the general will, the law that determines their actions ceases to be something other) but also because it provides individuals with a distinctive set of projects and attachments that rounds out and enriches their otherwise merely particular lives. Moreover, life within the state is for Hegel more than simply one further way of being a self, equal in significance to all others. Rather, it represents—by virtue of embodying the moment of universality—the highest of these possibilities. That is, political life most closely approximates the ideal of self-sufficient subjectivity (which is to say, spirituality) because it is the arena within which citizens, as a body, determine themselves in accord with universal principles arrived at through the exercise of their own socially constituted, public reason.

5

Objective Freedom, Part II:
Social Conditions of Individuals' Freedom

In this chapter I turn to the portion of Hegel's doctrine of objective freedom that can be loosely characterized as Rousseauean. This part of Hegel's view exhibits an affinity with Rousseau's in that it conceives of objective freedom in terms of the social conditions necessary for individual social members to possess free wills rather than locating it in those features of *Sittlichkeit* that make the social world as a whole into a self-determining entity. At the same time, however, this part of the theory of *Sittlichkeit* is Rousseauean only in its basic principle. At the level of concrete detail Hegel's social theory diverges quite substantially from Rousseau's, primarily because the two theories rest on different accounts of how rational social institutions make possible the freedom of their individual members. More precisely, Hegel's account differs from Rousseau's along two main dimensions. The first involves differences in content among the conceptions of freedom that rational social institutions are said to condition; the second concerns the specific ways those institutions are thought to secure the conditions of their members' freedom.

My first task, then, is to specify the conception, or conceptions, of freedom at issue in Hegel's basic claim that the institutions of *Sittlichkeit* secure the social conditions necessary for their members to possess free wills. Whereas Rousseau conceives of the general will as bringing about the conditions citizens need in order to enjoy what he calls *civil freedom* (the ability of individuals to act unconstrained by the wills of others within a private sphere of activity external to the community's vital interests), the Hegelian version of this claim is considerably more complex. This is because, as we have already seen, Hegel recognizes three

145

distinct conceptions of practical freedom that are ascribable to individuals and relevant to social theory: *personal freedom* (the freedom to pursue one's own arbitrary ends, unhindered by others, within a private sphere bounded by the rights of other persons), *moral freedom* (determining one's will and action in accord with one's own understanding of the good), and what I have been calling throughout *social freedom* (the cornerstone of Hegel's social theory and the primary object of my investigations here). The question, then, is: Which of these conceptions of freedom does Hegel claim to be conditioned by rational social institutions? The short answer to this question is: all three.

This interpretive claim poses no special difficulties with respect to the first two conceptions of freedom. It is relatively unproblematic to show that part of Hegel's defense of the institutions of modern *Sittlichkeit* consists in demonstrating that they secure the social conditions without which personal and moral freedom could not be realized.[1] But it is much less clear what sense it could make to say that the doctrine of objective freedom also provides an account of the conditions that make social freedom possible. The difficulty here is easily seen if we recall (1) that social freedom is conceived of as a unity of two elements (an objective and a subjective element), each of which is sometimes referred to as a species of freedom in its own right (objective freedom, on the one hand, and the freedom realized in the subjective dispositions of social members, on the other); and (2) that individuals are said to enjoy social freedom when these two moments are conjoined—that is, when they have the appropriate subjective relation (the subjective disposition "befitting of freedom") to those institutions that fulfill the criteria for rational institutions as defined by the doctrine of objective freedom. Since objective freedom, then, is a component of social freedom, it seems odd to regard it also as a condition of the latter. Apart from the obvious point that a composite cannot be realized if one of its essential parts is lacking, what more is being claimed when objective freedom is said to secure the conditions of social freedom? The key to understanding Hegel's position here lies in reformulating it more precisely: one aspect of the objective freedom embodied by rational social institutions consists in their securing the necessary conditions for the possibility of *the subjective component* of social freedom. In other words, part of the doctrine of objective freedom concerns itself with the features social institutions must have if individuals are to achieve the subjective disposition that enables them to see their social participation as their own, freely undertaken activity. As we shall see in much greater detail later, the most important claim here is that if individuals are to be able to find their particular identities through their social membership, the institutions of *Sittlichkeit* must be constituted so as to be able to satisfy what Hegel calls "the particularity of the subject" (VPR1, 81), by which he means the welfare, or well-being, (*Wohl*) of each particular individual.

 The guiding idea of the present chapter, then, can be summarized as follows: social institutions embody objective freedom—that is, they meet the demands of reason, defined in terms of what is required for self-determination to be realized in the world—only if they secure the necessary social conditions of personal and moral freedom and also satisfy the particularity of individual social members in a way that enables them to find their identities within those institutions and subjectively embrace them as their own.

The second important difference between Hegel's and Rousseau's accounts resides in the specific ways social institutions are thought to secure the conditions of their members' freedom. As we saw in chapter 2, Rousseau locates the objective freedom of the political order in its ability, through laws informed by the general will, to restructure the natural, prepolitical dependence of individuals in such a way that subordination to the wills of others ceases to be an inescapable consequence of human neediness. Hegel's account, in contrast, understands rational social institutions to condition the freedom of their members in a number of ways and is therefore more difficult to summarize in a single statement. I have already alluded to one way Hegel thinks such institutions condition their members' freedom: by satisfying the needs associated with "the particularity of the subject," they make it possible for individuals to acquire the subjective disposition that is an essential part of their social freedom. I shall postpone a discussion of this part of Hegel's view until the final section of this chapter and begin instead by focusing on his extensive account of how the institutions of *Sittlichkeit* secure the social conditions of personal and moral freedom.

Here it is possible to divide the ways in which social institutions secure the conditions of individuals' freedom into two main categories, according to whether those conditions are internal or external to the individuals whose freedom is at issue. The latter category comprises the external social conditions that are necessary in order for persons and moral subjects to be able to realize their freedom in the world. This part of Hegel's theory is relatively straightforward and uncontroversial, and for this reason I shall have little to say about it here. The principal example of such conditions is the apparatus of governmental institutions—the courts and law enforcement agencies treated under the heading "Administration of Justice" (§§209–229)—whose purpose is to realize the principles of Abstract Right by enforcing the laws that safeguard the rights of persons, including their legitimate property claims, and to protect the rights of moral subjects to live their lives in accord with their own understanding of the good, insofar as this is consistent with the freedom of others and of the state as a whole.

The former category, the internal conditions of freedom, is the basis of the more interesting and distinctively Hegelian claim that one of the central tasks of the institutions of *Sittlichkeit* is to fashion the subjectivities of social members so as to make them into the kind of agents who are capable of achieving self-determination.[2] Such agents must meet two basic conditions. First, they must value, and therefore be motivated to achieve, their freedom as persons and moral subjects. Second, they must possess the basic subjective capacities that are needed in order to realize their aspirations to be free in both of these senses.[3] According to this part of Hegel's doctrine of objective freedom, then, rational social institutions have as one of their essential tasks the *Bildung*—that is, the formation or education—of social members into agents who are subjectively capable of realizing themselves as bearers of free wills. This part of Hegel's view will be taken up in the next section, which will be followed by a shorter discussion of how satisfying the needs of particularity makes social freedom possible. Each of these sections can be thought of as addressing one of the following questions raised by the preceding overview of Hegel's doctrine of objective freedom: First, how do the institutions of *Sittlichkeit* contribute to the realization of freedom through the *Bildung* of social members? Second, in what ways do those institutions satisfy the particularity of social members, thereby making it possible for them to find their particular identities in their social participation?

The Formative Tasks of Social Institutions

As my earlier remarks suggest, *Bildung* for Hegel is inseparably connected to freedom; indeed, emancipation (*Befreiung*) is said to be its "absolute mission," or end (§187A). *Bildung,* then, is not simply formative experience of any type but formative experience that has a specific end, namely, self-determination. Formulated more precisely, *Bildung* refers to a kind of formative experience that results in the transformation of un-formed, "natural" individuals (or peoples) into subjects who both aspire to be free[4] and who possess the subjective capacities they need in order to realize their freedom. The importance accorded to *Bildung* in both Hegel's social theory (where the subjects transformed are human indi-viduals) and his philosophy of history (where *Geist,* or humanity in gen-eral, is the subject of *Bildung*) is a consequence of his understanding of the basic quandary of human existence: although it is the essential na-ture of human beings to be free, freedom does not come naturally to them. That is, in their natural, immediate state—prior to being trans-formed through *Bildung*—human beings are neither inclined nor suit-ably equipped to realize the freedom that constitutes their essence.[5]

Since unformed subjects lack even the aspiration to be free—they lack both the knowledge of their true essence and the desire to achieve it—it is intrinsic to the nature of *Bildung* that it take place unconsciously and involuntarily, behind the backs, so to speak, of the very subjects who un-dergo the process of formation. Or, more accurately, individuals and peoples participate in the process of *Bildung* without an awareness of the formative significance of the activity in which they are engaged (§187) and therefore without intending its freedom-promoting consequences. From this fact alone it is clear why Hegel's account of the formative func-tions of *Sittlichkeit* counts as a part of the doctrine of objective freedom: *Bildung* represents one way in which individuals are made to be free (here: they come to be outfitted with the necessary subjective conditions of their freedom) independently of their knowledge or consent.

But the involuntary nature of *Bildung* is not to be explained solely from the fact that unformed individuals have no desire to be free and therefore lack a motive for undertaking the measures necessary to achieve that end. *Bildung* is necessarily involuntary for the further rea-son that the subjective capacities required for the realization of freedom are for the most part acquired only by experiencing the severity of a dis-ciplinary regimen,[6] such as is to be found in labor (the form of discipline distinctive to civil society) or in subjection to the will of a more power-ful other (the basis of discipline in the family) (§174N).[7] This means that individuals submit to the process of formation only out of necessity, and this fact makes the institutions of *Sittlichkeit,* especially the family and civil society,[8] particularly well-suited to carry out *Bildung's* tasks. For individuals belong to the family and civil society not out of choice but because their neediness—including both their helplessness as children and their enduring need for the means of survival—leaves them no other option.[9] Human neediness, then, provides a guarantee that individuals will take part in the family and civil society, and those institutions qualify as rational for Hegel (in the particular respect at issue here) when they are able not only to satisfy the basic needs that necessitate individuals' participation in them but also to put that neediness to work in service of the higher end of freedom. The latter condition requires that institutions be constituted such that the satisfaction of need within them is simultaneously, and unbeknownst to the participants, a process of formation through which they acquire the subjective features required of persons, moral subjects, and (to a lesser extent) citizens.[10] Since the family and civil society are the primary arenas within which the *Bildung* of social members takes place, it is natural to divide this discussion of the formative functions of *Sittlichkeit* into two main parts. I shall first examine the various ways in which the family works to transform its members into self-determining beings and then do the same for civil society.

The general thesis that rational social institutions have the formation of individuals as one of their essential aims is relatively uncontroversial in the case of the family, since the rearing of children (*Erziehung*) is clearly one of the central concerns of family life. What is not immediately obvious, however, is how child rearing serves the specific end of freedom. In what ways, in other words, does the modern family contribute to the formation of children into subjects who are capable of acquiring self-determined wills? According to Hegel, the formative significance of the family has three separate aspects, distinguishable in terms of the different forms of freedom the rearing of children is said to make possible: as members of a properly functioning family, children acquire subjective capacities necessary for realizing the freedoms of (1) personhood and (2) moral subjectivity, and (3) for acquiring the subjective disposition befitting of free citizenship.[11]

Of these three ways the family contributes to the *Bildung* of social members, the easiest to articulate is the one that serves the end of moral subjectivity. In this context the most important aspect of family life is parental discipline. The significance of parental discipline resides less in the teaching of specific moral precepts than in its effect in providing children with a particular subjective capacity—in this case a capacity of the will—that is essential to the kind of self-determination that characterizes moral subjects. The rational end of discipline, as Hegel conceives it, is to raise children out of their original condition of "natural immediacy" (§175), where the will is simply determined by the "drives, desires, and inclinations" nature provides it with (§11), to a condition in which the will is no longer simply identical with, and therefore no longer determined by, its natural content. The subjective capacity that discipline instills in children, then, is the ability to say no to their immediate (unreflected) desires and to determine their wills instead in accord with an external, "objective" will (the dictates of the more powerful, punishing parent) that is distinct from immediate desires, takes precedence over those desires, and (in the case of good child rearing) exhibits a constancy that is lacking in a will determined by caprice or momentary urges.[12] Although determining one's will in accord with the will of a parent clearly falls short of the ideal of self-determination implicit in Hegel's conception of the moral subject (the determination of one's will in accord with one's own reasoned understanding of the good), a period of subjection to parental authority is an essential part of the formative process that must be undergone by originally immediate beings like ourselves in order to achieve that end.[13]

A second aspect of the *Bildung* children receive in the family relates to their capacity later in life to enjoy the particular form of freedom (a subspecies of social freedom) that Hegel associates with membership in the political sphere. More specifically, an essential task of the family is to provide children with a kind of "subjective foundation" (VPR1, 257) without which they would be unable to acquire the subjective disposition required of citizens if their participation in the state is to be free (in the sense articulated in chapter 3) rather than an instance of determination by an external other. The point Hegel has in mind here is expressed in the following statement: "In family life the [basis of] the ethical [*das Sittliche*] is to be brought forth and secured in children. It is essential that one first know ethical life in the form of unreflective love and trust . . . Nothing can make up for the lack of this unity and intimacy" (VPR2, 144; VPR1, 257). The subjective foundation of citizenship at issue, then, is provided by children's earliest emotional experiences in the family, where their relations to others are informed by a feeling of trust grounded in the love family members feel for one another (and recog-

nize the others as having for them in turn). Here it is important to remember that what makes the relations among family members similar to
those among citizens is not the love and intimacy that mark the former
but rather the attitude of trust. Hegel's claim is that children who lack
the early experience of trust within the family miss out on a crucial formative experience without which it becomes impossible (or at best extremely difficult) for them to establish relations of trust later in life, including those required by the nature of citizenship. The basis for this
claim is to be found in the circumstance that both the family and the
state, as "substantial" social unities, depend on the ability of their members to adopt collective ends as their own and to recognize those ends as
having precedence (at least sometimes) over their merely private interests. Doing so, however, presupposes a belief on the part of individuals,
a kind of faith or confidence, that they can count on their fellow social
members to do the same when their own private ends are irreconcilable
with the good of the whole. The formative function of the family in pre-
paring individuals to take on the roles of citizens consists, then, in its
providing children with an early and deeply ingrained experience of a
life shared with others in which they learn that fellow social members
can be relied upon to forgo private ends when the good of the whole requires it. Moreover, and perhaps more important, family life fosters children's capacity for trust in that it teaches them the benefits of a social
union in which the good of one's fellow members and the good of the
whole help to constitute the ends one takes as one's own. What is most
important here is not that children learn that social membership can be
of instrumental value as a means to securing their private ends but
rather that they develop an appreciation and longing for the distinctive
rewards inherent in living a life with others that includes the joint pursuit of shared final ends. Without having spent their early years as members of some such substantial unity, it is unlikely that, as adults, individuals will be capable of the subjective feat required of self-determining
citizens, namely, the (partial) abandonment of the standpoint of an independent self who is motivated solely by his own private good. Thus,
contrary to Plato's assumption, family life is not a threat to the well-being of the state but a necessary condition of individuals' taking their
proper part within it.[14]

Finally, the family also plays an essential formative role in enabling individuals to achieve the freedom of persons. The first way the family

contributes to the *Bildung* of persons resides in the special function it performs in forming the particular identities of its younger members. Membership in the family provides children with what we might call their "natural particularity," or with what Hegel at one point refers to as their "natural self" *(natürliches Ich)* (VPR4, 421). One's natural particularity is to be understood as the wide range of contingent, particular qualities—a mixture of the inherited and the learned—that one acquires more or less passively from one's family membership. These qualities—including such traits as one's skill at athletics or love of music, one's spirited temperament or penchant for hard work—can be thought of as the self's given content, or the raw material that, regardless of how it may be refashioned in later life, makes up the indispensable (and inescapable) basis of the particular being one ultimately becomes. Membership in the family, then, furnishes children with an initial, given content for their identities in the quite straightforward sense that it is by far the most significant source of the particular qualities, capacities, and inclinations that figure into who they are, and who they will become, as particular selves.

There is, however, a further, more important aspect to the family's function in forming the particular identities of individuals. Beyond merely providing children with a set of particular qualities, the family also has the task of instilling within them an affirmative attitude to their natural particularity, one that enables them to value and take pleasure in their own distinctive, contingent natures. It is not enough that children enter adulthood simply as the bearers of a set of particular qualities; they must also have confidence in the worth of their natural particularity in order to be able to form ends on the basis of it and to pursue those ends with sufficient determination. The family's ability to achieve the latter depends on the same feature of the family that explains how family membership makes it possible for individuals to take on the subjective disposition of citizenship, namely, the love children receive from their parents. The aspect of parental love that is relevant here, however, is not its ability to provide children with the experience of a substantial social unity but its nature as an unqualified affirmation of the loved one's particular being. The love children receive from their parents is unqualified in the sense that, unlike the recognition earned in civil society, it is not conditional on children's competence or their usefulness to others. By experiencing the parents' unqualified love for them just as they are, children take over their parents' attitude of unconditional acceptance of their natural selves and learn to value and take pleasure in their own contingent natures.[15] This is essential to realizing the freedom of personhood because being free to pursue one's own arbitrary ends unhindered by others has value only if one *has* arbitrary ends of one's own and is motivated to pursue them, and this is precisely what affirming one's natural particularity enables one to do.

The second respect in which the family promotes the development of children into persons has a more prominent presence in Hegel's texts than the one just discussed. The general aim of this formative function of the family is to foster children's independence (*Selbständigkeit*) from their parents. More precisely, it consists in "raising children out of the natural immediacy in which they originally find themselves to a condition of independence and free personhood, thereby providing them with the capacity to leave the natural unity of the family [in order to enter the sphere of civil society]" (§175). The independence at issue here is clearly meant to be related to, but also something more than, the freedom of personhood as we have understood it thus far (the "abstract" right to pursue one's own arbitrary ends, unhindered by others, within a private sphere bounded by the rights of other persons). In the present context children's independence from their parents includes material self-sufficiency, the ability to support oneself financially as a successful, working member of civil society. One obvious way parents accomplish this task is by teaching (male) children the skills and attitudes they will need if they are to be materially self-reliant once they reach the age of majority and leave the protected sphere of family life. Yet, strictly speaking, this formative task of the family can be regarded as an aspect of *Bildung,* of education that aims at some form of *freedom,* only if we take material independence to be somehow included in the ideal of (free) personhood. But this is possible only if we expand our conception of the person beyond the mere notion of an arbitrary chooser of ends who is recognized by society as a bearer of ("abstract") rights. Hegel signals his intention to do just this when, at the beginning of his treatment of civil society, he invokes the idea of the "concrete person" and proclaims it to be one of the ideals, or "principles," of civil society (§182). The concrete person is said there to be "a totality of needs, a mixture of natural necessity and free choice [or arbitrary will] [*Willkür*]" (§182). Thus, the concrete person, in distinction to the abstract, is more than simply a freely choosing will; it is, in addition, a bearer of *needs* (by "natural necessity"), and its freely chosen acts are directed, in large part, toward satisfying them.

That the move from "Abstract Right" to "Ethical Life" includes an enrichment of the idea of the person implies that Hegel means to criticize, as incomplete, the abstract conception of the person on which the former doctrine is based. His implicit claim is that merely guaranteeing social members the formal *right* to act as they choose (within the boundaries imposed by the universal actualization of freedom in all of its forms) fails to give full expression to the ideal implicit in personhood, the ideal of a self-standing, individual will that freely chooses its own ends. Perhaps the best way of formulating this claim is to say that the idea of the concrete person adds something to the abstract conception of personhood by recognizing that humans are more than just the free choosers of their ends. This description of the person leaves out the important consideration that most, or many, of the real-life choices humans make are guided by the desire to satisfy natural needs. The point of this move is not to deny the claim of "Abstract Right" that a person's arbitrarily chosen acts have an inherent right to the respect of others even if they are not directed at the satisfaction of needs—such acts are still the expression of a kind of self-determination—but only to assert that, given what human beings are like concretely (given their natural neediness), most expressions of free personhood will occur in the context of, and hence be conditioned by, the quest to satisfy natural needs. In other words, taking the basic fact of human neediness into account results in an expansion of the core ideal of personhood: the person, understood concretely, is someone who aspires to satisfy his needs (and to achieve other, more arbitrary ends as well) through his own freely chosen actions.[16] The modern family encourages the realization of this ideal insofar as it prepares children to leave its protected confines and to succeed in the rather less hospitable arena of civil society.

Hegel's texts point as well to a second, less obvious way in which the family fosters the independence and self-sufficiency of children and thus contributes to their *Bildung* as persons. This particular formative effect is due not to the content of what children learn from their parents (such as the various skills and attitudes necessary for self-sufficiency) but rather to a specific structural feature of the modern family. It is important to emphasize that this structural feature belongs not to the family in all of its conceivable forms but to the modern family in particular, for it plays a crucial role in distinguishing the modern family from its traditional, premodern predecessors and in accounting for the rational superiority of the former over the latter. The feature in question derives from the basic fact that the family of modern *Sittlichkeit* is the nuclear family, which, in contrast to the traditional extended kinship group or clan *(Stamm)*, consists (typically) of two parents and their minor children and endures only for a single generation.[17] In the present context the most important feature of the nuclear family is that "children . . . , when they come of age, are recognized [*anerkannt*] as legal persons and as capable both of holding their own free property and of founding their own families, . . . families in which they now have their substantial determination and with respect to which their first family diminishes in significance and the abstraction of the clan loses its rights" (§177). Thus, one of the most important features of the modern family is that it normally dissolves— more accurately, it diminishes in its right to make claims upon individual members—when its sons and daughters reach the age of majority. Hegel's claim is that the modern family represents an advance over the traditional family because its nuclear structure makes it better suited to carry out the formation of its members into independent persons and more hospitable to the expression of their personal freedom. In the first place, the nuclear family effects a kind of *Bildung*—it encourages the development of children's independence—simply by virtue of the fact that its very structure makes it necessary, and makes that necessity clear to its members early on, that sons (and now, for us, daughters) be prepared to support themselves when they come of age rather than rely on family resources for their means of subsistence. Second, the nuclear family has a formative effect on children by contributing to the development and reinforcement of their self-conceptions as persons. This it accomplishes through a kind of *recognition*[18] of their status as independent agents who, as adults, have the right to make important life decisions on their own, undetermined by the needs or wishes of the members of their "first family" and unbound by the constraints of family tradition. By giving their adult sons and daughters free rein in the choice of a career, a spouse, and a place of residence, parents acknowledge the diminished force that family obligations now have in comparison with the rights of their offspring's own arbitrary (or "choosing") will *(Willkür)*. This recognition of sons and daughters as independent persons is not only embodied in the customs and attitudes that typify the modern family; in the rational social world it also finds expression in the realm of law—for example, in the fact that parents have no legal rights over the property of their adult children and in the legal prohibition of traditional inheritance practices that, by excluding daughters from being heirs[19] or favoring eldest sons at the expense of their siblings (§180), violate the principle of equality implicit in the (similarly modern) notion of universal personhood.

I shall turn now to the second major social institution involved in Hegel's doctrine of *Bildung*, civil society. Two questions arise here at the very start: First, which types of freedom does participation in civil society condition? And, second, how—by what mechanism—does participation in this social sphere form individuals so as to be capable of realizing those types of freedom? I can best begin to answer to these questions by considering in full the paragraph in which Hegel most comprehensively describes the formative significance of civil society:

> As [members of civil society], individuals are private persons, who have their own interest as their end. Since this end is mediated by the universal, which thus appears to individuals as a means, they can achieve their end only by determining their knowledge, will, and activity in a universal way and making themselves into a link of this social chain. The rational significance [*das Interesse der Idee*] of this process, of which the members of civil society as such are unaware, lies in its making use of natural necessity . . . in order to elevate the individuality and natural immediacy[20] of those members to *formal freedom* and to the formal *universality of knowing and willing;* that is, its rational significance lies in the *forming* [*bilden*] of subjectivity in its particularity. (§187; some emphases omitted)

I shall now attempt to determine what answers are given here to the two questions posed here. In response to the first—which freedoms does *Bildung* in civil society condition?—Hegel fails to provide a clear answer couched in the terms we have by now come to expect. Rather than specifying the self-determination at issue to be personal or moral freedom, he characterizes it only as "formal." More promising for us is his description of the subjective capacity necessary for freedom that participants in this sphere allegedly acquire, namely, the capacity for achieving a kind of universality of will that stands in contrast to the volitional immediacy and individuality (or arbitrariness) characteristic of the natural state. Hegel's response to the second question—concerning the mechanism of *Bildung*—is somewhat clearer. The formative effects of civil society are said to depend on the fact that individuals are able to attain the private ends they pursue within that sphere only on the condition that they shed their natural immediacy and arbitrariness and become universal beings (in a sense yet to be determined). Since the ends pursued in civil society are grounded in natural needs, individuals have no real choice but to conform to the conditions imposed by civil society on the satisfaction of ends and therefore no real option other than to undergo the formative process peculiar to that social sphere. Although it is far from evident from this passage alone exactly what the resulting universality of will consists in, the process through which it is achieved is indicated somewhat more clearly: members of civil society lose their volitional immediacy and arbitrariness by making themselves into links of the social chain, that is, by adopting those qualities of will that enable them to fit into the system of social production and exchange.

How are we to synthesize these various points into an account of the formative process distinctive of civil society? One possibility is suggested by the following two passages:

> The absolute mission [*Bestimmung*] of *Bildung* is liberation, . . . [and] this liberation within the subject consists in *hard labor* that works against the mere subjectivity of conduct, against the immediacy of desire, as well as . . . the capriciousness of arbitrary will . . . Yet it is through this labor of *Bildung* that the subjective will achieves *objectivity* within itself. (§187A)

> Practical *Bildung* through labor consists [both] in . . . the limitation of one's activity—partly in accord with the nature of the material, but especially in accord with the wills of others—and in a habit, acquired through this discipline, of *objective* activity and *universally valid* skills. (§197)

The thrust of these passages seems to be that it is primarily the performance of labor—more specifically, *socially productive* labor—that effects the *Bildung* individuals undergo within civil society. This interpretive suggestion gains in plausibility when one recalls the essential role played by one form of socially productive labor (the bondsman's labor for the lord) in the formation of *Geist* in *The Phenomenology of Spirit*

(PhG, ¶¶190–196; 150–155).[21] According to the passages just cited, the formative significance of socially productive labor lies in its fostering of qualities of will that Hegel denotes by the terms 'objectivity' and 'universality'. But what, more precisely, does Hegel mean by these two terms, and how might we understand his claim that the phenomena they name are promoted or brought about through the performance of socially productive labor?

I shall begin with Hegel's statements that characterize labor as objective activity and as the means by which a subjective will achieves objectivity. Labor qualifies as objective activity in two different senses. First, labor is objectively determined (determined by the object) in the sense that it consists in "conduct . . . dictated by the . . . properties of its object" (§187Z) rather than by subjective caprice or immediate desire. The need to produce a shoe that serves its purpose compels the shoemaker to do to the unformed piece of leather what its peculiar properties and the shoe's purpose require of him, not whatever he happens to feel like doing at the moment. In producing an object capable of satisfying human need, "the laborer produces the thing as it ought [*soll*] to be" (§197Z) and therefore determines his activity in accord with a sort of imperative—the thought of how the object *ought* to be made—that claims priority over the laborer's own immediate desires and whose validity is grounded in something more substantial than a subject's arbitrary will. Labor is also objective activity in the sense (the third sense of objectivity spelled out in §26) that, as real activity within the world, it involves the translation of subjective ends (ends that are merely willed or intended) into the realm of objectivity ("external existence"): "in this sense of the term the will becomes *objective* only through the execution of its ends" (§26). Through productive activity, then, the will of the laborer achieves objectivity in two senses: first, the laborer learns to subordinate immediate desires to the dictates of objectively valid imperatives, or principles; and, second, he acquires competence in giving his ends objective existence, or in making "his behavior . . . accord with his will" (§187Z). The acquisition of both of these capacities is essential to the laborer's becoming "master over his own activity" (§197Z) and therefore to his realizing the ideal of self-determination inherent in Hegel's conception of moral subjectivity (successfully acting in accord with one's own understanding of the good).

Whereas the objective qualities of the will just discussed derive from labor's nature as productive activity in general, the universality referred to earlier depends on the requirement that labor in civil society be *socially productive* (that is, productive of goods or services that meet the actual needs of one's fellow social members).[22] Although members of civil society labor in order to achieve their own private ends, their labor takes place within a system of social cooperation marked by a division of labor. Since no individual can satisfy all of his needs through the immediate products of his activity alone—civil society is "a system of all-round dependence" (§183)—labor succeeds at attaining the end for which it is undertaken only to the extent that its products are needed by others. This implies that individuals in civil society must learn to tailor their productive activity in a way that takes into account the needs, wishes, and perceptions of other subjects and that is therefore "universal" in the very loose sense that it involves "the limitation of one's activity . . . in accord with the wills of others."[23] In other words, socially productive labor is activity that is informed by a kind of recognition of the subjectivity of others, a recognition both of the fact that one shares a world with other beings who have their own distinctive ends and of the necessity of letting the ends of others enter into the determination of one's own actions. As such, socially productive labor exhibits an important structural affinity to moral action that enables Hegel to regard the former as a source of *Bildung* in service of the latter. Although labor within civil society is not itself a species of moral action (since motivated solely by egoistic ends), it serves to develop within individuals a subjective capacity without which moral action would be impossible, namely, the ability to discern, and determine one's activity in accord with, the ends of one's fellow beings.

Given the specific conceptions of objectivity and universality that Hegel associates with the performance of socially productive labor, as well as the centrality of the latter to his account of civil society, it is tempting to conclude that moral freedom is the primary end to which the *Bildung* within this social sphere is directed. Yet, although Hegel does in fact espouse the views I have just outlined, they do not represent his only, or even his most important, claims concerning the formative significance of civil society. One way of gaining access to the rest of Hegel's position is to ask whether the account sketched earlier constitutes an argument for the rational character of the *modern* social world in particular. A review of that account reveals that the formative effects of civil society asserted there depend only on the requirement that individuals' labor be socially productive in a very general sense of that term (productive of goods or services that meet the actual needs of one's fellow social members) but not on any specifically modern way in which that labor is organized. This means that Hegel's view as articulated thus far amounts to an argument for the formative effects of any productive activity carried out within the context of a social division of labor and therefore cannot be construed as providing a defense of any distinctively modern social institution. Even slaves and serfs, it would seem, achieve through their labor the sort of objectivity of will referred to earlier, since they also learn to subordinate immediate desire to objective imperatives and acquire competence in translating subjective ends into external reality. The same holds for the quality of volitional universality, at least in the quite weak sense in which it is intended here: slaves and serfs, too, learn to allow the wills of others to play a role in determining their laboring activity.

How, then, can Hegel's account of *Bildung* within civil society be seen as delivering an argument for the rationality of the *modern* social world? I shall attempt to show here that, in addition to arguments about the formative effects of socially productive labor in general, Hegel's account of civil society includes the claim that participants in the modern economy are systematically required to take the wills of others into account in a quite specific manner and that the resulting, distinctively modern relations among economic agents endow them with wills that are universal in a more precise and richer sense of universality than the one employed previously. Moreover, this universality of will turns out to be an essential part of individuals' being constituted as persons (and hence a necessary condition of the realization of personal freedom).[24]

Before proceeding directly to this topic, though, it is advisable to say a word about Hegel's use of the term 'civil society'.[25] Unlike the terms 'family' and 'state', 'civil society' refers exclusively to what Hegel takes to be a distinctively modern social institution.[26] Thus, although it makes sense to speak of the modern (nuclear) family and to distinguish it from the traditional family (or extended kinship group), 'modern civil society' is redundant; 'civil society', as Hegel uses the term, designates a specifically modern form of economic organization. The present question, then, concerns how civil society distinguishes itself from other, premodern forms of economic organization with respect to the *Bildung* of its participants. More specifically, what feature unique to civil society is responsible for its having a formative function beyond those that follow merely from the general requirement, implicit in any social division of labor, namely, that labor be socially productive?

I have already suggested that the feature we are seeking resides in a certain way the members of civil society relate to one another, or take each others' wills into account, in determining their productive activity. The key to reconstructing this point lies in Hegel's claim, unemphasized and barely explicated in the text, that the relations individuals have to one another in civil society are *abstract* (§192). Throughout the section he calls "The System of Needs," Hegel uses the term 'abstract' to describe a number of aspects of civil society, including the *needs* individuals have as members of civil society (§190), the *goods (Mittel)* they collectively produce to satisfy those needs (§191), and the *labor* by means of which they do so (§198). In all of these cases 'abstract' is synonymous with 'particularized' (§190), or 'specialized'. Thus, one of the features of the modern economy Hegel points to is the fact that both the needs of individuals and the goods produced to satisfy them are far more particularized than in past societies. (Think, for example, of how the need for water-decaffeinated, Colombia-grown French roast replaces the more simply defined need for coffee in general.) Contrary to what one would initially expect, Hegel calls such specifically determined needs abstract because they attach themselves to very particular features of their object (the unique taste of Colombian French roast or the distinctive advantages of the water-decaffeinating process). This, however, presupposes that the subjects of need possess a highly developed capacity for breaking down an object with a manifold of attributes (coffee) into its single qualities and distinguishing among them. Focusing in this way on a single determinate quality of the object of need involves, according to Hegel, an act of abstraction, since to pick out one quality among many interconnected ones is at the same time to abstract from all the rest.[27] Along with the increasingly abstract nature of needs and goods in civil society goes the increasingly abstract nature of labor. By the latter Hegel clearly means to refer to the highly specialized division of labor characteristic of the modern social world.[28] In this case the qualifier 'abstract' intuitively makes more sense, since a highly developed division of labor can easily be thought of as dividing a complex production process into its many simple components and assigning each individual to perform only one (or perhaps a few) of these "abstract" tasks.

What, though, does it mean to say, as Hegel does, that *relations* among individuals in civil society are abstract? And how is this fact connected, as I am claiming it is, to the *Bildung* of persons? Given the applications of 'abstract' just mentioned, it is tempting to take Hegel's talk of abstract relations within civil society as referring simply to the fact that individuals occupy highly specialized positions within the social division of labor. I shall argue, however, that Hegel is best understood as referring to a different characteristic of civil society that, though probably a necessary concomitant of a highly developed division of labor (and therefore easily confused with it), is in fact a conceptually distinct feature of the modern economy. Although there is very little textual evidence in the published version of the *Philosophy of Right* that explicitly supports my claim, other versions of that work, together with considerations concerning the requirements of Hegel's argument, provide sufficient grounds, both interpretive and philosophical, for locating the abstract relations said to exist among economic agents in something other than the fact that each occupies a specialized position within the social division of labor. What, then, is this something other?

Hegel comes closest to articulating his point explicitly in the following statement taken from a student transcript of his university lectures in 1817–1818: "out of the mediation [inherent in] *the universal exchange of labor and goods* the individual becomes, and goes forth as, a self-consciously free will [*freie Willkür*] . . . which is also universal. From here comes the idea of formal right" (VPR1, 125; emphasis added). Here one of the formative effects of civil society is unambiguously traced back to the distinctive way modern producers relate to one another and to the system of production as a whole in pursuing their particular ends— namely, by becoming participants in a "universal exchange of labor and goods." Thus, labor within civil society is essentially the production of *exchangeable* goods.[29] The point here is not simply that the fruits of one's labor can in fact be exchanged for the products of others but rather that production is carried out with, and determined from the very beginning by, the conscious intention to do so; in civil society production is undertaken *for the purpose of* exchange.[30] Moreover, the exchange at issue here is not a direct exchange between producers (a system of barter, unmediated by money) but one that takes place within a "universal" system of exchange; it is, in other words, exchange mediated by the institution of a market and therefore by a conception of the abstract *value* of goods (or, in Marx's more precise terminology, the exchange value of commodities).[31] This means that productive activity in civil society is carried out not with the aim of meeting the needs or wishes of determinate individuals but with respect to a consideration of the value of one's products, a value that is expressed in terms of the amount of money they can command on the free market; in the modern economy "one produces objects only in relation to their value" (VPR2, 160). Because their interactions are mediated exclusively by a universal, propertyless[32] commodity (money), members of civil society do not relate to one another as concrete, particular individuals but only as "abstract" buyers and sellers who are identical in all relevant respects to all other buyers and sellers.

But how does this feature of civil society contribute to the formation of its members as persons? In the statement just cited, participation in a universal exchange of labor and goods is credited with fostering a kind of self-consciousness among members of civil society—consciousness of oneself as a free, universal will—that is also said to be one of the foundations of "formal right." The nature of this self-consciousness is articulated more clearly in §209, which, not accidentally, also marks the transition from Hegel's discussion of the system of needs to his treatment of the administration of justice (which includes as one of its central concerns the enforcement of the abstract rights of persons): "A consciousness of the individual in the form of universality—that I am taken to be a *universal* person, identical to *all*—is a part of *Bildung,* of thinking. The human being counts as such because he is a human being, not because he is a Jew, Catholic, Protestant, German, Italian, etc." (§209A). Hegel's claim, then, is that participation in a universal system of exchange of labor and goods forms the consciousness of social members in a way that is essential to the systematic realization of personal freedom. Such participation encourages individuals to think of themselves and others as beings who, despite their many concrete differences, are alike in one fundamental respect, namely, that all possess "the form of universality." More precisely, they come to conceive of themselves and their fellow social members as *persons,* who, as such, are identical to all other persons and who count as persons (as the recognized bearers of the same set of rights) not because of any particular qualities they possess but solely in virtue of their status as a human being.[33] Thinking of oneself as one person among others presupposes a particular subjective capacity that Hegel regards as fundamental to all spiritual phenomena: the ability to establish a relation of identity to that which is not identical—to what is "other"—to oneself. A person exhibits this capacity insofar as he is conscious of himself as a fully particularized being, qualitatively different from all others, and at the same time as an abstract, universal subject, identical to other persons with respect to the rights and obligations that derive from that common status. The idea underlying Hegel's claim must be that participation in civil society helps to form individuals as persons because it requires them to conceive of themselves and their relations to others in a structurally analogous manner.[34] Insofar as their economic transactions are mediated by the market, individuals encounter one another not as concrete beings with distinctive qualities but as abstract agents stripped of all particular determinacies; that is, they encounter one another simply as buyers and sellers, identical to all others with respect to their rights and obligations as economic agents. The reason for this lies in the fact that economic relations are mediated by the market and by the concept of value it presupposes. As members of civil society, individuals are able to achieve their particular ends only to the extent that their products (or labor power) can be translated into the universal language of value, a language that necessarily abstracts from all of its objects' particular qualities. In the context of the market, then, individuals, too, count (are able to command commodities) only on the basis of their abstract qualities, as the bearers of money, or possessors of a certain quantity of value. And, like the persons posited by abstract right, they are regarded as qualitatively identical to their fellow social members, and hence worthy of the same rights and privileges as all others.

Social Institutions and the Satisfaction of Particularity

The final aspect of Hegel's doctrine of objective freedom that I shall consider here is his claim that rational social institutions further social freedom by securing the conditions that make its subjective component possible. This part of Hegel's theory concerns itself with the features institutions must have if their members are to acquire the subjective disposition that enables them to regard their participation within them as their own self-determined activity. As I have asserted previously, the most important claim here is that the institutions of *Sittlichkeit* must be able to satisfy what Hegel calls "the particularity of the subject" if individuals are to be able to find their particular identities through their social membership and hence participate freely in social life. The central concept of this part of Hegel's theory is well-being *(Wohl)*, or welfare, and its principal claim is that social institutions must be able to satisfy the basic material needs of all of its members if they are to constitute a rational, or good, social order. As we shall see in more detail in chapter 7, showing that the institutions of *Sittlichkeit* promote the basic well-being of all individuals is essential to demonstrating their *goodness,* since the good as Hegel defines it unites right *(Recht)* with "universal" well-being (§§129+Z, 134). The implication of this concept of the good is that a social order that attended to its members' rights of personhood but not to their basic well-being would fall short of realizing the good. But the importance of well-being for Hegel's social theory can be understood from the perspective of *freedom* as well, since a social order in which fundamental human needs were consistently unmet could not be freely embraced by its members, who, besides being subjects of consciousness, are also material beings with natural, bodily needs.[35] In other words, one of the conditions that enables members of *Sittlichkeit* to embrace their social roles as constitutive of their own identities, and hence to participate freely in social life, is that those roles, along with the institutions that serve as their framework, allow them to satisfy their material needs.

Not surprisingly, this aspect of Hegel's view has a clear analogue in Rousseau's political theory. To see this, recall that in formulating the central problem of political philosophy, Rousseau distinguishes two fundamental types of human interests that a rational state must promote, namely, interests in freedom and in material well-being.[36] Rousseau, like Hegel, recognizes that material neediness is a central fact of human existence and that one of the principal (and most obvious) benefits individuals receive from social life is the increased efficiency with which they can satisfy their needs by cooperating with others in producing life's necessities. Rousseau's thought, like Hegel's, is that a society that addressed its members' purely spiritual needs[37] while leaving their material needs unmet would be neither sustainable nor (morally) legitimate. But beyond providing a general statement of what the material well-being of citizens requires—the preservation of life, personal security, and a certain quantity of basic resources—Rousseau devotes relatively little attention to how a rational state provides for its citizens' material needs.[38] Because his theory of *Sittlichkeit* extends beyond the state to include nonpolitical institutions, Hegel is able to offer a more complete account than Rousseau of how, in a rational social order, the work of satisfying the basic material needs of all converges with the more spiritual task of actualizing practical freedom. In order to reconstruct Hegel's position, I shall need to examine both what he takes the essential components of well-being to be and how he thinks rational institutions work to secure them.

Before doing so, it is necessary to clear up an ambiguity surrounding Hegel's concept of well-being. The question is whether this concept refers exclusively to material well-being or whether it also includes what we might call spiritual well-being. In at least one passage Hegel appears to equate well-being with happiness *(Glückseligkeit)* (§123).[39] At an earlier point he defines well-being as the satisfaction of the will's "*immediately* present content," which he identifies as "the *drives, desires, and inclinations* by which . . . nature determines the will" (§11). These naturally given drives, desires, and inclinations—which animals, too, possess (§11Z)—give rise to needs *(Bedürfnisse)* (§11A), the satisfaction of which constitutes a central component of human well-being.[40] Although well-being is initially defined as the satisfaction of those needs bestowed on us by nature, there are several passages in which Hegel states that human well-being includes not only these "sensible" *(sinnliche)* needs but also "spiritual" *(geistige)* needs (§§124, 11N; VPR1, 80), the most prominent of which is the need for recognition by others (§124). (The need for recognition is not a natural need in the sense at issue here because it presupposes a degree of self-consciousness—the possession of a self-conception, along with the desire to have it confirmed in the eyes of others—that elevates it above the sphere of the merely natural.)

In the present context I shall take 'well-being' to refer only to material well-being and to denote the satisfaction of the natural, or sensible, needs of human beings. I adopt this narrower conception of well-being here only because I have already examined, in chapter 3, how the institutions of *Sittlichkeit* accommodate the principal part of "spiritual" happiness, namely, the respect gained from the recognition of others. If we understand 'well-being' in its more inclusive sense, these claims of chapter 3 can be taken to have shown that by providing sufficient opportunities for all social members to achieve a wide variety of forms of recognition—as persons, moral subjects, family members, producers, and citizens—the rational social order secures (at least a large part of) the conditions of individuals' spiritual well-being. What remains to be seen is how Hegel's account of the rational social order accommodates those needs that derive from our purely natural drives, desires, and inclinations.

It should be acknowledged here that the notion of a purely natural (uncultivated) drive, desire, or inclination is highly problematic. Even the most superficial acquaintance with history confirms what Rousseau means to illustrate in his *Discourse on Inequality*, namely, that human desires, and the needs they engender, are susceptible to formation in innumerable ways by cultural and historical circumstances. Moreover, this is true of even the most rudimentary biological drives. The nutritional needs of the inhabitants of the twentieth century, for example, differ so radically from those of prehistoric humans that what would count as satisfaction for one group would be unrecognizable as such to the other. Hegel, following Rousseau, does not mean to deny the nearly infinite plasticity of human needs and desires. At the same time, he recognizes that the human being is not a blank slate on which simply any configuration of needs and desires can be inscribed. Although there is no fixed and determinate "human nature," human biology does impose certain inescapable constraints on the psychological makeup of concrete, historically formed individuals that social theory cannot ignore. There are, in other words, human drives that, despite the myriad concrete forms they are capable of assuming, are so much a part of human beings by nature that to close off all avenues of their expression would be both futile and tyrannical. A theory of the rational social order needs to take cognizance of these constraints and to ensure that the institutions it endorses provide sufficient means for satisfying the human needs they imply.

Since Rousseau takes freedom to be the essential character of human beings (SC, I.4.vi)—that property without which they fail to be truly human—a central concern of his social theory is to show that there is no necessary conflict between universal freedom and the satisfaction of humans' basic material needs. (This is the import of the well-known question with which he begins the *Social Contract*: whether it is possible, "taking men as they are," to devise laws "as they can be" [SC, I.1.i].) Hegel, as we have seen, agrees that freedom is the human being's "substantial nature" and that the rational social order must allow for the satisfaction of material needs in a way that accommodates this point. The most important respect in which Hegel's position diverges from Rousseau's is that for Hegel the quest for material well-being is not merely compatible with freedom but plays a substantive role in its actualization. It is not just that well-being and freedom are able to coexist; rather, reason makes positive use of human sensibility in order to realize its ends. How is this to be understood?

I shall consider first how freedom and material needs relate within the family. We have already seen that the family is a rationally necessary institution because it contributes in a number of crucial ways to the actualization of freedom: it provides its members with particular identities that enable them to freely subordinate their private wills to the requirements of the collective good; it furnishes the social order with the human individuals it needs in order to be a self-sustaining whole; and it subjectively forms children into persons, moral subjects, and citizens. What the part of Hegel's view now being considered adds to this account is the claim that one of the "moments," or ends, of family life is "the satisfaction of the sexual drive" (VPR2, 130). In other words, a further respect in which the family qualifies as rational is that in institutionalizing monogamous sexual love it enables its adult members to express one of the strongest of human drives in a way that is consistent with the actualization of freedom. But, as I have indicated, Hegel means to claim more than just that natural drives and needs are compatible with freedom. In the case of the family, the sexual drive contributes positively to the realization of freedom because it is one of the powerful forces that bring two adults together in marriage and help to keep them united for the long and difficult task of child rearing.[41] Since this is required for the realization of freedom, it can be said that the family exploits human sexual needs for rational ends, thereby bestowing ethical significance on an otherwise purely natural drive. Hegel expresses this point as follows: "Marriage contains a natural moment . . . [In it] the natural relation is transfigured into a spiritual one without being given up . . . The ethical moment consists in nature being overcome. On the other hand, this natural relation is not to be regarded as something degrading or wrong, or as a defect one is subject to merely as a result of the imperfection of human nature" (VPR2, 130–131).

Even though the natural element of marriage remains subordinate to the ethical—it is of lesser value and "possesses dignity only by being incorporated into an ethical unity" (VPR2, 132)—it is an essential element nonetheless: "[There are] sects that [realize] God's will through the most rigorous abstinence . . . [This] is not such an elevated virtue. As a living being, the human must possess the [sexual] drive, satisfy it, and elevate himself above it" (VPR1, 253). The point made here—against the Platonic ideal of love—is that a marriage that accomplishes its higher tasks without sexual fulfillment is a less perfect union than one where, in addition, sexual attraction remains alive. This is because "a relation [of this type] embraces the entire totality of the person—not only mind and sentiment but also the sensible being" (VPR1, 253). In other words, within such a marriage the imperatives of nature are in a more complete harmony with those of spirit; natural and ethical demands are united, each reinforcing the other. This is to say, to use a phrase encountered earlier, that there exists an "interpenetrating unity" of nature and freedom.

That civil society promotes the material well-being of its members is obvious. The economic cooperation it facilitates enables human beings to produce the goods they need to survive reliably and efficiently. And in the modern world civil society enables the majority of individuals not only to survive—to satisfy "universal needs like food, drink, clothing, etc." (§189Z)—but also to achieve a level of material comfort and luxury (§§191Z, 195) that, in its scope, is unprecedented in human history. Following Smith, Hegel locates the primary source of modern productivity not in any distinctively capitalistic feature of civil society but in its extensive division of labor (§198),[42] which allows for complex productive processes to be broken down into simple tasks and thus to be performed, with greatly increased efficiency, by separate individuals. A further feature of civil society that Hegel emphasizes—and, though he does not say so explicitly, probably also regards as contributing to its remarkable productivity—is the fact that production is market-governed. Here, too, Hegel accepts the substance of Smith's claim that the unregulated market—where society's work is not centrally coordinated but undertaken instead by large numbers of independent agents motivated only by their own economic gain—is a highly efficient way of organizing production and ensuring maximal overall output. Because it so effectively harnesses the forces of self-interest to promote the material well-being of society in general—it works on the principle: "in furthering my end I further the universal" (§184Z)—the market plays an indispensable role in actualizing practical freedom and is one of modernity's most important contributions to the fully rational social order.[43]

Finally, civil society's success in furthering the well-being of its members contributes to the realization of freedom in more than just the sense that, by making individuals better off, it provides them with material incentives that enable them to participate, uncoerced, in an objectively rational (freedom-actualizing) institution. Like the family, civil society, too, makes indirect use of the material neediness of its members to achieve freedom's ends. The principal respect in which it does so finds expression in Hegel's characterization of civil society as "a system of all-round *dependence*" in which "the individual's subsistence and well-being . . . are intertwined with the subsistence . . . and well-being of all . . . and are actual and secure only in this context" (§183; emphasis added). Thus, as Rousseau clearly recognized, the extensive division of labor that civil society relies on to produce the necessities of life makes thoroughgoing dependence on others a prominent and inescapable feature of the modern world. Unlike Rousseau, however, Hegel regards this dependence as primarily a boon to freedom rather than a threat. This is because, as we saw earlier in this chapter, it is precisely this dependence on others that forces individuals to step out of their merely particular points of view and to adopt a universal perspective—one that takes appropriate account of the needs and perceptions of abstract others—in determining their own (socially productive) activity. Civil society, then, serves not only as a highly efficient means of satisfying material needs; it also makes hidden use of those needs to effect the *Bildung* of its members into persons and moral subjects.

It is important to note that Hegel's treatment of civil society does not end with these points from Smith in praise of the market and the division of labor. For Hegel is more keenly aware than Smith of the intrinsic deficiencies of a wholly unregulated economy. Although the market is a highly efficient producer of goods, it does not by itself constitute a fully rational means of satisfying the material needs of society's members. The most important reason for this is that while the market promotes the production of large quantities of goods, it does not guarantee their rational distribution.[44] The latter requires not just that enough goods be present to satisfy the material needs of society overall but, more stringently, that they be distributed so that the material needs of every individual are met. (The good, as Hegel conceives it, incorporates not merely the well-being of the whole but the well-being *of all* [§§125, 230]; and, so, in civil society, "the welfare of all individuals ought to find its satisfaction" [VPR2, 189].) If it is to be possible for all social members to endorse civil society and to be "at home" (and thus free) in their roles within it, they must be able to know that social prosperity will not be accompanied by their own private misery; thus, the true end of civil society's massive productive capacities is not the creation of wealth per se but the *assurance* of each individual that his needs will be met (§230). Yet, as Hegel recognizes, vast disparities of wealth, including extreme poverty, are the inevitable consequences of an unregulated economy (§§185+Z, 241–245), where "contingent circumstances" (§§200, 241) determine the financial success of individual participants and hence the access they have to the goods that social cooperation produces. For this reason civil society can fully succeed at satisfying the material needs of its members only when the market is accompanied by two further institutions, the corporations and what Hegel terms "the police."

Insofar as they address the problem of poverty, the corporations' main task is to provide for the needs of their own members who may be out of work or otherwise affected by the "contingent circumstances" that not infrequently conspire to prevent individual participants in civil society from achieving self-sufficiency (§§252, 253A). Yet the corporations are obviously not in a position to eliminate poverty entirely, since many members of civil society—day laborers and unskilled workers, for example (§252A)—do not belong to one. If Hegel envisages a general solution to the problem of poverty, then—and many have argued that he does not[45]—it must reside in his account of the police (what we might call the public works authority).

With respect to the satisfaction of material needs, the principal business of the police is to facilitate the exchange of goods, care for public health, and ensure the quality of the necessary commodities of life (§§235–236; VPR2, 190; VPR4, 597). It also appears to be charged with ensuring that all members of civil society have access to the goods they require to satisfy their basic material needs: "For the *poor* the [public] authority takes over the role of the family with respect to their immediate want" (§241). Yet despite protracted attempts to do so, Hegel (to his credit) never actually finds a solution to this preeminently modern (§244Z) social ill that he can wholeheartedly endorse. Although a system of public welfare may seem an obvious response to the problem of poverty, and well within the purview of the police, Hegel is famously ambivalent about such a proposal. (The closest he comes to endorsing a state-funded welfare system is an ambiguous reference to "public poor-houses" [§242A].) His reason, which is not irrelevant to contemporary debates about the "culture" of poverty, is that while assistance in the form of handouts may address the problem of material need, it does so in a way that prevents the poor from achieving (what he takes to be) the more important good available to participants in civil society, namely, the "spiritual" satisfaction—self-esteem and the recognition of others—that comes from fulfilling one's material needs through one's own labor and effort (§§244+Z, 245).

Hegel also rejects the suggestion that the public works authority might alleviate poverty by creating jobs with state moneys. In this case his reasons are economic rather than ethical: the artificial creation of jobs can only exacerbate the phenomenon that gives rise to poverty in the first place, overproduction. If the underlying problem is, as Hegel believes, that more goods are being produced than can find buyers in the marketplace, then more jobs will only mean increased production and, eventually, an even greater loss of jobs in the private sector (§245). (Hegel, of course, does not consider the Keynesian remedy of using state funds to hire the unemployed for public works projects that improve the quality of life but do not contribute to the overproduction of goods.) After considering private charity, a poor tax, leaving the poor to fend for themselves, and even state-issued begging licenses (§245+Z), Hegel admits that modern poverty has no fully satisfactory solution consistent with the principles of civil society (§245): "Thus civil society in general lacks the power to eliminate poverty. It can find help only in a power that is not its own, in the ownership of land. This is not something civil society has within itself; rather, it must look to something other. This shows the necessity of *colonization*" (VPR2, 198; emphasis added).

The conclusion that colonization—or, more plainly, imperialism—must be relied on to alleviate poverty constitutes a serious blow to Hegel's theoretical ambitions. This solution manifestly fails to meet his own criteria for rational social institutions, for it implies that the modern social order is precisely not a stable, self-sufficient system but must instead rely on something outside of itself in order to achieve its ends. It will not do here to turn our attention from the individual nation-state and consider the earth as a whole as the unit that aspires to self-sufficiency. For, apart from the very serious question of how imperialism could be compatible with the freedom of the original inhabitants of colonized lands, Hegel's proposed remedy is at best a temporary solution, one that can work only as long as there are uncolonized portions of the earth. How, after that, could Hegel's vision of the fully rational social order be actualized?

Hegel himself admits that the intractability of poverty points to "a deep defect in the concept of civil society" (VPR2, 201). Given this, it is hard to see how one can avoid drawing the further conclusion that, by his own criteria, Hegel has failed to demonstrate the complete rationality of the modern social world. It is important to recognize, however, that this failure by no means constitutes a refutation of the normative standards that Hegel's theory of *Sittlichkeit* uses to evaluate the social order. Since my aim here is to defend and elucidate those standards rather than to argue that our own world measures up to them, I shall not consider whether a satisfactory solution to poverty can be found that would allow the basic features of civil society to remain intact. It is sufficient for my purposes to have made clear why persistent poverty must be unacceptable to a Hegelian social theorist and, in addition, to have indicated one point at which a contemporary critique of civil society might find a foothold in Hegel's account of what counts as a rational social order.

6

Hegel's Social Theory and Methodological Atomism

The previous three chapters have been concerned with filling in many of the details of the two basic parts—the subjective and objective components—of Hegel's conception of social freedom. Now that we have seen how these two elements work together to form the groundwork of the theory of *Sittlichkeit,* we are in a position to think more productively about one of the fundamental philosophical issues that has surfaced here from time to time but still remains unresolved, namely, the relation between individual and collective goods that underlies Hegel's account of the rational social order. More precisely, it is time now to determine the extent to which we can agree with Allen Wood's assertion, already noted in chapter 1, that in Hegel's social theory "collective goods have value because they have value *for individuals.*"[1] I shall understand this assertion as the claim that for Hegel collective goods are reducible, without remainder, to the good of individuals.

Determining Hegel's position on this issue is not a simple task, first because the claim that collective goods are reducible to the good of individuals admits of a variety of interpretations and, second, because Hegel nowhere explicitly states his position on this issue in precisely these terms. The closest he comes to addressing the question directly is a statement to the effect that social philosophy cannot "proceed atomistically" or "ascend from a foundation of individuality" (§156Z). A further, more substantial resource for reconstructing Hegel's view can be found in his critique of social contract theory, which he sets out in a variety of enigmatic remarks scattered throughout his writings.[2] In the present chapter I intend to examine some of those remarks with the aim of reconstructing Hegel's view on the relation between collective and individual goods. In doing so I shall concentrate primarily on the very complicated question concerning the extent to which his social theory is consistent with some version of what I shall call *methodological atomism*.[3] It is important to note that, as I discuss it here, methodological atomism has nothing to do with the view that philosophers of the social sciences frequently call methodological individualism, namely, the epistemological doctrine that all explanation in the human sciences is reducible to claims about the actions and states of individuals. As considered here, methodological atomism is not concerned with the *explanation* of social phenomena but with their *evaluation*. It is a general method or procedure employed by normative social theory to determine, or "construct," the rational ends of some social entity, such as the state.

The particular version of methodological atomism I shall focus on here is suggested by a phrase Hegel employs in characterizing the fundamental doctrine of social contract theory. According to him, the distinctive feature of social contract theory is that it takes *"the interest[s] of individuals as such"* to be the final end of political association (§258A). I shall explain this idea in more detail later, but for now the methodological atomism that Hegel is concerned with can be characterized as the view that the principles that define the collective good of a social group can be exhaustively constructed from a starting point that takes into account only the interests that members of the group have when regarded *as individuals*—that is, when viewed atomistically, in abstraction from their membership in the particular social institution under consideration. This doctrine, I take it, when applied to the sphere of *political* institutions, is an essential feature of social contract theory in all of its versions (including those of Hobbes, Locke, Rousseau, and perhaps even Rawls), but it is also central to other forms of liberalism, including some utilitarian theories. Thus defined, methodological atomism is not a content-neutral procedure that can be adopted by any social or political theory whatever. On the contrary, it contains a substantive claim about the possible content of any admissible conception of the collective good of social groups, namely, that the good of the social whole includes no ends that cannot be derived from, or constructed out of, the interests of the individuals (considered as such) who make up that whole.[4]

Characterized in this way, methodological atomism is one plausible and historically influential way of construing the thesis that collective goods are reducible without remainder to the good of individuals, but it is important to recognize at the outset of this discussion that it is not the only way of doing so. To see this, consider the example of a voluntary association that has been formed by a group of dance enthusiasts for the purpose of practicing together, performing for one another, and engaging in mutual criticism. The good that the members of this association realize cannot be understood simply in terms of the satisfaction of interests they have *as individuals*. For dance as it is practiced here is an inherently social activity; that is, the participation and reactions of their fellow members are constitutive of the ends individuals seek to achieve by belonging to the group, and it is impossible to achieve one's own good within the group without also furthering and caring about (some part of) the good of one's associates. In this case the desire to dance includes, as internal to itself, the desire to establish certain noninstrumental relations to others. In spite of this, it might still be the case that the good realized by this association can be reduced to the good of its individual members. There might, in other words, be no good that is realized by the association as a whole apart from the various ways its individual members benefit from participating in it. If so, this association would be an example of a group in which the collective good was reducible to the good of individuals, but not to their good *as individuals*. The methodological atomism that is implicit in social contract theory takes a narrower view of the relation between individual and collective goods within the political sphere; it asserts that the ends of the rational state can be derived entirely from the interests its individual members have apart from, and prior to, their membership in that institution (though not necessarily apart from their membership in any social group whatever).[5]

I shall argue in the end that Hegel's social theory rejects the doctrine that collective goods are reducible without remainder to the good of individuals on *both* of these interpretations and holds instead that the rational social order realizes a good that is both higher than and irreducible to the good of its individual members. At the same time, however, I shall seek to show that Hegel's position is closer to the former doctrine, in both of its versions, than is normally thought. Most important, I shall claim that the theory of *Sittlichkeit* operates, albeit implicitly, with a conception of the good (or fundamental interests) of individuals *as individu-*

als and that it uses this idea to place constraints on how the rational social order may be organized. More precisely, it takes the satisfaction of
those interests for all social members as one of the conditions a social order must meet in order to count as fully rational. This means that the
strongly holistic good that the rational social order allegedly realizes
must be compatible with the satisfaction of the fundamental interests of
all of its individual members considered as such. Demonstrating these
claims will require a detailed examination of Hegel's much-discussed but
rarely understood attempts to distance himself from social contract theory and, more generally, from the methodological atomism it presupposes.

It will no doubt seem obvious to many readers that Hegel, perhaps the
most vehement of modern critics of the social contract tradition, deserves, if anyone does, to be counted among the opponents of methodological atomism. Although ultimately I shall not deny that this judgment is in some sense correct, I want to proceed here by calling into
question this received assumption about Hegel's position in order to get
clear on both precisely where it diverges from methodological atomism
and what the significance of that divergence amounts to. This means
that I shall not simply take at face value Hegel's apparent rejection of social contract theory but instead attempt to determine, with more clarity
than Hegel himself achieves, the extent to which his basic philosophical
strategy for justifying rational social institutions differs in kind from that
employed by Rousseau, the social contract theorist nearest to him in
spirit.[6]
    One reason that determining the relation between individual and col-
lective goods in Hegel's social theory poses an especially difficult challenge is that, according to the reconstruction I have provided here, the
primary good realized in *Sittlichkeit,* social freedom, is a holistic property in both the stronger and weaker senses distinguished in chapter 1.
Thus, on the one hand, the social order itself (but not the individuals
who compose it) is considered to be self-determined because, as a
whole, it is self-sustaining and exhibits the rational structure of the Concept. On the other hand, individual members of *Sittlichkeit* are said to
enjoy a distinctive species of (social) freedom consisting in the fact that
(1) they find their particular identities through a form of social participation in which, because they embrace the general will as their own,
they remain subject only to their own wills and therefore subjectively

free; and that (2) the social order in which they willingly participate satisfies, independently of their subjective disposition, the requirements of a rational social order as defined by the doctrine of objective freedom. (That is, the social order secures the conditions necessary for actualizing the freedoms of personhood and moral subjectivity, as well as the subjective disposition of social members, and does so in such a way that the social order itself remains self-sustaining and affords individuals the full range of types of social membership in the three essential social spheres.) Social freedom, then, is actualized only in a social order that, as a whole, achieves self-determination in one sense (it is self-reproducing and structured according to the Concept) and at the same time is made up of individual members whose social activity is self-determined in another, less peculiarly Hegelian sense (roughly, they obey no foreign will).

This account raises a number of interrelated questions concerning the value Hegel ascribes to social freedom in the strongly holistic sense and the relation that value has to the good of individual social members: Is the self-determination achieved by the social whole valuable only because it in some way secures the good of individuals, or is it also good in itself, independently of whatever instrumental value it has in realizing the good of individuals? Conversely, is the self-determination enjoyed by individual social members important only because it is essential to the social order's achieving self-determination in the strongly holistic sense, or does it possess an independent value of its own? Or is it rather that, regardless of their interrelations, each form of self-determination is valuable for its own sake? And if that is the case, is there a hierarchy among those goods such that one of them counts as higher than the other? As indicated earlier, my suggestion is that we approach these issues by first addressing the closely related, though distinct, question posed by the issue of methodological atomism: Can we arrive at a complete account of the basic ends of the rational social order by starting from an account of the rational ends social members can be said to have *as individuals,* apart from the interests they acquire through their social membership itself? In other words, does the rational social order as Hegel depicts it pursue any ends (or achieve any good) beyond either the ends individuals have independently of social membership or ends that are defined solely in terms of the rational coordination of those individual ends? If so, what kinds of ends are they?

There are many reasons it is initially difficult to take seriously the suggestion that Hegel's social theory might be, or come close to being, reconstructible in accord with the strictures of methodological atomism. Let us note here two of those reasons. First, Hegel's texts abound with passages that characterize the rational social order as realizing an unconditioned or divine good that appears to belong to an order of goods entirely distinct from (and higher than) those ascribable to finite human individuals. To cite several well-known examples, Hegel describes the state (best understood here as the entire ensemble of rational social institutions) as "that which is rational in and for itself" (*das an und für sich Vernünftige*) and, further, as an "absolute, unmoved end in itself . . . that has the highest right in relation to individuals, whose highest duty is to be a member of the state" (§258; emphases omitted). And, more notoriously: "The existence of the state is God's march in the world" (§258Z).

A second reason for believing that Hegel rejects methodological atomism is that a large portion of his critique of the social contract tradition appears to be directed explicitly at the primacy it gives to the good of individuals, atomistically conceived. In a passage that belongs to his fullest mature elaboration of that critique, Hegel decries those political theories that make "*the interest of individuals as such*" into "the final end for which they are united" (§258A).[7] Immediately thereafter Hegel gives a characterization of his own view that he takes to stand in direct conflict with the position just described: "[The state], however, has a completely different relation to the individual. Because the state is objective spirit, it is only as a member of the state that the individual itself achieves objectivity, truth, and ethical life. *Association* [*Vereinigung*] as such is itself the true content and end, and the vocation of individuals is to lead a universal life" (§258A). If individuals achieve "objectivity" and "truth" only by leading a "universal life" within a rational social order, if association itself is the final end of social life, then—so it would seem—the interests individuals have *as individuals* (in abstraction from the attachments they acquire through the forms of social membership under investigation) will not be an appropriate starting point for social theory. As the passage just cited makes clear, Hegel's reasons for rejecting theories that derive the rational ends of social institutions solely from the interests of individuals as such are bound up with his assumption that doing so commits one to understanding the value social membership has for individuals as purely instrumental (as opposed to "association as such" being "the true content and end" of social membership). This assumption appears plausible if we restrict ourselves to the kinds of individual interests mentioned here, namely, "security and the protection of property and personal freedom." Hegel's thought is that, for a theory that begins with only interests such as these, social membership (here, *political* membership more narrowly construed) can have significance only as a means for individuals to achieve their common but separate ends rather than being the source of the substantive social bonds and shared final ends that have such a prominent place in Hegel's theory of *Sittlichkeit*. If the only ends admitted into the construction of rational social institutions are the ends individuals have prior to (in abstraction from) their familial, corporative, and political attachments, what grounds can there be for claiming that individuals' engaging in social activity for its own sake—their taking "the universal interest" of their institutions as "their final end" (§260)—is an essential feature of the rational social order?

I shall argue later that the first of these points—Hegel's description of the state as an unconditioned, divine good—does indeed pose genuine problems for any attempt to reconstruct his theory as a version of methodological atomism. (I shall postpone discussion of this issue until the end of this chapter.) It is important to see now, however, that the second set of considerations represents considerably less of an obstacle to such a reconstruction. Hegel's rejection of social contract theory as it is depicted in the preceding paragraph rests on an overestimation of the extent to which the methodological atomism inherent in social contract theory necessarily translates into a theory that is individualistic *in substance* (as, for example, the view that social membership is nothing more than a means for achieving the ends of individuals as such and that in order to achieve those ends individuals need not take the good of others as one of their own final ends). This is a misunderstanding that is easily acquired but difficult to be freed of, and for this reason it will be necessary to explain here in some detail why Hegel's implicit assumption concerning the substantive implications of methodological atomism is false.[8]

The first step toward this end is to clear up a crucial ambiguity inherent in formulating the issue at hand as a question about the way in which membership in the rational social order is good for the individuals that compose it. This ambiguity is best brought out by focusing on two different meanings that can be ascribed to the word 'for' in that formulation. Construed in one way—as 'for' in the subjective sense—it refers only to an individual's conscious attitude to what is said to be a good for him. On this interpretation, something is a good for me if, and only if, I in fact attach a value to it, or *take it to be* part of my good. Thus, the fact that a father values his participation in family life is sufficient to make it a good for him in this sense. If 'for' is understood in the second, objective sense, the assertion that social membership is good for individuals refers not to their own assessment of the value of that membership but to the objective value it has for them. Taken in this way, it is a statement made from a philosophical perspective that may be external to the actual consciousness—or, in Hegel's terminology, the subjective dispositions—of social members. To say that the rational social order is good for individuals in this sense is to make the claim that social membership satisfies *interests* that can be attributed to all individuals as such, independently of their consciously held values.

Hegel's doctrine of the subjective disposition of social members holds that in a rational social order social participation will be more than a merely instrumental good for individuals in the first of these senses: they will take their activity on behalf of collective ends to be valuable for its own sake. The claim that follows from the methodological atomism inherent in social contract theory, however, is that the rational social order is good for individuals in the second of these senses: it satisfies the fundamental interests of individuals as such. It is, of course, far from obvious that these two different assertions could be coherently unified within a single social theory, for it still seems that a position grounded solely in an account of the good (fundamental interests) of individuals considered apart from their social attachments will be unable to arrive at the view that individuals must be able to embrace the collective ends of their families, corporations, and the state as their own final ends if the social world is to be fully rational. The part of Hegel's critique of social contract theory referred to earlier is implicitly based on precisely the appearance that the two assertions just delineated are incompatible.

Here it is necessary to recall that Hegel's espousal of this claim depends on a crucial assumption he makes about the kind of interests that qualify as the interests of individuals as such ("security and the protection of property and personal freedom"). What is significant about the kinds of individual interests Hegel has in mind when criticizing social contract theory is that they can be pursued and satisfied by agents who maintain radically individualistic self-conceptions—that is, conceptions of themselves as sovereign, self-standing beings who have no noninstrumental concern for the good of others. While it is likely that achieving the end of personal security will require such individuals to join forces with other self-standing beings in a common project of mutual defense, there is no reason for individuals who are united solely for this purpose either to incorporate the good of their fellow associates into their own final ends or to think of their social cooperation as anything more than an efficient means for achieving an end they have independently of their association with others. The same point can be made with the help of a term I introduced in chapter 3 when defining the voluntative identity supposed to hold between members of *Sittlichkeit* and their institutions: the individual interests Hegel has in mind when criticizing social contract theory are interests that agents can pursue and satisfy without surrendering their wholly *private* wills (that is, each can continue to have a will directed exclusively at his own interests as a discrete, unattached individual).

The discovery that Hegel's rejection of methodological atomism relies on this assumption about the nature of the interests individuals have as individuals should lead us to ask the following question: What if, contrary to Hegel's assumption, there existed a good of which it were true both (1) that its achievement represented a fundamental interest of individuals (as such); and (2) that it could not be universally *achieved* by individuals unless they were the sort of subjects who regularly took (at least some part of) the good of their fellow associates as one of their own final ends? In other words, what if among those interests ascribable to individuals as such there were an interest whose satisfaction (as revealed by philosophical reflection on the conditions of satisfaction for all) required that individuals conceive of themselves not as radically self-standing units but as beings for whom their relations to others within certain social groups constitute an intrinsic part of who they are, with the consequence that they acquire the ability to will the collective good for its own sake, even at the expense of (some of) their private ends? The answer, of course, is that if there were such an interest, it would be far less obvious than Hegel takes it to be that his own social theory is incompatible with all versions of methodological atomism. But does such an interest exist? I shall argue here that both Hegel and Rousseau are implicitly committed at the deepest levels of their social theories to maintaining that there is such an interest and that, moreover, both of them conceive of that interest as an interest in *freedom*. In order to get a clearer idea of how methodological atomism is compatible with the view, espoused by both Hegel and Rousseau, that it is an essential feature of the rational social order that its members regard their social participation—their activity in the service of universal ends—as having more than merely instrumental value, it is necessary to spell out in more detail how these two positions are united within Rousseau's account of the social contract and, more specifically, how his understanding of freedom as a fundamental interest of individuals enables him to bring the two together.

Rousseau

That Rousseau does in fact intend to unite these two positions is clearly evidenced by a prominent feature of his account of the social contract that has been a constant source of puzzlement for interpreters.[9] The feature to which I am referring is Rousseau's insistence that the solution to the central problem faced by political theory requires that citizens of the rational state have a radically different subjective makeup from that of the hypothetical inhabitants of the state of nature with which his theory begins. The individual of the state of nature is said to be "by himself . . . a perfect and solitary whole" (SC, II.7.iii), a being who considers only himself (SC, I.8.i) and is motivated solely by his "private" (purely egoistic) interest (SC, II.7.ix). A citizen, in contrast, is supposed to regard himself as "a part of a larger whole from which [he] receives, in a sense, his life and being" (SC, II.7.iii) and is able, by virtue of this self-conception, to "want constantly the happiness of each" (SC, II.4.v). According to other passages, citizens do not "perceive their own existence . . . except as part of the state's"; they "identify themselves in some way with this larger whole" and "feel themselves to be members of the homeland" (PE, 222). The puzzle raised by these claims is the very same thought that underlies Hegel's rejection of social contract theory in the passage cited earlier: if it is true, as Rousseau states, that "among the motives causing men to unite . . . nothing relates to the union for its own sake" (GM, 158), how can he possibly arrive at a view that requires individuals to be subjectively constituted such that they regard the good of the whole as a constitutive part of their own good? Answering this question requires that we first make clear to ourselves the basic argumentational structure of Rousseau's political theory and the sense in which it qualifies as a version of methodological atomism.

The methodological atomism of Rousseau's theory can be seen in the fact that its logical starting point is an account of the fundamental interests of individuals as such. In the context of that theory the category 'interests of individuals as such' is given content by thinking of the interests individuals would have if they existed in a world (the state of nature) that lacked those social relations specific to the particular form of association whose justification is the subject of inquiry (here, the state). Isolating these fundamental interests is essential to Rousseau's theory because the principles that govern legitimate political association will be (exhaustively) constructed by determining the principles of social interaction that best coordinate those interests. The legitimate, or rational, state will be defined as one that allows for the fundamental interests of all citizens to be satisfied. The specific interests Rousseau ascribes to individuals as such are set out in his formulation of the central problem political philosophy is to solve: "Find a form of association that defends and protects the person and goods of each associate with all the common force, and by means of which each one, uniting with all, nevertheless obeys only himself and remains as free as before" (SC, I.6.iv). Two distinct classes of interests are attributed to individuals here: first, those that could be described as interests in one's material *well-being* (including the preservation of life, personal security, and the basic goods necessary for well-being) and, second, a moral, or "spiritual," interest in maintaining one's *freedom,* which is defined as "obeying only oneself."[10]

The existence of these two kinds of fundamental interests seems to present an irresolvable dilemma for the designer of rational political institutions, for while the interests associated with material well-being can be satisfied only through extensive social cooperation, the natural consequences of that cooperation appear to be directly incompatible with the conditions required for the maintenance of freedom. In fact, the necessity of social cooperation poses two distinct obstacles to the maintenance of freedom, each of which must be grasped if the complexity of the problem addressed by Rousseau's political thought is to be fully appreciated. The first of these obstacles is articulated in the point, already familiar from chapter 2, that the dependence engendered by social cooperation, when left in its natural, unreconstructed state, makes it virtually impossible for individuals to continue to obey only their own wills (and thus makes freedom a virtual impossibility). The second obstacle to the maintenance of freedom has its source in a different feature of social co-operation: since effective cooperation must be regulated by a collective will directed at the common good (including the material well-being of all), the need to cooperate with others will require individuals to adjust or curtail their actions in accord with interests beyond their own private good. This seems to imply, however, that individuals will have no option but to let their actions be determined by a will other than their own and thus to surrender their freedom; for as long as individuals consider only themselves and are motivated solely by their own private good, laws aimed at realizing the common good cannot but appear to them as external constraints on the pursuit of their own good. Although the threat of punitive sanctions might in fact induce such individuals to comply with laws directed at the common good, their compliance would involve submitting to a foreign will rather than obeying themselves.

The possibility of resolving the dilemma posed by the existence of the two fundamental interests—and hence the central insight of Rousseau's political theory—ultimately rests on the fact that it is possible to conceive of a variety of forms of practical subjectivity (what Hegel will call configurations of the free will), each of which satisfies the essential requirement of freedom, namely, that one obey only oneself. This is precisely the point underlying Rousseau's crucial distinction between natural and moral freedom. As Rousseau understands it, natural freedom consists simply in the absence of all constraint by the wills of other individuals. The unassociated beings of the original state of nature (as depicted at the beginning of the Second Discourse) enjoy this freedom in that they pursue the satisfaction of their needs and desires more or less unhindered by others. In the absence of enduring contact with their fellow beings, they escape determination by a foreign will and therefore obey only themselves, which in this case means nothing more than that they are free to follow, unimpeded by others, the impulses of their own particular (private) wills.[11] It is important to note here that it is this conception of freedom that is invoked (implicitly) in formulating the dilemma posed by the competing interests of material well-being and freedom.[12] Fortunately, though, this is not the only possible way of envisioning how individuals can remain obedient only to their own wills. Another possibility is offered by what Rousseau calls moral liberty (*la liberté morale*), defined as "obedience to the law one has prescribed for oneself" (SC, I.8.iii).[13] Underlying this conception of freedom is the thought that if the laws governing the rational state can be understood as having their source in the wills of the individuals who are subject to them, then compliance with those laws can be regarded as a form of obedience to oneself and therefore as a kind of freedom. Thus, individuals' need for social cooperation (in order to promote their interests in their material well-being) can be rendered compatible with their interest in freedom only if the principles governing that cooperation, including those directed at the material well-being of all, can be regarded as coming from their own wills in some meaningful way.

It is Rousseau's doctrine of the general will that is supposed to provide a solution to the complex problem said to lie at the heart of political philosophy. It does so by imposing two different kinds of conditions on the laws that regulate citizens' interactions within the rational state (conditions that correspond, respectively, to Hegel's doctrines of objective and subjective freedom). First, those laws must have a certain content in order to qualify as a true expression of the general will: they must in fact further the material well-being of all (the fundamental interest that originally motivates their association [SC, I.6.i; GM, 157–158]); and, as we saw in chapter 2, they must effectively mitigate the freedom-endangering consequences of social cooperation by restructuring natural dependence so as to make it realistically possible to avoid subjection to the particular wills of other individuals. (In accomplishing this, the general will secures the necessary conditions of a negatively defined conception of freedom, civil freedom [SC, I.8.ii], conceived of as the ability to act unconstrained by the particular wills of others within a sphere of activity external to the vital interests of the community as a whole.)[14] Second, in order to satisfy the requirement that individuals obey only themselves, the laws that in fact advance their fundamental interests as individuals must also be recognized by the citizens who are subject to them as products of their own wills. In many places Rousseau clearly regards citizens as the actual fashioners of their laws; (moral liberty, remember, is said to consist in *prescribing* laws to oneself). In other passages (SC, II.1.iv), however, he seems to impose only a weaker condition—closer to the one subsequently adopted by Hegel, who believed that the size of modern states made radically participatory forms of democracy impracticable—namely, that citizens merely *affirm* the laws that govern them as good. In either case, if individuals are to recognize rational laws as products of their own wills—if they are to be free in their subjection to those laws—they must be able to be moved by their assessment of the common good and to assent to laws that (sometimes) subordinate their private good to that of the whole.

This summary account of the basic structure of Rousseau's political theory provides us with the resources necessary to begin to articulate how his methodological atomism—his beginning only with the interests of individuals as such—can result in a view that makes political membership into more than a purely instrumental good for individuals and requires that they be subjectively constituted so as to regularly take (some part of) the good of their fellow associates as a part of their own good. The most important part of the argument that underlies Rousseau's view can be summarized in the following claims:

1. Individuals considered as such have two kinds of fundamental interests: their own material well-being and their freedom.
2. In order to further their interests in material well-being, individuals must engage in social cooperation.
3. But social cooperation poses a threat to the freedom of individuals because (a) the relations of dependence it involves make it difficult to escape subjection to the wills of others; and (b) the principles of the common good that govern cooperation will at least sometimes be at odds with their private good and therefore appear as external to their own wills.
4. Hence if the requirements of material well-being are to be reconciled with those of freedom, one condition that must be met is that the interactions of individuals be regulated by laws (implicit in the concept of the general will) that both advance the common good and restructure their interdependence so as to be less detrimental to freedom.
5. But if this condition is fully to satisfy freedom's requirement that individuals obey only themselves, it must also be the case that individuals can consciously embrace the laws dictated by the general will as their own.
6. Since these laws have the common good as their content—they aim to advance the interests of all citizens—individuals can be free in their subjection to those laws (recognize the laws that govern

them as their own) only if they can will the common good. Their freedom, therefore, requires that they have more than merely private wills.

Membership in the rational state, then, serves to realize the freedom of citizens in two respects: the laws dictated by the general will mitigate the freedom-endangering consequences of dependence (thereby securing the necessary conditions of a negatively defined civil freedom), and citizens who embrace the general will as their own enjoy a kind of self-determination (*la liberté morale*) that consists in obeying self-prescribed laws. The latter point is crucial to understanding how a political theory can start only from the interests of individuals as such (including their interest in freedom) and yet view political association as having a value beyond the purely instrumental role it plays in securing the fundamental interests of individuals as such. This is because political participation itself—both the framing of laws, jointly undertaken in accord with a shared conception of the common good, and the actual compliance with laws recognized as one's own—is more than just a *means* to being free; it is also, and more important, *constitutive of* a kind of freedom, for in acting in accord with laws they give to themselves, citizens do nothing other than obey their own wills.[15] Because this form of freedom presupposes that citizens have a standing commitment to the common good, one of the conditions necessary for its realization is that individuals be able to will the good of their political community as a whole (including the good of their fellow citizens). Thus, given the need for social cooperation that sets up the central problem of political theory, the aspiration of human individuals to be free can be fully realized only on the condition that they acquire general wills. The same point is sometimes formulated by Rousseau as the claim that the subsistence of the rational state as such depends on the *virtue* of its members (SC, III.4.vi; PE, 222), where virtue is defined simply as the "conformity of the particular will to the general will" (PE, 217). Since discerning the common good is by its nature a joint enterprise, carried on in a public arena and requiring the input of other citizens, the realization of freedom is possible for individuals only by becoming members of a collective subject—a body, composed of all citizens, that strives to know, will, and determine its activity in accord with its general will. Put in terms reminiscent of those

Hegel uses to characterize spirit: the 'I' achieves its freedom only as part of a 'we'.[16]

Just how deeply, though, must the 'I' be constituted as a 'we' in order to be free? At precisely what level of the will must a commitment to the common good be incorporated into the subjective disposition of free citizens? Or, equivalently, how radical a transformation in self-conception would the inhabitants of the state of nature have to undergo in order to take their place as free members of the rational state? Strictly speaking, Rousseau's argument as articulated thus far establishes merely that in order for individuals to remain subject only to their own wills as members of the state, they must be able to will the common good (which is to say, here, that they must be able to assent to legislation that furthers the common good). It does not by itself show, however, that in order to do so citizens must possess a self-conception that differs as radically as Rousseau claims it must from the self-conceptions characteristic of the hypothetical individuals with which his account of the social contract begins. More precisely, the argument summarized earlier does not yet demonstrate that the realization of their freedom within the rational state requires that individuals conceive of their political association as *intrinsic* to who they are and therefore aim to achieve the good of the whole for its own sake, because the flourishing of their community (and of their fellow citizens) is regarded by them as good independently of its relation to their own good as separate individuals. In other words, this argument shows that in order to be free, citizens must be able to will the common good but not yet that they must will it noninstrumentally, as a *final* end.[17]

In fact, the argument summarized here enables us to see more clearly how it would be possible for an individual to possess a general will to the extent required in order to be free (being able to will the common good even at the expense of some of one's private ends) while remaining, ultimately, a wholly self-interested being. For what that argument shows is that the satisfaction of one's fundamental interests as an individual is inextricably bound up with the existence of a political community in which the same interests are satisfied for all. Presumably, then, a recognition of this fact would make it possible for citizens to endorse legislation directed at the common good while regarding the achievement of that good as valuable only instrumentally, as simply a means to the satisfaction of their own fundamental interests as individuals. In such a case the ability to will the common good when it conflicts with one's private ends would require nothing more than the ability to distinguish one's fundamental interests as an individual from other, less fundamental ends one has and consistently to give priority to the former over the latter; in other words, it would require only that an individual have learned, as Rousseau himself expresses it, "to prefer his properly understood interest to his apparent interest" (GM, 163).

It is important not to overlook the fact that even this vision of the subjective disposition appropriate to citizenship would require a substantial reconfiguration of the subjective makeup of individuals who were not yet constituted as citizens, a reconfiguration that could legitimately be called a radical transformation in self-conception. It is no minor distance that separates the inhabitants of the state of nature, who aim only at their own particular good, from beings who consistently will the common good because they recognize that their own fundamental interests are best served by doing so. The self-conception at work in the latter scenario consists in identifying most deeply not with one's own particular good but with interests one shares with all other individuals (one's fundamental interests as an individual) and in recognizing that the fundamental interests of each can be satisfied only by promoting the fundamental interests of all. Yet this subjective change, however substantial, falls short of the radical alteration Rousseau thinks is required if natural *men* (and women) are to be transformed into *citizens*. For the latter, as Rousseau says again and again, regard the good of the political community as logically prior to their own, willing it for its own sake and not merely as a means to satisfying their own interests as individuals.[18] What grounds does Rousseau have, though, for requiring this more socially spirited disposition of free citizens?

The key to understanding at least one of the motivations behind this part of Rousseau's view lies in appreciating the importance of a theme that runs throughout all of his major works, namely, the difficulty human beings naturally have, due to passions that distort their vision and pull them in the wrong direction, in keeping sight of and acting in accord with their own best interest.[19] It is this feature of human beings that makes it necessary for political philosophy to concern itself with the *formation* (SC, II.7.x), or education—or, as Hegel calls it, the *Bildung*—of citizens. In order to be reliable willers of the common good, individuals who attributed no intrinsic value to the good of the whole would have to possess what Rousseau regards as nearly superhuman qualities: the ability always to bear in mind the essential link between the common good and one's own fundamental interests as an individual, and a constant disposition to give precedence to those (long-term, sometimes barely palpable) interests while resisting the pull exerted by one's (more immediately perceptible) purely particular good.[20] For Rousseau, a political theory that required these qualities to be widely distributed among citizens in order for the state to succeed in securing the fundamental interests of all would violate the very first principle to which such a theory must conform: in attempting to devise "laws as they can be," it would take insufficient account of "human beings as they are" (SC, I.1.i.). The general unreliability of human beings' ability to discern and will their fundamental interests implies that if citizens are consistently to relate to the general will as their freedom requires—if they are to be "safeguarded against the seduction of particular wills" (SC, II.6.x)—their subjective disposition ought to include an attachment to the common good that is less dependent on the effectivity of their reason.

This is surely one reason for Rousseau's view that citizens must have a deeper attachment to the common good—and therefore be more thoroughly constituted as a 'we'—than his argument seems at first to warrant. Although it is not always completely clear in his texts, Rousseau responds to the problem raised here by locating the primary ground of citizens' commitment to the common good not in an understanding of the unseverable connection between that good and their fundamental interests as individuals but in an affective bond they have to their political community and, by extension, to their fellow citizens. Thus, the freedom of citizens turns out to depend, for the vast majority of individuals, not so much on rational (or philosophical) insight into the identity of individual and collective interests as on "love of country" (*l'amour de la patrie*), an enduring concern for "the fate of the republic" (PE, 224), which is reinforced, if not instilled, by a consciously undertaken program of political education. This affective attachment to their political community provides citizens' wills with a force that, because itself a passion, is better suited to counteracting the promptings of their particular wills than a force more purely rational in nature. It is love of country, then, that above all else enables citizens to have the effective concern for the good of their fellow members—gives them the capacity to "constantly want the happiness of each" (SC, II.4.v)—that is essential to having a general will.[21]

Although Rousseau himself does not explicitly mention it, there is perhaps a second consideration motivating his view that citizens must will the common good for its own sake. This consideration, however, is not connected to the realization of *freedom* in a precisely Rousseauean sense of that term (which is to say that, strictly speaking, it is not based on the mere requirement that citizens end up obeying only their own wills). Rather, this consideration is grounded in the somewhat different concern that one's political membership and participation be more directly expressive of one's self-conception, and more immediately related to the final ends implicit in that self-conception, than is possible for citizens who accord no value of its own to achieving the good of the whole. Let us consider again the subjective disposition of individuals who regularly will the common good but do so only because they know that it is the sole guarantor of their fundamental interests as individuals. It follows from Rousseau's definition of freedom that such individuals are free in complying with the general will, because in acting in accord with the common good they do only what their own wills prescribe. It might even be true that for such individuals political participation—determining with others what the common good requires and playing one's part in bringing it about—is experienced as having a certain value in and of itself, since that participation is not merely a means to securing their fundamental interests but also constitutive of a certain kind of self-determination (prescribing laws to oneself) that they enjoy in the rational state.[22] Yet there is one respect in which the political participation of such individuals could be said to fall short of being fully "their own," a deficiency that is located in the very fact that the immediate object of their deliberation and activity as citizens (the common good) possesses no intrinsic value for them. Although their participation in the state meets the formal requirements of freedom (they avoid subjection to a foreign will), there is an important sense in which its content—the end to which it is immediately directed—is, though not antithetical to their wills, nevertheless external to what they ultimately care about. The thought here is that if the attachment individuals have to the common good is rooted solely in self-interest, there remains too great a distance between the immediate object of their will and activity as citizens (the common good) and the final ends (the satisfaction of their fundamental interests) that account for their ability to will it. This distance, when characteristic of a significant portion of one's practical involvement in the world,[23] can plausibly be regarded as a kind of alienation from oneself and one's activity. Although this thought belongs more obviously to Hegel's understanding of the subject's aspirations than to Rousseau's—it is an essential part of Hegel's demand that individuals be "with themselves" (*bei sich*) in their social institutions—it is at least hinted at as well in Rousseau's general concern that individuals achieve not only free wills but also a wholeness or integrity of will that includes a harmony of feeling and reason.

What Rousseau offers us, then, is an account of the legitimate state that is constructed in accord with the strictures of methodological atomism and yet prescribes as rational a subjective disposition in which citizens regard their political membership as an end in itself and take the good of the political community as a final end of their own. Moreover, it is not only from within the subjective dispositions of citizens that membership in the state appears as valuable for its own sake. For the philosopher, too, political membership turns out to have more than instrumental value (as a means to satisfying the interests of individuals as such). This is because participation in the rational state—creating, with others, the laws that govern one's own actions—is not merely a means to achieving freedom but is itself a species of freedom, one that is in fact necessary if the ideal of obeying only oneself is to be realized fully and universally. Thus, what might initially appear to require an act of philosophical legerdemain is accomplished instead by an argument whose strategy depends on effecting a transformation in how we conceive of political freedom. This transformation is brought about by establishing two claims: first, that under conditions of human dependence a social world based on natural freedom alone would in fact be a world of universal subjection to the wills of others; and, second, that if individuals are to submit themselves to a collective will for the sake of advancing their fundamental interests as individuals and at the same time be free, the freedom they enjoy as citizens must consist in a more complex form of obeying only oneself than the idea of natural freedom allows for: it is only in *embracing the general will as their own* that citizens remain subject only to their own wills.

It is important to see that Rousseau's argument does not simply replace its initial conception of freedom with a second, wholly unrelated one. On the contrary, his argument depends on there being an essential commensurability between the two conceptions such that from the perspective of the first the second can also be recognized as a conception of freedom. Moreover, this commensurability consists in the fact that each conception represents a different way of giving content to freedom's defining quality, obedience only to oneself. Thus, although Rousseau's argument involves no change in its definition of the abstract essence of freedom (freedom always consists in obeying only oneself), it does require a change in the way that abstract essence is specified or made determinate. Or, using the terminology introduced by Rawls, we could say that the move from natural to moral freedom represents a transformation in the *conception,* but not in the *concept,* of freedom.[24]

Thus, one of the distinctive features of Rousseau's political theory is that while it starts by considering only the fundamental interests individuals have as such, it ends up with an account of the rational state that requires citizens, in effect, to surrender (some of) their original individuality—it requires them to cease to think of themselves only as separate individuals—in order that those interests be universally satisfied. This basic feature of Rousseau's theory can be translated into the general claim that although it is possible to identify or define the fundamental good of individuals independently of their social relations, it is not possible fully to specify the content of that good (to determine concretely what that good will consist in when realized in the world) without envisaging the individual as integrated into a political community such that he no longer conceives of his own good as essentially separable from the good of the whole. Rousseau's claim is not simply that the individual's fundamental interest in freedom can only be satisfied within the framework of a certain political order but, more radically, that the freedom realized by individuals in the rational state must be social in its very content, a freedom that *consists in* citizens discerning and endorsing the collective will of their political community and doing so not as independent individuals with separable interests but as substantially integrated members of a single, indivisible body.

This reconstruction of Rousseau's position shows, then, that, contrary to Hegel's assumption, methodological atomism in political theory—making "the interests of individuals as such" into "the final end for which they are united"—is not necessarily incompatible with at least some of the claims Hegel himself wants to advance concerning the relation between individuals and the rational social order, namely: that "it is only as a member of the state that the individual itself has objectivity, [or] truth"; that "association as such is itself the true content and end" of social membership; and that "the vocation of individuals is to lead a universal life" (to have a general will) (§258A). In other words, Rousseau would agree with Hegel's conclusion that it is only as members of the state that individuals attain objectivity (become the kind of beings they by nature ought to be) but deny that doing so consists in anything more than satisfying a fundamental interest that can be ascribed to them *as individuals*, since, as citizens, they succeed in realizing their freedom, the quality that defines their essential nature as human beings.

Finally, it is important to note that, contrary to appearances, Rousseau's methodological atomism does not commit him to the view that the *only* goods that make citizenship in the rational state valuable for those who enjoy it are goods that could also be appreciated as such from the perspective of the unassociated, purely self-interested individuals of the state of nature. Rousseau's argumentational strategy as I have reconstructed it here leaves room for the view—one explicitly embraced by Rousseau himself (SC, I.8.i)—that citizenship brings with it certain goods (for example, the good intrinsic to having enduring, noninstrumental attachments to others and in pursuing with them common projects informed by shared final ends) the value of which can be recognized only by individuals who already have the subjective dispositions appropriate to citizens.[25] This implies, then, that what makes the rational state good for its members need not be *exhausted by* its success in satisfying their fundamental interests as individuals. In fact, Rousseau's argumentational strategy commits him only to the claims that a concern for the fundamental interests of individuals as such is itself *sufficient* to generate a complete account of the ends of the rational state and, further, that the satisfaction of those interests (especially the realization of freedom) represents the *most fundamental* good individuals achieve through membership in the state.[26]

The position I have attributed here to Rousseau can easily appear deeply paradoxical. For the subjective disposition it prescribes to social members seems to be expressly at odds with the normative perspective it employs to justify that disposition and the social order it counts as rational. More precisely, Rousseau's view posits affective, substantive attachments to particular others as necessary and desirable and at the same time accords supreme normative weight to a perspective that abstracts from those prerational, identity-constituting relations to others and evaluates the social order from a perspective that recognizes only the in-

terests of unattached individuals. In other words, Rousseau establishes
that the actual citizens of a rational state must be constituted as a 'we' (if
they are to be free), but his argument establishing this claim is addressed
to beings who are each constituted as an 'I' (in that it recognizes only individual goods as ultimately valuable and so seeks to ground the value of
social participation in relation to the interests individuals have as such).
(To anticipate, again: it is in according supreme normative weight to a
perspective that recognizes only the interests of unattached individuals—in addressing us each *only* as an 'I'—that Rousseau's theory differs
most importantly from Hegel's. I shall argue later that Hegel's theory implicitly relies on the Rousseauean strategy I have articulated here, insofar as it maintains that the rational social order realizes the good of all
individuals (as such). But Hegel's theory goes beyond Rousseau's in that
it also recognizes a strongly holistic collective good (and hence a further
justification of social participation), namely, the "self-determination" he
ascribes to the rational social order considered as a whole. Thus, for
Hegel, membership in the institutions of *Sittlichkeit* is rational from both
perspectives: because they satisfy individuals' fundamental interests and
because together they constitute a self-sufficient, rational whole that realizes the ideal of self-determination more completely than any human
individual.)

One way of bringing out the apparent paradox of Rousseau's argument
more clearly is to ask, If social members already conceive of themselves
primarily as members of substantive social wholes rather than as isolated individuals, what normative force could they find in a justification
of their institutions from the perspective of methodological atomism?[27]
Are not individuals who believe that legitimacy can be bestowed by a social contract committed to viewing the satisfaction of the interests of unattached individuals as the highest criterion of a rational social order?
And does this not contradict Rousseau's claim that, if they are to realize
their freedom, individuals must regard the collective good as integral to
their own and think of themselves, first and foremost, as members of a
larger whole?

In fact, Rousseau's position is not paradoxical, and seeing why it is not
is essential to grasping a basic feature of his—and also of Hegel's—view
of what rational justification in social theory must accomplish. We have
seen that Rousseau's theory, like Hegel's after him, emphasizes the importance of identity-constituting social bonds that exist prior to and

independently of rational reflection. Moreover, both theorists believe that membership in substantive social wholes brings with it goods that cannot be appreciated as such from outside of those groups. In these respects their views have deep affinities with those of contemporary communitarians. But unlike the latter, Hegel and Rousseau are also committed to the idea that the social wholes within which individuals find their identities are subject to stringent, nonparochial standards of rational acceptability. For them, in order to be rationally affirmable, a social order must be able to withstand the scrutiny of "universal" reason, one criterion of which is that the integrity of all its members *as individuals* be fully respected. In the case of both Hegel and Rousseau, this criterion includes the requirement that no collective ends be achieved at the expense of the fundamental interests (in freedom and material well-being) of any of its members. The kind of social members Hegel and Rousseau envisage, then, are individuals who have affective, identity-constituting attachments to others but at the same time feel the necessity of stepping back from their particular social relations in order to ask, But do these attachments satisfy the requirements of reason? And this, for modern subjects, includes the question, Do the institutions I belong to sufficiently recognize the worth of human individuals as such by ensuring that the fundamental interests of all can be met? One implication of this is that in the fully rational society individuals must conceive of themselves not only as members of particular social groups but also as *rational agents in general*—as subjects for whom the demands of universal reason are ultimately authoritative[28]—and as *individuals* who, as such, possess interests distinguishable from those of the groups to which they belong (and are justified in claiming the right to satisfy them). This is precisely what Hegel means to assert in claiming that the institutions of ethical life, in order to be fully rational, must be affirmable by moral subjects. How his vision of *Sittlichkeit* satisfies the demands of moral subjectivity is the topic of chapter 7.

Hegel

It is time now to return to the main topic of this study and attempt to answer the question that naturally arises from the preceding discussion: How does understanding the argumentational strategy of Rousseau's political theory shed light on the foundations of Hegel's theory of *Sittlich-*

keit? Hegel certainly does not appear to be (and indeed is not) a methodological atomist, but how exactly does his view of the relation between individual and collective goods differ from Rousseau's? More specifically, to what extent could Hegel agree with Rousseau that a complete account of the rational social order can be constructed in accord with some version of methodological atomism?

One's initial reaction to the latter question is likely to be a flat-out rejection of its suggestion that Hegel's approach to social theory might share something of significance with Rousseau's methodological atomism. There are at least two reasons this reaction is natural: First, Hegel quite clearly does not actually proceed by constructing rational social institutions on the basis of some antecedent account of the fundamental interests individuals have as such (a fact that is most readily seen in the absence in his theory of an account of the state of nature). Second, and less obviously, Hegel, unlike Rousseau, is not engaged in *constructing* social institutions at all. Rather, the social order described at length in the *Philosophy of Right* is made up of institutions Hegel claims to find already existing, at least in their basic outline, in his own time and place (which is to say, in some parts of western Europe in the early nineteenth century). For him the job of constructing a rational social world—or, more accurately, of laying its foundations—is one that has already been accomplished, in reality and not merely in thought, by the course of history. Given this view, Hegel conceives of his task as philosopher to be one of demonstrating that the social order we inhabit in fact satisfies in its basic outline the demands of reason (is hospitable to the realization of practical freedom), thereby enabling those of us who regard that order as indifferent or hostile to our aspiration to freedom to be reconciled to it. Yet even though Hegel does not set out to construct a rational social order from the bottom up, his assessment of the basic social institutions of modern Europe must make use of some conception of what makes those institutions rational, or good, and therefore worthy of their members' affirmation. For this reason it is still meaningful to ask how the normative standards at work in Hegel's social theory conceive of the relation between the interests social members have as individuals and the good that is thought to be achieved by the rational social order. In answering this question it is important not simply to assume that Hegel's refusal to employ the device of a state of nature implies that his social theory makes no appeal to an account of the interests individuals have as such. The question I want to focus on here is whether the foundation of Hegel's theory—his conception of social freedom—implicitly depends on some such account and, if so, what importance is accorded to those interests in his judgment that the family, civil society, and the state are, in their modern forms, rational institutions.

To pose this question is, in effect, to ask what lies behind Hegel's claims, cited earlier, that "it is only as a member of the state that the individual itself has objectivity, truth, and ethical life" and that "the vocation of individuals is to lead a universal life" (§258A). More specifically, what entitles Hegel to equate the individual's achievement of "objectivity" (the fulfilling of his "vocation") with leading a universal life within the rational social order? I have already investigated in detail the argument that enables Rousseau to put forth similar claims about the centrality of social membership to individuals' achieving an existence befitting of their nature as human beings: leading a universal life (in willing the general will) is the only way individuals who must engage in substantial social cooperation can advance their interests in their material well-being and at the same time obey only their own wills; in other words, leading a universal life is how they achieve their freedom.

It is clear that Hegel's basic position is in agreement with Rousseau's at least to the following extent: for Hegel fulfilling one's vocation (achieving "objectivity" or "truth") is essentially linked to one's social membership because *freedom* (in some sense of the term) constitutes one's essential nature as a human being and because such freedom is fully realized only in the rational social order. This much is unmistakably asserted by statements such as the following (already familiar from chapter 4): "It is because the determinations of ethical life constitute the concept of freedom that they are the . . . universal essence of individuals" (§145Z).[29] Beyond statements like this there are numerous passages that, in articulating what makes the institutions of *Sittlichkeit* rational, emphasize the point that social members achieve "substantial freedom" within them (§§149, 257). Yet despite such assertions, it is extremely difficult to determine the precise degree to which Hegel's basic argumentational strategy is similar to Rousseau's, primarily because Hegel never spells out in a completely unambiguous way what the freedom referred to in such passages consists in. The decisive issue here is whether the normative foundations of Hegel's social theory admit of reconstruction by means of an argument that possesses the same basic structure as Rousseau's. More precisely, to what extent does the value of those features of modern *Sittlichkeit* by virtue of which it qualifies as rational derive from the role they play in realizing some essence, or in advancing some fundamental interest, that could meaningfully be ascribed to individuals independently of their social membership? Is it possible to understand Hegel's position as invoking, even if only implicitly, some notion of the essence of human individuals that, like Rousseau's concept of freedom, can be abstractly defined (but not fully specified) independently of their social membership and whose primary theoretical function is to supply a general criterion for the kind of existence social institutions must allow individuals to achieve if their essential nature is to be realized? It is not difficult to find statements made by Hegel that lend themselves to being interpreted in this way, for example: "If one asks how individuality attains its highest right, the answer is the spiritual universality that is the state itself. Only in the state does the individual have objective freedom" (VPR2, 209–210). The claim that *individuality* has a "highest right" that is both defined in terms of freedom and satisfied only by achieving universality within the state (construed broadly as the social order in general) certainly suggests—though, admittedly, does not itself prove—that something akin to Rousseau's strategy is also at work in Hegel's account of *Sittlichkeit*.

The question on which the resolution of this issue turns is whether the freedom through which individuals achieve their highest right can meaningfully be regarded as *individually their own,* as a kind of self-determination that is in some significant sense won by each member of *Sittlichkeit* rather than merely by the social order considered as a whole. In other words, is it a freedom that, though realized only when individuals are incorporated into the social order as dependent members of a whole, nevertheless *resides* in the wills of individual social members and not simply in the social order's overall structure? With respect to Rousseau's conception of political freedom, the answer to the latter question is clearly yes: the freedom that is realized when citizens embrace the general will as their own can sensibly be said to belong to each social member rather than to the whole as such. Although there is an important sense in which Rousseau thinks free citizens must cease to conceive of themselves as—and hence cease to be—individuals (they must learn not to regard themselves as wholly self-standing beings whose primary good is distinct from the good of the social whole), his account of the rational state continues to accord a significant degree of integrity to citizens as individual units of agency. That the political freedom Rousseau champions is still a self-determination of the individual is seen in the fact that subjection to the general will counts as freedom (as *full* political freedom, which excludes being forced to be free) only if individual citizens, each regarded as the bearer of a distinct will, actually endorse the general will that governs them, as opposed to simply being the object of its commands. The freedom the rational state aims at realizing, then, depends on an affirmation of the general will by all in which the 'yes' is pronounced by each subject.

This brings us to a point that is of the utmost importance to the reconstruction of the foundations of Hegel's social theory: for Hegel, no less than for Rousseau, the realization of freedom within the rational social order requires that each individual affirm the laws and norms that govern the social participation of all. Social freedom is fully realized only insofar as *each* social member takes the universal ends of his institutions as his own: "The state . . . is the actuality within which the individual has and enjoys his freedom *but [only] by knowing, believing in, and willing the universal*" (PH, 38/XII, 55; emphasis added).[30] Hegel's insistence that social freedom comes about only by individuals having a conscious, voluntative relation to the collective will—only by their "knowing . . . and willing the universal"—implies that his social theory is no less committed than Rousseau's to securing a species of freedom that can be ascribed severally to its individual members and that is more or less identical to the freedom Rousseau believes citizens acquire by embracing the general will.[31]

Moreover, it is important to recall here that in addition to this Rousseauean point there is for Hegel a further sense in which individuals achieve a kind of self-determination through their social membership: in carrying out the various social roles with which they identify, they give real determinacy to their "selves" insofar as they realize their particular self-conceptions and achieve a socially recognized standing as a self of value. In establishing such identities for themselves within the world, social members achieve the state of being-with-oneself-in-another that Hegel identifies as the essential character of actualized freedom. Both of these points help to explain how, even from the philosopher's normative perspective, having a general will is not of merely instrumental value for individuals. For, as is true for both of the senses of self-determination distinguished here, "knowing, believing in, and willing the universal" is not simply a means to freedom but constitutive of it.

The conclusion to be drawn from these claims is that with respect to the realization of individuals' freedom the conditions Hegel's social theory imposes on rational social institutions are similar in content to and no less stringent than those Rousseau is led to adopt by an argumentational strategy that takes into account only interests that can be ascribed to individuals qua individuals. On this point Hegel's theory is in effect indistinguishable from a position, such as Rousseau's, that defines, without fully specifying, the essential nature of individuals independently of their social membership and then employs that concept to place constraints on acceptable institutional arrangements. In Hegel's case, as in Rousseau's, those restrictions imply that collective ends (the good of the family or state as a whole) may be achieved only through institutions that also allow each of their members to avoid subjection to a foreign will.

But if the theory of *Sittlichkeit* implicitly operates with a conception of the fundamental interests individuals have as such and uses that idea to place constraints on how the rational social order may be organized, why is Hegel not to be counted as a methodological atomist? What makes his basic approach to social theory different from that of a thinker like Rousseau? In broadest terms, the answer is that Hegel denies that a consideration of the interests individuals have as such is *sufficient* to ground a complete account of the rational social order. He claims, instead, that a fully adequate social theory must include the idea that the rational social order, considered as a whole, realizes a good—a species of self-determination—that is both higher than and irreducible to the goods or freedoms ascribable to individual social members. As we shall see, this feature of Hegel's view explains not only why he is not a methodological atomist but also why he rejects all weaker versions of the doctrine that collective goods are reducible to the good of individuals, including the one sketched at the beginning of this chapter. (Recall the example of the dance collective in which the good realized by the group was reducible to the good of individuals, but not to their good *as individuals*—that is, independently of their membership in that group.) This view concerning the irreducibility of collective goods finds expression in two distinctively Hegelian claims about the state—that the state is *un-*

conditioned and that it is *organically organized*—and each of these corresponds to a specific criticism Hegel brings against social contract theory in general. The best way to elucidate these two claims is to return briefly to Hegel's critique of the social contract tradition and to situate them within a more systematic consideration of what that critique amounts to.

The scattered remarks Hegel directs against social contract theory are notoriously elusive, but their main ideas can be formulated in terms of three relatively independent theses. The first is the claim, discussed at length earlier, that deriving the ends of the state from the interests of individuals as such commits one to regarding the state as having only instrumental value for its members. I have argued here that this criticism rests on a misunderstanding of the implications of social contract theory's individualistic starting point and that, contrary to Hegel's claim, social contract theory does not rule out the possibility of holding, as both he and Rousseau do, that in the rational state association with others is itself a final end of social members. The other two theses do, however, mark genuine differences between Hegel's position and social contract theory. One is the claim, alluded to at the beginning of this chapter, that the good realized by the rational state is unconditioned (or "divine") and therefore not reducible to the good of its individual members considered as such. The other thesis is expressed in Hegel's statements to the effect that social contract theory is incapable of doing justice to the state's true nature as an "ethical organization" (*sittliche Organisation*) (NL, 124/II, 519).[32] This point can be reformulated as the following claim: by taking into account only the fundamental interests individuals have as such, and by regarding those individuals "abstractly" (§303A)— as equal beings with identical interests, capacities, and natures—social contract theory renders itself incapable of understanding the state as an organically organized whole within which citizens occupy distinct and specialized roles. As we shall see, it is primarily the first of the two latter theses that is of interest in this reconstruction of the philosophical foundations of the theory of *Sittlichkeit;* yet given the large amount of confusion surrounding Hegel's critique of social contract theory in general, it will be worthwhile to consider what is at stake in the second claim as well and to determine its relevance to the main issue that concerns us here: the relation between individual and collective goods in Hegel's account of the rational social order.

I shall begin with the charge that social contract theory necessarily fails to do justice to the state's nature as an organic whole. How is this objection to be understood? As we saw in chapter 4, one of the important elements of Hegel's conception of social freedom is the idea that the social order as a whole embodies objective freedom when it is a teleologically organized, self-reproducing entity whose internal structure mirrors that of the Concept, or of reason itself. Included in this picture is the requirement that social members occupy specialized roles within society in order to carry out the various complex functions necessary for the social order to reproduce itself as the kind of being it essentially is. If one thinks only of the sphere of civil society, Hegel's claim is unremarkable, for it is a thoroughly familiar point that even a minimally complex system of production will require of its participants a degree of specialization that is likely to result in substantial diversity among the lifestyles and outlooks of those who occupy different economic roles. The complexity of the social order's economic needs requires that there be farmers and city folk, merchants and manufacturers, soldiers and civil servants, and it will not be surprising if this diversity of roles demands correspondingly diverse types of individuals. No serious social theorist of the modern world (the young Marx excepted) would take issue with this point. What distinguishes Hegel from social contract theorists such as Locke and Rousseau—indeed, from liberals of all stripes—is his insistence that the specialization found in civil society spills over into the political sphere and shapes the particular rights and duties individuals have in their roles as citizens. This is precisely the point Hegel means to express in statements such as the following: "The concrete state is a whole that is articulated into its particular spheres; the member of the state is a member of such an estate [of civil society], and it is only in his objective determination as such that he can be taken into account in the state" (§308A; emphases omitted).

In my view this doctrine represents the most important respect in which Hegel's understanding of the state diverges from liberal political theory. I shall argue, further, that it is the *only* aspect of Hegel's position that is unequivocally and irreconcilably at odds with the fundamental tenets of liberalism. I shall also claim that this unattractive and archaic doctrine is a relatively expendable part of Hegel's social theory that has little bearing on the relation between individual and collective goods. More precisely, it is possible to reject Hegel's claim that *as citizens* individuals relate to each other as specialized parts of an organic whole (the state) without ridding his theory of all, or even the most important, of its distinctive features. Moreover, overlooking that doctrine alters nothing of substance with respect to the question of whether the theory of *Sittlichkeit* accords primacy to individual or collective goods. But first let us see what this view of citizenship comes to.

The claim that individuals figure in the state only as members of a particular estate (or social class) implies that the rights and duties of citizenship are not assigned uniformly to individuals, regardless of social position, but differentially, according to the estate to which each belongs. Thus, for Hegel there is no general answer to the question, What are the rights and duties of citizens in a rational state? that does not take into account the role an individual occupies in civil society. This means that the specific ways in which citizens are allowed to take part in the affairs of the state are determined by their class membership. The most important example of this principle is that members of different estates play different roles in the legislative process through which the general will is constituted and expressed. For, as we saw briefly in chapter 4, civil servants participate directly in the formation and execution of laws according to their occupation within the state bureaucracy; members of the commercial class elect representatives to the legislative assembly through their particular corporations; and the interests of the agricultural class, both peasants' and landowners', are represented by unelected members of the landed aristocracy.

It should be obvious that this view of citizenship is incompatible with one of the fundamental tenets of social contract theory. For in setting out to derive the principles of political association from the idea of individuals who are free and equal in the state of nature, social contract theory commits itself to allotting the same basic rights of citizenship to all members of the state. No version of methodological atomism that begins with the assumption that individuals are qualitatively indistinguishable (in all politically relevant respects) can consistently uphold a view, like Hegel's, that assigns different rights of political participation to different classes of individuals. The fact that Hegel's political theory differentiates among individuals in this way may also appear to conflict with the claim I argued for earlier, namely, that the theory of *Sittlichkeit* implicitly operates with a conception of the fundamental interests individuals have as such and that it recognizes a set of social institutions as rational only if the fundamental interests of each, most notably the interest in freedom, can be realized within them. Further reflection, however, shows this impression to be mistaken: in Hegel's theory of *Sittlichkeit* the demand that the rational social order accommodate the fundamental interests of all individuals translates into the requirement that the organically structured social whole be constituted such that all individual members are able to maintain a free will while contributing in their own particular ways to reproducing their society in accord with the kind of being it essentially is. In the narrower context of Hegel's political theory this implies, among other things, that it must be possible for each member of the state to acquire a general will—to know and endorse as one's own the laws that govern society as a whole—in order to avoid being subject to a foreign will in one's role as citizen. In effect this requirement imposes two main conditions on rational political institutions. It means that the state must be structured so as to ensure not only that the particular interests of each class are taken into account (represented) in the legislative process but also that each (male) individual has available to him a means of gaining access to a point of view from which he can regard as good, and hence endorse, the laws that express the general will of his society.

Hegel's doctrine asserting differential rights of citizenship can be seen as the product of his attempt to satisfy the second of these conditions in light of his belief that the economic complexity of modern society requires diverse types of individuals who will have varying capacities and resources for reasoning about the common good and how to achieve it. The result of this attempt is the view that while all (male) individuals must have access to a universal standpoint from which they can affirm the general will, their having different natures[33] means that they must arrive at that standpoint through different routes. This is the thought underlying Hegel's claim that peasants come to affirm the general will on the basis of a relatively unreflective trust (E §528); that the business class does so through political participation mediated by the corporations; and that civil servants (who alone possess the requisite time and expertise) take part directly in the formation and execution of the general will. The aspect of Hegel's view that my reconstruction emphasizes is not the fact that individuals take different routes to arrive at a universal standpoint but the more fundamental requirement that there be some such route for each citizen.[34] Thus, although there is an obvious and important sense in which Hegel's political theory, in opposition to liberalism, treats citizens as unequals (they relate to the general will in different ways and have unequal say in its formation), there is another, more fundamental level of the theory at which individuals figure as equals (the particular interests of all must be represented, and each must be able to affirm the laws governing the whole). In short, Hegel's view is that while citizens are to be treated as equals in the sense that all are taken to have a fundamental interest in being free, the concrete ways in which they achieve their freedom will of necessity vary from class to class.

I shall now turn to the second of the two theses that differentiate Hegel's view of the state from social contract theory, the claim that the state embodies an unconditioned good that cannot be broken down into the good it achieves for its individual members. Although assertions to this effect can be found throughout Hegel's texts, by far the fullest statement of the view appears at the beginning of the *Philosophy of Right*'s discussion of the state in section three of "Ethical Life." Fragments of this passage have been cited earlier, but it will be helpful to have a more complete version of the passage before us now as we attempt to make sense of Hegel's claim:

> The state is . . . that which is *rational* in and for itself [*das an und für sich Vernünftige*]. This substantial unity is an absolute, unmoved end in itself in which freedom achieves its highest right, just as this final end possesses the highest right in relation to individuals, whose *highest duty* is to be members of the state . . . The state in and for itself is the ethical whole [*das sittliche Ganze*]—the actualization of freedom—and it is the absolute end of reason that freedom be actual [*wirklich*]. The state is spirit [*Geist*] that stands in the world and *consciously* actualizes itself therein . . . The existence of the state is God's march in the world; its foundation is the power of reason actualizing itself as [free] will (§258+Z).[35]

Appended to this passage, and highly relevant to the critique of social contract theory, is a statement directed against Rousseau in which Hegel asserts that understanding the state on the model of a contract has the consequence of denying the state's status as divine—as something that "exists in and for itself"—and therefore "destroys its absolute authority and majesty" (§258A).

In addition to the claim of primary concern to us here—that the state possesses unconditioned value (is an "absolute end in itself")—this passage makes four closely related assertions about the state:

1. The state is *rational;* (it is an "absolute end of reason").
2. The state is *free;* (it is the highest, most completely realized embodiment of practical freedom).
3. The state is *divine;* (it is a form of spirit, or *Geist,* that exists "in and for itself").
4. The state possesses *absolute authority* and *majesty* in relation to human individuals; (their "highest duty" is to belong to the state).

Statements 1 through 3 are to be understood as enumerating three properties of the state—rationality, freedom, and divinity—that are the source of the unconditioned value Hegel thinks it has. Statement 4, in contrast, articulates what Hegel takes to be one of the consequences of the state's having such value, namely, that it possesses both majesty and absolute authority over its members. In order to understand Hegel's view that the state realizes a good above and beyond the good it has for individuals, we must examine each of these points in some detail.

Before doing so, however, it is important to note that in the passage cited here Hegel explicitly equates the state with "the ethical whole" (*das sittliche Ganze).* This is significant, for it means that the characteristics I have just identified apply not to the specifically political institutions of *Sittlichkeit* taken on their own but to the social order as a whole, which comprises not only the state narrowly construed but also civil society and the family. One important implication of this point is that the social entity Hegel characterizes as having an unconditioned value (the social order as a whole) covers a much larger domain than the set of institutions that social contract theory aims to give an account of (the state in the narrower, strictly political sense). Apart from making the import of Hegel's critique of social contract theory even more difficult to assess, this fact is significant because it points to a further way in which Hegel's own view of the state in the narrow sense diverges from that put forth by standard versions of liberalism: for Hegel the political sphere is not a detachable, relatively self-standing realm but one that is integrally related to the other (nonpolitical) institutions that make up the social order as a whole. This is to say that it is impossible to formulate the principles of rational political association independently of an account of which nonpolitical social institutions are rationally necessary (necessary in order for practical freedom to be realized) and an understanding of how they contribute to that end. For, on Hegel's view, the proper ends of political institutions are themselves partially defined in relation to the needs of the other required institutions; thus, one of the primary ends of rational legislation is to ensure the flourishing of the family and civil society, without which the will's freedom could not be realized.

With this point in mind I shall begin to examine the three properties of the social order by virtue of which it is claimed to have an unconditioned value. To say that the social order is rational—that it is an "absolute end of reason"—is, in this context, simply to say that it serves the end of realizing freedom. ("It is the absolute end of reason that freedom be actual.") It might seem that an explanation of what makes the social order rational ought also to make reference to the fact that it is organized in accord with the Concept, or with what Hegel takes to be the structure of reason itself. But in fact this quality of the social order is not something distinct from its freedom-promoting character properly understood. For, as we saw in chapter 1, the structure Hegel ascribes to the Concept is derived from a consideration of how an entity must be constituted in order to exist as self-determined (here in the sense that its particular properties are determined by itself, by what it needs in order to achieve its essential nature). The Concept is equated with reason—with "that which is rational in and for itself"—only because to embody its structure is to achieve a certain form of self-determination. Thus, the task of explicating the first property attributed to the social order leads directly to a consideration of the second: What makes the social order an embodiment of freedom? In response to this question the passage cited here has little to add to the view I have set out at great length in the preceding chapters: the social order endorsed by the theory of *Sittlichkeit* realizes freedom because (1) as a whole, it is self-determining in the sense of being self-sustaining and exhibiting the rational structure of the Concept; (2) it secures the necessary conditions of personhood and moral subjectivity; and (3) its members find their particular identities by participating in it, and, in embracing the general will as their own, they remain subject only to their own wills.

In explicating what Hegel means when he characterizes the social order as rational and free, I have thus far failed to make mention of a number of puzzling, closely related terms that recur throughout the passage cited earlier: in addition to being rational and free, the state is said to be spiritual, absolute, existing "in and for itself," and "unmoved" (by anything other than itself). These predicates are all bound up with the third assertion I have isolated here, the claim that the state is divine (or, as Hegel says elsewhere, "something divine on earth" [§272Z]). It is really the ascription of this quality to the social order that adds something new to the account of *Sittlichkeit* already given and is most directly connected to the view that the rational social order realizes a good that cannot be analyzed in terms of the good of its individual members. But what does Hegel mean to convey to us by comparing the state to God? Characterizing the state as something divine on earth is his way of expressing the view that (except for world history when regarded as a meaningful whole) the rational social order is the worldly entity that comes closest to fully embodying the attributes he associates with a divine being. This view is closely connected to the assertion, made frequently throughout Hegel's texts, that *Sittlichkeit* is a *substance* (§§144, 146, 156).[36] What Hegel has in mind is best brought out by calling to mind Spinoza's definition of substance and his identification of it with God. For Spinoza substance is defined primarily in terms of the quality of self-sufficiency (or independence), as "that which is in itself and conceived through itself, i.e., that whose concept does not require the concept of another thing, from which it must be formed."[37] In other words, substance is that which is fully self-sufficient, both ontologically (with respect to its existence) and conceptually (with respect to its "concept," or essence). And, as we saw in chapter 1, Hegel follows Spinoza in associating this idea with freedom, or self-determination, because to be self-sufficient in this way is to be the sole source of one's own determinations, or qualities. Moreover, since substance thus defined is completely independent of anything external to itself, Spinoza argues that it must be infinite (unlimited by anything external) and therefore godlike. In Hegel's terminology such a being also qualifies as absolute because it has an unconditioned existence and nature (unconditioned by anything other than itself).

Thus, Hegel's provocative assertion that the rational social order is divine can be translated into the claim that the institutions of *Sittlichkeit*, taken together, embody to a high degree Spinoza's ideal of ontological and conceptual self-sufficiency. With respect to its existence, the rational social order approximates complete self-sufficiency and comes closer to achieving it than any human individual can, because its specialized organic structure (the topic of chapter 4) enables it continually to reproduce itself with all of its essential qualities. Of course, the modern state itself falls short of full ontological self-sufficiency, since its coming about depends on historical preconditions external to itself, including, for example, the ancient Greek experience of freedom in the polis, the development of Christianity, and Napoleon's extension of the French Revolution to western Europe. This is the basis for Hegel's view, alluded to earlier, that world history as a whole represents a more perfect example of divinity on earth than the modern state.

The claim that the institutions of *Sittlichkeit* embody conceptual self-sufficiency is more difficult to spell out, but I want to suggest that, if completely thought through, it shows itself to be identical to the assertion, already familiar to us, that the rational social order is organized in accord with the Concept.[38] It may help to begin by thinking of conceptual self-sufficiency as a kind of explanatory self-sufficiency:[39] a being is conceptually self-sufficient when an explanation of it can be given without making reference to anything other than itself. The problem with this suggestion is that explanations are of many different types, and so it is necessary to specify the kind (or kinds) of explanation at issue here. There are, I think, two senses in which Hegel considers the modern state to be explanatorily self-sufficient. The first involves the idea that the various features of the rational social order can be explained teleologically, that is, explained not in terms of something external to the state but in relation to itself (to its own essential nature as self-determining). To the extent that the modern state can be shown to be constituted as it is because its particular features serve the end of realizing practical freedom, it can be said to depend only on itself for an explanation of what it is. The other sense in which the rational social order is explanatorily self-sufficient is a bit closer to Spinoza's definition of substance as that whose *concept* does not depend on the concept of anything other. The thought here is that we can explain what the state as a whole is—we can grasp its essential nature—without referring to some concept beyond its own (beyond the concept of freedom itself). In the present context this is best understood as the claim that explaining the *value* the rational state has—understanding the realization of its essence as a worthy end—requires no reference to any end or value other than its own. This is simply to say that the state's value does not derive from some role it plays in service of an end other than that of achieving its own essence; instead, the rational state is an "unmoved" end in itself.

In this context it is important to note that Hegel's conception of the divine includes one crucial element that is absent from Spinoza's definition of substance: God—or in Hegel's terminology, *Geist*—is not merely ontologically and conceptually self-sufficient; it is also conscious of itself as such. It is this element of self-consciousness that makes the divine being not simply a substance but also a subject. (And, as *The Phenomenology of Spirit* famously pronounces, it is the conjunction of these two qualities—substantiality and subjectivity—that defines spirit [PhG, ¶17; 23].) In this respect, too, the rational social order approximates the attributes of divinity, for, as Hegel tells us in the passage cited earlier, "the state is spirit that . . . *consciously* actualizes itself [in the world]."[40] Although Hegel is clearly committed to the idea that the rational state possesses a collective consciousness (and will) that exist above and beyond the consciousness (and will) of any of its individual members, there is no need to think of this consciousness as involving some mysterious, superhuman species of awareness (§257). Rather, the self-consciousness of the rational state consists simply in the fact that its activity is governed by laws that are (1) publicly known; (2) consciously self-prescribed through the political participation of its members; and (3) (if social freedom is perfectly realized) fully transparent in the sense that all citizens recognize them as good.

We are now in a position to return to the issue that led us into the topic of divinity in the first place: Hegel takes the rational social order to embody a good that is both higher than and irreducible to the good of its individual members because the institutions of *Sittlichkeit,* considered as a single whole, constitute a will-governed being that embodies the ideal of perfect self-sufficiency more completely than any human individual can. Because the rational social whole comes closer to achieving divine independence than the finite wills of individuals, it occupies a higher place on Hegel's scale of values, or realizes a higher good, than its less self-sufficient parts.[41] Moreover, it is important to recognize that what gives the social whole its higher status on Hegel's view cannot simply be reduced to the ways it furthers the interests of its individual members as such. For the qualities of the rational social order that make it divinely self-sufficient (or nearly so) are strongly holistic properties that reside in that order as a totality—in how its parts work together as a whole—rather than in the individual parts themselves (just as the property of self-sufficiency can be ascribed to a self-sustaining organism as a whole but not, properly speaking, to the individual cells that make it up). At most—and I shall return to this later—we can meaningfully say that as members of *Sittlichkeit* individuals *partake of* the divine qualities of their social order but not that they themselves exhibit them.

Given this account of the source of the state's unconditioned value, the question that remains to be answered is what implications the state's divine character has for its individual members and their relation to it. This question brings us back to Hegel's claim, set out earlier in statement 4, that in relation to human individuals the rational social order possesses absolute authority and majesty. In ascribing a kind of majesty to the state, Hegel means to claim that the self-sufficient social order deserves to be revered by its members as something greater than themselves, as a living being that both surpasses their own more limited capacity for self-determination and, in surviving the deaths of its own individual members, comes as close as is earthly possible to overcoming human finitude.[42] Hegel clearly believes that the fully rational social order—this self-standing, enduring, harmoniously ordered organism whose every part and function is subordinated to a single rational end—ought to inspire in human beings a feeling of awe similar to what we experience when regarding a perfectly achieved work of art. Yet the reverence a social member feels for the state differs crucially from that evoked by a work of art, for the being whose majesty the social member beholds is not some external object, essentially unconnected to himself, but a being to which he inseparably belongs and whose qualities are therefore, in at least a limited sense, his own: not only does he partake of the state's divine qualities as a dependent member of the completed whole, he is also the (partial) cause of those qualities, since his social participation contributes to their achievement.

Moreover, this is true for members of *Sittlichkeit* in more than just the sense in which it could also be said of the cells of a biological organism that they partake of and contribute to the organism's self-sustaining quality. This is because the members of *Sittlichkeit,* unlike the cells of an organism, are themselves subjects who are capable both of forming a conception of themselves (a conception of what is essential to who they are) and of taking a conscious, affirmative (or negative) attitude to the whole to which they belong. This means that human individuals have the capacity to *identify with* the larger entity of which they are part; they are able, in other words, to regard their social order as one with themselves and (for that reason) to take pride in its properties as their own. With this thought I return to one of the fundamental Hegelian doctrines referred to in chapter 1, namely, that the distinctive characteristic of subjectivity—a characteristic that is indispensable to the capacity for freedom—is the subject's ability to regard itself as distinct from its object and at the same time to overcome, or negate, the otherness of the object by seeing it as in some sense identical to itself. In the case of social membership, being a subject enables individuals both to recognize the social order as something greater than (and therefore not strictly identical to) themselves and, simultaneously, to think of themselves as one with the whole in such a way that enables them to regard not only its ends but also its properties as their own. Thus, as conscious subjects, the members of *Sittlichkeit* can partake of the divine qualities of their social order in a way that would not be available to them if, like the organism's cells, they lacked subjectivity. Through their conscious identification with the whole, individuals are able not only to be aware of their partaking of and contributing to the state's godlike qualities but also to find a kind of satisfaction in that fact, as if those qualities were their own. What Hegel means to claim, then, is that belonging to the rational social order and having the appropriate conscious relation to it affords social members the opportunity to realize—more fully than if they were, or took themselves to be, nothing more than individuals—what his philosophy takes to be the deepest, *spiritual* aspirations of human beings as embodied in the ideal of substantiality, namely, the aspirations to be fully self-determining and to overcome one's own mortality by achieving a more enduring existence than one has on one's own, an existence that approximates the indestructible, self-standing, "substantial" being of things.[43]

Although Hegel's view that the state's proper mission is (in part) to satisfy certain spiritual needs of its citizens is likely to seem alien to modern readers, it is no doubt his claim that the state possesses absolute authority in relation to its individual members that is most jolting to our modern (liberal) ears. If there is a single tenet that unites the many versions of liberal political thought, it is surely the idea that the state's legitimate authority is not absolute but limited to serving the common good of its members (and, in the case of social contract theory, to doing so without violating the fundamental interests of any one of them). But, again, before concluding that Hegel departs so radically from the main-stream of modern political thought, we should pause to consider what exactly his claim amounts to: What sort of "absolute" authority is implied by the state's godlike nature?[44] As the passage cited earlier makes clear, one implication of the social order's divine status is that the "highest duty" of human individuals is to belong to the state. Yet, as we have already seen, this view itself need not mark a divergence from the social contract tradition, since Rousseau arrives at essentially the same position by arguing that only as a fully integrated citizen of the rational state can each individual realize his nature as a free being. Once again, the real worry for liberals comes down to whether Hegel's view, in ascribing absolute authority to the state, gives it license to disregard or sacrifice the legitimate interests of individuals for the sake of achieving its own, allegedly higher ends. This worry is reinforced by the fact that Hegel makes a number of statements that appear to support precisely this conclusion. In discussing the state's right to protect itself militarily and to call on its citizens to risk their lives in its defense, Hegel speaks of war as a phenomenon that reveals the state's "absolute power over everything individual and particular, over life and the rights of property" and that "brings to consciousness . . . the nullity of those spheres" (§323). More famously, Hegel's philosophy of history abounds with references to human individuals as the "unconscious tools" (§344) of world history who are necessarily "sacrificed and abandoned" (PH, 33/XII, 49) to its own higher aims. According to that view, world history achieves reason's ends not merely without the knowledge or consent of the individuals who carry them out but also at the expense of their own happiness and interests. As a process that realizes an end whose greatness exceeds the merely human, history "requires that many an innocent flower be trampled and many things crushed on its path" (PH, 32/XII, 49).

In assessing the import of statements such as these, it is important to distinguish clearly between two apparently similar but in fact quite different types of claims Hegel makes, each of which is exemplified by the two assertions cited here. The first assertion aims to articulate the nature and content of the state's legitimate authority and to specify what duties citizens have to the state by virtue of that authority. As such, it clearly belongs to Hegel's theory of *Sittlichkeit* and, more specifically, to his account of the state in its narrower, strictly political sense. The second claim occupies a different place in Hegel's system, namely, his philosophy of history. The crucial difference between these two philosophical projects is that the first concerns itself with phenomena of will (understood as the activities of social institutions and their members) that are part of the here and now and constitute an ongoing system of activity that fully satisfies the requirements of reason. In the modern state, as Hegel describes it, reason has achieved a complete, and therefore final, realization of its ends. In this sphere of philosophy, to comprehend a particular social practice as rational (as freedom-promoting) is at the same to endorse it as a worthy undertaking for those who inhabit the modern world.

The second philosophical project, in contrast, is a purely retrospective, contemplative enterprise aimed exclusively at enabling us to adopt a particular attitude to the past—one in which, by understanding the past as serving the ends of reason, we become reconciled to it.[45] Its primary concern is to make it possible for us to affirm, and hence to become reconciled to, a history that appears at first to be nothing more than a senseless, endlessly recurring series of events in which evil, servitude, and suffering consistently win out over good, freedom, and happiness. In this sphere of philosophy, revealing the rationality of a part of the past does not amount to recommending it as a course of action for modern individuals; rather, to comprehend a part of history as rational is to grasp it as a necessary developmental phase in the cosmic process through which spirit achieves its defining end, that of making the world into a fully rational, self-comprehending substance. Since this mode of philosophical understanding justifies the past by seeing it as a historically necessary condition of spirit's achieving its supreme goal, it will regard some aspects of the past as *instrumentally* rational only—that is, necessary as a means to the full realization of reason's ends but not themselves part of a world where those ends are finally and perfectly achieved. Thus, the claim of Hegel's philosophy of history that the sacrifice of individuals for the sake of spirit's higher goals is rational and necessary does not commit him, as a philosopher of the rational social order, to the view that a similar sacrifice is required or acceptable in the modern state, where reason is fully realized.

I have already made known my belief that it is possible to appreciate the force of the main ideas underlying Hegel's vision of the rational social order without accepting his theodicean account of history. For this reason my aim here is not to assess the merits of that account but only to draw attention to the basic difference between it and the philosophical project undertaken in the theory of *Sittlichkeit* in order to show that the claims Hegel makes in his philosophy of history as to the expendability of individuals have no direct implications for how he thinks individuals will relate to the state in the fully achieved, perfectly rational social world. Thus, of the two issues raised earlier, the only one directly relevant to our concerns here is the alleged duty of citizens to risk their lives in defense of their homeland, for it alone addresses the question of what kind of authority over individuals Hegel's theory confers on the state and whether the fully rational social order is one in which society as a whole has its own higher ends that must (or may) be achieved at the expense of individuals' fundamental interests. How, then, does Hegel's discussion of the military obligations of citizens help to clarify what he means by ascribing absolute authority to the state?

First, it is extremely important to note that the *only* concrete duties Hegel infers from the state's alleged absolute authority over individuals are the obligations of citizens to risk their lives in military service for their homeland[46] and, less important, to surrender their property to the state when the exigencies of war require it (§324). Moreover, the conditions under which the state has the right to demand such sacrifices of its citizens are precisely specified: "[Only] when the state as such—its self-sufficiency [*Selbständigkeit*]—is endangered, does duty call on all citizens to defend their state" (§326); only for "the maintenance of the state's independence and sovereignty" (§324) can individuals be required to risk their lives in war. Statements such as these make it clear that in asserting the state's authority over individuals to be absolute, Hegel does not mean that there are no, or only very few, limits to its legitimate authority but rather that in certain rare and precisely defined circumstances the state has the right to demand of its citizens that they put at risk something that is "absolute" from their perspective as individuals, namely, their own lives. When this point is made explicit, it becomes more difficult to see where the disagreement lies, or even whether there is one, between Hegel and liberals concerning the nature of the state's authority. It is hard to imagine that liberal political theories would want to deny Hegel's conclusion that citizens have the obligation to risk their lives defending their own (just) state when its sovereignty is endangered. As Hegel himself understands it, the disagreement between his position and social contract theory on this issue is not over whether citizens have this particular duty but over the more fundamental question of what philosophical principles are required in order to justify the claim that they do. In setting out his own position, Hegel argues that a theory of the state based on the idea of a contract (or any species of methodological atomism) is incapable of explaining how citizens could have a duty to risk their lives for their state and, by implication, that only a theory that recognizes the social whole as realizing a good of a higher type than the finite ends of its individual members has the resources to do so: "If the state is regarded only as civil society and its final end located in *the protection of the life and property* of individuals, the requirement to make this sacrifice [of one's life] is based on a severe miscalculation; for such protection is not achieved by sacrificing what is supposed to be protected" (§324A).

But here again Hegel is mistaken in his claim that social contract theory, or methodological atomism in general, is incapable of grounding the duty of citizens to risk their lives in defense of their state. Moreover, his belief in this claim rests on the very same assumption that was at work in the critique of the social contract tradition considered previously, namely, that its methodological atomism commits social contract theory to regarding the protection of individuals' life and property as the ultimate end of political association. If Hegel's assumption were true, he would perhaps be correct in concluding that his imagined liberal opponents are unable to account for the duty of citizens to risk their lives in military service, and this for the reason he implicitly appeals to in the passage quoted here: if political authority is legitimate only insofar as it protects the fundamental interests each individual has independently of membership in the state, and if the most basic of those interests is the preservation of life, then putting their lives on the line for the good of their country can only be seen as exceeding the bounds of what the state can rightfully require of its citizens. We have already seen, however, that there is no reason that a theory committed to methodological atomism must limit the ends of political association to the protection of individuals' lives and property and that at least one important version of social contract theory—Rousseau's—avoids doing so by including the interest in freedom among the interests it ascribes to individuals as such and by arguing that freedom cannot be fully realized unless individuals take their membership in their political community to be a constitutive part of their own identities. Moreover, this (methodologically atomist) strategy suffices to give Rousseau the resources for explaining both why individuals have a duty to risk their lives for their homeland[47] and how they could be motivated to do so. For if belonging to the state is both an expression of one's own conscious identity and necessary for realizing one's essential human nature (as free), then the loss of one's state is tantamount to the loss of oneself (or, more precisely, to the loss of a substantial part of oneself, since membership in the state does not exhaustively constitute one's identity). For such individuals the willingness to put one's life on the line for the sake of the state's sovereignty and independence is simply an expression of the attitude that selfhood has a higher value than mere life and that it is sometimes reasonable to risk the latter in order to avoid the more horrible prospect of an existence absent of one's self.

Because Hegel takes over the Rousseauean principle that human individuals cannot realize their essential nature as free beings (cannot satisfy a fundamental interest they have as individuals) unless they are able to regard their membership in a political community as (partially) constitutive of their own identity, he is wrong to think that his ascription of divinity or unconditioned value to the social whole is necessary in order to explain either the duty citizens have to put their lives at risk when their state's independence is endangered or their motivation for doing so. Since Hegel has no quarrel with the social contract tradition over whether citizens of the rational state have such a duty, nor a need to reach beyond the resources of methodological atomism in order to make sense of it, is there, then, no real difference between Hegel and methodological atomists on the nature of the state's authority? Such a difference exists, I believe, but it turns out to be both less significant and of a different nature than we are likely at first to expect. Hegel's divergence from traditional liberalism on this issue is located not in the actual duties each assigns to citizens but rather in the attitude, or frame of mind, the respective theories envisage members of a rational political order as having when making the sacrifices demanded by the state. This suggestion brings us back to Hegel's point concerning the majesty of the self-sufficient social order and his claim that it deserves to be revered by its members as a being greater than themselves, as an entity that both achieves the ideal of self-determination more perfectly than they are capable of and surpasses, as greatly as possible, the limits of human finitude. The aspect of Hegel's view that distinguishes it from Rousseau's and from other versions of methodological atomism is the idea that members of *Sittlichkeit* regard the legitimate demands their state makes on them as authoritative not only because they subjectively identify with the social whole—not only because they regard it as an extension of themselves and as "of their own essential nature" (§147)—but also because they revere its quality of self-sufficiency (*Selbständigkeit*) for itself (§146) and recognize it as a higher good, and hence a worthier goal, than the satisfaction of their own merely particular ends.[48] In other words, maintaining the state's independence and sovereignty is an important project for them not only because it is necessary for achieving their own particular ends and for realizing their essential nature as free but also because the idea of a self-sufficient, perfectly achieved will carries weight with them and has the power to motivate them to do what they can in order to give that divine ideal an earthly existence.

The fact that Hegel's theory of *Sittlichkeit* invokes a version of Spinoza's conception of divine substance in order to explain the state's authority is no doubt one important reason for the widespread perception among contemporary philosophers that his theory does not merit serious attention as a vision of the rational social order. One obvious objection to this aspect of Hegel's theory is that it implausibly supposes that human individuals could, or even ought to, care whether or not the social order exhibits a property like self-sufficiency in Spinoza's sense. While showing the social order to be conceptually and ontologically self-sufficient may suffice to persuade a confirmed Spinozist that it is worthy of our reverence, those qualities seem far too abstract to be of much concern to ordinary members of society, or even to philosophers who do not share the presuppositions of Spinoza's metaphysics. But this objection can be answered if we bring to mind all that is included in the concept of self-sufficiency as it is actually applied in the theory of *Sittlichkeit*. Doing so reveals that, for Hegel, to revere the social order for its divine self-sufficiency is nothing more than to revere it as a set of institutions that is *systematically rational* in the sense that it both coordinates and realizes the various components of the good, as he conceives it. According to this view, the self-sufficient social order is an enduring, self-contained, self-reproducing system of institutions rationally organized so as to realize the practical freedom of individuals (in all its various senses), to harmonize that freedom with their basic well-being, and to accomplish these aims with the full awareness of its members.

A second, more fundamental objection to Hegel's use of the concept of divine substance brings us back to one aspect of the primary issue this chapter has attempted to address. The charge here is that regarding the state as something absolute, or unconditioned, inevitably makes the interests of finite individuals into a secondary concern of political theory, resulting in a view that permits those interests to be easily overridden for the sake of the community's higher, collective ends. One of the most important achievements of the present chapter is to have demonstrated that this objection, too, is unfounded. It is predicated on the natural but mistaken assumption that Hegel thinks of the divine as a transcendent being separate from, rather than immanent to, the realm of the finite. In other words, the error underlying this objection could be characterized as the failure to appreciate sufficiently the *pantheistic* character of the divine as Hegel (again following Spinoza) conceives it. Still, in order to draw the proper conclusions from this feature of Hegel's position it is necessary to distinguish two possible ways of understanding the pantheistic thesis that all is god. On one of those interpretations Hegel's position merely incorporates a secularized version of the view that a spark of divinity dwells within every human individual. Thus, 'all is god' would mean that all human beings by nature exhibit important similarities to god and that these similarities obligate us to accord a certain dignity and inviolability to each individual. Something like this view can indeed be ascribed to Hegel, insofar as he—in essential agreement with Rousseau, Kant, and other social contract theorists—makes it a condition of the rational social order that its members' activity be governed by laws that can be affirmed by all, thereby accommodating the freedom, and hence the essential dignity, of each (male) individual. According to the second, more genuinely pantheistic reading, 'all is god' means not that each unit that makes up the whole has something godlike within it but rather that divinity pervades the entirety of what is and consists in some (strongly holistic) quality that belongs to the whole only when its otherwise finite and imperfect parts are properly ordered. This view finds expression in Hegel's theory in his implicit claim that the divine resides in, and is nothing more than, a certain systematic arrangement of elements that in themselves are finite but that, taken as a whole, embody the qualities of a fully self-sufficient being. Because Hegel subscribes to both of these versions of the pantheistic thesis, the divinity of the whole, as he conceives it, cannot compete with the integrity or dignity of the human individuals that are its parts. On the contrary, part of what constitutes the majesty of the fully rational state for Hegel is that it achieves its collective ends while also accommodating the fundamental interests its members have as individuals, including (most important) their interest in being free. For it to achieve the strongly holistic properties of ontological and conceptual self-sufficiency at the expense of the freedom or other fundamental interests of its members would be to fall short of the very demanding ideal Hegel thinks modern social institutions are capable of measuring up to. That Hegel's conception of social freedom is one in which the freedom of the whole includes the freedom of individuals as one of its essential components is made evident by his explicit disavowal of "a concept of the general freedom of all that is dissociated from the freedom of individuals" as an "empty abstraction" (NL, 88–89/II, 476). (This at least captures the basic intent of Hegel's theory. In the next and final chapter I shall consider in detail the extent to which Hegel succeeds in reconciling what might be called the rights of the whole with the aspect of individual dignity that worries his liberal critics most, the rights of moral subjectivity.)

Before bringing this chapter to a close, I wish to articulate more concisely what we have learned concerning Hegel's relationship to methodological atomism. First, we have seen that, contrary to appearances, Hegel's theory of *Sittlichkeit* operates with a conception of the fundamental interests individuals have as such and makes it a necessary condition of the rational social order that those interests be realizable for each social member. (In addition, Hegel's understanding of what those interests are and how they are realized within society is closely related to the account of the same given by a prominent adherent of methodological atomism, Rousseau.) This important point of agreement between methodological atomism and the theory of *Sittlichkeit* can be expressed more loosely as the claim that the social order's being good for individuals, as individuals, is a necessary condition of its being rational. Moreover, this formulation of the point represents the proper interpretation of Allen Wood's correct but imprecise assertion, cited earlier, that for Hegel collective goods have value because they have value for individuals.

Second, we saw that Hegel's divergence from methodological atomism can be located in his denial that a consideration of the fundamental interests of individuals as such is *sufficient* to ground a complete account of the rational social order, and this for two reasons: first, because methodological atomism cannot do justice to the organic character of the rational social order (including the different rights and duties individuals are said to have in their roles as citizens); and, second, because it cannot account for the social order's status as unconditioned, or divine. The second, more fundamental point is the basis for Hegel's claim, in opposition to methodological atomism, that satisfying the fundamental interests of individuals is not the *highest* good achieved by the rational social order. By claiming that the latter is godlike, and by locating its divinity in certain (strongly holistic) properties it has only when regarded as a whole, Hegel commits himself to the view that it realizes a collective good that is higher than, and irreducible to, the finite goods it secures for individuals. This conclusion points to an important qualification that must be made of the general assertion that in Hegel's social theory collective goods have value because they have value for individuals. For it implies that Hegel recognizes an aspect of the good realized by the rational social order that cannot be understood as a good of individuals. It is more accurate to say, then, that the social order's being good for individuals is a necessary condition of its being rational but is not exhaustive of its goodness. Another way of expressing this point is to say that it is not possible to reconstruct Hegel's social theory by beginning only with an account of the fundamental interests of individuals in a hypothetical state of nature. (This is the point Hegel means to be making in §156Z, when he distinguishes two possible starting points of social theory, "individuality" and "substantiality," and explicitly rejects the methodological "atomism" inherent in the former.) The crux of Hegel's argumentational strategy, in contrast, is to begin with an abstract account of the properties a will would have to exhibit in order to qualify as fully self-determined (or self-sufficient) and then to ask, What concrete phenomenon most fully embodies the properties of a self-determined will? The nonindividualistic aspects of Hegel's theory of *Sittlichkeit* are the result of his answer to this question, namely, that the will of a single human individual can realize those properties only very imperfectly and that only a rational community, considered as a whole, can come close to achieving the highest ideal of practical philosophy, complete independence from determination by an other.

7

The Place of Moral Subjectivity
in Ethical Life

The principal question addressed by this chapter is whether social freedom as Hegel conceives it is compatible with the freedom of moral subjectivity. In other words, can individuals who find "their own essence" (§E514) within their social roles also think of themselves as, and be, independent moral subjects? In order to answer this question it will be necessary to undertake a more detailed examination of Hegel's conception of moral subjectivity and to extend our grasp of how the institutions endorsed by his social theory are supposed to accommodate the important fact that their members are moral subjects.

In chapter 1 I provisionally located the central feature of moral subjectivity in the capacity to determine oneself to act in accord with one's own understanding of the good. I also noted that moral subjectivity is closely bound up with a kind of practical freedom, or self-determination of the will, since it involves the will's giving itself ends in accord with ethical standards that derive not from external, or foreign, sources but (in a sense to be further specified) from the will itself. Another way of expressing the basic ideal implicit in Hegel's account of moral subjectivity is to say that human agents ought to be more than simply subject to (governed by) the rational standards of the good that obligate them; they ought also to be the source of those standards. For only when those standards are in some significant sense the subject's own can behavior that is governed by them be regarded as free, or self-determined. Formulated in yet another way, Hegel's point is that individuals realize themselves as moral subjects only when they find the source of moral authority within themselves rather than in something merely external. Moral subjects, then, are supposed to be deeply and radically free in the sense that, as self-sufficient arbiters of the good, they need rely on nothing external to their own subjectivity in order to know what duty requires of them. With respect to the dictates that obligate its will, a moral subject is, in the words of one of the principal originators of this modern ideal of moral agency, "a perfectly free lord of all, subject to none."[1]

Since the fundamental idea behind Hegel's theory of *Sittlichkeit* is that social institutions are rational because, and to the extent that, they realize practical freedom, the question to be raised here is easily discerned: How do the institutions Hegel endorses help to realize the kind of self-determination appropriate to moral subjects? Because this freedom appears to consist in something wholly internal to the individual—a relation merely between one's understanding of the good and one's own actions—it may not initially be clear how social institutions could be implicated in its realization. Although a full answer to this question cannot be given without the more precise account of moral subjectivity provided in the following, the sketch just presented enables us to recognize two general ways in which social institutions could be regarded as fostering the freedom of moral subjects. The first of these has already been touched upon in chapter 5 under "the objective component" of social freedom. One of the central doctrines of this part of Hegel's theory is that rational social institutions secure the preconditions of practical freedom through a process of *Bildung*, or education—that is, by forming social members in a way that furnishes them with the subjective capacities necessary for the exercise of practical freedom in its various forms. Applied to the present context, Hegel's claim is that the institutions of *Sittlichkeit*—most important, civil society and the modern family—play a crucial role in forming individuals into subjects who regard themselves as both able and entitled to discern for themselves what the good consists in.[2]

The second general respect in which rational social institutions might contribute to the realization of moral freedom concerns not the formation of moral subjectivity but ways in which the social order can further the ability of its members, once they are already constituted as moral subjects, to *exercise* their moral subjectivity (that is, to act successfully in accord with their own understanding of the good). Thus, one way Hegel's conception of moral subjectivity could have consequences for social theory is by making it a condition of a rational social world that its members be guaranteed a certain quantity of basic resources that is minimally necessary for any vision of the good life to be successfully realized. This is essentially the idea that leads Hegel to demand of the institutions of *Sittlichkeit* "that the subsistence and well-being of individuals be secured, that particular well-being be treated as a right and realized" (§230). (This thought is by no means foreign to contemporary political theory, since one of Rawls's reasons for focusing on the just distribution of primary goods is that he takes them to be necessary means for successfully realizing any conception of the good life.[3] Thus, translated into Hegelian language: Rawls regards primary goods as important in part because they are necessary conditions for the actualization of moral subjectivity.)

Another respect in which social theory could concern itself with enabling its adult members to exercise their moral subjectivity follows more or less directly from the emphasis placed by that conception of subjectivity on what could be called the "inner affirmation" of ethical norms by those who are subject to them. The most obvious idea here, in very general terms, is that rational social institutions must be able to accommodate the central requirement of moral subjectivity that individuals' wills be bound only by principles they themselves recognize as good. In Hegel's own words, one implication of his account of moral subjectivity is that "ethical . . . determinations ought not to lay claim to the obedience of the human being merely as external laws or as the dictates of an authority. Instead, they ought to find assent, recognition, or even justification in his heart, disposition [*Gesinnung*], conscience, insight, etc." (E §503A). In other words, the rational social order will need to satisfy what Hegel characterizes as the most important right of moral subjects (§132), namely, that all practical dictates that govern their lives, including the prevailing laws and imperatives of social life, be recognized as good and affirmed as such by the individuals whose actions they determine. It is this aspect of the relationship between social institutions and moral subjectivity that the present chapter aims to examine. Its task is to articulate, understand, and evaluate the measures Hegel's social theory envisions for ensuring that individuals' participation in social life not be in conflict with their right, as moral subjects, to be bound only by their own ethical standards. As we shall see more clearly later, its central problem could be formulated as the question, What rights and freedoms of *conscience* does a Hegelian social order provide for?

Even at this preliminary stage of our inquiry, it is worth noting that the issue to be addressed here is but a version of the question that much of the liberal tradition regards as the fundamental problem of political philosophy. Rawls's theory of justice is no doubt the clearest example of this approach, since its principal task can easily be construed as one of devising principles of justice that give adequate recognition to the moral status of "persons" (roughly, the Rawlsian analogue to Hegel's moral subject), one of whose defining features is "the capacity to form, to revise, and rationally to pursue" one's own conception of the good.[4] Since Rawls's understanding of the problem that motivates a theory of justice emphasizes the ineliminable divergence among modern individuals' conceptions of the good, his answer to the question of how political association ought to accommodate moral subjectivity gives pride of place to the idea of securing respect for the moral status of individuals regarded as the authors of their own conceptions of the good. This emphasis on respect manifests itself in a number of ways in Rawls's theory, but one of its most prominent effects is to place limits on what the state can legitimately require a citizen to do. Such limits to the state's authority are regarded as morally necessary in order to avoid coercing individuals to act in accord with conceptions of the good that are not their own, hence violating their status as persons (or, as Hegel would say, as moral subjects). Rawls's concern for the respect due to persons is just one version of a more general doctrine that, in one form or another, plays a central role in all liberal theories of the state, namely, that one of the primary tasks of legitimate political association is to protect the status of its members as moral agents by securing for them an arena, protected from incursion by the state and other individuals, within which they are free to act as they, guided only by their own assessment of the good, find appropriate. Despite the important affinities between Hegel's and Rawls's theories—affinities that are both deeper and more numerous than initial impressions suggest—we shall see later that Hegel's solution to the problem of how to reconcile the demands of moral subjectivity with those of social cooperation does not rely primarily on the liberal idea of respect and the need to place clearly defined limits on the authority of the state to command its citizens. (We shall also see, however, that such liberal notions figure more prominently in Hegel's theory than is commonly thought.) Instead, Hegel's solution focuses first and foremost on making the fundamental goodness and rationality of the modern social order transparent to its members so that compliance with its norms and laws can be achieved without violating the ideal of moral subjects whose actions are determined only by their own understanding of the good. Nevertheless, the undeniable differences between Hegel and Rawls (and other liberals) on this score should not blind us to the important fact that both positions are motivated by a concern to ensure that the social order give adequate expression to an ideal of moral subjectivity that, in essence, the two theories share. Keeping in mind this point of contact between Hegel and the liberal tradition will aid us not only in understanding how the theory of *Sittlichkeit* handles the problem of moral conscience but also in assessing the merits and weaknesses of that solution.

Hegel's Conception of Moral Conscience

In order to gain a more precise understanding of the problem addressed by this chapter, it is first necessary to undertake a detailed analysis of its principal concept, moral conscience (*Gewissen*).[5] Conscience is the appropriate focal point of this discussion because it is the central feature of moral subjectivity as Hegel understands it.[6] In other words, to ask whether *Sittlichkeit* can accommodate the moral subjectivity of its members is to ask, first and foremost, whether it can allow for the full expression and realization of conscience. Finding a clear answer to this question is made difficult by the fact that conscience appears in two distinct guises in Hegel's texts. One of these is conscience in its "true" form, which is held to be fully realizable within a rational social order. The other is an overly abstract and individualistic conception of moral authority that Hegel criticizes as tantamount to arbitrariness and as one step away from evil itself.[7] Both configurations of conscience incorporate versions of the central idea of moral subjectivity that the individual is the autonomous source of whatever ethical standards bind its will. The first to appear in the *Philosophy of Right* is the "bad," overly individualistic form—that is, conscience as seen from the abstract perspective of "Morality." This is followed by Hegel's discussion in "*Sittlichkeit*," which amounts to several scattered remarks referring to conscience in its "true" form. For this reason it makes sense, in characterizing the present task, to speak, as commentators frequently do, of attempting to determine which elements of moral conscience are preserved, or *auf-*

gehoben, within modern ethical life. This means that at the end of this discussion I will need to say, more explicitly than Hegel ever does, which elements of the rejected form of conscience are excluded by his social theory and whether the form he incorporates into his account of *Sittlichkeit* does justice to the ideal of the wholly self-legislating, individual subject that the standpoint of "Morality" is supposed to contribute to Hegel's vision of the fully rational social order.

I can begin my analysis of conscience by recalling Hegel's statement, cited earlier, emphasizing the importance of social members' inner affirmation of whatever "ethical determinations" they are bound to follow: if moral subjectivity is to be given its due in the institutions of *Sittlichkeit,* then the laws and norms that govern participation in those institutions "ought to find assent, recognition, or even justification in [one's] heart, disposition [*Gesinnung*], conscience, insight, etc." (E §503A). The reference here to the disposition of social members should remind us of chapter 3, which analyzed Hegel's understanding of the subjective disposition, or frame of mind, appropriate to free social membership and showed it to be the central idea in his account of social freedom in its subjective aspect. This could easily lead one to think that the question raised here concerning individuals' inner affirmation of social norms and laws could be dealt with simply by reinvoking the ideas already explored in chapter 3. It could appear, in other words, that the only condition the social order must satisfy in order to accommodate the moral subjectivity of its adult members is that the latter subjectively identify with (find their practical identities within) the institutions to which they belong in the sense articulated in chapter 3, namely, (1) they value and pursue the collective good of their social groups as a final end; (2) they find and express their own particular identities through their social participation; and (3) they view their institutions as sustained by their own activity and therefore as products of their own wills. The thought here is that by subjectively identifying with their social institutions in this sense individuals would, at least implicitly, be acknowledging those institutions as good, and hence in following the laws and norms governing social life they would be bound only by standards of the good they themselves affirm.

It is crucial for understanding the aim of the present chapter to recognize that subjectively identifying with one's social institutions in the manner just described is not of itself sufficient to satisfy the requirements of moral subjectivity as Hegel understands them. This claim is reflected in the fact that the quotation cited earlier refers not only to the disposition of social members but also to their "conscience" and "insight." The point is further confirmed by recalling that in Hegel's view the ancient Greeks, too, found their identities through their social participation—indeed, the very ideal of social freedom in its subjective aspect comes to us from the Greek city-state—and yet at the same time were incapable of realizing, or even conceiving of, all the forms of practical freedom that are available to and regarded as indispensable by the modern world. It is familiar to us by now that the intention of Hegel's theory of *Sittlichkeit* is not simply to reassert the ideals of classical Greece in their ancient (and primitive) guise but rather to reformulate them within a philosophy of freedom that incorporates two further conceptions of self-determination that (allegedly) postdate the culture of ancient Greece, the person and the moral subject.[8]

The most important element of moral subjectivity that Hegel takes to be missing from the subjective identification associated with classical Greece is indicated in his terse and somewhat startling remark that—with the notable exception of Socrates, who is taken to be the original source of this modern principle of subjectivity—the "Greeks had *no conscience*" (§147N).[9] We can best understand what Hegel takes this distinctively modern principle to consist in by retracing his account of its long historical development, beginning with one of his statements of the contribution Socrates makes to the history of moral subjectivity:

> It was in the time of Socrates that a moral standpoint first arose. The Athenians accused him of the crime of no longer following the laws of the fatherland and believing in his country's gods—of no longer being so immediately ethical [*sittlich*]. Socrates established the standpoint of inner reflection, of thinking over [for oneself] whether something is true. [His principle was] that the concept of God, of good and evil, . . . is not immediately binding [*gültig*] in itself but, in order to be recognized, must first have made its way through the interior of the human being. (VPR4, 301)

The two (related) hallmarks of the subjective attitude introduced by Socrates are said here to be the absence of immediacy—to be "immediately ethical" is to accept the ethical practices of one's society unreflectively—and the aspiration to think through social mores for oneself before accepting them as valid. Hegel's point appears to be, then, that by itself the subjective disposition described in chapter 3 falls short of the ideal of moral subjectivity because it is compatible with the very "immediacy" between individuals and social practices that Socrates's questioning of Athenian norms is intended to challenge. (As an example of this immediacy, recall Antigone's eloquent assertion—as transmitted by Hegel—of the unshakable and inscrutable character of the ethical laws she must follow: "They are not of yesterday or today but everlasting, and where they came from no one knows" [PhG, ¶437; 321–322].) Thus—anticipating the application of these ideas to his social theory—Hegel's view appears to be that in a fully rational social order individuals do not immediately (unreflectively) accept the laws and norms that govern them as good, regarding them, with Antigone, as laws and norms that simply "*are,* and nothing more." Rather, fully free social members must affirm the ethical standards that bind them in a manner appropriate to their status as beings of conscience—that is, in a manner that incorporates the ability and aspiration of moral subjects both to distance themselves from given practices and norms and to assess their merits rationally.

The idea of moral conscience originated by Socrates is both reinforced and elaborated in the religious doctrines of Christianity, which, according to Hegel, find their clearest and most consistent formulation in the theology of the Protestant Reformation. Part of Hegel's assessment of the philosophical significance of Luther's transformation of Christianity is expressed in the following excerpt from his university lectures on the philosophy of history: "Because the individual now knows that he is filled with the divine spirit, all relations of externality fall away. There is no longer a distinction between priests and laymen; there is no class that is exclusively in possession of the truth . . . Rather, it is the heart, the emotional spirituality of the human being, that can and should come into possession of the truth, and this subjectivity belongs to *all humans*" (PH, 416/XII, 495–496).

Two advances over the Socratic ideal of moral subjectivity are worthy of note here. First, Luther, along with Christian theology more generally, regards the moral authority of humans as dependent on their connection to a divine being whose status as absolute, or unconditioned, endows it with a relation to the world that transcends the limited perspective available to finite human individuals as such. As the preceding passage indicates, it is only because humans can be "filled with the divine spirit" that they are able to "come into possession of the truth" in moral matters and render competent judgments on the goodness of human norms and practices. On this view, the Socratic "standpoint of inner reflection"— the ability to determine the validity of ethical standards for oneself—requires access to a point of view that can furnish standards of the good that are absolutely, or unconditionally, valid. One consequence of this Christian innovation is that ethical judgments come to be regarded as susceptible to an absolute and final grounding. While the often inconclusive nature of Socrates's dialogues could be interpreted as casting doubt on the existence of ethical standards that can survive the sustained scrutiny of reason, Luther's view clearly presupposes that such ultimate standards exist and that human beings, by standing in the right relation to the divine, have access to them. For such a view, achieving truth in ethical matters is no longer a mere aspiration of the moral subject; the existence of a God who reveals himself to humans ensures both that such truth exists and that human subjects can possess it.

The second advance over Socrates's idea of moral subjectivity is located in Luther's explicit assertion that the source of moral authority resides within every individual regardless of birth or earthly position. (Recall his claim, as formulated by Hegel, that "this subjectivity belongs to *all human beings*.") Thus, for Luther the link between the human and the divine is not merely a relation between God and some selected human individuals, nor between God and the human community as a whole. Rather, each individual has, at least potentially, a direct connection to the absolute and hence unmediated access to the true criterion of the good. In other words, Luther sees each individual as a discrete and independent locus of moral authority, one that needs no external human assistance in order to know what true moral goodness requires.

Both of Luther's contributions to the development of the idea of moral subjectivity are succinctly captured in Hegel's summary of the Protestant creed: "This is the Lutheran faith: that the human being stands in relation to God and does so as *this* human being" (LHP, vol. III, 149/XX, 51). In view of our interest in their connection to the modern, or Enlightenment, understanding of moral conscience, it is relevant to note that each of these doctrines represents a respect in which the account of moral subjectivity implicit in Reformation theology could be regarded as universalistic. This is most obvious in the case of the second point distinguished here, the claim that moral authority is not the exclusive possession of a particular class of human beings but resides within all individuals. This position could be said to be universalistic in the sense that it upholds a belief in *universal access* to the true standards of the good. (And this Protestant doctrine, Hegel thinks, is nothing more than an elaboration of the universalism already present in early Christianity's belief in a single deity whose concern and authority extend to all human beings, whether Jew or gentile).[10] But a kind of universalism is also implicit in the assertion that the ultimate source of the true standards of the good is absolute. The idea here is that the ethical standards that bind human actions derive their supreme authority from the fact that they appear as good from an unconditioned perspective, one that is neither partial, nor limited in the sense that its vision of the good depends on, or is relative to, occupying a particular place within the moral universe. This position constitutes a form of universalism, then, because it takes well-founded moral judgments to require a *universal perspective* (one that transcends all particularly situated points of view).[11]

It is in the Enlightenment—most notably, in Kant's moral philosophy—that the idea of moral conscience attains its greatest prominence and its most complete articulation. The conception of conscience Hegel ascribes to the Enlightenment is to a large extent merely a synthesis of the Socratic and Lutheran views of moral subjectivity. Luther's emphasis on "emotional spirituality" as the basis of humanity's connection to the divine is discarded in favor of the older Socratic idea that the exercise of moral subjectivity relies not on feeling but on rational reflection—on cognitively distancing oneself from given norms and practices in order to assess their rationality—and to the related claim that such norms are morally binding only if they can withstand the scrutiny of reason. But the Enlightenment's understanding of what such reason consists in appropriates, in secularized form, three central ideas of Luther, namely, that there exists an ultimately authoritative truth in ethical matters; that such truth is in principle available to all individuals (universal access);[12] and that attaining such truth requires adopting a standpoint that abstracts from all merely particular points of view (universal perspective).

To all of this the Enlightenment adds a single, supremely important innovation of its own: "Luther won spiritual freedom [for humankind] . . . [by] triumphantly establishing that the human being's eternal destiny must be wrought out within himself. But the *content* of what is to be wrought out within him . . . Luther assumed to be something given, something that is revealed by religion. Now [in the Enlightenment] the principle has been established that this content must be present to me, something I can inwardly convince myself of, and that everything must be referred back to this internal ground" (PH, 441–442/XII, 523). The significance of this Enlightenment tenet lies in the thought that the source of unconditional ethical standards resides not in an external deity but within human reason itself. It is not just, as Luther asserted, that all individuals have access to the truth in ethical matters; rather, the very source of that truth—the *ground* of our ethical standards—is also present within each of us. The principal aspiration Hegel is ascribing to the Enlightenment here is to see the *content* of ethical standards as deriving from something internal to the beings who are subject to them. In the paragraphs that follow this passage, Hegel makes clear that what is required in order to satisfy this aspiration is not fully captured by the mere demand—more or less implicit already in the Socratic view—that subjects be bound only by ethical standards they can recognize as authorized by reason. For formulating the ideal of moral subjectivity in this way leaves open the possibility that reason could be conceived of as having its source in something extrahuman—as, for example, in Plato's equation of reason with the principles that underlie the cosmic order— with the consequence that in an important respect the content of moral duty would remain merely given to, or imposed upon, the human being from without. For the Enlightenment, in contrast, the ethical standards the moral subject is to recognize as rational must have an "internal ground," one that (in a sense yet to be explained) comes from itself. (Perhaps it is more illuminating to say that for the Enlightenment nothing could any longer count as reason that was not internal to the human being in this sense.) It is precisely this Enlightenment idea that Hegel means to communicate when he says in the *Philosophy of Right* that the ideal embodied in the notion of moral conscience includes an assertion of the subject's authority to know "what right and duty are" not only "within itself" (*in sich*)—that is, within its own consciousness—but also as "proceeding from itself" (*aus sich*) (§137A).

But how, more concretely, are we to understand this demand that the content of ethical norms derive from something internal to the human being? It is helpful in this context to recall that Hegel finds the paradigmatic formulation of this position in the Kantian principle of moral autonomy, which locates the source of duty in an "internal ground," namely, the will's self-legislative capacity. For Kant ethical duties could be said to come from something internal to the human being in the sense that the criterion that determines them, the universalizability of the will's maxims, is simply an expression of the most fundamental condition of the exercise of practical reason, the faculty Kant identifies with the will itself. According to Hegel, this account of the source of moral obligation has the important consequence that "right and ethics, which earlier were merely imposed externally upon the human being in the form of a divine command, are now regarded as grounded in the . . . human will" (PH, 440/XII, 522).

The concept Hegel places at the foundation of his own moral and social philosophy—"the free will that wills the free will" (§27)—is supposed to be an alternative way of expressing the core Kantian idea of autonomy and the concomitant claim that the content of ethical standards is to be derived from principles internal to the human will: "The will that wills itself is the ground of all right and all obligation . . . ; the freedom of the will itself, as such, is the principle and substantial foundation of all right" (PH, 442–443/XII, 524). As preceding chapters have attempted to make clear, Hegel's version of this Kantian strategy involves establishing the rational character of social norms and institutions by showing them to be necessary for the realization of practical freedom (to be necessary conditions of the will's achieving complete self-determination). Such a strategy makes the source of ethical standards internal to the human being because freedom is the human being's essence: "freedom of the will . . . is what makes the human being human; it is for that reason the fundamental principle of spirit" (PH, 443/XII, 524–525). Thus, the Enlightenment aspiration to find the content of ethical norms within the human being appears in Hegel's *Philosophy of Right* as the view that in order to be genuinely binding on human beings such norms must be recognizable by them, not merely as conforming to some possibly external standard of reason but as promoting a distinctively *human* end—indeed, the highest of all such ends, self-determination.[13]

As we have seen in earlier chapters, one distinctive feature of Hegel's social theory is that it recognizes a species of practical self-determination that cannot be predicated of individual wills but only of social groups considered collectively. (Recall the claim discussed in chapter 4 that the institutions of *Sittlichkeit* are themselves self-determining because they make up a self-sufficient social order that is both informed by the structure of the Concept and capable of reproducing itself, along with all of its essential qualities.) But, as I have been at pains to argue throughout, this feature of Hegel's view ought not to be construed as support for the frequently heard assertion that the freedom of the will on which the *Philosophy of Right* is founded is something more profound than merely human freedom. While it is true that Hegel's theory invokes a conception of self-determination that cannot, strictly speaking, be predicated of *individuals*—for he, like Rousseau, thinks of the social order as a collective subject with a unitary life and will (SC, I.6.x)—it is a mistake to think that this supraindividual form of self-determination must therefore be something other than *human* freedom. There are two reasons for this. First, part of what Hegel means in ascribing (objective) freedom to institutions themselves is that they secure the necessary conditions of the freedom of their individual members (in all three of its forms). Second, these "free" institutions do not have an existence that transcends the world inhabited by flesh-and-blood human beings; they are, instead, thoroughly human entities, created and sustained by the activities of human individuals, and even regarded by those individuals as continuous with their own selves. Thus, even where Hegel's theory posits a supraindividual will with a freedom of its own, this freedom remains inseparable, both conceptually and existentially, from the self-determined activity of human individuals.

Hegel's adoption of Kant's general strategy of conceiving of ethical norms as "laws of freedom"—as principles that follow from the will's basic character as self-determining—must not be allowed to obscure the important differences in how the two thinkers understand the concept of autonomy and the implications of its being the foundation of practical philosophy. Given the very rich account of the rational social order that Hegel takes to follow simply from the starting point of autonomy, it will come as no surprise that his conception of the freedom that characterizes the will is considerably broader than his predecessor's. The most striking respect in which the two conceptions diverge is reflected in the fact that for Hegel the moral principle thought to be internal to the will is not a merely formal principle of universality but includes a substantive conception of the *good*. For Hegel the principle that has its source in the nature of the (human) will is not the universalizability of an individual's maxims but a conception of the good that brings together the principles of abstract right (the principles that command respect for the freedom of all persons) with a systematic realization of human well-being (*Wohl*) (§§129+Z, 130, 134).[14]

The thought behind this doctrine is that "well-being is not a good without *right,* just as right is not the good without well-being" (§130). The reason Hegel makes this claim is that only a state of affairs in which the demands of right are in systematic harmony with general well-being can be fully satisfying to reason and hence affirmable by it as good without reservation. The well-being that is incorporated into this moral concept of the good is, of course, *universal* well-being[15] (§§125, 130) rather than merely that of the individual who, as a subject of conscience, is engaged in determining what the good consists in. At the same time, Hegel is at pains to make clear that the concept of the good employed by modern moral subjectivity takes universal well-being to refer not to what is best for some collective entity, such as the state (§126A), but to "the well-being *of all*" (§125), which includes the particular (and private) well-being of all individuals (§126A). This means that modern moral subjects can recognize as good only what unifies right and well-being in a specific way, namely, by systematically reconciling the personal freedom of all with the well-being of each individual. (It is instructive here to recall Rousseau's formulation of the fundamental task of the *Social Contract* as one of uniting "what right permits with what interest prescribes, so that justice and utility are not at variance" [SC, I.0.i].)

The fact that Hegel takes the principle that determines our duties to include human well-being as one of its components appears to belie his claim to be following Kant in deriving the content of ethical standards solely from the will's self-determining character. How, we are compelled to ask, can the good be regarded as a principle of *freedom?* Hegel's reasoning here is nowhere made explicit, but it appears to rely on the following idea: if the "laws of freedom" were understood in a way that excluded the promotion of well-being as one of their constitutive ends—as the principles of abstract right claim to do—then the highest principles to which moral subjects are bound would have no necessary connection to an important end that no human being can fail to have an interest in, namely, happiness. This would mean that morality might very well require individuals to act on principles that were, in their consequences, systematically indifferent, perhaps even antagonistic, to the fundamental human interest in happiness. Indeed, for such a morality *fiat iustitia* might well imply *pereat mundus.*

Hegel's rejection of such a possibility is based on the thought that, given their ineradicably sensuous character, human beings could never be fully reconciled to a morality that claimed supreme authority over their wills and yet made no, or merely a fortuitous, contribution to human well-being.[16] Beings like these who cannot fail to care deeply about their happiness would inevitably find themselves incapable of endorsing the commands of such a morality in a wholehearted fashion—that is, without a lingering sense that what present themselves as their highest laws fail to take account of something that matters vitally to them. But if a morality can muster no more than this kind of halfhearted endorsement, those who are subject to it cannot be fully free in following its dictates, for in such a case there will always be a substantial part of themselves that registers resistance to morality's demands. One point that recounting this line of thought brings more clearly into view is that, in contrast to the Kantian position, Hegel's understanding of what is required for the will's self-determination begins not from a purely a priori account of the nature of freedom but rather from a consideration of what beings who enter the world with certain natural needs and inclinations would be able to embrace as their highest principles without doing violence to, or alienating themselves from, their sensuous nature.[17]

Hegel's claim that ethical norms deriving from the concept of self-determination must incorporate considerations of human well-being implies a further respect in which his position diverges ultimately from Kant's. It is not enough for Hegel that morality incorporate human well-being in general as one of its essential ends and thus that compliance with its demands have the consequence of furthering "the well-being of all." It must also be the case, if individuals are to be able fully to embrace morality's demands, that doing one's duty be the source of a certain *particular* satisfaction for the individual who does it. Hegel's thought here is that if individuals are to be able to perceive morality as something more than a severe, demanding taskmaster, it must do more than merely command them to promote the freedom and well-being of their fellow humans; it must offer them an incentive for doing so that is more vivid than an abstract concern for the good of all, an incentive that also addresses their own interests as particular beings.[18] Since duty will often require individuals to sacrifice their private good for the good of others, Hegel believes that ethical demands can be systematically reconciled with the particular satisfaction of moral subjects only to the extent that the latter take on as their own the particular identities available to them through the three institutions of *Sittlichkeit*. Because (as we saw in chapter 3) these identities are thickly social—both particular and universal at once—they enable individuals to further the good of others while also affording them the particular satisfaction associated with giving reality to their own conceptions of who they are and of securing the recognition of others—their "honor and fame"(§124)—through the performance of socially beneficial roles.

Hegel's understanding of the legacy of the lengthy historical development I have just retraced is summed up in his brief statement of "the [moral] subject's highest right," sometimes referred to as "the right of the subjective will" (§132): "*Conscience* expresses the absolute authority of subjective self-consciousness, namely, to know what right and duty are both *within oneself* [*in sich*] and *as proceeding from oneself (aus sich)*, and to recognize nothing other than what it thus knows as the good; it also includes the claim that what it thus knows and wills is in *truth* right and duty" (§137A). On Hegel's view, then, the rights of conscience are fully accommodated only when all of the following conditions obtain:[19] (1) individuals are bound only by laws and norms they themselves *consciously endorse* as good; (2) their endorsement of the ethical standards that bind them is the *result of their own rational reflection*, which is predicated on the ability to step back from prevailing laws and norms and to evaluate them from a universal (nonparticular) perspective; (3) the ethical standards that individuals come to endorse on the basis of reasoned reflection constitute *a true representation of the good*; and (4) the goodness of those standards derives from the fact that they promote a *value internal to human beings*, namely, self-determination of the will. Any doubt regarding the centrality of rational reflection for this account of conscience is quickly dispelled by noting that Hegel also refers to this set of conditions—the moral subject's "highest right"—as the "right of insight into the good" (§132A), where insight is unambiguously characterized as conviction that is grounded in reasons. This view is stated with perfect clarity in Hegel's 1825 lectures on the *Philosophy of Right*, where he asserts that the subjective relation a being of conscience ought to have to ethical standards is "not merely a general acquaintance with the good"; rather, as a moral subject, "I ought to have insight into the good, and insight is something more than mere acquaintance . . . With reflection arises the demand that . . . I have insight into what is declared to be right and good, that I be convinced of its rightness and goodness [on the basis of *good* reasons]" (VPR4, 351–352).[20]

The Place of Moral Subjectivity in *Sittlichkeit*

As readers of Hegel are well aware, the view of conscience and its rights that has just been discussed is set out in Part II of the *Philosophy of Right* ("Morality"), before Hegel has turned his attention to the theory of *Sittlichkeit* and its account of how social institutions are implicated in the realization of practical freedom. The textual location of this discussion of conscience raises the obvious question of how, precisely, Hegel's view of *moral* subjectivity relates to his social theory. This question is easily recognized as an instance of a more general problem that attends the interpretation of any aspect of Hegel's philosophy, namely, What status do earlier parts of the system have once they have been dialectically "superseded" *(aufgehoben)* by later parts? Applied to the case at hand, the question becomes: To what extent are the rights of conscience preserved and not simply negated within the theory of *Sittlichkeit?* How precisely are the rights of moral subjectivity to be accommodated in a fully rational social order?[21]

Unsympathetic interpreters of Hegel have objected time and again that his theory of *Sittlichkeit* negates rather than preserves the most important elements of his own account of moral subjectivity. Their claim, more precisely, is that Hegel's vision of the rational social order accords its members no place for the genuine expression of moral conscience. In one of the most recent of such attacks, Ernst Tugendhat argues that "Hegel does not allow for the possibility of a responsible, critical relation to the . . . state. Instead he tells us that existing laws have an absolute authority . . . The independent conscience of the individual must disappear, and trust takes the place of reflection. This is what Hegel means by the *Aufhebung* of morality into *Sittlichkeit.*"[22] Tugendhat's charge that individual conscience has no place in Hegel's vision of the rational social order appears to draw support from a well-known passage from the *Philosophy of Right*'s most comprehensive discussion of the concept of *Sittlichkeit*, where Hegel does indeed say that "in *Sittlichkeit* . . . the independent conscience of the individual . . . [has] disappeared" (§152). And, as we have already seen in chapter 3, Hegel unambiguously asserts that trust rather than reflection is the hallmark of the subjective disposition of socially free individuals.[23]

Before examining Hegel's position at the level of detail it deserves, it is worth briefly noting three points that should make us hesitant to accept this familiar critique without further consideration. First, let us review the quotation cited earlier in support of Tugendhat's charge, this time in its entirety: "In *Sittlichkeit* the willfulness [*Eigenwilligkeit*] and independent conscience of the individual—a conscience that strives to be self-sufficient [*für sich*] in opposition to ethical substantiality—have disappeared" (§152). So, while it is undeniable that conscience *in some sense* is supposed to disappear within the rational social order, the fact that Hegel here associates conscience with willfulness (and with a drive always to oppose existing social reality) should make us wonder whether his critics have correctly understood precisely what aspect of moral subjectivity Hegel means to banish from *Sittlichkeit*. Second, and more important, even if Tugendhat is correct that Hegel's account of rational social institutions fails to give the rights of moral conscience their due, the conclusion we ought to draw from that is that he has been untrue to his own philosophy for having violated a fundamental doctrine of the "dialectical" method, namely, that earlier concepts (here, the elements of "Morality") are never simply discarded as the system progresses but are instead preserved in the stage that follows (*"Sittlichkeit"*) as components of a more comprehensive whole.[24] Hegel's failure, then, would call not for a rejection of the basic principles of his social theory but for a more localized rethinking of the role that the moral judgment of individuals ought, by the lights of his own philosophy, to play in the rational social order. Finally, Tugendhat's interpretation of Hegel's remark that conscience "has disappeared" in *Sittlichkeit* is extremely difficult to reconcile with many other statements made throughout the *Philosophy of Right*, including the claim that "conscience is . . . something sacred and its violation a sacrilege" (§137A).

Perhaps the only thing these three points establish conclusively is that Hegel's view of how the demands of moral subjectivity are accommodated within *Sittlichkeit* is too complex to be captured in a brief summary. This is undoubtedly due to the fact that, as we have seen, his conception of moral conscience brings together a number of disparate elements that are in need of careful sorting out. Thus, in order both to ascertain the role Hegel means to attribute to conscience within social life and to assess the merits of his detractors' charges, it will be necessary to proceed more methodically than I have thus far. More specifically, it will be necessary to determine exactly which of the various elements of conscience, as viewed from the perspective of "Morality," are intended to be preserved within *Sittlichkeit* and in precisely what form.

I shall begin with the issue of reflection and the charge that the attitude of trust Hegel imputes to social members is incompatible with their adopting a universal, nonparochial perspective from which they could ask whether the norms and practices of their social order are rationally justified. (As Tugendhat formulates this charge, in *Sittlichkeit* "trust *takes the place of* reflection," and this excludes the possibility of "adopting a rational perspective" on existing norms.)[25] The first thing to observe is that Hegel's texts abound with passages that straightforwardly contradict this objection, explicitly affirming that this aspect of conscience—the capacity for rational reflection on the goodness of one's social institutions—is meant to be preserved within modern *Sittlichkeit*.[26] Consider, for example, the following passage from Hegel's 1819 lectures on the *Philosophy of Right*:

> Now the good has many forms. First it can be characterized as the lawful, as that which is allowed or prohibited by law. I can know what is lawful, and my knowledge of it is merely the general cognizance that it is in force and is to be obeyed [*daß es gilt*]. A further kind of knowledge, however, is knowledge based on reasons, not merely immediately [as in the first case]. In this case the knowledge is called conviction. Higher yet is knowledge . . . based on the Concept [that is, full philosophical understanding]. *As a consequence of my moral right, I can demand that a thing be valid for me not merely as required by law or as based on specific reasons; rather it ought to be shown to be rational in accord with the Concept.* (VPR2, 106; emphasis added)

Moreover, after making the remark (referred to previously) that the ancient Greeks lacked a conscience—a lack he clearly regards as a shortcoming of the ancient world—Hegel spells out what he means by that claim by adding: "[They were] unable to give an *account*; [they had] no *conscience*, no *conviction*—[their affirmative stance was] unmediated by *reasons*" (§147N).

If there is plenty of textual evidence documenting Hegel's intention to include the capacity for rational reflection as part of the subjective disposition appropriate to members of *Sittlichkeit*, it may be instructive to ask why so many of his interpreters have insisted on ascribing to him the opposite view.[27] There are, I think, two reasons for this common misunderstanding. First, it is easy to gain the impression that moral conscience as Hegel understands it is irremediably at odds with the subjective disposition he ascribes to free social membership (as outlined in chapter 3). This is because the latter requires that individuals subjectively identify with their social institutions, while the former carries with it the apparently opposite requirement that individuals' attachments to their social roles be sufficiently loose to allow them to reflect on their social order from the detached, universal perspective that modernity takes as constitutive of reason. But this line of thought is predicated on a widespread but mistaken understanding of the sense in which Hegel claims membership in the institutions of *Sittlichkeit* to be constitutive of the identity of individuals. In fact, the reconstruction of that claim presented in chapter 3 provides us with the resources we need to dispel the common illusion that reflective moral subjectivity is incompatible with the perception free social members are said to have of their social world as "undifferentiated" from themselves and as embodying "their own essential nature" (§147). In this context it is crucial to recall the precise meaning I attributed there to the notoriously slippery concept of identity. As I argued in chapter 3, it is not Hegel's intention to claim, as contemporary communitarians sometimes do, that the social roles individuals occupy *exhaust* their practical identities such that individuals are nothing more than bearers of the various particular social roles they occupy. Instead, the assertion that individuals find their identities in the institutions of *Sittlichkeit* can be analyzed into two more modest claims: first, that social roles furnish individuals with what they take to be their most important ends and projects, those that could be said to constitute their life-defining activity; and, second, that a substantial part of social members' "sense of self"—their sense of themselves as individuals of "worth and dignity" (§152)—derives from the social recognition they receive as a result of successfully fulfilling their roles within *Sittlichkeit*. When 'identity' is understood in this more limited sense, there is nothing in Hegel's account of the subjective disposition of free social members that precludes the ability to distance oneself reflectively from one's social roles in order to ask, as a moral subject, whether the social order one inhabits is rationally justifiable.

A second reason Hegel's account of *Sittlichkeit* is so frequently thought to allow no place for the rational reflection of its members is that Hegel sometimes seems to say precisely that. In certain passages that acknowledge the wide spectrum of routes through which individuals can come to affirm the basic goodness of their social institutions,

Hegel appears to disparage the route of rational insight and to assert that the more immediate forms of affirmation are sufficient for free social membership and perhaps even superior to conviction mediated by reasons. Consider the following notes Hegel scribbled in his own copy of the *Philosophy of Right* just next to the paragraph of "Morality" in which he explicates "the right of the subjective will": "It can be wished that humans know the rational grounds, the deeper source of right—[but] this is not objectively necessary. Trust, faith, healthy common sense, customary morality [*Sitte*]—these are the ordinary objective way[s] of grounding [our ethical beliefs]" (§132N).[28] Moreover, the impression conveyed by comments such as these is only reinforced by those problematic passages already referred to in which Hegel appears to claim that in *Sittlichkeit* the individual's conscience disappears (§152) and trust takes the place of moral reflection (E §§514–515).

A careful reading of these passages, however, shows that they do not contradict the view that the subjective disposition Hegel ascribes to members of *Sittlichkeit* is meant to accommodate rather than exclude the modern moral subject's claim to be able to validate through reasoned reflection the ethical standards it embraces. Consider first the passage just quoted, which denies that it is necessary for individuals to know the rational grounds of their standards of the good. The key to interpreting this passage lies in observing that it says merely that rationally grounded insight into the good is not *objectively* necessary. By this Hegel means two things. First, the *obligation* social members have to obey laws and norms that embody the good is not diminished by lack of insight on their part into the reasons that make their social practices good.[29] That such reasons exist and are accessible to the human intellect is sufficient to ground objectively the obligation to comply with them. (I shall return to this point later in order to consider whether it can be reconciled with Hegel's claim that conscience is preserved in *Sittlichkeit,* for the view that moral obligation does not depend on the *actual* insight of moral subjects appears directly to contradict his characterization of the right of conscience as "the absolute authority of . . . self-consciousness . . . to know what right and duty are . . . and to recognize nothing other than what it . . . knows as the good" [§137A].)

Second, the fact that some social members lack such rational insight does not prevent the social order from being an adequate "objectification" of the Concept (§132) or, in other words, from living up to its ideal as a self-determined organism whose sustaining parts (human individuals) themselves have self-determined wills. As long as social members in some fashion inwardly affirm the laws and norms that govern them, their actions in compliance with those laws and norms are in harmony with their own wills rather than determined by an external will. The thing to say about such individuals is not that they are unfree, nor even that they lack the freedom of moral subjectivity in its most general form (determining one's actions in accord with one's own standard of the good), but only that, in being unable to give a rational account of the standard of goodness they affirm, they fall short of realizing the full range of moral freedoms available to modern subjects. This commits Hegel to the principle that a social order in which many individuals had a thorough understanding of the reasons their institutions are worthy of affirmation would be prima facie superior to one in which such insight were restricted to a few (since in the former society the ideal of modern subjectivity would be realized more extensively). But Hegel's view is that differences in the natural aptitudes of individuals, together with the substantial claims modern civil society makes on the time and energy of those who exercise a vocation, make it impossible, and hence unreasonable to demand, that the affirmative attitude of all or even most individuals depend on a complete grasp of their social order's rational foundations. Put another way, it is not necessary that all of its members be philosophers in order for a social order to measure up to its ideal as a realm where practical freedom finds full expression.

A second passage Tugendhat and other critics point to in support of their claim that moral reflection has no place in ethical life is Hegel's statement in the *Encyclopedia* that members of *Sittlichkeit* do their duty "without . . . reflection" (E §514). But here again it is necessary to examine Hegel's statement in its entirety. The claim Hegel actually makes is that members of *Sittlichkeit* "fulfill their duty *without the reflection of free choice [ohne die wählende Reflexion]*. They regard their duty as something that is their own and that has a stable being [*als das Ihrige und als Seiendes*], and in this necessity they win themselves and their actual freedom" (emphasis modified). Thus, a careful reading of this passage makes clear that what Hegel intends to exclude from the subjective disposition of social members is not reflection *simpliciter* but what he pointedly calls "the reflection of free choice." Tugendhat is apparently unaware that this phrase is a direct reference to preceding paragraphs of the *Encyclopedia* (E §§476–477), where Hegel discusses the "reflecting will" and equates it with *Willkür*. In earlier chapters I referred to *Willkür* as the arbitrary or choosing will, and in chapter 1, in the context of discussing Hegel's conception of personhood, I briefly defined it as the will's capacity to determine which among its given desires to act upon. In the paragraphs at issue here (E §§476–477), Hegel characterizes *Willkür* as the capacity "to *choose* among inclinations" and connects it to a kind of reflection as follows: "The will . . . distinguishes itself from the *particularity* of its drives and sets itself over and above their manifold content as the simple subjectivity of thought; in this way it is *reflecting* will." Thus, the reflection involved in the exercise of *Willkür*—the "reflection of free choice" mentioned earlier—is simply the will's ability to distance itself in thought from given inclinations—to stand above them, as it were—and then to determine, or choose, which of them to take up as "its own" as the basis for action.

In saying, then, that members of *Sittlichkeit* "fulfill their duty without the reflection of free choice," Hegel means to be making a point about how such individuals typically experience their own ethical action. The point is simply that when social members do what their roles as parents, professionals, and citizens require of them, they do not normally adopt a reflective attitude of the sort Hegel associates with free choice. That is, they do not normally "stand above" the contents of their will and regard the dutiful course of action as something they might choose to do but might equally well choose not to. Instead, for a member of *Sittlichkeit*, fulfilling one's duty is so intimately bound up with one's sense of who one is (one's fundamental identity, as discussed in chapter 3) that doing so appears more like a necessity—a necessity, given who I take myself to be—than an arbitrary choice. In view of the widespread misunderstanding of Hegel's account of ethical agency (including a vastly exaggerated depiction of his differences with Kant), it is important to recognize that nothing in this account of the everyday practical attitude of social members rules out their also being able at times to step out of this unreflective frame of mind in order to pose the question definitive of moral subjectivity, namely, whether their social institutions are in truth worthy of their allegiance. While Hegel clearly thinks that the act of stepping back from one's inclinations and choosing to do one's duty is not part of the everyday subjective disposition of free social members—imagine parents who regarded feeding their children as on a par with deciding which movie to see after dinner—he is most emphatically not a champion of a mindless compliance with social norms that never pauses to reflect on the social order and one's place within it from the perspective of a moral subject.

But all of this leaves one obvious question still unanswered: If Hegel recognizes the importance of rational reflection on the validity of existing social norms, what is it that he intends to exclude from *Sittlichkeit* when he proclaims the disappearance of "the independent conscience of the individual" (§152)? As I noted previously, the full text of Hegel's remark asserts the disappearance not of moral conscience per se but of "willfulness" and "conscience that strives to be self-sufficient in opposition to ethical substantiality." These phrases suggest that what Hegel intends to banish from *Sittlichkeit* is not conscience properly understood but a debased form of that phenomenon, one informed by an exaggerated version of the individual's claim to moral sovereignty. If so, what distinguishes the form of conscience Hegel endorses from mere willfulness? A clue to answering this question is provided by Hegel's description of the latter as "a conscience that strives to be *self-sufficient*" (emphasis added). The same theme appears in another passage where conscience in its distorted form is referred to as "moral self-conceit" and "the vanity of imagining one always knows better than others" (*die Eitelkeit des Besserwissens*) (VPR1, 91). Further references to the "erring conscience" (§137N) make clearer what the self-sufficiency involved in moral willfulness consists in, namely, "the empty thought that I depend only on my conviction and insight *as a particular being*" (§132N; emphasis added); "the subject taking *itself*, in its *singularity*, to be deciding on the good" (E §511); and "taking [into account] only what I find present in my conscience, not any other sources" (§137N).[30]

Passages such as these suggest that what Hegel calls willfulness and self-conceit is an overly individualistic form of conscience that, in attempting to determine the ethical standards it will embrace, gives insufficient weight to the testimony of other moral authorities that have at least an equal claim to knowledge of the good. Among these authorities Hegel includes not only other individuals but also the long-standing norms and practices of one's society (§132N). Willfulness in moral matters, then, must be the tendency to regard whatever understanding of the good one arrives at *entirely on one's own* as finally authoritative—that is, as immune to challenges from divergent views of the good that, if taken into account, might provide one with grounds for revising or rejecting one's own private judgment.[31] This belief in the perfect self-sufficiency of private conscience exaggerates the moral sovereignty of the individual by taking the particular, isolated moral subject—the individual "*in its singularity*"—as the supreme, unchallengeable arbiter of moral standards rather than regarding it as one among many participants in a collective quest to determine the good. Another way of putting this point is to say that by shutting out the testimony of others and refusing to subject one's own understanding of the good to possible acceptance or rejection by others, the purely private conscience eschews *rational* insight and thus falls short of a central aspect of the ideal of moral subjectivity. If, as Hegel believes, reason-giving is an inherently social practice in which the validity of reasons depends on their being accepted as such by other subjects,[32] then the conscience that aspires to rational insight cannot be as independent of the convictions of others as the wholly private conscience takes itself to be.

This raises the question of whether—and, if so, in what sense—the individual can still be described as sovereign in moral affairs, as a subject of conscience that is "perfectly free" and "subject to none." The best response available to Hegel, surely, is that his view preserves the sovereignty of the moral subject, but only if sovereignty is conceived along Rousseauean rather than Hobbesian lines. That is, true sovereignty is not the authority to make one's own arbitrary pronouncements into the law of the land; rather, to be sovereign with respect to the principles that bind one's actions is, first, to have a part in the collective project of determining those principles and, second, to comprehend the rational basis of the principles that come to be settled on through the just and inclusive exchange of reasons. On this view, each individual is capable of both discerning the good and grasping its rational basis, but only to the extent that he is open to a genuine exchange of reasons with fellow subjects, as carried out within the institutional framework provided by a rational social order. The "thinking *for* oneself" that characterizes sovereign moral subjects is not fundamentally a "thinking *by* oneself" but rather a "thinking together with others." Moreover, this way of interpreting the modern secular principle of universal access to the good faithfully echoes the Protestant doctrine from which it derives, which teaches that in principle every individual has access to the true ethical standards but that actual knowledge of those standards requires having the appropriate orientation to a subject other than oneself (in this case to an absolute subject, God). According to Hegel's secularized version of this doctrine, access to true ethical standards depends on standing in the right (institutionally mediated) relation to other individuals, who, like oneself, are sovereign moral subjects. To insist, whether to oneself or to others, that one's own private convictions are true regardless of the reception they receive from one's fellow moral subjects is not a manifestation of true moral conscience but of willful self-assertion (which, to extend the analogy, is nothing other than what Christians call "sin").

Hegel's distinction between willfulness or moral self-conceit, on the one hand, and the form of conscience that gives adequate recognition to the authority of its fellow moral subjects, on the other, raises an obvious concern that needs to be acknowledged here in anticipation of a more complete discussion of the matter later. The danger of Hegel's view is clear and frequently noted by his liberal critics: without a more precise statement of the conditions under which an individual is justified in rejecting divergent accounts of the good offered by other moral authorities, it is too easy for the Hegelian state to dismiss any disagreement with conventional norms, any criticism of existing social reality, as an expression of willfulness rather than the legitimate exercise of moral subjectivity. Thus, the worry expressed by Tugendhat and cited earlier might be reformulated as follows: even if Hegel wants individuals to reflect rationally on the acceptability of their social order, his distinction between willfulness and the reasonable exercise of conscience effectively identifies the latter with conformity to prevailing norms and thus excludes the possibility that reasonable members of *Sittlichkeit* will be critical of their institutions. The worry that Hegel sees reflection but not criticism as compatible with free social membership is perhaps reinforced by one of the quotations cited previously (§152), where it appears that moral willfulness is virtually *equated with* opposition to the existing social order. (Willfulness is glossed there as "striv[ing] to be self-sufficient in opposition to ethical substantiality.") In fact, there are two distinct questions raised by Hegel's view that will need to be treated separately in the following discussion of the issue. The first is whether Hegel's theory can recognize any forms of social criticism as rational, given his account of the subjective relation free social members must have to their social order, as well as his view that the institutions of modernity are fully justified. (And, if some types of critique are possible, which ones are they?)

The second question concerns how the state ought to treat those individuals who, whether out of moral willfulness or from reasonable moral conviction, do not recognize as good the laws and social norms that Hegel's theory takes to be fully justified. These are important questions that any account of the rights of conscience will need to take up, and liberals especially will want to know whether Hegel can answer them satisfactorily. The reason for postponing a discussion of them just now is that, although Hegel addresses these questions, he does not regard them as the most important issues his account of moral subjectivity raises for social theory. In order to do justice to the differences between Hegel's position and that of thinkers who fit more squarely within the liberal tradition, I shall first examine what Hegel himself takes to be the most important ways the rational social order accommodates the rights of conscience and only after that turn to the questions liberal theorists typically regard as primary.

Understanding how the theory of *Sittlichkeit* aims to accommodate the rights of conscience depends first on recalling that Hegel's account of conscience ascribes to moral subjects a number of aspirations. As noted previously, Hegel regards the aspirations of conscience as fully realized only when (1) individuals are bound exclusively by laws and norms they themselves endorse; (2) their endorsement of those laws and norms is grounded in rational reflection; (3) the ethical standards they endorse truly represent the good; and (4) the goodness of those standards derives from the fact that they promote a value internal to the human will (self-determination). The two questions formulated earlier—those that express central concerns of liberalism—implicitly focus only on the first of these conditions and ask what ought to be the case when it fails to obtain, that is, when certain individuals do not endorse the laws and norms their society expects them to obey. Hegel's primary concern, in contrast, is not to determine how to deal with such discord when it arises—when, in Hegelian language, there is disparity between the rational and the existent—but rather to articulate what a complete realization of the ideal of moral subjectivity would look like and to think about how the social order could be constituted in order to make the realization of that ideal more likely. Hegel's central question, then, is whether a social order in which *all* of these aspirations of moral subjectivity were widely and nonaccidentally fulfilled is a coherent and realizable ideal and, if so, under what conditions. Rather than focusing from the start on how to respond when one of the four conditions summarized earlier is unmet, Hegel's first concern is to ask whether the demands they represent are systematically compatible—that is, whether (and how) it is possible for them to be realized within a single human society.[33]

Hegel's view is that the greatest potential for conflict lies in a tension between the first and third of the four aspirations of conscience, namely, the claim to be bound only by laws and norms one endorses oneself and the claim to have access to the truth in ethical matters. (A complete solution to the problem Hegel poses will, of course, also need to incorporate conditions (2) and (4)—that ethical standards be reflectively grounded and that they embody the value of self-determination. But the discussion of these issues from previous chapters should make it clear how they fit into the picture once what Hegel takes to be the principal conflict is resolved.) This tension is precisely what is at issue in the distinction Hegel draws between the "true conscience" (*das wahrhafte Gewissen*), realized only within the rational social order, and the merely "formal conscience" (§137+A) championed by "Morality." True conscience is the form of moral subjectivity that reconciles the two aspirations noted previously—it regards only its own ethical standards as authoritative, and those standards are also objectively good—while formal conscience consists in the mere activity of determining for oneself what is good without regard to the content, and hence to the truth or falsity, of the standards endorsed. Hegel's point is that the merely formal conscience is not a complete realization of the ideal of moral subjectivity, since subjects of conscience aspire not only to determine for themselves what is good but also to be right about the ethical standards they endorse. By extension, a society in which individuals regarded prevailing laws and norms as good, but were mistaken in doing so, would not satisfy the demands of moral subjectivity. Those demands are completely met only when the laws and norms of existing social institutions are both good and recognized as such by its members.

Thus, the first condition a social order must meet if it is fully to accommodate the rights of conscience is that it in fact *be* good (and hence affirmable by true conscience). For Hegel, then, the single most important respect in which moral subjectivity is accommodated within *Sittlichkeit* is that social institutions are capable of withstanding the rational scrutiny of its members. This feature of the rational social order could be called its *reflective acceptability*.[34] In the terms employed by Hegel's theory, a social order meets the requirements of reflective acceptability when its institutions realize social freedom in its objective aspect (that is, when they meet the criteria for free social institutions outlined in chapters 4 and 5). The second condition Hegel's account of conscience imposes on the rational social order follows from the requirement that social members be bound only by laws and norms they themselves endorse: if compliance with prevailing laws and norms is to be consistent with the central ideal of moral subjectivity (determining one's actions in accord with one's own understanding of the good), then the institutions of *Sittlichkeit* must not only *be* rational, they must also be apprehended as such by their members. A second principal requirement of the rational social order, then, is that its rational character be apparent to its members. Apart from simply being good, the most important way the institutions of *Sittlichkeit* accommodate the rights of conscience is by making their goodness transparent to those who belong to them. In sum, the basic thought behind Hegel's strategy for giving moral subjectivity its due within *Sittlichkeit* is that if both of the earlier conditions are met, then (1) social participation will not systematically conflict with the requirement that individuals be able to follow only their own (true) consciences, and (2) the social order will be constituted such that those consciences are likely to be "true" rather than merely formal.

We have already seen in chapter 4 how the ideal of rational transparency informs Hegel's account of the political institutions he endorses. For one of the central aims of that account is to specify how the legislative process must be structured if citizens are to be able to regard the laws that result from it as rational and hence worthy of their assent. But the rational transparency Hegel's theory aims at concerns more than just particular laws and norms internal to the various institutions; it also includes an understanding of the basic structure of the social order itself. That is, Hegel's ideal requires that social members have a general grasp of the purpose of each of the social spheres to which they belong and of how the three principal institutions constitute a complete and coherent whole. Ultimately, only a *philosophical* account of the social order— something akin to the story being reconstructed here—can completely satisfy the demand for rational transparency. (And this perhaps implies that in a rational society the study of philosophy must be made available to all who want and are able to undertake it.) Yet Hegel makes it clear that there are more widely accessible forms of comprehension that fall short of full philosophical knowledge but still provide individuals with suitable rational grounds for affirming the social order. One example he offers is the "science" of contemporary political economy, as represented by the writings of Smith, Say, and Ricardo (§189A+Z). These thinkers contribute to a genuine understanding of the rational character of the modern, market-governed economy by uncovering its basic principles of operation and showing how they work to satisfy both particular and universal interests. The account of civil society they provide starts with certain human needs and shows that the modern economy's central mechanism, the market, is better at satisfying them than any other known form of economic organization. For Hegel these theories qualify as limited—though not for that reason as untrue—because as they stand in the writings of the political economists (and in contrast to how they are incorporated into the *Philosophy of Right*), they remain insufficiently self-standing,[35] which is to say that they are not yet truly systematic. What this critique amounts to is the charge that political economy demonstrates the rationality of civil society relative to contingent human needs but fails to appreciate its deepest rational significance. The latter is achieved only by a philosophical account, like Hegel's, that traces the value of social institutions back to an unconditioned good, human freedom. Although political economy is not ignorant of how its object of study helps to realize certain kinds of freedom (the freedoms of unrestrained commerce and personal choice more generally), it lacks the resources to provide a systematic account of the multiple and often hidden respects in which modern civil society serves the end of freedom. (That is, it does not reveal how civil society works in concert with the family and the state to secure the preconditions of both social freedom and the freedom of moral subjectivity, and to constitute a social whole that is self-determining and complete.)

Hegel's view that there are different ways of appreciating the rationality of the social order can be of service to his theory only if he also takes there to be a substantial continuity between these different forms of comprehension—that is, if what distinguishes them is primarily a difference in scope, or in the extent to which they penetrate to fundamental philosophical principles, rather than, say, radically divergent understandings of what the goodness of institutions consists in. If the judgment that the modern social order is good is to be both rationally grounded and available to more than a very select segment of society (those trained in philosophy), then the standards in terms of which the majority of individuals evaluate their social institutions must approximate or be continuous with those employed by philosophy. What primarily distinguishes higher from lower forms of comprehension cannot be that the latter are false, distorted, or misleading but that they are incomplete. This implies that what makes for the true goodness of the family, civil society, and the state, as revealed by philosophy, cannot be so hidden from their participants' eyes that their reasons for affirming their institutions are of a radically different kind from those offered by the philosopher. This point is borne out by reconsidering the case of political economy. For Hegel does not regard its understanding of the rationality of civil society in terms of the satisfaction of human needs as in competition with his own view but, instead, as a constituent part of a complete philosophical account. That civil society is well suited to satisfying basic human needs is an important part of what makes it good (since the good, for Hegel, unites both well-being and right), as well as part of what makes individuals able to affirm the market's operating principles and to accept the restrictions such principles place on their activity as limits that proceed from their own will.

Objections

Now that I have examined what Hegel takes to be the most important ways the institutions of *Sittlichkeit* accommodate the rights of conscience, it is time to revisit the two questions frequently raised by Hegel's liberal critics that were postponed earlier. We have already seen that, contrary to Tugendhat's charge, Hegel's account of the subjective disposition of free social members does not exclude the possibility of rational reflection on the merits of existing institutions. On the contrary, Hegel regards affirmation that is mediated by such reflection as a highly valuable expression of moral subjectivity. But as noted earlier, this view alone does not respond to all of the liberal's worries about Hegel's treatment of the rights of conscience. For there remains the concern that Hegel's theory lacks the resources for ascribing any value to the right of individuals to adopt an attitude to the existing social world that is not merely reflective but genuinely *critical* (oppositional) in character. As Tugendhat expresses it, the theory of *Sittlichkeit* has no room to acknowledge "the freedom to be able . . . rationally to take a position *in op-*

position to existing norms."[36] While Hegel grants that it is desirable for
individuals' affirmation of the social order to be based on good reasons,
his exclusive focus on the value of *true* conscience—manifest in the fact
that it, not formal conscience, is what he takes to be sacred and inviola-
ble—can indeed appear to exclude the freedom to disagree with conventional norms or to criticize existing social reality in accord with the legitimate rights of moral subjectivity. But to what extent is this appearance
true? As I suggested previously, this issue is best treated by dividing it
into two sets of questions. The first concerns whether Hegel's theory
possesses the *philosophical* resources that would make some form of rational social criticism possible: Does Hegel's judgment that the modern
social order is good render all criticism of existing reality rationally impossible? And, if not, is the subjective disposition he attributes to free
social members compatible with their actually engaging in the forms of
criticism his theory allows for? The second set of questions concerns
whether Hegel's theory can allow any *political* space for criticism of the
social order by those who remain unreconciled to its basic features. Most
important, how ought the state to treat individuals who on the basis of
their own conscience—perhaps even their moral willfulness—cannot
affirm the laws and norms of their society?

The charge that the theory of *Sittlichkeit* fails to recognize the freedom
to criticize the existing social order as an essential right of moral subjectivity comes closer to hitting its mark than the other objections considered here thus far. There are, for example, no passages in the *Philosophy
of Right* that acknowledge the importance of social members having the
freedom to engage in public discourse that is critical of their social institutions. One place we would expect to find such an acknowledgment is
the discussion of the press's role within political society (§319+A). But
here Hegel completely ignores the function a free press could serve as a
forum for rational, critical debate. Instead he appears to defend freedom
of the press (in a very limited form) only because it satisfies the need of
individuals "to express even their subjective opinions concerning the
universal" (§308A) and because the falsity, distortion, and derision that
are likely to result from such freedom can do little damage in a well-constituted state. Here, as in his discussion of public opinion more generally
(§§316–319), the freedom to express one's opinions publicly seems to be
viewed more as a concession to the vanity of individuals who need to
"put in their own two cents' worth" than as a precondition for a public,

reasoned debate about the merits and shortcomings of the social order. Views such as these can only reinforce the fear expressed earlier that Hegel is able to see social criticism only as an expression of caprice and willfulness rather than a valuable manifestation of moral subjectivity.

It is tempting to respond here that Hegel simply is not interested in less than ideal cases (where freedom is imperfectly actualized) but only in articulating the standards for a fully rational social order and in showing that the actual institutions of the modern world constitute such an order. But even if we grant the latter description of Hegel's project (which is, after all, correct), we are still quite far from the conclusion that social criticism can have no place in his theory. In fact, the contrary is the case, and the truth of this is unmistakably revealed by an obvious but frequently overlooked feature of his view. This feature is the simple fact that the social order the *Philosophy of Right* depicts and lauds as "actual" *(wirklich)* nowhere exists in precisely the form in which Hegel presents it there. Despite Hegel's reputation as an apologist for the Prussian state, the institutions he endorses are obviously not identical to those of nineteenth-century Prussia. It is precisely here—in the disparity between real (existing) institutions and those that are actual in Hegel's technical sense—that the possibility for social criticism is to be found. For the theory of *Sittlichkeit's idealized* account of modern social institutions provides us with the resources for seeing where existing institutions do not fully measure up to what they should be and for thinking about how they can be made to conform to their own (immanent) rational principles.

That the critical potential of Hegel's social theory is so often overlooked is no doubt due in part to a natural misunderstanding of his claim that the primary aim of philosophy is to reconcile human beings with the actual world. But in this context it is important to recognize that, properly understood, reconciliation is not incompatible with social criticism directed at the reform, as opposed to the radical overhaul, of existing institutions. Criticism and reform are consistent with the spirit of Hegel's theory, insofar as they aim at transforming institutions so as to make them conform more faithfully to the rational principles already implicit in their existent practices. This is just to say, in Hegelian jargon, that the proper object of our reconciliation is actuality (*Wirklichkeit*), not existing reality (*Realität*). Actuality, as Hegel conceives it, is not to be identified with whatever exists; it is, instead, the *unity* of existing reality

(*Existenz*) and its rational essence (EL §142).[37] This means that actuality includes, beyond mere existence, a philosophical comprehension of the rational principles that inform existing reality and make manifest its inherent goodness. Applied to the social world, 'actuality' refers to existing social reality as reconstructed within rational (philosophical) thought— thought that aims to clarify and bring into harmony the basic principles underlying the various existing social orders that typify western European modernity. As such, actuality represents a purified version of existing reality that is more fully rational than any particular existent social order but that is not for that reason independent of, or out of touch with, the existing world. To say that the object of reconciliation is reality that has been reconstructed in thought is not to saddle Hegel with an airy form of idealism that reduces actuality to "mere ideas" (or even "mere ideals"). Rather, the ideas (and ideals) that characterize the actual social order are already to be found, though in imperfect form, in existing institutions. Thus, the normative standards Hegelian social criticism brings to bear on existing reality are actual, and not "merely ideal," in the sense that they are not externally imposed upon, but already belong to, the existing object of criticism. (To take an example from American democracy: the practice of "one person, one vote" embodies an ideal of political equality that is imperfectly realized as long as political campaigns are financed by the "donations" of a few wealthy individuals or corporations. Thus, criticism of the existing order is possible in the name of ideals that already govern existing practices.) A further sense in which the normative standards employed by Hegelian social criticism are more than mere ideals is that realizing them (or approximating them) is an achievable end rather than a utopian dream. This is so, first, because the rational reconstruction that results from "comprehending" the social order guarantees that there is nothing intrinsic to its idea that would preclude its perfect realization and, second, because the survey of existing reality that first yielded the ideals employed by the theory of *Sittlichkeit* confirms that the basic preconditions of rational institutions are already in place and that such institutions already exist in basic outline.[38]

Finally, these points help to explain how a critical perspective on social reality is compatible with the basic subjective disposition that Hegel's theory requires of free social members. These two attitudes can easily appear to be in direct conflict, since finding one's identity in one's social membership requires a kind of affirmation of the existing social order that seems to be incompatible with criticizing it. Now, however, we are in a position to see that no such conflict exists, since, strictly speaking, the proper object of our affirmation as socially free individuals is not institutions as they presently exist but something like "our institutions as they aspire to be, almost are, and in principle could be (if only we worked hard enough to bring them better in line with their own ideals)." There is nothing contradictory in thinking that a single individual can both take his American citizenship to constitute a substantial part of who he is (in the sense required by Hegel's theory) and hold that in their present form American political institutions do not completely measure up to their own immanent ideals. What *is* required for this synthesis to be possible is that existing institutions come close enough to realizing their own ideals so as to be recognized either as genuine, albeit imperfect, embodiments of the actual (rational) social order or as on their way to becoming such.[39]

It is clear, then, that Hegel's theory has the resources for regarding at least some forms of social criticism not only as consistent with the affirmative disposition essential to free social membership but also as a legitimate, even necessary, exercise of moral subjectivity. Why, then, does it appear otherwise? One reason is that Hegel's discussion of this issue is distorted both by exaggerated worries about the dangers of criticism that originates "from below" and by an excessive confidence that a "universal class" with its professional intellectuals can serve as a society's sole or primary mouthpiece of moral conscience. (One of the obvious dangers of the latter—more obvious to us than it was to Hegel—is that members of an intellectual elite may be too comfortable in their relatively privileged positions to carry out their critical mission with sufficient vigor.) It is important to recognize that the source of Hegel's failure to appreciate public opinion and a free press as positive forces of social criticism does not lie in a general inability of his theory to accommodate a critical perspective within the subjective disposition appropriate to *Sittlichkeit* but rather in his mistrust of their *popular* (and hence undisciplined) character. Although this mistrust of the masses' capacity for judgment is not completely extrinsic to Hegel's larger view—it is bound up with the belief that only philosophy (and trained philosophers) have a fully comprehensive perspective on the social order's good[40]—it is not essential to his most fundamental theoretical commitments, those concerning the nature of freedom and the social conditions of its realization. There is nothing intrinsic to these fundamental commitments that accounts for Hegel's skittishness about the masses or for his failure to emphasize that certain kinds of social criticism are compatible with, perhaps even required by, his account of the different forms of practical freedom.

A second reason it can seem that the theory of *Sittlichkeit* excludes social criticism in any guise is that Hegel goes to great lengths to express his opposition to the particular type of critique for which his theory indeed has no place. The kind of critique Hegel thinks is at odds with the fullest realization of freedom—first, because it is incompatible with finding one's identity in one's social membership and, second, because in the modern world such critique is untrue—is what one might call *radical* social criticism. Radical critique can take two forms: the first involves a rejection of the basic values that existing institutions embody (or seek to embody), whereas the second accepts those values as worthy ideals but insists that the existing social order is in principle incapable of realizing them and must therefore be replaced by new institutions that, as yet, exist only on the drawing boards of social engineers. An example of the first kind of critique would be the claim that the individualistic values encouraged by civil society—self-reliance, private enrichment, and the achievement of self-chosen professional identities—are unworthy ideals, perhaps because they preclude the formation of genuine bonds to others, or because they distract human beings from pursuing more important goods such as eternal salvation or national honor. Familiar examples of the second kind of radical critique include the claim that the essentially patriarchal nature of the nuclear family makes it a site of enslavement rather than liberation (at least for its female members), and the charge that the principles of free-market exchange make it impossible for most participants both to support themselves economically and to engage in meaningful, identity-constituting work.

It is easy to see how adopting a radically critical stance toward existing institutions is in conflict with the realization of social freedom as Hegel conceives it, since doing so is incompatible with finding one's identity within one's social roles in the sense in which his theory requires. This point alone, however, is not sufficient to establish the undesirability of radical criticism, for it is possible to imagine cases in which subjective identification with one's social order can take place only by, in effect, relinquishing one's status as a moral subject. For if existing institutions are fundamentally bad—if they stand in the way of, rather than promote, the realization of freedom in its various forms—then social members who affirm those institutions put themselves in conflict with the good and hence with their own (true) conscience. In other words, Hegel does not believe that radical social criticism is unwarranted in all historical circumstances, nor that it is always an expression of willfulness, or moral self-conceit. On the contrary, radical social critique counts as unwarranted and willful only in the modern (Western) world, and this is because modernity's three social institutions are, in basic outline, rational. In historical circumstances in which the latter condition does not obtain, refusing to affirm the existing social order must be regarded as a legitimate expression of moral subjectivity.[41]

An obvious question arises here concerning the plausibility of the claim that undergirds Hegel's opposition to radical social critique—that the modern social order *merits* no such critique—but before turning to that issue in the final section of this chapter, it is important simply to clarify the implications of Hegel's view. What, more precisely, does it mean to say that the theory of *Sittlichkeit* allows no philosophical space for radical critique? It means, first and foremost, that individuals who do not affirm and subjectively identify with social institutions that are in essence rational, or who inhabit a social order so bad that it cannot be rationally affirmed, fall short of realizing the full range of freedoms available to modern subjects. Since in both situations individuals experience the laws and norms that govern social life as imposed on them from without, both are instances of unfreedom, or of alienation from the social world. No matter what the reason for such alienation, Hegel regards it as a lamentable falling short of the ideal of reconciliation. But apart from this judgment as to the unfree or alienated status of those who engage in radical social critique, what does the theory of *Sittlichkeit* have to say about how a rational social order ought to treat those who fail to affirm its basic institutions? Does it, in other words, attribute any importance to such individuals having the *political* freedom (or right) to communicate their dissatisfaction to others, no matter how alienated or willful true theory might show it to be? This question leads directly back to the second of the liberal concerns distinguished earlier, namely, how the Hegelian state proposes to treat individuals whose consciences do not allow them to recognize as authoritative the laws and norms that the theory of *Sittlichkeit* takes to be fully justified.

To this question Hegel's texts offer, at best, conflicting answers. In several passages, all located in "Morality," Hegel appears to assert quite clearly that the merely formal conscience has no protected status within the rational state:

> The state cannot recognize conscience in its distinctive form (that is, as *subjective knowledge*) any more than subjective *opinion* . . . has validity within science." (§137A)

> On the one hand, conscience is a sacred place; on the other hand, however, it is not to be respected. It depends on whether its content is true, whether it contains the principles of objective duty. (VPR4, 362)

> In general nothing is to be ceded [*ist darauf nichts zu geben*] when someone says in response to demands made of him by the state that it is against his conscience to fulfill them. (VPR2, 107)

Nowhere in these passages does Hegel suggest that individuals ought to be guaranteed certain rights to disobey, or to express their opposition to, laws or social norms that the theory of *Sittlichkeit* regards as justified but that they, as beings of conscience, cannot endorse. The statements cited here might be charitably interpreted as merely making the weak and unobjectionable claim that simply disagreeing with legitimately constituted laws is not sufficient to dissolve one's obligation to obey them. But given both the absence of explicit statements to the contrary and the frequency with which Hegel associates social criticism with willfulness, even reasoned public dissent appears to fall within the province of Hegel's pronouncement that merely formal conscience "is not to be respected."

A more nuanced picture emerges, however, when we turn to those passages in "*Sittlichkeit*" where Hegel takes up a concrete example of conscientious dissent by considering the status of religious minorities, such as Jews, Quakers, and Mennonites. The first thing to be noted is that here Hegel explicitly recognizes something very close to the rights of religious conscience as upheld by orthodox liberalism: "the state can have no say in the content [of religious belief], insofar as this content relates to the internal dimension of representational thought" (§270A).[42] Moreover, his support for such rights is explicitly grounded in his account of moral subjectivity (more precisely, in a respect for each individual's right to determine for himself what is true in religious matters): "[Religious] *doctrine* itself has its province within conscience and enjoys the right of the subjective freedom of self-consciousness—the sphere of inwardness, which as such lies outside the province of the state" (§270A). Since these passages repeatedly draw attention to the distinction between "internal" belief and "external" action, it can easily appear that the rights of conscience Hegel recognizes pertain exclusively to religious belief and hence not to *actions* required by the laws and norms of *Sittlichkeit*. Yet Hegel's actual statements concerning the treatment of religious minorities clearly grant them a degree of "external" freedom not to comply with their political duties:

> A state that is strong because its organization is fully developed can adopt a more liberal attitude . . . and can completely overlook particular matters that might affect it, or even tolerate communities whose religion does not recognize even their direct duties to the state (although this of course depends on the numbers concerned). The state does this by entrusting the members of such communities to civil society and its laws, and is satisfied if they fulfill their direct duties to the state passively, for example, by commutation or substitution [of an alternate service]. (§270A)

In expressing the view that a well-constituted state ought to *tolerate* dissenting communities, Hegel clearly means to stop short of claiming that conscientious objectors have a *right* (in at least some sense of that term) to be exempted from the legitimate duties of citizenship.[43] But what his view ultimately comes to (or ought to, given the basic principles of his theory) is the claim that such dissenters have no *unconditional* right to be exempted from the duties that membership in the state normally imposes on those who belong to it. For, as the passage quoted here indicates, there are certain circumstances—for example, when dissenters become too numerous—in which no such exemption can rightfully be demanded. This view must not be confused with one that advocates the toleration of dissenting communities on merely prudential grounds (for example, because doing otherwise would be too difficult or costly, or would give rise to social unrest). Hegel's view, in contrast, (or at any rate the view that follows from his own principles) endorses toleration on moral grounds but denies that those grounds imply an unconditional right to follow one's conscience in defiance of the state.[44] As we have seen, the theory of *Sittlichkeit* is constructed around the idea that practical self-determination assumes a variety of forms and that these forms can be hierarchically ranked according to how close each comes to embodying the ideal of complete self-determination. This view, together with Hegel's commitment to the value of self-determination in all of its forms, implies that some degree of moral value (and hence respect) is to be accorded the exercise of conscience regardless of whether the ethical standards an individual takes as authoritative are objectively valid. An individual who determines himself to act in accord with standards of the good that are false but nevertheless "his own" clearly fails to achieve the highest level of self-determination to which modern moral subjects aspire. Yet Hegel is committed to holding that such an individual achieves a degree of self-determination that, however incomplete, merits the respect of others and of the state in whatever ways are consistent with the systematic realization of freedom in its various forms.

Ascribing this position to Hegel requires nothing more than applying the same principles that inform his account of the nature and limits of abstract right (the rights of persons) to the case of moral subjectivity. For there, too, a form of freedom is at issue—choosing which of one's given desires to act upon—that falls short of complete self-determination but is nevertheless important enough to ground a system of rights that a rational social order must respect and enforce. The freedom that defines personhood bears an important similarity to the type of self-determination I am ascribing here to the merely formal conscience in that it, too, is independent of the will's actual content (the ends the person chooses as his own). In order for the person's ends to count as self-determined, and hence as prima facie worthy of others' respect, it is enough that those ends be freely chosen. This criterion is formal because it is indifferent to what one chooses: choosing an end suffices to make it "mine."[45] A further similarity between the two cases is that both generate only conditional rights. The rights of persons, like the rights appropriate to the merely formal conscience, can be overridden in those rare circumstances where they conflict with another, more compelling "right," such as the social order's continued existence. The consistent Hegelian position on this issue, then, brings together the following three claims: (1) conscientious dissenters ought to be accorded a right to public criticism of the social order and to noncompliance with laws that violate their understanding of the good; (2) this right is grounded in their dignity as moral subjects rather than in prudential considerations; and

(3) this right can be overridden only when the state's very existence, or some other compelling interest in freedom, is at stake.[46]

In response to the objection that the theory of *Sittlichkeit* allows no room for moral subjects to engage in conscientious criticism of the existing social order, I have attempted to establish two main points: first, that the sense in which Hegel's theory requires individuals to find their identities within their social roles is compatible with their adopting a substantive, though limited, critical stance with respect to the social world, namely, one that envisages the reform, though not the radical overhaul, of existing institutions so as to bring them in line with their own immanent ideals; and, second, that the reason Hegel regards more radical critique as undesirable is not that his theory places too low a value on moral subjectivity—requiring it to give way in any circumstance to whatever demands the state might make—but rather because he is convinced that a radical critique of modern social institutions would be *mistaken* and hence would entail the subjective alienation of individuals from a social order that was in truth essentially good.[47] While it is true that Hegel regards "being at home" in the actual social world as the highest practical good, *taking* the world to be a home—being *subjectively* reconciled to it[48]—is desirable only when it can be achieved without compromising one's status as a moral subject.

Thus, liberal critics are clearly right in arguing that Hegel's theory, without going so far as legally to prohibit radical social critique, fails to recognize it as having a value in the modern world that would warrant its being specially protected or encouraged, or even thought worthwhile. As was pointed out earlier, this charge finds support in a central feature of Hegel's view, namely, that its strategy for accommodating the rights of conscience within *Sittlichkeit* gives priority to the task of making the rationality of the modern social order transparent to its members and thus underplays the importance of maintaining a political space within which divergent understandings of the social good can compete for public acceptance. What is less clear, however, is the extent to which liberal critics are justified in regarding this feature of Hegel's position as an irremediable defect that signals the failure of his theory as a whole. Settling this issue will require a more detailed examination of the specific doctrine that grounds this aspect of Hegel's view, the claim that in

their modern form the institutions of *Sittlichkeit* adequately embody objectively true standards of the good and that they stand in need of no further substantive transformation in order to be fully rational. The question we shall need to consider is how deeply Hegel's theory as a whole
depends on this doctrine, and to what extent the theory's plausibility
and relevance are diminished if we find ourselves unable to share Hegel's
assurance that our own standards of the good—and, derivatively, of the
rational social order—are demonstrably final and beyond all need of
revision.

Before addressing this question directly, it is necessary to say a word
about the scope, or "thickness," of the conception of the good that the
theory of *Sittlichkeit* relies on. This issue arises here because when asked
whether we can plausibly take our own standards of the good to be ultimate and unrevisable, the contemporary response is likely to be that, insofar as we are referring to "thick," or substantive, conceptions of the
good, talk of "our" conception is no longer meaningful. How can we, at
the end of the twentieth century, ask whether our standards of the good
are finally true, if, as is generally assumed to be the case, the very absence of substantive consensus about the good is a defining feature of
our historical situation? Taking this thought one step further, doesn't
this feature of the contemporary world imply that Hegel's account of the
rational social order, with its reliance on the idea of a universally shared
understanding of the good, amounts to little more than the elaborately
constructed fantasy of a backward-looking romanticism? Doesn't his
theoretical edifice simply collapse when confronted with what Rawls
terms "the fact of pluralism"?

The short answer to this question is that while Hegel's theory does require there to be substantive agreement among social members concerning the good, what they are expected to share is a considerably thinner
conception of the good than is normally assumed.[49] It can easily appear
that Hegel's theory ultimately rests on something like the classical doctrine of the one rational good, which posits a final end (or ordered set of
ends) that exhaustively specifies the good of individuals, fixes their sta-
tions and duties, and defines what it is right or rational for them to do in
any circumstance.[50] Yet despite some undeniable affinities between the
theory of *Sittlichkeit* and Plato's social philosophy, the appearance that
Hegel is closer to the ancients than to modern liberalism is illusory.

A first step toward clarifying Hegel's relation to the value pluralism that motivates much of contemporary liberalism is to notice that the concept of the good at work in the theory of *Sittlichkeit* is not relative to particular individuals. As Hegel employs the concept, my conception of the good is not a conception of what is good *for me*. Rather, 'the good' is a universal moral concept that is taken to have the same content for all subjects. Its grammar is such that judging a thing to be good entails both taking oneself to have a moral duty to do what one can to bring it about (E §507, §133+Z) and believing that any similarly situated individual would have the same obligation. This usage, however, stands in sharp contrast to what liberal theorists usually mean by 'the good' when they refer to divergence among individuals' conceptions of the good in the modern world. Rawls, for example, explicitly characterizes a conception of the good as an individual's understanding of what constitutes his own rational advantage or, alternatively, of what plan of life is most rational for him, as the particular individual he is.[51] This means that whatever agreement about the good Hegel's social theory requires, it is not agreement about which life is best for all individuals, or for any particular individual. Rather, the theory of *Sittlichkeit* explicitly allows for a wide divergence among both the "life plans" individuals make for themselves and the conceptions of *their own good* that such plans express. Indeed, the theory *requires* such divergence, since the tasks a social order must carry out are numerous and varied and can be done well only by individuals who adopt rather specialized forms of life. Farming, trading, philosophizing, and (for Hegel) raising children are examples of essential social functions whose differing natures demand differing commitments and values—and hence differing styles of life—of those who execute them.

To be sure, Hegel's theory places some general constraints on the kinds of lives that will be available for most individuals to lead. That is, the rational social order will not be possible unless its members, or many of them at least, lead lives centered around a threefold commitment to family, work, and (usually to a lesser extent) the cultural and political life of the nation. It is important, though, that the nature of these constraints be correctly understood. First, as I have already suggested, these general constraints are compatible with there being a rich diversity among the concrete forms of life and final ends that individuals choose as best for themselves. With respect to this issue, the theory of *Sittlichkeit* is best understood as providing a broadly drawn picture of the kinds of lives the majority of social members must be able to find meaningful and well suited to their own natures if the social order is to reproduce itself and fulfill its essential task of realizing practical freedom. Second, the constraints Hegel's theory places on the kinds of lives available to most individuals have no legal status, nor are they in any way coercive. There is no thought here of consigning individuals to socially necessary roles against their will, since doing so would blatantly violate a basic principle of self-determination (the principle of personhood). Hegel's view, rather, is that in a well-functioning social order individuals will typically grow up having acquired the desires and values that lead them to embrace the sanctioned roles of *Sittlichkeit,* not merely voluntarily, but as constitutive of the very projects that give their lives significance. Socialization, as part of the *Bildung* of individuals, is the only tool the rational social order has at its disposal to help ensure that its manifold essential functions are carried out. Hegel is not at all disturbed—and neither should we be—by the thought that the lives individuals will come to want for themselves will display a high degree of conformity to established norms in the broad sense that most will aspire to establish a family, to seek fulfillment in a career, and to have some part in their nation's cultural and political life. What is important from his perspective, rather, is that the social roles that are widely available to individuals—and by extension the institutions that define them—are *worthy* of being taken up by generation after generation, which is to say that they can be justified as good according to the standards implicit in the modern ideal of moral subjectivity.

Finally, there is no reason that Hegel's theory need make outlaws, or even social outcasts, of the minority of individuals who lead more idiosyncratic lives at the margins of bourgeois respectability. So, for example, his defense of the family as an institution essential to the realization of freedom does not imply that a rational social order will require or expect *all* social members to marry or *all* married couples to raise children.[52] It does imply that individuals who have no children or who live outside of a committed sexual relationship will miss out on an especially deep kind of social bond that gives meaning and substance to most people's lives. The lives of such individuals can rightfully be said to be impoverished in fundamental respects, but this should not be taken to mean that no degree of compensatory enrichment can be had by developing other aspects of one's identity, nor that all individuals would be

better off overall if they married and raised a family. What is most important from the perspective of Hegel's social theory is that sufficient numbers of individuals be motivated to enter into the commitments of family
life so that the family, as a social institution, can flourish and reproduce
itself. Beyond this, it is also important that there be general agreement,
among both those who are in families and those who are not, as to the
fundamental value of the family as an institution and the importance of
whatever social measures—subsidized child care, say, or parental leave
laws—are needed to reinforce it. There is nothing that precludes an individual who chooses the single life as best for himself (as part of the most
rational life *for him*) from recognizing the family as a good institution
(good in Hegel's impersonal sense) and from assenting to social measures that strengthen it. All that is necessary, then, for social members to
be able to agree on the fundamental importance of the family is a (more
or less articulated) understanding of the role it plays in realizing practical self-determination and a belief in the general value of those elements
(including a relatively thin conception of what is good for all, or most,
human individuals) that enter into Hegel's rather expansive understanding of self-determination.

Generalizing from the example of the family, it becomes clear that
what Hegel's vision of *Sittlichkeit* requires is a consensus among social members that the three institutions of modernity provide the basic
framework within which most human individuals will be able to lead
good and meaningful lives. The shared understanding of the good on
which such a consensus depends amounts to a general agreement about
the importance for all individuals of those goods the institutions of
Sittlichkeit are distinctively suited to secure: personal and moral freedom, social recognition and self-esteem, substantive attachments to others, and satisfaction of the fundamental human needs to love and to be
productive. It is difficult to see how any theory, liberal or otherwise, that
takes sufficient account of the general requirements of human satisfaction and also recognizes the need for individuals to affirm the norms and
structures that govern their social life could dispense with all manner of
agreement concerning not just the liberties individuals deserve but also
the basic kinds of goods the social order must enable them to pursue.
Rawls's brand of liberalism, for one, does not forgo such agreement, nor
does it aim to. Indeed, if we take seriously Rawls's assertion that his theory of justice requires consensus on a thin conception of the good,[53] his

insistence that self-respect is a primary good that just institutions must promote,[54] and his view that nonpolitical institutions—most notably, the family—play an essential part in realizing the just society,[55] then the differences between his theory's use of the good and Hegel's appear to signal minor disputes over the content and scope of that concept (as it is relevant to social theory) rather than a fundamental disagreement over social theory's need to rely on some general account of what constitutes the basic, or "primary," goods of a human life.

One possible objection to this attempt to see Hegel's doctrine of the good as more compatible with (Rawlsian) liberalism than is normally assumed can be formulated as follows: although Hegel's theory may leave social members plenty of room to determine for themselves what concrete form of life is best for them, the philosophical justification of that theory ultimately rests on something very close to the kind of comprehensive conception of the good[56] on which Rawls and many other liberals believe it is impossible, even undesirable, for modern individuals to agree. Thus, so the charge goes, at the foundation of the theory of *Sittlichkeit* lies a comprehensive metaphysical vision of the world that grounds the norms that define the rational social order by situating them within a systematic account of all realms of value, including the religious, the philosophical, the aesthetic, and the moral. There is clearly some basis for this objection, insofar as Hegel's social theory is part of a larger, overtly metaphysical[57] account of the meaning of human history, the availability of spiritual redemption, and the ultimate value of all things. Yet the fact that Hegel's account of the rational social order fits into a more comprehensive vision of the nature and purpose of the universe as a whole does not imply that what makes the rational social order good on his account can be grasped and appreciated only within the context of his theodicy. Indeed, one of the persistent aims of this book has been to show that the normative standards that inform Hegel's social theory can be made plausible and compelling in detachment from his secular theodicy simply by articulating how they have their source in the ideal of practical freedom—or, more precisely, in a variety of forms of that ideal that are generally recognizable as good by modern subjects. My claim, in other words, is that one need not accept Hegel's view that the whole of reality is at bottom rational, nor his understanding of the historical role the rational social order plays in realizing divine ends, in order to find the normative standards of his social theory compelling.

One reason for this is that, contrary to what is usually assumed, Hegel's argument that the modern social order is essentially rational is, in one important sense, logically prior to his grander claim that reason (or God) pervades all of reality. For establishing the latter view depends, in part, on being able to show first that the social order, as one piece of all reality, is rational. What makes it possible to comprehend the institutions of *Sittlichkeit* as rational prior to the conclusion of Hegel's system is not some recognition that they serve a greater end beyond themselves, nor that they fit into a larger story about how divine purpose is realized throughout the world. On the contrary, Hegel is able to find a place for the rational social order within his theodicy only because, considered just on their own, the institutions of *Sittlichkeit* can be shown to realize one particular form of the divine, or unconditioned, good of self-determination, namely, the self-determination of the will. This claim—that the modern social order can be recognized as good in detachment from Hegel's most comprehensive metaphysical views—finds reinforcement in Hegel's explicit acknowledgment that social members need not be of a single religious faith in order to live harmoniously within the state and to recognize one another as fellow citizens who share a general will. Rather than lamenting the fact of religious diversity, Hegel regards the division of the Christian church as "the most fortunate thing that could have happened to the church and to thought" (§270A).[58] Clearly, then, Hegel himself does not believe that embracing divergent philosophical or religious views of the world makes it impossible for social members to share an allegiance to the secular, nonparochial values of self-determination that underlie his defense of the institutions of modern *Sittlichkeit*.

Having established that the theory of *Sittlichkeit* need not require social members to agree on a comprehensive conception of the good in the sense most liberals have in mind when they deny that such agreement is possible for us, it is time to return to the question posed earlier concerning how deeply Hegel's theory depends on the claim that the standards of the good he ascribes to the modern age are not merely "ours" (the ones we happen to share) but are objectively true and unrevisable, and that the social institutions he takes to embody those standards are therefore in need of no further substantive transformation in order to be fully rational (and, thus, are not the proper object of radical critique). As suggested previously, this question arises out of an apparent tension between the requirements of moral subjectivity—more specifically, the demand that what one's conscience endorses be not only "one's own" but also rationally defensible—and Hegel's central claim that identifying with the social roles available through the institutions of *Sittlichkeit* is an essential part of the full freedom of modern individuals. The potential for conflict here resides in the fact that identifying with one's social roles in the way Hegel's theory requires is incompatible with being radically critical of existing institutions or in doubt about their basic goodness, since identifying with one's roles entails regarding the institutions they are part of as fundamentally good, if not so in all details. But affirming existing institutions in a way that excludes the possibility of radical critique can be regarded as rational—as part of the realization of self-determination in *all* of its forms—only on the assumption that one's normative assessment of the social order is not subject to fundamental doubt. Thus, the importance Hegel places on individuals' identification with their social roles appears to rely quite heavily on his conviction that modern standards of the good have the status of ultimate truths and that existing institutions are for the most part adequate to them.

The specific worry that arises here is that the kind of subjective affirmation of institutions endorsed by Hegel's theory makes it unlikely, perhaps even impossible, that social members will be disposed to give a serious hearing to any form of radical social criticism, some instances of which might, for all we know, turn out to be worthy of consideration. This worry gains force for us from the simple fact that we inhabit a historical era subsequent to Hegel's and that significant parts of what looked rational to his age appear hopelessly reactionary to ours. Our historical experience appears to demonstrate that no set of social institutions, even as idealized in accord with their own immanent standards, deserves to be taken as a finally adequate expression of unshakable standards of the good. And if the finality of one's account of good social institutions cannot be guaranteed, then the kind of identification with social roles that Hegel's theory emphasizes—one that appears to preclude consideration of the possible need for substantive social change—seems to be of ambiguous value at best. In that case might not the very opposite of this identification—*alienation* from existing institutions—also be of ethical value, insofar as it represents a subjective precondition of progress toward an even better social order?

One of the reasons these issues acquire particular urgency for us is that historical developments since Hegel's time have made it impossible to ignore at least two powerful arguments that cast doubt on the fundamental goodness of the institutions the theory of *Sittlichkeit* endorses: first, the critique of feminists that the essentially patriarchal character of the bourgeois family makes it, at least for its female members, a site of oppression rather than liberation; and, second, the socialist critique that the principles of a free-market (capitalist) economy make it impossible for productive activity to be a source of meaning and identity for most of its participants. Developments such as these not only make it impossible for us to accept Hegel's claim to have delivered a final, unrevisable account of rational social institutions; they also make clear that if his account of social freedom is to be reconciled with the demands of moral subjectivity, something more is required beyond merely taking measures to ensure that *insight* into the rational character of the social order is accessible to all of its members. In addition, it is necessary to show that finding one's identity within one's social roles is not incompatible with the ability to criticize even certain basic features of social institutions—the exclusion of women from civil society and the state, for example—and be motivated to work toward bringing about substantive changes in the very institutions with which one identifies.

One possible response to the recognition that aspects of Hegel's account of the actual (fully rational) social order can no longer be accepted would be, first, to retain the Hegelian ideal of a social order in which individuals find their particular identities by participating in social institutions that perfectly accommodate all of the aspirations of self-determining subjectivity but, second, to deny Hegel's further claim that existing institutions have the potential to realize that ideal. The task of social philosophy, then, would be to redesign social institutions through measures—for example, communalizing ownership of the means of production—that would make identification with the social order, and reconciliation to the world, possible. This, in essence, is the Left Hegelian response. The problem with this position is that it both follows and breaks with Hegelian social theory in precisely the wrong places. In lieu of the more modest critique Hegel's theory allows for, it substitutes a radical form of social criticism that seeks to obliterate existing institutions and replace them with the untried fabrications of utopian speculation. Hegel's observation of the Jacobin Terror was sufficient to convince him of the danger and ultimate futility of this form of social critique. At the same time, the Left Hegelian position tends to retain Hegel's eschatological faith in the achievability, in this world and in our own time, of a social order that is fully and finally rational. This position preserves the dubious Hegelian ideal of a social order that will satisfy, once and for all, the whole of reason's demands; it diverges from Hegel's eschatology only in asserting that the perfected social order is just around the corner rather than already here. The question I am raising here, in contrast, is whether a Hegelian social theory can incorporate a more open-ended attitude to its own account of what constitutes a good social order—that is, an attitude to its own standards of the good that allows for individuals to affirm their social roles as constitutive of their own identities but also takes those normative standards to be open to substantive revision in the face of unanticipated historical developments.

Since the feminist critique of the family is the more widely accepted of the two contemporary critiques mentioned here, it is the natural place to begin a discussion of the extent to which Hegel's theory can relinquish its claim to be in possession of the final truth about the rational social order without thereby abandoning its central doctrines concerning the nature of social freedom. The solution to this problem, if there is one, must lie in showing that while the social changes implied by the feminist critique of the family are clearly substantive on some ordinary meaning of that term, they are not radical in the sense (defined earlier) that would make them irreconcilable in principle with the theory of *Sittlichkeit*. In other words, what needs to be demonstrated is that Hegel's theory is able to accommodate a kind of social criticism that involves more than merely bringing existing institutions in line with their own immanent ideals but something less than a wholesale rejection of those institutions from a perspective external to the basic values they aspire to embody. I shall argue here that it is possible to understand the feminist critique of the family, in at least one of its widely accepted versions, as an instance of precisely this kind of social criticism—that is, as an example of what could be called "substantive immanent critique."[59] An implication of this thesis is that women who accept the feminist critique of the family can do so without ultimately relinquishing their practical identities as wives and mothers. What the feminist critique of the family requires of them is not that they stop wanting to be mothers, wives, and daughters but rather that they—and ultimately, of course, the men they live with—substantively revise their conceptions of what properly belongs to those roles.

The need for substantive revisions in Hegel's understanding of the modern family has its source in a head-on conflict between the subordinate role the Hegelian family assigns to women and a widespread contemporary belief in the basic equality of men and women that is the legacy of more than a century of feminist thought and activism since Hegel's time. Although Hegel thinks of himself as incorporating some form of equality between men and women into his account of the family (§167N), the hollowness of this equality comes to light in his unambiguous assertion that, at least in its dealings with the external world, the husband is the family's head and the wife his subordinate (§171). It is extremely important for understanding the source of the oppression of women—both in Hegel's account of the family and in the real world—to note that the wife's subordinate role in the family follows directly from her exclusion from the spheres of civil society and the state—from the fact, in other words, that while "the man has his actual substantial life in the state . . . and in work and struggle in the outer world," the woman "has her substantial vocation [only] in the family" (§166). Moreover, Hegel explicitly traces this difference in the "substantial vocations" of the sexes back to alleged natural differences between male and female (§165): men are by nature powerful, active, and rational—in short, they have the capacity for freedom—whereas women, because they are naturally quiet, passive, and immersed in "subjective" feeling, are best suited to receiving direction from others (§166+Z).

Hegel's reliance on the supposition that the natures of men and women diverge in ways that are both clearly identifiable and ethically significant constitutes a major obstacle to the acceptance of his account of the family in the late twentieth century, for, quite simply, few of us continue to believe that such differences exist. Yet to reject this doctrine is to deny a nontrivial element of Hegel's account,[60] which is to say that criticizing the Hegelian family for being patriarchal cannot plausibly be regarded as an instance of the kind of critique the theory of *Sittlichkeit* has already been shown to be able to accommodate (critique that aims merely at bringing existing institutions in conformity with their own immanent ideals). Thus, it becomes important to ask whether the kind of identification with social roles that Hegel's theory envisions would make it impossible for women who initially identified with their roles in the patriarchal family to come to recognize their own subordination within it and to be motivated to change it without thereby surrendering their own identities as wives and mothers in ways that would constitute a fundamental alienation from the institution of the family as such. I shall argue that this kind of substantive immanent critique of institutions is not in fact ruled out by Hegel's emphasis on the identity-constituting character of free social participation. The point here is not to claim that either critique of this sort or the struggle to effect the transformations it implies can avoid being painful and disruptive for those who undertake it; the point is merely to show that the Hegelian ideal of finding one's identity through one's social roles need not prevent those who realize it from being the agents of the kinds of social transformation we have come to regard as inevitable and, indeed, to welcome as essential to historical progress.

Making this argument depends on distinguishing what is fundamental in Hegel's account of the family from those of its elements that, though not accidental, are less central to its main purposes. My claim will be that the strictly defined gender roles Hegel endorses belong to the second of these categories and thus that the core of what makes the family rational on his account is independent of the dogma of male superiority. If this is correct, it will be possible to understand in principle how women can reject the patriarchal features of the modern family while remaining fundamentally committed to the projects of marriage and motherhood. This is also to say that it will be possible to understand how substantive social transformation can be effected by agents who at the same time identify with their roles in the very institutions they seek to change.

In order to assess the extent to which sexual inequality is essential to the Hegelian family, it is necessary to recall the main reasons Hegel regards the family as an indispensable part of the rational social order. Formulated most generally, the family is good, or rational, because it is an arena within which human beings can find satisfaction of their basic needs for sex and love in a way that also imbues those natural needs with ethical significance. To say that sexual and affectional needs acquire ethical significance within the family is simply to say that satisfying those needs as parents and spouses do is part and parcel of the ethical project of actualizing freedom. The various senses in which freedom is actualized in the family should by this point be familiar: as a procreative unit the family furnishes the human material necessary for the continued reproduction of the social order and thus contributes essentially to its character as self-determining substance (chapter 4); in its child-rearing function the family forms the subjectivities of social members so as to give them the capacities they need to exercise the freedoms of personhood and moral subjectivity (chapter 5); membership in the family provides individuals with projects and commitments that are constitutive of their particular identities and that enable them to embrace collective goods as their own final ends and thus to remain free while acting in their service (chapter 3); finally, the family itself represents a "natural" or "immediate" form of spiritual existence—a kind of "being-with-oneself-in-another"—in that the love that binds its members entails a surrender of self-sufficient individuality and a finding of oneself in others that, in giving substance to subjectivity, realize spirit's defining characteristic (chapter 4).

The claim I mean to be making here is that none of these fundamental functions of the family is decisively threatened by abandoning the principle of sexual inequality. Although such inequality may have always been part of the family as history has known it, there is no reason to think that procreation, child rearing, and the bonds of familial love depend essentially on women's subordination to men. If this is true, then it must also be the case that women who come to reject the patriarchal character of the family can in principle do so without giving up their basic aspirations to be mothers and wives. This is because the projects that bind them most deeply to those roles retain their coherence and appeal in the absence of sexual inequality. Some historical evidence for this claim can be found in the resilience the modern ideal of family life has exhibited in the face of social developments that earlier generations would have taken to be straightforwardly incompatible with essential features of the family, developments that include not just the commitment to sexual equality but even a rejection of the presumption that spouses must be of opposite genders. This resilience shows itself in the large number of individuals in recent decades who have found themselves at odds with basic features of the family as it is usually understood—women who refuse their subordination to men, lesbians and gays who appear to be ineligible for parenthood because of their sexual orientation—and yet have not abandoned their aspirations to be parents and spouses but instead have devoted great energy to redefining the family in ways that allow them their own recognized place within it. (Contrary to what contemporary advocates of "family values" proclaim, same-sex marriages represent not the demise of the family but a creative reconfiguration of it, one that enhances the family's ability to reproduce itself by making it less restrictive without compromising its essential ethical significance.) These examples demonstrate that taking certain social roles to be central to one's identity in the way Hegel's theory envisages is not incompatible with rejecting some basic features of those roles and struggling to refashion them in ways that bring about the kinds of substantive social change that an account of the rational social order ought to allow for.[61]

I shall conclude this chapter by taking stock of the various ways in which Hegel's social theory responds to the challenge of creating a suitable place for moral subjectivity within ethical life. Does his theory succeed in its quest to preserve the ideal of the self-legislating, individual subject as furnished by the standpoint of "Morality"? To what extent is it true that, even though bound substantially to others, the member of *Sittlichkeit* remains "a perfectly free lord, subject to none"? Or, equivalently, what sense does it make to claim that in ethical life individuals are self-sufficient arbiters of the good, dependent on nothing external to their own subjectivity for knowledge of what duty requires? One way of addressing these questions is to begin by recapitulating the features of the debased, overly individualistic version of conscience (as depicted in "Morality") that Hegel intends to exclude from ethical life and then to ask whether the form of conscience he is left with can still be recognized as embodying a tolerably robust ideal of individual moral self-determination.

A careful review of this chapter would reveal that Hegel's critique of morality's overly individualistic conception of conscience can be reduced to two points. First, Hegel rejects any understanding of conscience that construes the autonomy of the moral subject as implying that an individual must actually endorse a moral principle in order to be obligated by it. As I have indicated earlier, the individual moral subject is not the "absolute lord" of his actions in the sense that he alone is entitled to judge whether a particular moral principle is binding for his will. Although Hegel attributes to the moral subject "the absolute authority . . . to recognize nothing other than what it . . . knows as the good" (§137A), he does not take a subject's actual insight into the rationality, or goodness, of a moral requirement as a necessary condition of its validity. (And, significantly, in this respect his view is no different from those of earlier proponents of this ideal. Neither Luther nor Rousseau nor Kant believes that a duty ceases to be a duty simply because an individual fails to recognize it as such.) Another way of formulating this point would be to say that the configuration of moral subjectivity that Hegel's theory reveres as a "sacred" power with "absolute authority" is conscience in its *true* rather than merely *formal* guise. Expressed in terms of this distinction, Hegel's point is that the failure of the merely formal conscience to achieve insight into the principles that derive from its own nature as a self-determining will implies not that it is unbound by those (true) ethical principles but only that, in being subject to laws it does not itself endorse, it falls short of achieving genuine moral autonomy.

As we have seen, this ideal of moral subjectivity is fulfilled in Hegel's vision of the rational social order only when social norms and laws both have their ultimate source in the essential character of the subject's own will (practical self-determination) and are sufficiently transparent to ordinary human reason that all social members are capable, in principle, of appreciating their legitimacy and, hence, of embracing them as their own. The complete sovereignty of the individual moral subject—its being bound exclusively by laws that derive from its own will—is not to be understood as a license to obey only those laws to which one actually assents but rather as an ideal that modern individuals *aspire* to realize, the ideal that any ethical principle that binds us will "first have made its way through the interior of the human being" (VPR4, 301). One of the central points of Hegel's theory of *Sittlichkeit* is that this moral ideal *can* be universally realized, but only in a modern social order where a panoply of rational, freedom-promoting laws and norms both in fact prevail and are affirmed as such by its members.

The second aspect of morality's conception of conscience that Hegel rejects is its implicit assumption that the self-determining moral subject is, or can be, an *isolated* individual, free of all relations to other legitimate moral authorities. Although Hegel holds that all individuals have (in principle) access to a true understanding of the good, this access is viewed as something they possess not as separate beings but as participants in a collective enterprise to determine the good and, hence, as subjects who are appropriately receptive to the moral testimony of others. Thus, properly understood, the self-sufficiency of moral subjects is not the authority to decide merely by oneself what duty requires; nor does it rest on the conceit that one's own perspective on the good is, simply because it is one's own, superior to everyone else's. Instead, genuine moral self-sufficiency is the ability individuals have to achieve a true understanding of the good by arriving at their own conclusions through a process of thinking together with others. This implies that in order to realize fully the freedom of moral subjectivity (including the requirement that one's ethical convictions be true), an individual must, in Rousseauean fashion, be dependent on the opinions of others while maintaining the intellectual autonomy implicit in the Enlightenment ideal of "thinking for oneself."

At the same time, it is important to bear in mind that even though he focuses on the "true" conscience and the conditions under which it can be achieved in the real world, Hegel's attitude to less perfectly realized forms of moral subjectivity is not one of simple disparagement. As I have argued earlier, in holding that "the sphere of inwardness . . . lies outside the province of the state" (§270A), Hegel commits himself to recognizing something very close to the political rights of conscience as understood by traditional liberals. Although conscientious dissenters cannot be granted an unconditional exemption from all laws and norms they do not themselves endorse, they deserve, as moral subjects, as much political space to act in accord with their consciences as is consistent with the continued existence of a free social order. For simply to follow the dictates of one's own conscience, even when it is merely "formal," is to achieve a degree of moral self-determination that, however incomplete, merits the conditional respect of others and of the state. Hegel's aim here, as well as in his philosophy of *Sittlichkeit* more generally, is not simply to dismiss those expressions of human freedom that fall short of complete self-determination but rather to inquire whether a social order is possible in which practical freedom, in all its forms, can be fully realized. His answer to this question is that such a world is not only possible but real; it is the world we already inhabit.

NOTES

INDEX

NOTES

Introduction

1. One notable exception is Michael O. Hardimon's recent book, *Hegel's Social Philosophy: The Project of Reconciliation* (Cambridge: Cambridge University Press, 1994). Although Hardimon provides a reliable and genuinely philosophical reconstruction of Hegel's social theory, he pays relatively little attention to the conception of *freedom* that is at work in the theory and to how that conception grounds Hegel's account of the three basic institutions. Although I agree with much of the substance of Hardimon's interpretation, my account differs from his primarily in that it gives pride of place to a systematic analysis of the concept that Hegel himself regards as the cornerstone of his theory, namely, freedom.

2. This claim is complicated by the fact that Hegel recognizes two basic forms of *Sittlichkeit,* modern and ancient. I shall be concerned here primarily with social freedom as it is realized in modern social institutions. But it would not be wrong to think of the ancient Greeks as realizing a primitive version of social freedom, one that does not yet incorporate the (historically later) freedoms of personhood and moral subjectivity. This is discussed further in chapter 1.

3. A quite different account of how the concept of freedom figures in Hegel's social and political philosophy is given by Terry Pinkard in *Hegel's "Phenomenology": The Sociality of Reason* (Cambridge: Cambridge University Press, 1994), chap. 7. The topic is also addressed by Allen W. Wood in *Hegel's Ethical Thought* (Cambridge: Cambridge University Press, 1990), chap. 2; by Robert B. Pippin in "Hegel, Ethical Reasons, Kantian Rejoinders," *Philosophical Topics* 19 (fall 1991): 99–108; and by Hardimon, *Hegel's Social Philosophy,* 111–116, 119.

4. SC, IV.2.viii. Here I am in essential agreement with Robert Pippin's assertion that "to understand Hegel's strategy, we need . . . to recall that [he] inherits a tradition that begins with Rousseau." See Pippin, "Hegel, Ethical Reasons, Kantian Rejoinders," 100.

5. Wood, *Hegel's Ethical Thought*; Hardimon, *Hegel's Social Philosophy*.
6. This qualification is necessary because, although social freedom is the freedom that is most important to Hegel's theory, the rational social order must also accommodate the freedoms of personhood and moral subjectivity.
7. Hardimon, *Hegel's Social Philosophy*, 25–26, 95.
8. A recent example of the latter is found in Ernst Tugendhat's *Self-Consciousness and Self-Determination* (Cambridge, Mass.: MIT Press, 1986). Tugendhat explicitly denies what I assert here, namely, that Hegel has a substantive answer to the question, "What constitutes the rationality of the state [or social order]?" (319). In stark contrast to the view I argue for, Tugendhat claims that "Hegel's philosophy is consciously and explicitly . . . the justification of the existing order, quite irrespective of how this existing order may be constituted" (317).
9. For example, much of the critique of modern society that has been inspired by the Frankfurt School can plausibly be viewed as informed by ideals that derive from Hegel's social theory. This point was driven home to me by a recent article by André Gorz, "Die Gesellschaft als Megamaschine," in the excellent German weekly *Freitag* (October 22, 1993). Gorz demonstrates his endorsement of many of the normative criteria of Hegel's social theory in criticizing modern society for the following shortcomings: fostering anomie; lacking transparency and intelligibility; failing to demonstrate to individuals how their particular interests converge with the common good; being unable to provide all of its members with meaningful work; destroying and failing to replace social structures that provide members with a sense of identity; and offering few opportunities for individuals to find concrete social recognition by carrying out socially constructive roles that enable them to see themselves as integral parts of their social order. For an excellent discussion of the views of the Frankfurt School, see Raymond Geuss, *The Idea of a Critical Theory: Habermas and the Frankfurt School* (Cambridge: Cambridge University Press, 1981).
10. One objection that could be raised here is that the normative standards Hegel's theory endorses could not possibly serve as the basis for a radical critique of existing reality because those standards *derive from* that reality in the sense that they articulate the underlying, or "immanent," rationality of institutions that already exist. But this objection is founded on a misunderstanding. To say that an ideal is internal to a social institution—that is, implicit in its existing practices—does not imply that that ideal is *realized*, or even realizable, by that institution. For Hegel, norms are internal to an existing social order in the sense that the functioning of institutions depends on participants having an implicit conception of the value and purpose of their institutions. But this is compatible with an institution being unable to

realize the ideals it presupposes. That such a disparity is conceptually possible is demonstrated by Hegel's own struggle to reconcile the poverty civil society inevitably produces with its implicit claim to provide an opportunity for all social members to further their well-being through their own productive activity.

11. Because I am talking here about moral philosophies in general, I use 'moral' and 'ethical' interchangeably and hence (in this introduction) ignore the important distinction Hegel draws between *Moralität* and *Sittlichkeit*. Strictly speaking, Hegel's account of *Sittlichkeit* constitutes only a part—although a central one—of his ethical philosophy and social theory, since the former must be supplemented by the doctrines of *Moralität*, the latter by the principles of abstract right.

12. To this it will no doubt be objected that Hegel's ethical philosophy incorporates, or "sublates" (*aufhebt*), Kantian moral principles rather than dispensing with them altogether. While it is true that *Sittlichkeit* in some sense preserves the standpoint of Kantian *Moralität* (this is discussed in detail in chapter 7), it is not clear to me that Hegel intends to leave any room for the kind of moral reasoning involved in applying Kant's categorical imperative. Interpreters of Hegel's ethical philosophy have generally failed to make clear what role a principle like the categorical imperative has, or could have, in his ethics. See, for example, my response to Wood's reconstruction of Hegel's position in my review of his book in the *Journal of Philosophy* 89 (1992), 316–320.

13. This is true even in civil society, where professional identities imbue labor with a more than merely instrumental significance and also serve as the basis for bonds of solidarity among members of the same profession.

14. This issue is fruitfully discussed by Raymond Geuss in three articles: "Auffassungen der Freiheit," *Zeitschrift für philosophische Forschung* 49 (January–March 1995): 1–14; "Freedom as an Ideal," *Proceedings of the Aristotelian Society*, suppl. vol. 69 (1995): 87–100; and "Freiheit im Liberalismus und bei Marx," in *Ethische und politische Freiheit*, ed. Julian Nida-Rümelin and Wilhelm Vossenkuhl (Berlin: de Gruyter, 1998), 114–125.

15. This is the principal claim examined by Hardimon (*Hegel's Social Philosophy*) in his interpretation of Hegel's social theory.

16. The "constructive potential" that Amy Gutmann finds in communitarianism—"the potential for helping us discover a politics that combines community with a commitment to basic liberal values" (49)—is precisely what I am claiming can be found (in a much more developed form) in Hegel's social theory. See her helpful discussion of the liberal-communitarian debate in "Communitarian Critics of Liberalism," *Philosophy and Public Affairs* 14 (summer, 1985): 308–322. For two good accounts of German romantic

thought, see Frederick C. Beiser, *Enlightenment, Revolution, and Romanticism: The Genesis of Modern German Political Thought, 1790–1800* (Cambridge, Mass.: Harvard University Press, 1992), chaps. 8–11; and Charles Larmore, *The Romantic Legacy* (New York: Columbia University Press, 1996), 33–64.

1. Hegel's Conception of Social Freedom: Preliminaries

1. I shall use 'actualization' and 'realization' interchangeably throughout. Both are possible translations of *Verwirklichung*, which is closely related to Hegel's technical term *Wirklichkeit* (actuality or reality). ('Actuality' and its derivatives are sometimes preferred because they preserve the connection to 'to act' *(wirken)* that is implicit in Hegel's term.) Something that is "actual" or "actualized" is both (1) fully rational and (2) realized in the world (determinately existent in space and time). For more on this concept, see Michael O. Hardimon, *Hegel's Social Philosophy: The Project of Reconciliation* (Cambridge: Cambridge University Press, 1994), 53–59; and Allen W. Wood, *Hegel's Ethical Thought* (Cambridge: Cambridge University Press, 1990), 10.

2. One could also call it "the freedom of ethical life," or simply "ethical [*sittliche*] freedom." I prefer "social freedom," even though Hegel himself does not use this term, because it makes clear that I am interested in his account of *Sittlichkeit* as a social theory rather than as an ethical philosophy. This freedom is appropriately called "social," because, as we shall see later, it is achieved only in and through the basic social institutions. Social freedom is equivalent to the freedom referred to when, for example, Hegel says that social members achieve their "substantial freedom" (§257) in ethical life.

3. Hegel uses this term in the present sense at NL, 89/II, 476.

4. The importance of Spinoza's conception of substance is unmistakable here. I expand on this theme in chapter 6 in explaining why Hegel thinks of a social order that is self-determining in Spinoza's sense as godlike, or divine.

5. "A freedom for which something were truly external, or foreign, [would not be] freedom; its essence and formal definition is precisely that nothing is absolutely external" (NL, 89/II, 476).

6. This doctrine is a consequence of Hegel's acceptance of Spinoza's principle *omnis determinatio est negatio* (LHP, vol. III, 285–286/XX, 164–165). The principle that all determination is negation implies that ascribing a quality x to an entity always involves situating that entity with respect to what it is not (not-x) and hence relating it to something other than itself.

7. For example, §7Z. For an expanded discussion of the meaning of *Beisichselbstsein in einem Anderen,* see Wood, *Hegel's Ethical Thought,* 45–51.

8. Art and religion also accomplish the kind of reconciliation referred to here,

but because they do not involve a purely rational relation to the world, Hegel regards them as inferior to speculative philosophy. Together these three regions of experience—art, religion, and philosophy—make up the realm of "absolute spirit."

9. It is no accident that *bei* in everyday discourse commonly means 'at the home of.' Thus, *Beisichselbstsein in einem Anderen* could also be rendered as 'being-at-home-in-an-other.' In fact, Hegel sometimes explicitly uses the locution 'at home' (*zu Hause*) to characterize freedom (§4Z).

10. Interpreters of Hegel often deny the distinction I am highlighting here between speculative and practical freedom. In support of their view they point to Hegel's claim in §4Z that "thinking and willing . . . are not two faculties; rather the will is a particular mode of thinking." But a careful reading of this and other passages supports rather than undermines my interpretation. Hegel does not espouse the absurd position that thinking and willing are indistinguishable; rather, he claims only that willing depends on, and is "a mode of," thought. This means that, though speculative and practical freedom can be distinguished, they are not wholly independent of one another. For a modern individual who is subjectively alienated from his society, speculative philosophy can reveal the essential goodness of his social order, enabling him to embrace it and hence participate in it freely (with a free will). In such a case, practical freedom depends on speculative. But it is clear—and this point must be insisted on, if we are to understand Hegel's social theory—that not all types or degrees of practical freedom (freedom of the will) require speculative insight into the rationality of all reality (*Wirklichkeit*). A member of *Sittlichkeit* who endorses his institutions but understands not a word of Hegel's philosophy can still be practically free. I am indebted to Dudley Knowles for encouraging me to clarify this issue.

11. As will become clearer in the following, each form of practical freedom—personal, moral, and social—will imply a distinctive interpretation of what it is for one's action to be one's own, or to proceed from one's own will rather than from an external source. But in none of these cases does freedom consist in what Kant calls "transcendental freedom" and defines as "the power of beginning a state . . . through spontaneity" (KRV, A445/B473). In other words, practical freedom for Hegel is not, and does not presuppose, a capacity to initiate action through an act of will that is exempt from causal determination. I am indebted to Robert Pippin for a helpful discussion of these points, as well as of a number of other issues related to the topic of self-determination in general.

12. I use 'self-actualization' here in a weaker sense than Wood intends when he claims that Hegel's ethical theory is a theory of self-actualization (Wood, *Hegel's Ethical Thought*, 17–19). The weaker sense applies whenever the self

actualizes some conception it has of itself (whether rational or not). The stronger sense carries more robust normative implications: the conception of the self that is actualized is not just any conception but one that accurately captures the self's true (or rational) nature. When (as in the three forms of practical freedom) the self actualizes a conception of itself *as free* (as a self-determining will), it qualifies as self-actualizing in the stronger sense. Thus, I do not disagree with Wood's claim that Hegel's view is a theory of self-actualization in the stronger sense. I am grateful to Bill Bristow for making this point clear to me.

13. This formulation comes from Raymond Geuss, who, without mentioning Hegel's name, provides an excellent discussion of the basic features and problems of the Hegelian conception of practical freedom as self-actualization. See Raymond Geuss, "Auffassungen der Freiheit," *Zeitschrift für philosophische Forschung* 49 (January–March 1995): 10–11.

14. One example of how the basic features of our world enter into Hegel's account of the *actualized* versions of the various conceptions of the self-determining will is the claim, considered in more detail in chapter 5, that rational social institutions must be structured so as to be able to satisfy the basic natural needs of humans (for example, sex and food), if members' participation in them is to be voluntary (and therefore free).

15. Most of the main ideas of Hegel's theory of abstract right are to be found already in Fichte's *Grundlage des Naturrechts,* published in 1796. Fichte's conceptions of formal freedom and individuality (sometimes referred to as "personhood"), and his account of how individual rights follow from those conceptions, are nearly identical to the corresponding parts of Hegel's theory. For an extended discussion of Fichte's theory, see my paper "Fichte and the Relationship between Right and Morality," in *Fichte: Historical Contexts/ Contemporary Controversies,* ed. Daniel Breazeale and Tom Rockmore (Atlantic Highlands, N.J.: Humanities Press, 1994), 158–180.

16. Although this term appears in Hegel's discussion of the abstract forms of the will in the introduction (§12), it also applies to the wills of persons. This claim is supported by the fact that Hegel explicitly connects both personhood and the resolving will to *Willkür.* The connection between personhood and *Willkür* is made explicit at E §492 and VPR2, 145.

17. *Willkür* could also be rendered as 'the choosing will' or (as translators of Kant sometimes call it) 'the faculty of choice.' Hegel's understanding of *Willkür* has obvious affinities with Kant's characterization of the human will as "pathologically affected" but not "pathologically necessitated" (KRV, B562): "Human choice (*Willkür*) . . . is *affected* but not *determined* by sensible impulses . . . *Freedom* of choice is this independence from being *determined* by sensible impulses" (6: 213). An excellent discussion of Kant's

conception of *Willkür* is found in Henry Allison, *Kant's Theory of Freedom* (Cambridge: Cambridge University Press, 1990), 55, 129–136.

18. This is to say only that such a will is unlimited by *other wills;* natural laws, for example, will continue to put constraints on the will's ability to realize its ends.

19. A good discussion of Hegel's view of property and its relation to personal freedom is offered by Dudley Knowles, "Hegel on Property and Personality," *Philosophical Quarterly* 33 (January 1983): 45–62.

20. Thus, I take personal freedom to be identical to what Hegel elsewhere, following Rousseau, calls civil freedom: "not being restrained in one's inclination, *Willkür,* the execution of one's skills, etc." (VPR2, 150).

21. Wood's more extensive discussion of personhood and abstract right is especially helpful; see *Hegel's Ethical Thought,* 22, 49–50, 77, 94–107.

22. Hegel's term is *Moralität,* which he distinguishes systematically from *Sittlichkeit,* or ethical life. For discussions of this important distinction see ibid., 127–173, 195–196; Charles Taylor, *Hegel* (Cambridge: Cambridge University Press, 1975), 370–378, 385–388; and Joachim Ritter, "Morality and Ethical Life: Hegel's Controversy with Kantian Ethics," in *Hegel and the French Revolution* (Cambridge, Mass.: MIT Press, 1982), 151–182. Hegel's distinction between morality and abstract right is a direct descendant of Fichte's most important innovation in political philosophy, the separation of right *(Recht)* from morality (Neuhouser, "Fichte and the Relationship between Right and Morality," 158–180). Not surprisingly, Hegel's distinction between moral and personal freedom is also closely related to the distinction Fichte employs to demarcate the boundary between right and morality (the distinction between "formal" and "material" freedom). For a discussion of the latter, see my book *Fichte's Theory of Subjectivity* (Cambridge: Cambridge University Press, 1990), 117–166.

23. Hegel most often uses the term 'subject' *(Subjekt)* to refer to the subject of *Moralität,* but I shall use 'moral subject' in order to avoid confusing this particular conception of subjectivity with other uses of 'subject' throughout Hegel's philosophy that have little to do with *Moralität.* Examples of the latter are his claim that the absolute is to be conceived of as both substance and subject (PhG, ¶17; 23), his characterization of the person as a kind of subject (§34), and passages that equate subjectivity with self-consciousness in general (§25).

24. A further condition must be met if moral freedom is to be *fully* realized: the understanding of the good one acts on must be true, or objectively valid. This brief account of moral subjectivity is based on Hegel's characterization of the moral subject as one that strives "[1] to have insight into the good, [2] to make the good its intention, and [3] to bring about the good through

its activity" (E §507; emphases omitted). Like the passage just cited, my account here emphasizes only what Hegel calls the "highest right of the subject" (§132A). It ignores some important aspects of Hegel's highly complex conception of moral freedom, including the rights of "knowledge" (§117), "intention" (§120), and "subjective satisfaction" (§124+A). Chapter 7 provides a fuller account of moral subjectivity in its examination of Hegel's conception of moral conscience.

25. Hegel expresses this point in terms of the lower forms' lack of full self-sufficiency: "the abstract [or lower] forms reveal themselves not as existent on their own [*für sich bestehend*] but as untrue" (§32Z).

26. This is true even for the highest form of practical freedom, social freedom, insofar as Hegel's treatment of *Sittlichkeit* gives way to his account of world history (§340, E §548). The point that motivates this transition within Hegel's system is that even the rational social order does not fully achieve the ideal of self-determination, since its existence is historically conditioned (is made possible only by earlier social orders that are not in themselves fully rational). Thus, if we are to succeed in finding a truly self-subsistent reality, the course of human history must itself be comprehended as a self-determining whole. This is the task Hegel's system moves on to once it has understood the realm of ethical life.

27. This step in the argument illustrates the (partially) teleological character of the dialectical arguments that make up Hegel's system and refutes the idea that they are strictly transcendental in nature. In fact, these arguments often make use of both teleological and transcendental strategies. The dialectical transition from a lower configuration *x* to a higher configuration *y* typically instantiates the following general procedure: Begin by defining an abstract conception of self-determination, *x* (for example, "self-determination is to choose one's own ends"). Then ask, Under what conditions can *x* be realized in the world? That inquiry will reveal either: (1) that *y* is necessary as a condition of *x*'s being actualized (the transcendental strategy); or (2) that, although *x* may be realizable without *y*, it needs to be supplemented by *y* in order that *x*, in its actualized form, remain consistent with the essential character of self-determination (the teleological strategy). The picture is further complicated by the fact that some transitions make use of both strategies. This is true of the transition from "Morality" to "*Sittlichkeit*," since the latter is both a necessary condition for the actualization of personhood and moral subjectivity, and a higher configuration of the self-determined will that is required in order that the lower forms, together with the conditions of their actualization, constitute a whole that is itself consistent with the essential character of self-determination. The notorious obscurity of Hegel's dialectical transitions is due, in part, to the amazing fact that

he never explicitly articulates their very complex structure. Even more amazing perhaps is that, for the most part, careful analytic techniques can elicit from those transitions consistent and compelling argumentational strategies.

The transition from "Abstract Right" to "Morality" is of the teleological type, since moral subjectivity is deduced not, strictly speaking, as a condition of the possibility of its predecessor but as a configuration of the will that must supplement personhood in order for personal freedom to be actualized in a manner consistent with the initially posited ideal (telos) of the will's complete self-determination. Thus, contrary to what is often supposed, the claim implicit in this transition is not that a society made up only of persons (of individuals who were only persons and not also moral subjects) is a conceptual or practical impossibility but that such beings could not fulfill the requirements of universal personhood and at the same time exist as fully self-determined.

28. It is important to note that this argument only establishes the necessity of a will that possesses the structural complexity attributed to moral subjectivity. On its own it does not account for every feature Hegel eventually ascribes to the moral subject, for example, its being bound by principles of the *good,* which include but also extend beyond what is required for the realization of personhood (namely, the principles of *right*).

29. The deduction is only quasi-logical because it involves more than purely conceptual analysis. For example, the inadequacy of personal freedom becomes apparent only by considering the conditions under which it would be realized in the world we inhabit.

30. It would be wrong to claim that 'the good' lacks *all* nonarbitrary content for the detached moral subject. As Hegel indicates in §134, the standpoint of morality can rightfully claim at least this much: the good consists in following the principles of abstract right and in furthering human welfare, both one's own and that of others. The point is that this characterization of the good is still quite distant from a concrete account of the particular acts or social institutions that satisfy these criteria.

31. The point here is that the status of personhood was extended to Romans and non-Romans alike and did not depend on ethnic membership.

32. As I present it here, the freedom characteristic of classical Greece is merely a forerunner of Hegel's social freedom for two reasons: First, it incorporates only the *subjective* component of social freedom as Hegel understands it (what he calls the *Gesinnung,* or subjective disposition, appropriate to social membership). Second, the Greeks identified with their polis in a way that left no room for a robust conception of themselves as, at the same time, *individuals;* in other words, the form of freedom enjoyed by the Greeks was un-

able to accommodate the freedoms of personhood and moral subjectivity that arose in later epochs.

33. See also §261Z, where the state is identified as the "organization of the concept of freedom."

34. The interpretation I attribute to Ilting comes primarily from his illuminating notes to the student transcripts of Hegel's lectures edited by him in VPR1, 287–363, but also from his article "Hegel's Concept of the State and Marx's Early Critique" in *The State and Civil Society: Studies in Hegel's Political Philosophy*, ed. Z. A. Pelczynski (Cambridge: Cambridge University Press, 1984), 93–113.

35. VPR1, 312 n. 165, 309 n. 151; emphasis added.

36. VPR1, 309 n. 151.

37. I have translated Ilting's talk of the ethical community being *fully* adequate to the concept of freedom into the weaker claim that it is the *most* adequate embodiment of practical freedom, because the latter more accurately represents Hegel's view. No actually existing social order can be fully adequate to the concept of self-determination, since any such order will be determined by its place in history and therefore dependent on historical conditions— something external to itself—in order for it to be (to have become) what it is. This thought underlies the transition in Hegel's system to a philosophy of history (§340, E §548), which, regarded as a single, coherent process, embodies an even more substantive form of self-determination than any particular social order can.

38. Hegel's characterization of the state as "the actuality of the ethical idea . . . that thinks and knows itself and brings about what it knows [that is, itself] in so far as it knows it" (§257) suggests that the kind of self-determination *Sittlichkeit* is supposed to embody is modeled on Fichte's conception of self-positing subjectivity. (See Neuhouser, *Fichte's Theory of Subjectivity,* chap. 3.) Hegel's point, on this reading, could be formulated as the claim that only the rational social order and not, as Fichte thought, the individual subject can fully realize the aspirations of self-determined subjectivity. I do not pursue this fascinating thought here.

39. As will be described in Chapter 4, this conception of self-determination could also be explicated in terms of the idea of an organism (a teleologically organized, self-reproducing whole). Hegel's understanding of a fully self-determined being is derived from Kant's account of an "organized product of nature" (KU, §§65–66). The two principal features Kant ascribes to the latter—teleological organization and the capacity to be self-organizing— roughly correspond to the Hegelian criteria for self-determination I am highlighting here: a structure that accords with the Concept and the capacity for self-reproduction.

40. Hegel explicitly associates self-reproduction ("that substance continually produces itself") with both self-determination and freedom at VPR1, 151.

41. The structure of the Concept is often characterized as consisting of three "moments" (or essential elements), which are designated either as universality, particularity, and individuality or as immediate unity, difference, and mediated unity. I discuss this characterization of the Concept in greater detail in chapter 5.

42. In this formulation I have replaced 'individual' of the previous sentence with 'particular'. Although Hegel's *Logic* makes a technical distinction between individuality *(Einzelheit)* and particularity *(Besonderheit)* (EL §163), in other contexts Hegel often ignores the distinction and uses the two terms interchangeably. My talk of the interpenetrating unity of universality and particularity fits better with the terminology of universal and particular wills inherited from Rousseau and is warranted by Hegel's occasional use of the same terminology, for example, "Actuality is always the unity of universality and particularity" (§270Z).

43. In chapter 3 I make clearer how the unity of universal and particular wills that characterizes civil society falls short of the more thoroughgoing unity of wills found in the institutions Hegel takes to be paradigmatic of *Sittlichkeit,* the family and the state.

44. Another implication of this demand is that the social spheres must be constituted such that the kinds of identities and interests individuals acquire in each are compatible with those required in the others. Civil society, for example, must not be so competitive and individualistic that the forms of community characteristic of the family and state are made impossible. Also, the mutual dependence requirement implies that it is the role of the state, by virtue of its perspective on the whole, to foster, protect, and regulate civil society and the family through legislation, just as it is the role of the family and civil society to produce (and educate) individuals who have the capacities they need in order to carry out their duties as citizens, including the ability to take a perspective on, and will, the good of the whole.

45. VPR1, 309 nn. 150, 152. See also 312 n. 165.

46. Ilting himself comes to precisely this conclusion. He calls the state as it is described in the 1820 *Philosophy of Right* "authoritarian" and attempts to trace this feature back to the (alleged) fact that "it is not the freedom of the citizens that is actualized in the . . . state" but rather "the freedom of the state" (Ilting, "Hegel's Concept of the State," 103–104).

47. VPR1, 309 n. 150. See also Karl-Heinz Ilting, "Die Struktur der Hegelschen Rechtsphilosophie," in *Materialen zu Hegels Rechtsphilosophie,* vol. 2, ed. Manfred Riedel (Frankfurt am Main: Suhrkamp, 1975), 68. Hardimon also construes the good individuals attain through social membership in terms

of individuality (including the freedoms of persons and moral subjects) rather than (social) freedom. See Hardimon, *Hegel's Social Philosophy*, 146–153, for a clear account of the concept of individuality.

48. This claim is, strictly speaking, compatible with the charge that at the level of institutional detail (for example, in his discussion of the role of public opinion within the state), Hegel's theory gives too much weight to measures that ensure the smooth functioning of the social order and too little to the requirements implicit in the ideal of free citizenship. This objection was raised to me by Michael Theunissen and is suggested in his paper "The Repressed Intersubjectivity in Hegel's Philosophy of Right," in *Hegel and Legal Theory*, ed. Drucilla Cornell, Michel Rosenfeld, and David Gray Carlson (New York: Routledge, 1991), 3–63. If this charge is true, the problem lies in Hegel's failure to apply his own foundational principles consistently, not in those principles themselves.

49. See also §153 for support of my claim that *individuals* achieve a distinctive sort of freedom as members of *Sittlichkeit*. Hegel speaks there of membership in ethical life as fulfilling "the *right of individuals* to their *subjective determination to freedom*."

50. Identification with the general will is but one instance of the overcoming of otherness referred to previously in the discussion of being-with-oneself-in-an-other: a subject negates the apparently alien character of the general will through an act of consciousness (that is, by grasping that will as identical to itself).

51. The difference I am pointing to is expressed, more clearly than in his published work, at VPR1, 269–270, where Hegel distinguishes the organic nature of *Sittlichkeit* from a more mechanistic, less spiritual type of organized whole. The latter is one in which "the [subjective] disposition may be lacking if only each accomplishes his appointed task." In a rational social order, in contrast, "the individuals must know that in their particular labor they are acting for the whole and must have this whole as their end."

52. This formulation comes from Wood, *Hegel's Ethical Thought*, 259.

53. Taylor, *Hegel*, 375, 373.

54. Ibid., 374.

55. Ibid., 373–374. Later, when Taylor is no longer considering the basic philosophical strategy of Hegel's social theory (383), he characterizes the freedom of *Sittlichkeit* as subjectively identifying with society's norms and ends (a theme I treat in chapter 3 and designate as the subjective component of individuals' social freedom). But this is not the dominant element in his account of the freedom of *Sittlichkeit*.

56. Ibid., 387.

57. Of course, Taylor, too, wants to combat the view that Hegel's social theory is inherently totalitarian. This is successfully accomplished in many parts of

his book, but the philosophical strategy he sets out in his account of the distinctive freedom individuals achieve in *Sittlichkeit* does not effectively exclude the totalitarian interpretation. That account is compatible with the commonly held view that in the first two parts of the *Philosophy of Right* Hegel pays lip service to the good of individuals—their freedom as persons and moral subjects—and then in *Sittlichkeit* subordinates their essential interests (qua individuals) to the (strongly holistic) ends of the social whole.

58. It is important to emphasize that, contrary to common belief, reconstructing Hegel's account of social freedom independently of his philosophy of history is completely consistent with his own self-understanding. On Hegel's view, it is possible to provide a justificatory account of the rational social order by focusing on how that order realizes practical freedom, without regard to its relation to the historical mission of absolute spirit. Hegel does hold, however, that such a reconstruction would not embody the *deepest* perspective from which the rationality of the social order can be assessed, since it would ignore the role played by ethical institutions in spirit's historical process of comprehending all of actuality (including the whole of history) as identical to itself, thereby realizing itself as a—indeed, the only—completely self-related, or self-determined, being. My position diverges from Hegel's only in its implication that a successful reconstruction from the less inclusive perspective would count, for us, as a sufficient, fully satisfying demonstration of the rationality of the modern social world.

59. Further clues to the meaning of subjective and objective freedom are found in the following statement: "Objective freedom, the laws of real [*reellen*] freedom, demand the subjugation of the contingent will, for it is merely formal. When the objective is rational in itself, the insight [of social members] must be adequate to this reason, and then the essential moment of subjective freedom is present" (PH, 456/XII, 540).

60. In one of his lectures on the *Philosophy of Right* Hegel articulates the two components of social freedom (subjective and objective) and then explicitly links this bipartite structure to the central idea of Rousseau's political philosophy, the general will: "The assembly of estates . . . contains the moment of the general will in its dual sense: first, as the will that is rational in itself [that is, the objective component] and, second, the fact that it is the general will not only in itself but also for itself in that each has his self-consciousness within it [that is, the subjective component]" (VPR1, 176).

2. Rousseau: Freedom, Dependence, and the General Will

1. LHP, vol. III, 401/XX, 306. See also §258R.

2. Although his *Lectures on the History of Philosophy* devotes only three pages to Rousseau—far fewer than my assessment of his influence on Hegel would

seem to predict—I do not believe that this undermines my claim that the normative foundations of Hegel's social theory are best understood as an elaboration of those implicit in Rousseau's political philosophy. In addition to Hegel's acknowledgment, cited earlier, that Rousseau is the first thinker to hit upon the proper first principle of political philosophy (the free will), my interpretive thesis finds historical support in the testimony of one of Hegel's fellow students at Tübingen: "Metaphysics was certainly not Hegel's special interest during the four years that I knew him well [1788–1792]. His hero was Rousseau, whose *Émile, Social Contract,* and *Confessions* he read constantly." Cited by Bernard Cullen in *Hegel's Social and Political Thought: An Introduction* (Dublin: Gill and Macmillan, 1979), 4.

3. It could be argued that Hegel intends the last two sentences of this quote as a critique of Rousseau rather than as an indication of what he takes from him. Hegel's text is not absolutely clear on this point, but I do not think this is the best reading of it. On this interpretation, Hegel would be claiming that Rousseau takes natural freedom to be freedom in its fully actualized form. This is a highly implausible interpretation of Rousseau, given the importance he ascribes to moral freedom (autonomy) and the clarity with which he insists that such freedom is possible only through the general will and hence only within the state. Hegel himself says only that Rousseau's thought contains an "ambiguity" on this point, which seems to me an acknowledgment that the latter recognizes, at least in part, that freedom can be fully actualized only in the state. The ambiguity Hegel refers to is most likely bound up with Rousseau's talk of natural freedom. Hegel would deny that freedom of any type could exist in a state of nature. (I take Rousseau to be claiming the same, but since he never clearly states this view, Hegel's charge of ambiguity is certainly justified.) I am indebted to Tony Laden for pointing out this textual difficulty.

4. Rousseau's term *liberté morale* easily misleads twentieth-century readers, who are apt to take 'moral' to refer to the ethical, to that which has to do with right and wrong. Rousseau very often uses 'moral' in a broader sense that denotes the intellectual, mental, or spiritual aspects of human reality, in contrast to the material or physical. It might be better to call the autonomy Rousseau describes here "spiritual freedom" in order to avoid confusing it with Kant's notion of moral autonomy, which is moral in both the broad and narrow senses.

5. This term, as well as much of the following description of this conception of freedom, comes from Joshua Cohen, "Reflections on Rousseau: Autonomy and Democracy," *Philosophy and Public Affairs* 15 (summer 1986): 276–288.

6. A particular will is defined by Rousseau as a will that "tends *only* toward [one's] particular [or private] advantage" (SC, III.2.v; emphasis added). It is

also sometimes referred to as a "private" (SC, I.5.i) or "individual" will (SC, III.2.vi). It is identical to a purely self-interested, or purely egoistic, will.

7. I have changed Masters's 'private will' (*avis particulier*) to 'particular opinion' in order to make it consistent with the translation of *avis* as 'opinion' in the previous sentence.

8. For examples of this way of interpreting Rousseau's passage, see the editor's notes to *On the Social Contract,* 138, and W. T. Jones, "Rousseau's General Will and the Problem of Consent," *Journal of the History of Philosophy* 25 (January 1987): 115, 128.

9. This distinction between the issues of obligation and freedom is also made in the second of the two passages cited previously, most explicitly at SC, IV.2.vii. After establishing that "the vote of the majority always *obligates*" (emphasis added), Rousseau goes on to ask how being forced to obey the law to which one is obligated can be consistent with *freedom.* While it is essential to distinguish the issue of obligation from that of freedom, it is also important to note that Rousseau's solution to the former is parasitic on his account of the latter, since he intends to ground our obligation to obey the general will in the more fundamental imperative that calls on us to realize our nature as free beings.

10. This interpretation is suggested by a passage from the Geneva Manuscript (GM, 178), that was left out of the *Social Contract,* as well as by N. J. H. Dent in *Rousseau* (Oxford: Basil Blackwell, 1988), 179–180. Dent, however, goes on to give an account of the "forced to be free" passage that is much closer to the one I develop later.

11. John Plamenatz is one (otherwise reliable) interpreter who equates the two concepts ("Ce qui ne signifie autre chose qu'on le forcera d'être libre," in *Hobbes and Rousseau,* ed. Maurice Cranston and Richard S. Peters [Garden City, N.Y.: Doubleday, 1972], 323–324). Rousseau himself sometimes fails to distinguish freedom from independence, for example, at *Emile,* 84. At other times he appears to make a distinction and to do so in a way that is consistent with my interpretation (DI, 156; GM, 159); in at least one other place he explicitly draws the distinction differently than I do (OC III, 841).

12. Here I take seriously Rousseau's statement (*Emile,* 108 n) that he does not always "give the same meanings to the same words" but that the thoughtful reader will always be able to discover the underlying coherence of his thought.

13. Rousseau speaks of "true" or "natural" needs (for example, *Emile,* 84, 86, 213, 333), but his use of these terms is inconstant. At DI, 137, he says that savage, as opposed to modern, man "felt only his true needs." The impression is often given that "true" (or "natural") means "given to the human by his biological nature" and hence that true needs are simply the primitive

physical needs of the original state of nature. I suggest that Rousseau's notion of true needs is better understood as referring, roughly, to those goods
that are essential to one's well-being properly understood, and that false
needs are those that are perceived as such but are in fact destructive of, or
not essential to, one's well-being properly understood. Thus, for Rousseau
an essential feature of true needs is that they are compatible with one's being
free.

14. The problems involved in finding a suitable English translation of *amour-
propre* are well known. For an excellent discussion of Rousseau's frequently
misunderstood view of *amour-propre,* see Dent, *Rousseau,* chap. 2.

15. Notice that the commodities of life are "for oneself," while the need for
"consideration" inherently involves others. I explain and emphasize this
feature of Rousseau's view later.

16. Although the two types of needs appear to stand in a one-to-one correspondence to the two types of dependence, their relation is more complex, since,
as we shall see, for civilized (as opposed to primitive) human beings *amour-
propre* plays a significant role in constituting economic dependence.

17. It is important to bear in mind that psychological dependence is not necessarily pathological; on the contrary, it is essential to being human. Emile is
dependent on Sophie's regard (and vice versa), and this is as it should be.

18. This point is echoed in *Emile,* 185: "So long as one knows only physical
need, each man suffices unto himself."

19. This is not to say that recognition by others cannot be, or is not typically,
mediated by things.

20. See also RSW, 83.

21. See *Emile,* 85: "Dependence on things, since it has no morality, is in no way
detrimental to freedom."

22. This point is consistent with the widely held view that there is a significant
moral difference between being forced to do something by natural necessity
and being coerced to do it by another agent. For Rousseau the view that natural necessity does not compromise human freedom is based on the idea
that the world of things is ordered by natural laws, which have a constancy
and necessity that the particular wills of individuals do not. This makes the
natural world reliable (and predictable) in a way that particular wills are
not. Moreover, Rousseau appears to believe that the fact that nature is ordered is sufficient to guarantee that it will be benign with respect to anything "natural," including human freedom (for example, *Emile,* 37).

23. This is consistent with Rousseau's statement of the fundamental problem of
political philosophy, which defines freedom as "obeying only oneself" (SC,
I.6.iv).

24. Obedience to a foreign will is a phenomenon that calls for an explanation,

because human beings by nature value being their own master and are prima facie strongly disinclined to cede to a will that is not their own. This is *one* of the claims implicit in Rousseau's view that human beings are naturally free.

25. Or, more succinctly: "What yoke could be imposed on men who need nothing?" (DSA, 36). See also DI, 139, where Rousseau depicts a state of perfect independence and asks, "How will [a man] ever succeed in making himself obeyed?"

26. The unrestructured dependence referred to here is "natural" in the sense that it is the result of a development that, as a whole, was not an object of human foresight, plan, or will.

27. Another important example is Rousseau's analysis of how the needs generated by inflamed *amour-propre* lead to inevitable clashes among wills. For a discussion of this and the distinction between inflamed and benign *amour-propre*, see Dent, *Rousseau*, chap. 2.

28. This interpretation of the Second Discourse is confirmed at GM, 159. There Rousseau also rules out a return to the "golden age" (described at DI, 151) as a possible solution to the problem of dependence. In this case, too, he rejects the idea of returning to a more primitive society not because such a return would be impossible but because the golden age is "a state foreign to the human race."

29. It is important to bear in mind that the sociopolitical measures espoused in the *Social Contract* are not in themselves a sufficient response to the problem of dependence. Individuals must also be internally constituted in accord with the principles outlined in *Emile,* if their psychological dependence is to admit of being structured in a way that is compatible with freedom. The most important consideration here is whether *amour-propre* appears primarily in its benign or inflamed form.

30. See also Rousseau's advice to the Corsicans: "The fundamental law of your constitution must be equality" (OC III, 909–910).

31. See SC, II.11.i, where equality is said to be one of the two principal objects of law for the reason that "freedom cannot last without it."

32. Rousseau advises the Poles: "The tendency of your laws should be toward a continuous reduction of large inequalities of wealth and power, . . . a chasm that the cumulative operation of natural forces tends unavoidably to widen further" (GP, 65). See also SC, II.11.ii.

33. The first two proposals are made at OC III, 945 and PE, 234. Rousseau's critique of capitalist class relations is explicit at SC, II.11.ii ("no citizen should be so opulent that he can buy another, and none so poor that he is constrained to sell himself") and implicit in his depiction of a golden age without economic classes (DI, especially 151). For a detailed discussion of these

themes in Rousseau, see Andrew Levine, *The Politics of Autonomy* (Amherst, Mass.: University of Massachusetts Press, 1976), chap. 5.

34. For example, OC III, 491–492, 842–843.

35. This formulation is suggested by Frederick Barnard, *Self-Direction and Political Legitimacy: Rousseau and Herder* (Oxford: Oxford University Press, 1988), 27.

36. Rousseau acknowledges that the universal applicability of law (the sense under consideration here) does not preclude distinctions among classes of citizens but only references to particular individuals (SC, II.6.vi).

37. My understanding of Rousseau's statement that legitimate law must "come from all" is indebted to Dent's excellent treatment of this topic, (*Rousseau,* 179–184).

3. The Subjective Component of Social Freedom

1. For now worries about the apparent circularity of this formulation can be alleviated by assuming that what social freedom (its objective component) conditions is not itself but the two other forms of freedom discussed earlier, personal and moral freedom. In chapter 5 I shall argue that there is a sense in which objective freedom secures the conditions not only of personal and moral freedom but of social freedom as well. But this complicating feature of objective freedom can be ignored for now.

2. Hegel also uses the term 'ethical disposition' (*sittliche Gesinnung*) (E §515), and sometimes simply 'disposition' (§158), to refer to this frame of mind. 'Subjective disposition' makes clear that this disposition is what secures the subjective component of social freedom, in contrast to the objective component. It is not, however, to be confused with the distinctively modern form of *moral* subjectivity that Hegel treats in Part II of the *Philosophy of Right.* The subjective disposition at issue in the present chapter is subjective in the (broader) sense that it is a phenomenon of consciousness, consisting in the consciously held ends and attitudes of social members. As I shall make clear later, the subjective disposition appropriate to *Sittlichkeit,* and hence the subjective component of social freedom, can be characterized independently of Hegel's account of moral subjectivity. Thus, Antigone could be said to have a free subjective disposition in the sense discussed here, even though she is not a moral subject. If Hegel is to succeed at his task of uniting ancient ideals with the demands of modern moral subjectivity, the subjective disposition I describe here must be compatible with moral subjectivity, but it does not, strictly speaking, require it. Chapter 7 investigates how and whether the frame of mind required by *Sittlichkeit* is compatible with being a moral subject.

A further complicating point here is that Hegel sometimes speaks of *Gesinnung* as not merely a subjective attitude but a *true* subjective attitude. For example, at §268 he defines the political *Gesinnung,* patriotism, as a subjective attitude ("certainty") that "is founded on truth." Strictly speaking, when I talk of *Gesinnung* as a subjective attitude, I am referring to what Hegel calls *Gesinnung* as certainty *(Gewißheit)* independently of its truth *(Wahrheit).* My approach here is supported by Hegel's reference to *Gesinnung* as certainty alone as a kind of freedom: "their *certainty* of their own freedom has its *truth* in . . . objectivity" (§153). This section of the chapter articulates what it means for individuals to have "the *certainty* of their freedom" in their social membership. See §§153, 268 for this talk of "certainty" and "truth."

3. Thus, as I use it here, 'identical unity' refers to a sameness or oneness that is claimed to exist between social members and their institutions. I emphasize that 'identical unity' here means sameness in order to distinguish it from the concept of identity I introduce later, which plays a central role in my reconstruction of Hegel's view. 'Identity' in the latter, more prominent sense refers to "who one is" and makes its appearance in Hegel's theory in the claim that the particular identities of social members are constituted by the roles they carry out within the family, civil society, and the state.

4. See note 21 for my reasons for diverging from Nisbet's translation of this passage.

5. Although, strictly speaking, §257 describes only the subjective disposition involved in membership in the state, this threefold account clearly applies as well to the *Gesinnung* appropriate to *Sittlichkeit* in general. See the nearly identical accounts at §152, E §514, and VPR2, 123.

6. I borrow this term from Christine Korsgaard's discussion of the topic in *The Sources of Normativity* (Cambridge: Cambridge University Press, 1996), 100–107. 'Identity' is used here in the second of the two senses I refer to in note 3.

7. See N. J. H. Dent's definition of 'particular will' in *A Rousseau Dictionary* (Oxford: Blackwell, 1992), 187–189.

8. When discussing social contract theory Hegel refers to these universally shared, egoistic interests as "the interests of individuals as such" (§258A). This concept will play a prominent role in the argument of chapter 6.

9. Although a particular quality always distinguishes its bearer from some other members of its species, it does not necessarily distinguish its bearer as a *unique* individual (that is, as different from *all* other members of its species). Thus, being a mother counts as a particular determinacy because it distinguishes mothers from humans who are not mothers, but it is clearly a quality shared by many. This implies that particular qualities do not neces-

sarily set individuals' interests at odds with one another but can also be the source of a commonality of ends (that is, among individuals who share a particular quality).

10. Hegel typically uses 'inclination' (*Neigung*) to refer to natural, purely sensible inclinations, which he characterizes as immediate ("immediately present"), contingent, subjective, and animal-like (§11+Z, E §§473–474). But he also speaks of spiritual or rational inclinations (§11N, E §474A), which are distinguished from their natural counterparts by their rational content (they correspond to one's ethical duties); their mediate nature (they are not naturally given but the results of character formation within society); and their spiritual character (they are the expressions of one's self-conception and therefore possible only for spiritual, or self-conscious, beings). Desiring to care for one's children and wanting to vote in an election are examples of spiritual inclinations, and it is primarily this type of inclination that is at issue here.

11. To say that socially free individuals are *inclined* to further the collective good does not imply that they never experience conflicting desires in situations where the requirements of social roles collide with their private, or purely egoistic, ends. When my child's need for attention conflicts with my desire to read my newspaper in peace, I may have to exert some effort to deny that desire in order to do what is best overall. The point is that in such a case any hesitation I experience is not a struggle between inclination, on the one hand, and reason, on the other, but between two inclinations—two kinds of particular satisfaction—one of which is less central to who I am, and therefore less spiritual, than the other. Overcoming my desire to read, then, is not a case of the universal winning out over the particular but of one particular interest defeating another because it represents for me a deeper source of (particular) satisfaction.

12. This use of 'private' is warranted by two circumstances: first, Rousseau uses the terms *privé* and *particulier* interchangeably to refer to this kind of interest; second, Hegel, too, sometimes uses derivatives of *privat* in this way, for example, in describing members of civil society as "*private persons (Privatpersonen),* who have their own interest as their end" (§187).

13. See also Allen W. Wood, *Hegel's Ethical Thought* (Cambridge: Cambridge University Press, 1990), 210–211.

14. Hegel's doctrine of objective freedom can be understood as complementing his account of the subjective disposition of ethical life by demonstrating that members of *Sittlichkeit* do not suffer from false consciousness but are correct in regarding their activity for universal ends as constitutive of their own good.

15. It is in fact true for Hegel that social members also regard their institutions,

and not merely their roles, as their own essence, but, as we shall see later, in the discussion of trust, the former attitude is predicated on the latter: the ability of social members to recognize their institutions as having the same essence as themselves presupposes that they find their basic identities as particular individuals in the roles they occupy within those institutions.

16. Thus, I am interpreting Hegel's claim that social members find their own essence in the institutions of *Sittlichkeit* as the claim that they find their basic identities in the particular roles they occupy within those institutions. It is possible to read Hegel as making a different point here, namely, that social members recognize an identity between their essential nature (as a form of Spirit) and that of their society (which embodies the same Spiritual structure). Although Hegel does mean to assert the latter claim, recognizing one's identity with one's social world in this sense belongs to the realm of speculative metaphysics (and hence to the province of "absolute Spirit"). The forms of freedom realized through participation in a rational social world—including social freedom—belong to the realm of objective Spirit and thus do not, strictly speaking, depend upon individuals having achieved full philosophical comprehension of that world. This means that there must be some way of construing Hegel's claim about the unity of essence that does not require attributing comprehension of the absolute to individuals who enjoy social freedom. My account of how individuals find their basic identities in their social institutions satisfies this condition; moreover, it is clearly a phenomenon that Hegel deals with and regards as essential to free social membership. (See, for example, the passage from §158 referred to in the following note.)

17. This is made clear, among other places, at §158, where Hegel characterizes the *Gesinnung* of a family member in terms of finding one's "essentiality" in "the self-consciousness of one's *individuality* in this [family] unity" (emphasis added). The identities constituted within civil society are also particular rather than abstractly universal, since they presuppose limiting oneself to one particular sphere of productive activity (§207). Even one's identity as a citizen is inherently particular, insofar as it is (as Hegel sees it) inseparably bound up with being a member of a particular nation (*Volk*) (§§156, 321–322; E §§540, 545). See also VPR2, 122, where Hegel characterizes *Sittlichkeit* as a realm in which "abstract universality [has] . . . disappeared."

18. This raises difficult questions about the relation between individuals' particular identities and their status as (abstractly universal) moral subjects. At the very least, the two kinds of identities must be compatible with one another, which in Hegel's theory translates into the demand that individuals be able to reflectively endorse their social world and their positions within it from the universal perspective of moral subjectivity. What this universal

moral perspective is, and whether it can be made consistent with the kind of social membership required by *Sittlichkeit,* will be the topic of chapter 7.

19. This is one way of understanding the idea of identity and its relation to social membership. It is espoused by Michael J. Sandel in *Liberalism and the Limits of Justice* (Cambridge: Cambridge University Press, 1982), 61–65.

20. Moral subjectivity, including the form of self-determination distinctive to it, is treated in "Morality," Part II of the *Philosophy of Right,* and will be the main topic of chapter 7. For clarification regarding different uses of 'subject' and 'subjectivity' in Hegel, see chapter 1, note 23.

21. Hegel's exposition of this point in §147 is badly put (and mistakenly translated by both Knox and Nisbet). Hegel does not say that individuals' relation to their social institutions is "immediate and closer to identity than even . . . trust" (Nisbet) but characterizes it rather as "a relation that *at first* [that is, immediately] is more identical than even . . . trust" (emphasis added). This construal of §147 is confirmed both by the remark that follows it ("[Unmediated] identity . . . can turn into a relation of identity that is mediated by *further reflection*") and by the corresponding passage in the 1819–1820 *Nachschrift* (VPR2, 123).

22. This interpretation is suggested by Wood, *Hegel's Ethical Thought,* 209.

23. 'Project' should not be understood in an existentialist sense, implying that the practical engagements in question are the results of some radically free, individualistic choice. They are projects in the sense of involving voluntary, lifelong, stable commitments to a set of ends, such as raising a family, being a good carpenter, or advancing the civil rights of an oppressed minority. They are also projects in the sense that the content of social roles is never completely defined and is thus subject to (some degree of) interpretation and revision by those who occupy them.

24. Hegel expresses this point as follows: "I am referring here to the activity of the human being based on particular interests, or special ends, such that [one] invest[s] the entire energy of [one's] will and character in these ends and sacrifice[s] . . . everything else to them. This particular content is so much of a piece with the individual's will that it constitutes his entire determinacy and is inseparable from him; he is what he is through that content" (PH, 24–25/XII, 38).

25. This interpretation is confirmed at §258, where the subjective disposition of citizens is characterized as implying that one takes being a member of the state to be one's "highest duty."

26. The Hegelian claims discussed here are strikingly similar to Korsgaard's provocative account of what it is to have a practical identity in *The Sources of Normativity,* 101, 105–106. She claims to find these ideas (or at least the seeds of them) in Kant's moral philosophy. This is an intriguing suggestion,

and it may even be true, but it is indisputable that it is Hegel who first explicitly articulates the idea of a practical identity and emphasizes the importance of *particular* practical identities (as opposed to an identity as a pure, rational being) to both social theory and moral philosophy. See also Michael Hardimon, "Role Obligations," *Journal of Philosophy* 91 (July 1994); 346, 357–362.

27. Michael Inwood, *A Hegel Dictionary* (Oxford: Blackwell, 1992), 104. As Inwood notes, Hegel also uses *Selbstgefühl* in a second sense to refer to "a vague awareness of oneself as an individual in contrast to . . . one's particular feelings." (See also §322+A, where *Selbstgefühl,* applied to nations, refers to a feeling of independence—*Selbständigkeit*—and pride.) I suspect that Hegel's concept *Selbstgefühl* derives from Rousseau's talk of one's *sentiment de sa propre existence,* which, like Hegel's term, refers both to self-esteem (DI, 179) and to a primitive awareness of oneself as an individual subject, distinct from one's surroundings (DI, 117).

28. "In love I am not taken as a self-consciousness, as a legal person, but as a natural subject [*Ich*], that is, in my entire particularity" (VPR4, 421). See also §162N: one is loved within the family "because of this particular quality." The idea that familial love represents a form of recognition is not found explicitly in the *Philosophy of Right,* but this suggestion is supported by Hegel's early emphasis on love as the paradigmatic case of finding oneself in the other. Cf. Ludwig Siep, *Anerkennung als Prinzip der praktischen Philosophie* (Freiburg: Alber, 1979), 56–61.

29. This is most evident in communitarian political theory and in the moral philosophy of Bernard Williams.

30. This formulation is indebted to Wood (*Hegel's Ethical Thought,* 212), whose understanding of Hegel's universalism I endorse.

31. This raises the interesting question whether institutions depend on the wills of their members only with respect to their existence or also for their having (some of) the particular features they do. In other words, do individuals simply reproduce their institutions exactly as they find them, or does their reproductive activity involve qualitative change? Although Hegel seems only to allow for the former possibility, I shall argue in chapter 7 that his theory both can include the possibility of the latter and is more attractive when it does.

32. See also §155N: "substantial *Sittlichkeit* . . . is *my* essence, it has existence through me."

33. Wood, *Hegel's Ethical Thought,* 37–39.

34. See ibid., 45–51. The second translation is justified by the facts that *bei* commonly means "at the home of" and that Hegel himself sometimes speaks explicitly of being "at home" (*zu Hause*) in the other (§4Z). As ex-

plained in chapter 1, this formula is Hegel's "most general" definition of freedom because it applies to all species of freedom Hegel recognizes, including the other kinds of practical freedom (personal and moral), as well as the theoretical, or speculative, freedom achieved through philosophy.

35. Hegel conceives of the speculative freedom achieved in philosophy (and, less adequately, in art and religion) as a reconciliation of subjects to a world that initially appears to them to be radically other—that is, hostile or indifferent to the basic aspirations of subjectivity. It is extremely important to distinguish this speculative reconciliation with the social world from the practical freedom social members enjoy in their real social participation. (See chapter 1, note 10.) Reconciliation with the social world is possible (in part) *because* it is possible to understand the social world as a realm within which freedom of the will is realized.

36. Notice that 'subjective' here is used in a sense, indicated in parentheses, that is distinct from its meaning in both 'subjective freedom' and 'moral subjectivity'. This is fully consistent with Hegel's explicit acknowledgment in §25 of the various senses of 'subjective'. The present usage corresponds to the third meaning (γ) distinguished there.

37. It is worth noting that despite Hegel's failure to acknowledge this point, it is consistent with the spirit of his thought, since doing so makes social participation similar in one more respect to the activity characteristic of Spirit, especially as it is construed by Charles Taylor, who emphasizes the role of self-interpretation in Spirit's self-expressive activity. See Charles Taylor, *Hegel* (Cambridge: Cambridge University Press, 1975), 16–18; and Wood, *Hegel's Ethical Thought*, 46.

38. This formulation was suggested to me by Paul Franks. See VPR1, 124 for the suggestion that social participation involves giving actuality to the self and that this is a part of the freedom Hegel ascribes to individuals in *Sittlichkeit*.

39. See Michael O. Hardimon's discussion of alienation in his *Hegel's Social Philosophy: The Project of Reconciliation* (Cambridge: Cambridge University Press, 1994), 119–122.

40. The most prominent of these potentially misleading passages is the discussion of Antigone and (ancient) *Sittlichkeit* in the *Phenomenology* (¶¶436–445). The tendency to blur this distinction can also be found throughout the student transcripts of Hegel's lectures. (See, for example, VPR1, 90–91, where Ilting notes in his capacity as editor the "*antikierende Tendenz*" of the passage in question.) I would argue that Hegel himself became progressively clearer about this distinction over time and that his texts do not implement it fully consistently until 1820, with the publication of the *Philosophy of Right*.

4. Objective Freedom, Part I: The Self-Determining Social Whole

1. As I point out later, Hegel explicitly characterizes the essence of individuals in terms of practical freedom at §145Z: "It is because the determinations of ethical life constitute the concept of freedom that they are the substantiality or universal essence of individuals."

2. To say that a social institution is inherently, or *an sich*, rational is to say both that it is truly rational, as opposed to merely being thought to be such (§258A), and that its being rational is independent of its members' consciousness of it as such. In its latter meaning *an sich* stands in contrast to *für sich*, and hence the unity of objective and subjective freedom—what I call full social freedom—is characterized as *das an und für sich Vernünftige* (§258).

3. "The state in and for itself is the ethical whole, the actualization of freedom, and it is the absolute end of reason that freedom be actual" (§258Z).

4. Hence the doctrine of objective freedom plays a primary role in carrying out the project of reconciliation that the *Philosophy of Right* takes as its principal aim. Note that Hegel's strategy requires that individuals who are subjectively alienated from existing institutions be committed nonetheless to the value of freedom. Grasping the doctrine of objective freedom is supposed to transform the alienated individual's conception of what freedom is and what it requires to be achieved in the world.

5. Once again, it is important to point out that this does not imply that the strongly holistic property on the basis of which institutions are justified is defined independently of the good of individuals but only that it is not defined in terms of their *freedom*.

6. Also relevant here is Hegel's claim that "the true actuality of freedom is the *organism* [of the state]" (VPR1, 269). Other passages that reveal the same tendency are §§144, 258A+Z, 261Z, 270Z; E §539.

7. One interesting (though perplexing) exception is Hegel's extended reference to Rousseau in his longest explicit discussion of objective freedom (§258A). Here Hegel both claims Rousseau as his forerunner with respect to the issue of objective freedom—he credits him with "having established *the will* as the principle of the state"—and criticizes him for conceiving of the general will "as something conscious" rather than as that which is objectively required for freedom to be realized, independently of "whether it is recognized and willed by individuals." As I make clear in chapter 2, I believe the second of these claims represents a serious misunderstanding of Rousseau's doctrine of the general will. I discuss Hegel's critique of Rousseau and social contract theory in general in chapter 6.

8. Or, similarly: "the true actuality of freedom is the *organism* [of the state], . . .

namely, its differentiation into . . . abstract [or fragmented] . . . tasks so that out of these . . . determinate labors and interests the universal interest and work results" VPR1, 269.

9. As mentioned in chapter 1, Hegel's concept of an organized whole derives from Kant's account of an "organized product of nature" (KU, §§65–66). The two criteria of such a being are (1) its parts—with respect to both existence and form—are completely determined by its end, or telos, as a whole; and (2) it is self-organizing in the sense that each of its parts contributes to producing (and reproducing) all other parts. (Growth in a biological organism is an example of the latter.) It is interesting to note that Kant, too, held that the rational state could be thought of as analogous to an organism: "in a recent . . . transformation of a large people into a state the word *organization* was frequently and very aptly applied to the establishment of magistrates, etc., and even to the entire body of the state. For each member in such a whole should indeed be not merely a means, but also an end; and while each member contributes to the possibility of the whole, the idea of that whole should in turn determine the position and function of each member" (KU, §65 n).

10. See VPR1, 148: "rationality is only the whole system; . . . the organization is rationality."

11. Kant articulates this feature of an organic whole in terms of the thing's end (*Zweck*) "determining a priori everything it is to contain" (KU, §65).

12. This marks an important difference with Rousseau, who generally views particular differences as a threat to the social unity required for there to be a general will.

13. Notice the similarity to the formulation in chapter 2 of what Rousseau takes to be the fundamental problem of political philosophy: how to devise a form of political association that reconciles the associates' need for social cooperation with their essential natures as free beings (SC, I.6.iv).

14. It is significant for understanding the development of Hegel's thought that this statement (or an equivalent) is missing from the corresponding passages of earlier versions of his social theory, as preserved in student transcripts of his lectures. (For clear evidence of this from as late as 1819, see VPR1, 270.) For this reason I conclude that Hegel's concern to give the spiritual nature of individuals its proper due is a rather late development, first made explicit in the published text of 1820.

15. See especially §144, where the "differences" that characterize *Sittlichkeit* are said to be "determined by the Concept," and §145, according to which "the *rationality* of ethical life resides in the fact that it is the *system* of the determinations of the Idea." Similar statements can be found throughout the *Philosophy of Right*, for example, at §§145Z, 260Z, 262, 263+Z, and 270Z.

16. The elements of this structure can also be specified as universality, particularity, and individuality *(Einzelheit)*, but when Hegel refers to the structure of the Concept in the context of *Sittlichkeit* (for example, §§157–158, 181), he normally employs the terms I use here.

17. This formulation is inspired by Charles Taylor, *Hegel* (Cambridge: Cambridge University Press, 1975), 374.

18. On this issue—it should be said explicitly—I am casting my lot with those Anglo-American interpreters for whom, in the words of Allen Wood, "Hegel's great positive achievements as a philosopher do not lie . . . in his system of speculative logic but in . . . his reflections on the social and spiritual predicament of modern Western European culture" (Allen W. Wood, *Hegel's Ethical Thought* [Cambridge: Cambridge University Press, 1990], 5). But I take my approach here to be warranted as well by the views of eminent interpreters from the Continental tradition who are less dismissive of the Logic. It is implicit, for example, in the writings of Michael Theunissen (especially in his attempt in *Sein und Schein* to understand Hegel's Logic in social terms) and explicitly stated in the work of Dieter Henrich: "[Hegel] always regarded the formal theory of speculative philosophy . . . as actually realized and confirmed only to the extent to which it allowed the entire complexity of [real] life relations . . . to be grasped and made transparent in a conceptual form that was peculiar to those relations and derivable only from them." See Henrich's "Logische Form und reale Totalität," in *Hegels Philosophie des Rechts*, ed. Dieter Henrich and Rolf-Peter Horstmann (Stuttgart: Klett-Cotta, 1982), 428.

19. It is an interesting example of the flexibility (or inconsistency?) Hegel demonstrates in applying his logical categories that he sometimes spells out the Conceptual structure of *Sittlichkeit* in terms different from those I make use of here. For example, at §260Z Hegel refers to the family and civil society as the moments of particularity and associates the state with universality. (The sense of this classification scheme is discussed briefly in chapter 1.)

20. See also VPR1, 268: "The state is not a family; [it is] a unity not of blood but of spirit."

21. The statement that the unity of the state is mediated rather than immediate because grounded in rational reflection may appear to conflict with the suggestion made earlier that the state embodies a mediated unity because it incorporates the atomism of civil society (by allowing individuals to participate as citizens without giving up their distinct particular identities and ends). But these two features are two sides of a single coin. Reason is the force that effects a substantial unity among (relatively) self-sufficient units.

22. Of course, simply apprehending the rationality of laws in this sense—grasping that they in fact further the interests of the whole—need not result in a

willing of them, if, for example, one is indifferent to the good of the whole. Thus, the claim that such insight brings individuals to embrace the general will seems to presuppose that they already have an attachment to their society that enables them to be concerned about its good. Indeed, Hegel does seem to think that some such prereflective attachment to one's *Volk* is needed in order to explain the possibility of adopting the standpoint required of citizens (§§346–347; E §§545, 552). Having said this, it is important to note that membership in a *Volk* is not a matter of shared blood (VPR1, 268) but of shared spirit, or culture (§§274, 349; E §540; VPR1, 148).

23. This interpretation is endorsed by Taylor: "these three [moments] cannot be brought to synthesis by being present in all citizens and harmonized in each of them. Rather the synthesis is achieved by a community in which the different dimensions are carried primarily by a specific group" (*Hegel*, 434). I discuss the limited validity of this interpretive claim in the text and in the second point of note 28.

24. This is implicit in Hegel's discussion of inheritance rights (§180A), where he recognizes women as potential owners of property and hence as legal persons.

25. The division of civil society into three estates is another instance where the structure of the Concept appears as a principle of social organization. The agricultural estate is "substantial or immediate"; the commercial estate is "reflecting or formal"; and civil servants constitute "the universal estate" (§202).

26. The features of Hegel's theory I have in mind here are (1) the fact that peasants appear to be represented in the legislature only by members of the landed nobility, who acquire this function "without the contingency of an election" (§307; VPR1, 181–182); (2) the exclusion of nonmembers of corporations ("day laborers, servants, etc.") from representation (VPR1, 183); and (3) repeated suggestions that members of the commercial class, because absorbed in pursuing their particular economic interests, are in principle unsuited to discern and execute the general will (for example, §§308, 310A).

27. Ilting appears to support this suggestion at VPR1, 361 n. 383. It should be noted further that in §262 of the published text Hegel still speaks (as he does in the lecture transcript of 1818–1819) of spirit's "allocating individuals" to the spheres of the family and civil society. As the rest of §262 makes clear, however, he is here making the point that in the rational social world individuals exercise choice over the particular positions they are to occupy in these two spheres. The thought that individuals limit themselves to occupying particular, chosen roles in the family and civil society (as opposed to

trying to fill a number of different roles within each sphere at once) is distinct from the claim, made in 1818–1819 but no longer in 1820, that large groups of individuals are "given over to . . . the limitedness of family . . . or . . . bourgeois life" (VPR1, 270).

28. Two qualifications of this claim are necessary in order to give a more complete picture of what I take to be Hegel's mature position: First, Hegel never abandons the idea that the rational social world as a whole embodies the moments of the Concept more completely and adequately than any individual social member is capable of doing. Moreover, he expects our recognition of this fact about the social world to furnish us with one more reason for affirming the institutions of *Sittlichkeit* and to reconcile each of us to the ways in which we as individuals fall short of the ideal of the well-rounded life implicit in the structure of the Concept. The idea that individuals can realize all three Conceptual moments only imperfectly reflects Hegel's recognition that, while this is an ideal the rational social world must strive to measure up to, the concrete circumstances inherent in the various forms of life required by the social organism make it impossible for each of the three identities to be fully developed within each individual. For example, Hegel thinks the businessman will have insufficient time—and the peasant insufficient understanding—to follow political affairs in as much depth as the noble landowner or civil servant, while the latter two figures will have less of a chance than members of the commercial class to pursue the private projects that characterize participation in civil society.

Second, as the example just mentioned indicates, regarding the structure of the Concept as furnishing an ideal for each individual social member is not necessarily incompatible with espousing a fairly robust form of organicism. The latter manifests itself in Hegel's political theory in his insistence (§§261A, 303+A, 305–308) that individuals have different concrete rights and duties as citizens, depending on which of the estates they belong to (and on their particular positions within that estate). Hegel's political theory treats individuals as equals in its fundamental requirement that conditions be such that every citizen can know and will the general will as his own (and thereby be free of subjection to a foreign will in the realm of the state), but this basic equality of citizens remains highly abstract in light of the further claim that different types of individuals will necessarily relate to the general will in quite different ways. (Roughly, the peasant comes to will the general will on the basis of relatively unreflective trust [E §528], the businessman through the corporation-mediated process of integration described here, the civil servant by participating directly in the general will's execution or formation.) The idea, then, is that the state is to be structured so as to accommodate the fullest degree of freedom compatible with the inherent limitations of each member's nature and social position. Once again, I am more interested in the basic ideals underlying Hegel's theory than in the concrete form they take in, for example, his detailed account of the nature of and differences among society's three estates.

29. Here again I substitute 'particularity' for 'individuality'. Even though the terms have different technical meanings, Hegel's usage often ignores that fact.

30. Wood, *Hegel's Ethical Thought*, 239.

5. Objective Freedom, Part II: Social Conditions of Individuals' Freedom

1. Recall here Hegel's statement, cited earlier, that personhood and moral subjectivity "cannot exist on their own" but "must have ethical life as their bearer and foundation" (§141Z).

2. In light of this distinction between the internal and external conditions of personal and moral freedom, my summary of this part of the doctrine of objective freedom can be restated as follows: social institutions qualify as rational only if they (1) provide a protected social space within which individuals can fully exercise their rights as persons and moral subjects; (2) form, or educate, individuals into agents who are capable of self-determination; and (3) satisfy the particularity of individuals in a way that enables them to find their identities within those institutions and freely embrace them as their own.

3. Although Hegel's account of *Bildung* concerns primarily personal and moral freedom, it is not, strictly speaking, limited to these. For, as we shall see later, one of the functions of the family is to provide children with a kind of experience that is necessary in order for them to acquire, as adults, the capacity for trust that is essential to the subjective disposition appropriate to free citizenship.

4. "*Bildung* engenders the sense for freedom" (VPR1, 50).

5. "What human beings ought to be is not achieved by instinct but must instead be won through their own efforts. This is the basis of the child's right to be reared" (§174Z). Not coincidentally, the same view of the human condition is found in Rousseau. Indeed, this thought is the central idea of the *Discourse on Inequality.*

6. In this context it may be helpful to recall the necessary roles played by servitude, fear, and labor in the formation of *Geist* as related in *The Phenomenology of Spirit* (PhG, ¶¶193–196; 152–155). The same idea is expressed in Hegel's remark that *Bildung* requires "the seriousness, suffering, patience, and labor of the negative" (PhG, ¶19; 24).

7. Although children's obedience may be partially grounded in their love of their parents, such love is insufficient to effect discipline (§174Z). For this the parents' superior power is also required. The challenge of good parenting (or one of many) is to unify both.

8. Although membership in the state is no more voluntary than membership in the family or civil society, the former is less directly connected to the satisfaction of individuals' most immediate needs. This helps to explain why the latter institutions have a greater significance as instruments of *Bildung* than the state. Despite this, the state is not without its own formative effects, one of which has already been treated in the earlier discussion of how the transparency of the legislative process helps to enable citizens to embrace the general will as their own. Hegel explicitly acknowledges this aspect of the legislative process as an instance of *Bildung* (§315+Z).

9. Here it is only relevant that family membership is involuntary for children, since they, not their parents, are the subjects of *Bildung* within the family. There is an obvious sense in which family membership is voluntary for adults who choose to marry and bear children.

10. This point suggests that the two aspects of objective freedom discussed in this chapter—*Bildung* and the satisfaction of social members' particularity—are more closely related than they initially appear, for both are inextricably bound up with the phenomenon of human need. *Bildung* requires and exploits human needs in order to achieve its end, and meeting those needs is central to the satisfaction of particularity.

11. It is possible to see a fourth formative function of the family in the circumstance that the latter forms children into individuals who, as adults, are disposed to marry and begin their own families. This feature of the family could be counted as a form of *Bildung* in Hegel's sense because it secures one of the subjective conditions of the enduring existence of the family as a social institution and because the family is essential (in a variety of ways) to the actualization of freedom. Hegel hints at this point at VPR1, 107.

12. See also §174Z; VPR1, 105–106.

13. A further respect in which the family educates children into moral subjects is that it teaches them to distance themselves from their immediate impulses in order to deliberate about which actions promote or conflict with the good of others, in this case the good of other family members with whom they are united through love. This point suggests that the unity of the family, though based in love, cannot be as "immediate" (unmediated by reflective distance to one's desires) as Hegel sometimes seems to imply. I am grateful to David Brink for discussion of these ideas.

14. The fact that family membership provides individuals with a subjective capacity that is a necessary condition of their becoming citizens can be re-

garded as an example of the kind of "harmony and mutual dependence" that must exist among the three social spheres if they are to meet the requirements implicit in Hegel's conception of a self-determined social whole as discussed in chapter 4 (that is, if they are to constitute a teleologically organized whole that exhibits the structure of the Concept).

15. According to Michael Theunissen, Kierkegaard characterizes precisely this valuing of one's own contingent nature as a kind of freedom, the freedom of self-acceptance. See his *Der Begriff Verzweiflung* (Frankfurt am Main: Suhrkamp, 1993), 41, 51f.

16. The masculine pronoun here is more significant than it might initially seem. One way of articulating the status Hegel's theory accords to women is to say that, although granted the abstract rights of personhood, they typically do not have the opportunity to realize themselves as concrete persons, due to their exclusion from civil society. Thus, the distinction between abstract and concrete personhood could serve as the basis of a critique of Hegel's treatment of women.

17. My account here is heavily influenced by Wood's brief but illuminating remarks on the nuclear family and its significance for free personhood. See Allen W. Wood, *Hegel's Ethical Thought* (Cambridge: Cambridge University Press, 1990), 26, 240, 281 n. 3.

18. As indicated by the passage just cited, Hegel clearly regards this parental attitude as a kind of recognition (*Anerkennung*) of children's personhood. The idea I attribute to Hegel here—that recognition is a form of *Bildung* because it instills in the recognized individual a particular self-conception—has its origin in Fichte's account of the role of recognition in the formation of persons. See Frederick Neuhouser, "Fichte and the Relationship between Right and Morality," in *Fichte: Historical Contexts/Contemporary Controversies,* ed. Daniel Breazeale and Tom Rockmore (Atlantic Highlands, N.J.: Humanities Press, 1994), 158–180.

19. Hegel's criticism of laws that exclude daughters from inheriting property exemplifies his view that the formal rights of personhood apply equally to both sexes even though women are prevented from developing themselves as concrete persons in the sphere of civil society.

20. Here I translate *Natürlichkeit* as "natural immediacy" because it conveys Hegel's meaning better than 'naturalness'. See §187A, where 'natural simplicity' is equated with 'immediacy and individuality'.

21. Although the *Phenomenology's* treatment of labor is surely relevant to the discussion of labor in the *Philosophy of Right,* it would be a mistake to assume that the former can simply be imported into the latter without taking account of the important differences between the two texts' basic projects. (One example of an interpretation that commits this error is Jeremy

Waldron's account of Hegel and property rights in *The Right to Private Property* [Oxford: Oxford University Press, 1988], chap. 10.) In the first text Hegel is interested in labor's significance for the historical formation of Absolute Spirit; in the second he is concerned with the role labor plays, in the context of rational social institutions, in realizing practical freedom. This difference in the systematic aims of the two texts results in substantial differences in the content of their discussions of labor: in the *Phenomenology* the primary significance of labor resides in its ability to transform the external, objective world in accord with the dictates of a subject, which enables self-consciousness to recognize the possibility of finding itself within the objective realm and hence of establishing an identity of subject and object. This point is missing from Hegel's account of civil society, replaced by those I emphasize in the text.

22. The connection between universality and the requirement that labor be socially productive is made explicit at §192Z: "The form of universality enters here because of the fact that I must take others into account [*nach dem anderen richten muß*]." Hegel characterizes socially productive labor only loosely, as "labor that stands in relation to the needs of others" (VPR1, 116). Notice that the effect of universality Hegel points to depends upon laborers being *conscious* of the requirement that their labor be socially productive, a condition that Marx believes is missing from capitalist production.

23. Note the connection between universality and "taking others into account" asserted in the preceding note.

24. Civil society could be said to effect a further kind of *Bildung* (in relation to acquiring the subjective disposition appropriate to citizenship), insofar as participation in that institution plays a crucial role in explaining how individuals come to be able to embrace the general will. I shall not develop this important claim here but merely note that it is grounded in the fact that corporate membership, which follows naturally from individuals' egoistic pursuits within civil society, is the crucial mediating link between private wills and the general will in the political sphere. The basic idea here is articulated in my account in chapter 4 of the role played by corporations in the transparent legislative process.

25. See Manfred Riedel, *Between Tradition and Revolution* (Cambridge: Cambridge University Press, 1984), chap. 6.

26. "The creation of civil society belongs to the modern world, which for the first time allows all determinations of the Idea to attain their rights" (§182Z).

27. See Hegel's reference to the "*breaking apart* and *distinguishing* of concrete need into its single components and aspects, which come to be different *particularized,* therefore more abstract, needs" (§190).

28. Unlike Marx, Hegel is not very interested in giving a causal explanation of the highly specialized division of labor distinctive of the modern world. (To the extent that he attempts to do so, he appears to give explanatory primacy to a basic tendency humans allegedly have, in contrast to animals [§190], toward the multiplication and specialization of needs [§198; VPR1, 117].) Although Hegel notes the connection (emphasized by Smith) between a highly developed division of labor and increased productivity, he fails to see how the former is the result of a demand for the latter that has its source in *capitalist* social relations. Indeed, the concept of a specifically capitalist mode of production is entirely lacking in Hegel's analysis. The feature of civil society Hegel singles out as fundamental is the market-regulated production and exchange of commodities. He pays no attention to whether the means of production are privately owned or whether production is carried out for the accumulation of surplus value. This raises the very interesting but complicated question of whether the economic system Hegel describes and defends must also be capitalist in form, or whether a socialist (Hegelian) civil society is also conceivable.

29. In the *Encyclopedia* treatment of *Sittlichkeit,* Hegel makes this point more explicitly than in other places; productive activity in civil society is characterized there as "the bringing forth of *exchangeable* goods through one's own labor" (E §524; emphasis added).

30. At VPR1, 117, Hegel explicitly says that production in civil society is undertaken for the purpose of creating a "surplus" that can be exchanged for others' products.

31. Like Smith before him, Hegel fails to distinguish adequately between a commodity's use value and its exchange value. This ambiguity is present, among other places, in his statement that human labor bestows value upon its products (§196). In the present context, and in all subsequent usage, 'value' must be interpreted as referring to exchange value.

32. More precisely, money lacks all *qualitative* properties and (as money) has only the quantitative property of being the measure of the (exchange) value of things.

33. Strictly speaking, Hegel's conception of the human being (*Mensch*) differs from that of the (abstract) person. A human being is a person thought of as having basic needs. So respecting human rights as opposed to personal rights narrowly understood involves caring for the satisfaction of those basic needs. If 'human being' is defined in this way, I see no difference between it and the concrete person as Hegel defines it.

34. Notice that here Hegel is making what Marx would consider to be a materialist claim, insofar as this is a version of the principle that social being determines social consciousness.

35. The connection between well-being and freedom is further discussed in chapter 7 in the context of Hegel's account of moral subjectivity and its central concept, the good.

36. One difference between the two is that Hegel subsumes issues of material well-being under the title of freedom, because being reasonably well-off is a necessary condition of affirming one's social order and hence of participating in it freely.

37. For Hegel a purely spiritual need detached from all materiality is probably impossible, given that spirit (for him) always unites both nature and consciousness.

38. Rousseau does consider this issue to some extent in Part III of his *Political Economy*; PE, 224–236.

39. Ilting denies this equivalence (VPR1, 305 n. 134), but it is hard to reconcile his claim with Hegel's usage in §124. Moreover, the passages Ilting cites in support of his claim do not seem to me decisive.

40. This part of Hegel's theory can be thought of as addressing what Rawls calls "the broad features of human desires and needs, their relative urgency and cycles of recurrence, and their phases of development." See John Rawls, *A Theory of Justice* (Cambridge, Mass.: Harvard University Press, 1971), 424.

41. Here again, human neediness—in this case, sexual neediness—reveals itself as reason's helpmate. It not only guarantees human participation in the process of *Bildung* but also provides a natural impetus for entering into a form of ethical engagement with others.

42. The division of labor that Smith and Hegel celebrate is, as Marx appreciates, not distinctive to capitalism, for it is also a feature of socialist production, in at least some of its forms. As Marx points out, capitalism is defined by the social form of production, not by its material mode. In capitalism the former includes certain class-based relations of production (where the means of production are privately owned, and the majority of individuals own no such means other than their own labor power), as well as a specific end for the sake of which production is undertaken (the limitless accumulation of privately appropriated surplus value). Interestingly, neither of these essential features of capitalism plays a prominent role in civil society as Hegel describes it.

43. Here again Hegel highlights a feature of civil society that is essential to, but not distinctive of, capitalism. It is a question worthy of further discussion whether some form of market socialism could accommodate the features of civil society that make it a rational institution in Hegel's eyes.

44. It must also be pointed out—though it is not clear that Hegel recognizes it—that the free market alone is also unable to guarantee that enough goods *of the right kind* are produced to satisfy the material needs of all. This is be-

cause the market responds to effective demand, not to the needs of those who lack the means to purchase what they need.

45. The literature on Hegel's treatment of poverty is vast. Some of the best accounts are Wood, *Hegel's Ethical Thought*, 247–255; Michael O. Hardimon, *Hegel's Social Philosophy: The Project of Reconciliation* (Cambridge: Cambridge University Press, 1994), 236–250; Shlomo Avineri, *Hegel's Theory of the Modern State* (Cambridge: Cambridge University Press, 1972), 146–151, 214–218; and Harry Brod, *Hegel's Philosophy of Politics* (Boulder, Colo.: Westview Press, 1992), 107–110.

6. Hegel's Social Theory and Methodological Atomism

1. Allen W. Wood, *Hegel's Ethical Thought* (Cambridge: Cambridge University Press, 1990), 259.

2. The most important textual sources for reconstructing Hegel's critique of social contract theory are §§29A, 75A+Z, 258A+Z; NL, 59–70, 85–92, 123–124/II, 440–453, 470–480, 518–519; LHP, vol. III, 401–402/XX, 307.

3. This term is inspired by Hegel's remark, cited previously, in which he denies that social philosophy can "proceed atomistically."

4. The phrases 'derived from', 'constructed out of', and 'reducible to' are far from univocal, and the sense in which collective ends are constructed out of individuals' ends varies widely among the liberal theories mentioned here. Still, each of these theories begins by ascribing a set of rational ends to hypothetical individuals prior to political association and then derives collective ends by asking how those ends are best coordinated. Later I examine in detail the specific version of this procedure used by Rousseau, the social contract theorist I am most interested in here.

5. In other words, social contract theory does not typically picture members of the state of nature as devoid of all social relations; it merely abstracts from all bonds of *political* association, since it is the state (and not, say, the family) that is the object of its inquiry.

6. One reason it is important to question the received view is that it is extremely difficult to weave Hegel's remarks on social contract theory into a coherent critique of some plausible interpretation of that approach to political theory.

7. In the same place he describes the position he is arguing against as one that takes "the principle of the individual will" as its "fundamental concept" (§258A) and therefore "starts out from individuality, from the individual self-consciousness" (§258Z).

8. Rawls makes a similar point in his discussion of "social union" and in his denial that social contract theory is committed to endorsing the ideal of a "private society." His contrast between these two kinds of association paral-

lels the distinction Hegel is concerned with here. See John Rawls, *A Theory of Justice* (Cambridge, Mass.: Harvard University Press, 1971), §79.

9. See, for example, Patrick Riley's *Will and Political Legitimacy* (Cambridge, Mass.: Harvard University Press, 1982), 110, which asserts—mistakenly, in my view—that this feature constitutes the central, irresolvable paradox of Rousseau's political theory.

10. As noted in chapter 2, 'obeying only oneself' should be understood as equivalent to the definition of freedom as "not being subjected to the will of others" (OC III, 841; RSW, 83). Although Rousseau does not mention it in his formulation of the basic problem of political philosophy, it could be argued that there is a third kind of interest that he thinks must also be addressed by the social contract, namely, achieving the recognition of others and thereby satisfying (some of) the needs associated with *amour-propre*.

11. In the *Social Contract* 'natural freedom' refers to a slightly different conception of freedom from the one attributed to the beings of the original state of nature in the Second Discourse. According to the former, natural freedom consists in the fact that individuals outside of political society have no *obligations* to submit to the will of others. Thus, they are naturally free de jure, whereas the unassociated beings depicted in the Second Discourse are naturally free de facto (their ability to satisfy their own needs enables them in fact to avoid submission to foreign wills).

12. More precisely, this conception of freedom is presupposed by my account of the second obstacle to the maintenance of freedom, since the problem at issue there arises only on the assumption that individuals are motivated entirely by their own private good.

13. Moral freedom for Rousseau is not identical with the form of freedom Hegel associates with moral subjectivity, which is, roughly, acting in accord with one's own understanding of the good.

14. Thus, civil freedom is roughly equivalent to Hegel's conception of personal freedom.

15. I take Joshua Cohen to be making roughly the same point when he says that "having a general will is not . . . a means to autonomy" but rather "what autonomy consists in." See Joshua Cohen, "Reflections on Rousseau: Autonomy and Democracy," *Philosophy and Public Affairs* 15 (summer 1986): 287.

16. In showing how 'the I's being constituted as 'a we' follows from Rousseau's brand of methodological atomism, I take myself to be filling in some of the details of the view implicit in Cohen's suggestion that Rousseau's emphasis on freedom as a fundamental interest of individuals means that "there is . . . an anticipation of the general will—something universal—present within the contractual situation itself, and therefore a basis for that will in the nature of human beings" (284).

17. To make this distinction more concrete by means of a contemporary exam-

ple: Do I support universal health care only because I am farsighted enough to see that ultimately my own freedom and well-being will be threatened in a community plagued by radical inequalities in basic goods such as health care, or do I attach some intrinsic value to my fellow citizens' basic needs being met?

18. This, I take it, is implied by Rousseau's talk of a "shared felicity from which each individual would derive his own" (GM, 158) and his claim that in the rational state "public felicity, far from being based on the happiness of private individuals, would itself be the source of this happiness" (GM, 160).

19. This conflict is not natural in the sense that it belongs even to the animal-like beings of the original state of nature but in the sense that it is a basic feature of the *human* condition. That is, it is a natural concomitant of the social dependence and the divergence among particular interests that come about once individuals acquire more than the very simplest of needs.

20. Rousseau formulates the problem at issue here in the following terms: "Each individual, appreciating no other aspect of government than the one that relates to his particular interest, has difficulty perceiving the advantages he should obtain from the continual deprivations imposed by good laws" (SC, II.7.ix).

21. This connection between love of country, political education, and the general will is nicely summarized in the following statement: "Love of country [*l'amour de la patrie*] is the most effective [means of teaching citizens to be good], for . . . every man is virtuous when his particular will conforms on all matters with the general will, and we willingly want what is wanted by the people we love" (PE, 218).

22. There is, admittedly, something odd in claiming that citizens might value their political participation for its own sake, even if they attach no intrinsic value to the common good or to their association with others. Perhaps it would be more accurate to say that their political participation satisfies or gives expression to a certain conception of themselves as self-determining beings and that the terms that govern that participation accord them a dignity appropriate to that self-conception.

23. This qualifier is important, for surely not all instrumentally valued activity is alienating.

24. The distinction between a concept and a conception (of justice) is found in Rawls, *A Theory of Justice*, 5–6.

25. Rousseau appears to take the same view of membership in the family (DI, 146–147). Presumably the good intrinsic to conjugal and paternal love, described here as "the sweetest sentiments known to men," could not be recognized by the unassociated beings who precede the development of families.

26. In this context it is important to recall that Rousseau's primary aim, as well as that of social contract theory more generally, is not to provide an exhaustive account of the good of political membership but to ask what conditions a state and its laws must meet if they are to be legitimate and thus obligate those who are subject to them.

27. I thank Richard Boyd for first articulating this problem to me.

28. I am indebted to Terry Irwin for drawing my attention to this point.

29. Other passages that explicitly link the essence of individuals to freedom are §§149Z, 153.

30. For other passages that emphasize the same point, see §§260, 264, and VPR1, 269–270.

31. The textual evidence in support of this claim has already been provided in chapter 1 (note 49) and chapter 4 (note 14). The former makes clear that social freedom is not fully realized if individuals remain mere cogs of a social mechanism that perform their particular functions without knowing and affirming the principles that govern the whole. The latter shows that Hegel initially adopted a Platonic position (emphasizing the specialized tasks of individuals without requiring that they know or will the ends of the whole) but by 1820 embraced a more Rousseauean view in which individuals perform specialized tasks but also aspire to, and achieve, a general will. The fact that Hegel initially adopted a Platonic model and then replaced it with the one I have sketched here is evidence for my claim that in his mature theory some conception of the interests of individuals as such works to place constraints on how the rational social order may be organized. In other words, the task of the theory of *Sittlichkeit* is not simply to conceive of a social order that is self-sustaining and organized in accord with the Concept but to conceive of such an order that also allows for the freedom of individuals to be realized. An account of the social order that fell short of satisfying the latter criterion would have failed to incorporate one of the crucial ideals bequeathed to modernity by Christianity, namely, the sacredness of all individuals, each of whom is a special object of divine concern.

32. See also §§303A, 308A; NL, 60/II, 440; and XII, 534.

33. Whether Hegel views these differences as innate (like Plato) or as acquired through the long-term occupation of specialized roles is of no relevance here.

34. This condition—together with the provision that individuals are free to choose their estates (§206)—is an important respect in which Hegel's theory differs from Plato's.

35. Related statements of Hegel's include: "The state is divine will made present as spirit *unfolding* as an actual configuration and *organization of a world*" (§270A); "the state is the world that spirit has made for itself; . . . therefore

the state must be revered as something divine on earth" (§272Z); and "the nation-state is spirit in its substantial rationality and immediate actuality; it is therefore the absolute power on *earth*" (§331).

36. For a more complete discussion of the concepts of spirit and substance as they relate to Hegel's social philosophy, see Michael O. Hardimon, *Hegel's Social Philosophy: The Project of Reconciliation* (Cambridge: Cambridge University Press, 1994), 43–52.

37. I am indebted here to Henry Allison's excellent discussion of these issues in *Benedict de Spinoza: An Introduction* (New Haven, Conn.: Yale University Press, 1987), 44–63. The cited passage appears on p. 46.

38. This suggests that Hegel's logical doctrine of the Concept can be understood as an attempt to think through the implications of Spinoza's idea of conceptual self-sufficiency by specifying how such a being would have to be organized in order to achieve independence in this sense.

39. This term is suggested by Allison, *Benedict de Spinoza*, 47.

40. See also §257, where the state is characterized as "ethical spirit, the *manifest,* self-transparent substantial will that thinks and knows itself and brings about what it knows [that is, itself] in so far as it knows it."

41. Thus, strictly speaking, Allen Wood is right to claim that "it is a serious distortion of Hegel's view to say that he regards true freedom as the freedom of a collective rather than the freedom of individuals" (238). For Hegel is not concerned with the freedom of a collective *rather than* the freedom of individuals. Nevertheless, he is concerned with a freedom of the collective that is not reducible to the freedom of individuals, and recognizing this is crucial to understanding how the normative structure of Hegel's social theory differs from other, more familiar views.

42. See Hegel's claim at §324A that in the perfectly achieved state nature is stripped of its finite character, two marks of which are mortality and transience.

43. Since individuals derive spiritual satisfaction from partaking of the strongly holistic qualities of their social order, there is a sense in which even those qualities could be said to realize a good for the individuals who make up the whole. This observation, though true, does not contradict my basic claim that for Hegel the rational social order achieves a good that cannot be reduced to the good it has for human individuals. The point is that the achievement of divine self-sufficiency is a good whose value transcends whatever value it might also have for the individuals who partake of (but do not themselves exhibit) that property.

44. In §146 the social order's self-sufficiency (*Selbständigkeit*) as substance is explicitly said to be the source of the absolute authority of ethical (*sittliche*) norms.

45. The difference between these two philosophical projects corresponds to the important but frequently overlooked distinction Hegel draws at §324A between the theodicean task of justifying past wars from the perspective of providence and the practical task of justifying a present war from the ethical perspective. The latter aims to provide a reason for taking a certain *action,* as opposed to becoming reconciled with the world as it already has become.

46. Even though defending the homeland is in principle a duty of all citizens, Hegel argues that in the modern state it will typically be carried out only by the members of a particular, nonhereditary estate *(Stand)* devoted exclusively to military service (§§325, 326A). This means that in Hegel's state normal citizens will only in extremely rare cases be asked to sacrifice more than their property in support of their country's wars.

47. Recall the suggestion made in chapter 2 that for Rousseau our duties to others are ultimately grounded in the duty we have to ourselves to realize our essential nature as free.

48. These two aspects of the subjective disposition appropriate to members of *Sittlichkeit* are distinguished by Hegel himself and discussed separately in §§146 and 147.

7. The Place of Moral Subjectivity in Ethical Life

1. Martin Luther, "The Freedom of a Christian," in *Luther's Works: American Edition,* vol. 31, ed. Harold J. Grimm (Philadelphia: Muhlenberg Press, 1957), 344.

2. This aspect of Hegel's social theory is the object of Jürgen Habermas's critique in "Moral Development and Ego-Identity," *Telos* 24 (summer 1975): 41–56. Habermas's claim is that Hegel's social theory, with its emphasis on individuals' identification with particularistic social groups such as the family and nation-state, does not allow for the development of universalistic "post-conventional identities." In my opinion this criticism rests on a misunderstanding of Hegel's view, since the kind of identity Habermas finds lacking in the theory of *Sittlichkeit* in fact bears crucial similarities to Hegel's concept of a moral subject. As this chapter aims to show, the realization of moral subjectivity is compatible with membership in the institutions of ethical life.

3. John Rawls, *A Theory of Justice* (Cambridge, Mass.: Harvard University Press, 1971), 93.

4. John Rawls, *Political Liberalism* (Cambridge, Mass.: Harvard University Press, 1993), 19. The idea that the principles of justice are derived from the moral concept of the person is more explicit in Rawls's later thought than in *A Theory of Justice* itself.

5. The best extended discussion of this topic in English is found in Allen W. Wood, *Hegel's Ethical Thought* (Cambridge: Cambridge University Press, 1990), chap. 10.

6. Hegel's conception of moral subjectivity is considerably more complex than my discussion of it here can convey. Although conscience is the most important, or "highest," element of moral subjectivity, it is not the only one. This is reflected in the fact that Hegel recognizes a number of moral "rights" (or freedoms) beyond the rights of conscience. These include the rights of "knowledge" (§117), "intention" (§120), and "subjective satisfaction" (§124+A). My claim that conscience is the central feature of moral subjectivity is based on the fact that Hegel refers to the freedom of conscience as "the subject's highest right" (§132A). For a more complete account of Hegel's idea of a moral subject, see Wood, *Hegel's Ethical Thought*, 134.

7. The latter conception is depicted in the *Phenomenology of Spirit* (PhG, ¶¶632–671; 464–494) and at §§138–139 and E §511. True conscience is discussed at §137.

8. In my discussion of the ancients I shall be concerned to articulate only Hegel's understanding of their conception of freedom (and of its shortcomings). I shall not try to establish the historical veracity of his claims about the Greeks, since I am most interested in the conceptual distinctions his view of ancient *Sittlichkeit* enables him to make.

9. "It can be said of the Greeks in the first and true form of their freedom that they had no conscience; for them [ethical life consisted] predominantly [in] the habit of living for the fatherland without further reflection" (PH, 253/XII, 309).

10. Hegel formulates this fundamental tenet of Christianity as follows: "[The Christian] God wills that *all* humans attain salvation. Thus, apart from all particularity, in and for himself, the human being, as human being, has an infinite worth that supersedes all particularity of birth and fatherland" (PH, 334/XII, 404).

11. It might be thought that this second brand of universalism is already implicit in the philosophical challenges Socrates poses to his fellow Athenians. The idea here is that in challenging his interlocutors to find reasons that would legitimate the traditional practices of Athens, Socrates is engaged in the search for a justification that transcends the parochial perspective of Athenians and purports to hold for all rational inquirers. In this regard, however, it is noteworthy that Hegel consistently identifies Socrates with the principle of "reflection" (or, equivalently, "negativity") (VPR4, 301) but not with universalism in this sense. While Socrates clearly invites his interlocutors to reflect rationally on their practices, it is not clear that the re-

flection he inspires is best thought of as aimed at establishing norms that could be endorsed by any rational inquirer. Its aim appears rather to be the more modest one of internal coherence.

12. It is important to note that Hegel ends up endorsing a weakened version of the principle of universal access. For him, truth in ethical matters is accessible only to all *modern* individuals, not to those who lived during earlier historical eras, before *Geist* was fully developed.

13. Given the confusion surrounding Hegel's doctrine of spirit—especially its account of how human ends relate to the ends of spirit—it is worth emphasizing Hegel's explicit claim in the passage cited here that it is because freedom is a *human* end (because it "is what makes the human being human") that it is "the fundamental principle of spirit."

14. Establishing the precise relation between Hegel's and Kant's moral theories is an extremely complicated matter. (I am indebted to David Brink and Michael Hardimon for pointing out some of these difficulties.) One important difference is that although Kant recognizes a general duty to promote the happiness of others, Hegel's theory begins with a determinate account of what the fundamental well-being of any individual must include and argues from that for the duty to participate in the particular system of social institutions that best realizes such well-being for all (that is, modern *Sittlichkeit*).

15. It is a matter of some controversy whether Hegel's moral theory requires concern for the welfare of all existing (and future?) human beings, or merely for the welfare of all who belong to one's own national community. (See §§125, 126A+N.) For the purposes of reconstructing Hegel's (and Rousseau's) social theory, it is sufficient to take 'universal well-being' to refer to the well-being of all of one's fellow citizens.

16. A similar thought is at work in Kant's argument for the practical necessity of belief in God's existence. His argument essentially depends on the claim that human beings could not be fully at home in a world—could never recognize a world as fully rational—in which the laws of morality had no systematic relation to the achievement of happiness (of those who are morally worthy of it). An important difference from Hegel here is that for Kant the concept of the good (the "highest good") enters moral philosophy only after the unconditional validity of the categorical imperative has been established. This means that the concept of the good is not required to demonstrate the binding character of moral duties. For Hegel the obligatory character of duties cannot be established without showing how they fit into a scheme of social institutions that systematically realizes the good, including human well-being.

17. Needless to say, this Hegelian move presupposes a rejection of the basic Kantian dichotomy between inclination, on the one hand, and reason and freedom, on the other.

18. Hegel refers to this principle as "the *subject's right* to find its *satisfaction* in the action" (§121), and as "the right of the subject's *particularity* to find satisfaction" (§124A).

19. These are the necessary and sufficient conditions for fully realizing the species of self-determination Hegel associates with moral conscience. As I note later, they are not identical to the weaker set of conditions under which ethical norms are binding on individuals. For Hegel ethical norms can be binding on individuals even though they fail to recognize them as such. In such a case, individuals would be morally obligated to follow those norms but would not fully enjoy the freedom of moral subjectivity. For they would be bound by objectively valid principles that they themselves did not consciously endorse.

20. Although 'on the basis of *good* reasons' (*aus guten Gründen*) does not appear in the particular passage cited, Hegel uses this locution at §132A.

21. Ludwig Siep discusses this question helpfully in "The 'Aufhebung' of Morality in Ethical Life," in *Hegel's Philosophy of Action,* ed. Lawrence S. Stepelevich and David Lamb (Atlantic Highlands, N. J.: Humanities Press, 1983), 137–155. See especially sect. IV.

22. Ernst Tugendhat, *Self-Consciousness and Self-Determination* (Cambridge, Mass.: MIT Press, 1986), 315–316, translation amended. Tugendhat also makes the more radical (and more obviously false) charge that "Hegel's philosophy is consciously and explicitly the . . . justification of the existing order, regardless of how this existing order may be constituted" (317).

23. Tugendhat cites E §§514–515 in support of his claim that the reflection appropriate to moral subjectivity is excluded from *Sittlichkeit* (315). I discuss this passage in more detail later, but for now it is sufficient to note that although Hegel does identify trust here as "the true ethical disposition," the reflection it is said to replace is qualified as "the reflection of free choice" (*die wählende Reflexion*). Since Hegel consistently characterizes choice (*Wahl*) as an incompletely rational form of willing (§14, E §§476–477)—equivalent, roughly, to selecting among a set of given options in accord with one's subjective preferences—the claim that "the reflection of free choice" is absent from *Sittlichkeit* cannot be taken to imply that all reflection is excluded, including that associated with moral subjectivity.

24. Tugendhat's critique runs deeper than my brief treatment of it here implies. He aims to show that the alleged exclusion of conscience from *Sittlichkeit* is not a mere oversight on Hegel's part but a necessary consequence of very fundamental features of his philosophy, including his commitment to the

"subject-object model" of consciousness and his "speculative" conceptions of identity and freedom. Although I am not ultimately persuaded by these charges, they are worthy of more attention than I can give them here. For a more comprehensive rebuttal of Tugendhat's critique, see Ludwig Siep, "Kehraus mit Hegel?" *Zeitschrift für philosophische Forschung* 35 (1981): 518–531.

25. Tugendhat, *Self-Consciousness and Self-Determination,* 311, 315–316; emphasis added.

26. In addition to the passages quoted here, see §147A, §268, and VPR2, 123–124, all of which unambiguously confirm that trust is compatible with higher forms of rational insight. Moreover, §5 makes clear that reflection—the capacity to abstract from "every given determinate content" of the will, including the prevailing norms of one's society—is an essential element of the will, without which full freedom is unrealized.

27. One commentator who clearly recognizes this aspect of Hegel's social theory is Andreas Wildt, who goes so far as to say that institutions are ethical (*sittlich*) to the extent that they make possible the formation of what Habermas calls "post-conventional identities." Although Hegel does include this as one mark of a rational social order, it is far from being its defining characteristic. See Andreas Wildt, *Autonomie und Anerkennung* (Stuttgart: Klett Cotta, 1982), 110.

28. See also §147+A, where it can seem that Hegel valorizes an immediate relation to the social order in comparison to the more mediated relations he mentions. Even here, however, rational insight is clearly characterized as compatible with the attitude of trust. For my reading of this confusing paragraph, see chapter 3, especially note 21.

29. Hegel expresses this in his statements at §132A that "the *right of the rational*—as the objective—over the subject stands firm against" the subject's right to have rational insight into any norms that bind it and that "what I require to satisfy my conviction concerning the good . . . in no way detracts from the *right of objectivity.*"

30. At §137N "erring consciences" are further characterized as those that "recognize as right only what they find in their own merely subjective consciences." See also §132N, which speaks of the need "to learn and become accustomed to taking my insight as something contingent, which involves recognizing my conviction as "only *one* authority" alongside the authority of "others, the state, and the world."

31. This interpretative claim coheres with Siep's conclusions concerning which elements of the conscience described in "Morality" are preserved in *Sittlichkeit*: "What [Hegel] rejects is simply the veneration for the decisions of conscience as being beyond criticism. Hegel holds that, according to its very

'idea,' conscience claims to be the 'rule for a rational, universal manner of acting that is valid in and for itself' (§137). Hence it cannot be placed beyond all intersubjective standards for examination." See Siep, "Kehraus mit Hegel?" 153.

32. Christine Korsgaard finds this Hegelian theme already in Kant. See her *Creating the Kingdom of Ends* (Cambridge: Cambridge University Press, 1996), 138–140, 290–291. It is implicit as well in Rawls's conception of the reasonableness of citizens; Rawls, *Political Liberalism*, 48–54.

33. Hegel also takes moral subjectivity to be realized in *Sittlichkeit* in the sense that the social order, *taken as a whole,* embodies the features of a moral subject insofar as it is governed by its own general will directed at the universal good: "the state . . . *knows* what it wills and knows it in its *universality,* as something *thought;* consequently, it acts and functions in accord with known ends and recognized principles and in accord with laws that are such not only *implicitly* but for consciousness" (§270).

34. The concept of reflective acceptability is introduced and helpfully discussed in Michael Hardimon, "Role Obligations," *Journal of Philosophy* 91 (July 1994): 348–354. As Hardimon points out, a social role (or institution) can be reflectively acceptable even though it may not actually have been reflected upon.

35. As Hegel puts it, knowledge that falls short of truly philosophical comprehension depends on grounds (*Gründe*) based on "presuppositions that are taken to be immediate [that is, underived or unexamined]" (VPR2, 124).

36. Tugendhat, *Self-Consciousness and Self-Determination,* 311.

37. For a helpful discussion of Hegel's concept of *Wirklichkeit,* see Michael O. Hardimon, *Hegel's Social Philosophy: The Project of Reconciliation* (Cambridge: Cambridge University Press, 1994), 53–63.

38. It is interesting to note that along this dimension Marx's social theory, though revolutionary rather than reformist, is much closer to Hegel's than to Rousseau's. For Marx, too, believes that the basic building blocks of the rational social order (communism) are already in place. For Marx both the *values* that are to be realized in the rational social order and the *real conditions of its achievement* are effects of capitalism's necessary pattern of development.

39. I would argue that a similar conception of reconciliation is at work in, and one of the central aims of, Rawls's political theory. Though the Hegelian roots of that theory are seldom explicitly acknowledged, something like Hegel's position is implicit in the method of reflective equilibrium. For that method aims to brings to explicit consciousness the obscurely recognized principles of justice that inform contemporary practice, and doing so is intended to reinforce our commitment to (and affirmation of) them, even as

we recognize that they are only imperfectly realized in the world we inhabit. Expressed in Hegelian language, the intended effect of Rawls's philosophy is both affirmation of "actual" political institutions and a recognition of how existing institutions can be brought closer to actuality.

40. The clear implication is that legitimate social criticism and reform will be more likely to originate from an intellectual elite than from an oppressed underclass, as Hegel's most illustrious successor would have it.

41. Even in these circumstances Hegel's preferred response is withdrawal from the social world rather than critique or social activism (§138Z). This is no doubt due to his belief that fundamental historical progress is never the direct result of human planning but takes place behind the backs of human participants, via the ruse of reason.

42. See also Hegel's statement later in the same passage that "as far as *doctrinal instruction* is concerned, . . . the state should not only grant the Church complete freedom in such matters, but should also treat its doctrinal teachings with unconditioned respect, regardless of what they may contain, on the grounds that the Church alone is responsible for determining them" (§270A).

43. The concept of toleration comes up again in a similar passage at VPR2, 107: "The Quakers do not take oaths because it is against their conviction; for the same reason they do not bear arms or remove their hats in front of others . . . The state—the objective, right action—has complete priority here; it cannot be asked what my particularity says against it. So, for example, it is always a matter of toleration when the state endures Quakers . . . At the same time, a state can be internally strong to the extent that it tolerates abnormalities of this kind within it. In general nothing is to be ceded when someone says in response to demands made of him by the state that it is against his conscience to fulfill them."

44. In fact, few liberals would claim otherwise. Certainly not Rawls, who writes: "There is a temptation to say that the law must always respect the dictates of conscience, but this cannot be right" (*A Theory of Justice*, 370).

45. Of course, *actions* resulting from such free choices must meet the further condition that they allow for the same degree of personal freedom to be accorded to all, if they are to be protected by the principles of abstract right.

46. A similar condition is laid down by Rawls when he discusses the rights of intolerant citizens: "[An intolerant sect's] freedom should be restricted only when the tolerant sincerely and with reason believe that their own security and that of the institutions of liberty are in danger" (*A Theory of Justice*, 220).

47. Kenneth Westphal has pointed out to me that Hegel has a further reason for thinking that a radical critique of *Sittlichkeit* will be unnecessary, namely,

that the rational social order includes a variety of institutions whose purpose is to ensure that social criticism from below is constantly taken notice of and responded to by government officials. See, for example, Hegel's discussion of the "public authority" (§§235–237) and the "administration of justice" (§216+A+Z). Westphal provides a wide-ranging interpretation of Hegel's social thought in "The Basic Context and Structure of Hegel's 'Philosophy of Right,'" in *The Cambridge Companion to Hegel,* ed. Frederick C. Beiser (Cambridge: Cambridge University Press, 1993), 234–269.

48. See Hardimon, *Hegel's Social Philosophy,* 95–96, for the distinction between subjective and objective reconciliation.

49. As Rawls uses the term, a "thin" conception of the good is one that commands the universal agreement of rational beings, since it includes only those goods (primary goods) that all such beings can recognize as good, regardless of differences among their more specific final ends or life plans. The goods recognized by Rawls's thin theory of the good are the means necessary for carrying out any (more comprehensive) conception of the good whatever (*A Theory of Justice,* 92–93).

50. I am indebted to Samuel Freeman for this characterization of the classical doctrine.

51. Rawls, *Political Liberalism,* 19; Rawls, *A Theory of Justice,* 92–93.

52. This claim appears to contradict Hegel's statement that "to enter the state of marriage is . . . an ethical duty" (§162A). But even if Hegel's ethical theory were committed to the implausible view that marriage is morally obligatory for all individuals, such a view is not essential to his social theory. All the latter requires is that the family be a flourishing institution generally. This means only that enough individuals must marry (and reproduce) to make society self-sustaining and that the value of the family as an institution must be widely recognized, even by those who choose not to marry.

53. Rawls, *A Theory of Justice,* 396–397.

54. Ibid., 178f., 440–441.

55. For example, Rawls takes the Hegelian view that life within the family plays a crucial role in fostering a sense of justice among citizens (ibid., 462–467).

56. Rawls, in *Political Liberalism,* defines comprehensive conceptions of the good as conceptions of the good that are "associated with comprehensive doctrines" (176)—that is, with religious, philosophical, or moral doctrines that cover "all recognized values and virtues within one rather precisely articulated system" and that purport to "hold for all kinds of subjects ranging from the conduct of individuals and personal relations to the organization of society as a whole" (13–14).

57. To say that Hegel's system is unabashedly metaphysical is not to say that the sense in which it is metaphysical is obvious or familiar. One of Hegel's most

profound contributions to philosophy is his attempt to defend the possibility of metaphysics in light of the Kantian challenge by transforming our understanding of what metaphysics is and how it can be had. This aspect of Hegel's thought has yet to be fully understood and appropriated. A fine beginning is made by William F. Bristow in "Hegel and the Transformation of Philosophical Critique" (Ph.D. diss., Harvard University, 1997).

58. The religious diversity Hegel recognizes as compatible with a rational social existence clearly includes non-Christians as well, since (in a footnote to §270A) he advocates full citizenship for Jews.

59. I would argue that the same is true of lesbian and gay critiques of the bourgeois family that reject the assumption that only members of the opposite sex are suited to marry or raise a family.

60. One reason the doctrine of sexual difference is nontrivial for Hegel's account is that it enables him to see the family as a "concrete," or "spiritual," whole, an entity that incorporates a variety of differentiated parts into an organic unity. Presumably a more up-to-date Hegelian account would attempt to recover this feature of the family by locating the essential differences between spouses in characteristics they have as different particular individuals rather than in characteristics they allegedly have merely by being a member of one sex rather than the other.

61. In this discussion of the family I have focused only on the claim that a theory that places great value on the identity-constituting nature of social roles need not be hostile to the prospect of future substantive transformations of "rational" institutions. The argument depends on showing that none of the fundamental ethical functions *of the family itself*—hence none of the essential sources of our deep attachment to it—is threatened by eliminating sexual inequality. This argument does not, however, address the further, very important question whether it is possible to institute gender equality within the family without severely disrupting its relation to the other two social spheres. The most urgent version of this question concerns the relation between the family and civil society: If gender equality in the family depends on both spouses being full and independent participants in civil society, how will the principal social task Hegel assigns to women—child rearing—be carried out in a world where women and men have equal status? Will the task of raising children take a backseat to parents' professional obligations? Will it lose its place in the domestic sphere and be sold, like dry cleaning, as just another service commodity that civil society can efficiently provide? Since both of these options look to be incompatible with the ideal of the family, the only satisfactory solution appears to lie in adjustments internal to civil society—job sharing, flexible work schedules for parents, generous family leaves, and so on—that would accommodate the child-rearing needs

of a two-worker family. Can civil society make such accommodations? Hegel would doubt that it could, since he believes that practicing a profession well requires a full-time commitment to it. But even if such changes are possible, they will certainly not come about from within civil society itself (merely through the operation of market forces) but will have to be imposed on it from without, that is, through public pressure and legislation by the state.

INDEX